BLUNDER

Blunder

Britain's War in Iraq

PATRICK PORTER

OXFORD
UNIVERSITY PRESS

OXFORD
UNIVERSITY PRESS

Great Clarendon Street, Oxford, OX2 6DP,
United Kingdom

Oxford University Press is a department of the University of Oxford.
It furthers the University's objective of excellence in research, scholarship,
and education by publishing worldwide. Oxford is a registered trade mark of
Oxford University Press in the UK and in certain other countries

© Patrick Porter 2018

The moral rights of the author have been asserted

First Edition published in 2018

Impression: 1

All rights reserved. No part of this publication may be reproduced, stored in
a retrieval system, or transmitted, in any form or by any means, without the
prior permission in writing of Oxford University Press, or as expressly permitted
by law, by licence or under terms agreed with the appropriate reprographics
rights organization. Enquiries concerning reproduction outside the scope of the
above should be sent to the Rights Department, Oxford University Press, at the
address above

You must not circulate this work in any other form
and you must impose this same condition on any acquirer

Published in the United States of America by Oxford University Press
198 Madison Avenue, New York, NY 10016, United States of America

British Library Cataloguing in Publication Data

Data available

Library of Congress Control Number: 2018943557

ISBN 978-0-19-880796-4

Printed and bound by
CPI Group (UK) Ltd, Croydon, CR0 4YY

Links to third party websites are provided by Oxford in good faith and
for information only. Oxford disclaims any responsibility for the materials
contained in any third party website referenced in this work.

For Jane, Mum, Dad, Em, Pat, Gus, and Molly
Con Amore

Acknowledgements

For the writing of this book, I am in the debt of many people.

My great thanks to Dominic Byatt at Oxford University Press for taking this project on, for his care and good cheer.

While writing, close friends help keep the flame burning. Thanks to my old friend Robert Saunders, for his friendly ear, incisive advice, and encouraging word even while he was writing a history of his own. Gratitude also to David Blagden, comrade and colleague, for the laughter, thought, and conversation. Ever since we first met, Huw Bennett has been a sharp interlocutor on Iraq, and much else besides. Mark Meredith's part was more of a cameo, but his dark humour beguiled the weary hours.

The book bears the footprints of many others: Roger Hutton; Marc Mulholland and Victoria Lill; Paul Newton; Kori Schake; Tarak Barkawi and Jennifer Luff; Emma Ashford; Chris Preble; Lawrence Freedman; John Bew; Ned Lebow; Jonathan Golub; Martin Robson; Sergio Catignani; Jason Reifler; Hew Strachan; Michael Clarke; Malcolm Chalmers; Andrea Berger; Anna and Nico von der Golz; Adrian Gregory; Nick Stargardt; Rob Dover; Nigel Biggar; Ryan Grauer; David Edelstein; Toby Dodge; Colin Gray; Christopher Layne; Barry Posen; Josh Shifrinson; Stephen Walt; John Mearsheimer; Matthew Kroenig; Andrew Monaghan; Jacques Hymans; James Ellison and Paul Domjan. For the chance to work with strategic minds and practitioners, I am also grateful to the Joint Command and Staff College and the Strategy and Security Institute at the University of Exeter.

My thanks to John Gay and the staff at the *National Interest* for publishing earlier pieces on which this draws; to the Oxford Strategic Studies Group and the Royal United Services Institute for inviting me to rehearse the argument; to Mick Cox, John Ikenberry, and Dan Deudney for debating the matter at the International Studies Association Conference; and to my students, who had less choice in the matter.

My family are the bedrock for everything: Brian and Muriel Porter, Emily, Pat, Gus, and Molly. For my wife Jane, gratitude is beyond telling.

Lastly, to those who suffered in this campaign, and in all tragic expeditions.

Patrick Porter

Oxford
25 April, 2018 (Anzac Day)

Preface

LEST WE FORGET

This book explains a decision for war. Britain's participation in the invasion of Iraq in the spring of 2003 was a momentous choice. 'Operation Telic' was the country's first military-strategic failure since the withdrawal from Aden and South Arabia in 1967,[1] its largest scale combat since Korea in 1950, its most failed outcome since Suez in 1956, and its most **polarizing** campaign since the South African war of 1899. Iraq was a hinge event in British political life in the first decade of the twenty-first century. It is never far from audits of how Britain's public life lost its way. Britain has waged preventive wars before, 'first strikes' to destroy distant perceived threats. Yet these anticipatory campaigns are distant memories within very different conflicts: the invasion of Iran in 1941 during World War II, to prevent Axis disruption of oil supplies to the Soviet Union, and the bombardment of the Dano-Norwegian fleet at Copenhagen in 1807 to deny it to Napoleon Bonaparte. This smaller war was born of great ambition. As a move to topple a regime, reconstitute a state, change a region, influence a superpower and interrupt a hypothetical danger, as a war intended to be both precautionary and revolutionary, it was a landmark. It is also part of the present. At the moment of writing, a set of resulting crises straddling Iraq and its neighbours draws multiple states into collision. The wars energized by the war have no end in sight. With a large archive of documents and testimonies now unearthed, we can better ask what happened and why, and discern its warnings. The battle over the war's memory continues. 'All wars are fought twice, the first time on the battlefield, the second time in memory.'[2]

Looking back, a reckoning with the campaign is not easy. People killed, died, and suffered for it, for disappointing results. To question the war is to doubt the value of sacrifice. And the very process of learning from history is a fraught and losing struggle. Our species has tried to educate itself through history, yet has failed often to prevent similar disasters. From the confusion of historical analogies, error can flow. Again and again, the mythologized memory

---

[1] Unless stated otherwise, all primary documents cited are drawn from the 'Chilcot' Iraq Inquiry. As Geraint Hughes observes, 'Iraqnophobia: The Dangers of Forgetting Operation Telic' *RUSI Journal* 157:6 (2012), pp. 54–60, p. 54.

[2] Viet Thanh Nguyen, *Nothing Ever Dies: Vietnam and the Memory of War* (Cambridge: Harvard University Press, 2016), p. 4. I am grateful to Dr Natalie Sambhi for alerting me to this reference.

of Nazi Germany and Munich has moved modern policymakers to identify adversaries as Adolf Hitler, to cast themselves as Winston Churchill, and to assume decisive quick victory. Major powers retain a propensity for self-inflicted wounds. They inflate threats and choose wars that are more costly and difficult than they realize. We have been here before. Studies of the United States' conflict in Vietnam (1961–75) did not arrest George W. Bush's drive for war in 2003. Five years before Iraq, Fredrik Logevall wrote a magisterial account of Lyndon Johnson's fateful decision for major escalation in Vietnam in 1965. He feared that 'something very much like it could happen again' if permissive conditions arose, that 'soldiers will again be asked to kill and be killed, and their compatriots will again determine, afterward, that there was no good reason why.'[3] So it went. But we have to try.

In March 2003, Britain joined a coalition led by the United States to invade Iraq and overthrow Saddam Hussein's tyrannical Ba'ath regime. Though not the most powerful state in the coalition, Britain was central to the war's articulation and rationale. The invaders overthrew Iraq's regime in three weeks. This came after twelve years of frustrated attempts to coerce Baghdad into verifiable disarmament, to contain it's ruler's aggression and shield the peoples he preyed upon, and to induce the ruler's downfall. They struck partly in the name of counter-proliferation, to destroy an arsenal of WMD (Weapons of Mass Destruction) that turned out to be non-existent. They struck partly to disrupt a perceived gathering threat, a potential union of terrorism, destructive weapons technology, and 'rogue states'. And as I argue, these were intensely ideological days. At its core, the war was one of ideas, large and real. Iraq was one front in the 'Global War on Terror', declared after the 9/11 terrorist attacks, to destroy 'terrorism' itself by spreading a liberating alternative. The invasion was supposed to help spread free markets and democracy. It was supposed to spearhead the emancipation of the Greater Middle East, to correct the conditions that spawned security threats. It was meant to accelerate the resolution of the Arab–Israel conflict and the birth of a Palestinian state. It was supposed to plant a wealthy, democratic, and compliant state in the heart of the Middle East. And in London, it was intended to strengthen and confirm British influence over the American superpower, to tame Washington and tie it into an international system that it might abandon. 'Operational Telic' was a war of many dreams. Warmakers articulated those dreams with disastrous eloquence.

'Telic' draws from the Greek *telos*, meaning 'direction' or 'purpose'. It is the unintended consequences, however, that the world must live with. The toppling of Saddam bred disorder, and disorder led to bloodletting. It killed and

---

[3] Fedrik Logevall, *Choosing War: The Lost Chance for Peace and the Escalation of War in Vietnam* (University of California Press, 1998), pp. 412–13.

maimed hundreds of thousands. It displaced millions who fled the country. It cost billions of pounds and trillions of US dollars more than was expected. It precipitated sectarian warfare and the influx of Sunni Islamists. By destroying a regime that had given up its chemical and biological weapons and abandoned its nuclear and ballistic missile programme, the war struck a blow against the cause of disarmament—not for the last time—by implicitly demonstrating to other hostile states the value of nuclear deterrence. It upended a rough balance of power in the region, empowering Iran. Iraq was not the only generating event behind today's turmoil in the Middle East. But it helped drive both sectarian strife and a geopolitical cold war between Iran and Saudi Arabia. As an effort to project and increase power, the war instead consumed it.

Worse than a crime, the war was a blunder. The blunder led to defeat. In March 2017, the unveiling of a memorial in Whitehall to the wars in the Gulf and Afghanistan underscored a tragic failure. One photographer captured a lonely former Prime Minister Tony Blair sitting Aztec-faced among chattering royals, officers, and dignitaries. The carefully crafted liturgy mentioned 'duty' and 'service', but never victory. This has the taste of ashes. If not defeat—and some find the notion crude—the campaign's result was at least a barely acceptable stalemate. In August 2007, with the city of Basra imploding around Britain's overstretched forces in southern Iraq, with dwindling domestic support and demand for the bolstering of embattled positions in Afghanistan, Britain's MI6 station chief quietly negotiated a deal with a senior leader of the Iranian-backed *Jaysh al-Mahdi* (JAM) paramilitary force, the 'Mahdi Army' that was besieging British bases. The militia agreed to stop targeting the British military in exchange for the release of detainees from British custody. British troops were permitted to withdraw from Basra Palace to the refuge of the airport without the loss of life, a withdrawal the militia graciously policed en route.[4] UK ministers framed this pullback as an efficient handover to Iraqi state security forces and the culmination of an effective operation. But as Prime Minister Winston Churchill warned the House of Commons after the Dunkirk evacuation in May 1940, it would be wrong to assign this deliverance 'the attributes of a victory'.[5] When an army charged to oversee the creation of a new state must retreat to safe passage under the cover of night, and only with the permission of a private force, obtained with bribes, that is humiliation. Basra's Shia militia subsequently brought the whip to uncovered women, intellectuals, and merchants, and a revived black market. These dividends of Britain's failed stewardship were only reversed later by a joint Iraqi–US

---

[4] Frank Ledwidge, *Losing Small Wars: British Military Failure in the 9/11 Wars* (Yale: Yale University Press, 2017), p. 51.
[5] *Hansard* 4 June 1940, vol. 361, cc. 787–98.

offensive of March 2008, launched with Britain sidelined. Britain's mission was supposed to democratize the state, emancipate women, and unite Iraqis above confession and ethnicity, and affirm the UK's strategic value to Washington. The results were perverse. Like other conflicts waged for wildly unrealistic aims in far peripheries, it exposed the deadliness of good intentions and the limits of Western power.

This book was conceived in the summer of 2016, a bitter season in British politics. I worried that Iraq would be part forgotten, and part misremembered. If humans are creatures of memory, they are also tempted to forget. I feared that upheavals since the Iraq War—like Britain's withdrawal from the European Union—would overshadow it. The long and painstaking inquest, the 'Chilcot' Iraq Inquiry, published its report in an hour when the Brexit fallout was all-consuming. Granted two days of parliamentary discussion over the Inquiry Report, only fifty MPs out of 650 took part in discussion on day one, falling at times to fifteen or twenty. Some decision-makers welcomed the diversion. Two foreign ministers who once pressed the case for military action, Jack Straw and Colin Powell, wished the matter gone. In leaked correspondence, Straw allegedly wrote that Brexit had a 'silver lining', reducing 'medium term attention on Chilcot', which has 'faded altogether'.[6] Powell noted gladly that Chilcot barely registered in Washington. Others also call for a process of forgetting. In making the case for military adventures today, those who carry the flame of warlike idealism talk of Iraq as a 'shadow'[7] that we must escape, or 'move on'[8] from, lest its memory arrest Britain's inclination towards heroic internationalism and morally charged military action. To linger over Iraq might induce 'isolationism', some warn, as though a concern for prudent war avoidance is tantamount to cancelling trade, aid, or alliances.[9] On 29 March 2006, a group of British writers, journalists, and scholars issued the 'Euston Manifesto', insisting that

> the proper concern of genuine liberals and members of the Left should have been the battle to put in place in Iraq a democratic political order and to rebuild the country's infrastructure, to create after decades of the most brutal oppression a life for Iraqis which those living in democratic countries take for granted—rather than picking through the rubble of the arguments over intervention.[10]

---

[6] Christopher Hope, 'Jack Straw boasted of how the "silver lining" from Brexit meant Chilcot criticism "faded" away', *The Daily Telegraph*, 14 September 2016.

[7] Fabian Society, *Outward to the World: How the Left's Foreign Policy can Face the Future* (London: Fabian Society, 2015), pp. x, 1; 'British Foreign Policy must emerge from the shadow of Iraq, argues Hilary Benn', *The Guardian*, 21 December 2015.

[8] David Batty, 'David Miliband: Time to Move on From Iraq', *The Guardian*, 22 May 2010.

[9] Joe Cox & Tom Tugendhat, *The Cost of Doing Nothing: The Price of Inaction in the face of Atrocities* (London: Policy Exchange, 2017), p. 13.

[10] [my italics] *The Euston Manifesto: For a Renewal of Progressive Politics* at http://eustonmanifesto.org/the-euston-manifesto/, accessed 28 October 2016.

'Rubble', 'shadow', 'move on'—this is the euphemistic language of amnesia. To encourage the forgetting of Iraq's memory would not only breach civic duty to commemorate the dead. It would do a disservice to the living and unborn, especially given that the war's consequences are still with us. The Euston group wished to separate the issues of whether to intervene and the commitment to Iraqi liberation, but the two questions are inseparably linked. The difficulties of remaking a state after breaking it, and the violence this can unleash, points back to the original question of whether to break it to begin with. Part of 'proper concern' for any conscientious citizen is precisely to argue over intervention, and argue again. Whether or not to take up arms is the ultimate political question. It will not leave alone countries that possess the capability to project power. We therefore must pick through the 'rubble' of the past. The rubble contains fragments of history, and history is the only guide we have. We are not entitled to 'closure'.

For the war is still with us. Our choice is whether to confront it, or wish it away. The war's notoriety, the gap between promises and reality, sets the terms and vocabulary of debate through which we contest the use of force: 'regime change' and 'exit strategy', 'forty-five minutes' and 'mushroom cloud', 'shock and awe' and 'war of choice', 'mission accomplished' and 'poodle'. As well as language, the seductive ideas that powered the invasion outlived the retired decision-makers, and are still with us. Under later governments, the ideas that drove the venture inflicted further mischief, from the chaos wrought by intervention in Libya to Western sponsorship of an Islamist-infected rebellion in Syria, to an escalating crisis triggered by threats of preventive war against North Korea. Expectations that the end of the Blair era meant the curtailing of adventures in 'regime change' proved naïve. The next government would assist a revolution in Tripoli and a failed one in Damascus, with results that were not uniformly excellent. As before, the reigning ideology, of transforming 'ungoverned space' through benevolent force, could return. This makes the inquest urgent.

I also wrote this book from fear that the war's memory would be reduced, turned merely into 'Blair's war', or into a tactical exercise about how to wage ambitious expeditionary wars better, 'next time'. Indeed, a counter-narrative has now formed, interpreting the Iraq War as a lesson in the need to be more determined to project military power, not less. Some find error not primarily in the war's launching, but its ending. They pin failure on Western abandonment and premature withdrawal, treating the state of Iraq as the West's to lose. On the other side of the divide, critics fixate too much on one actor, Prime Minister Tony Blair, and the 'Blairites', isolating culpability and exonerating others. This was Britain's war, not just Blair's. It was carried by assumptions widely shared and which outlive the warmakers, it held a quiet majority of support in the country, it was endorsed by a free vote in the House of Commons, and by a decisive margin. The glib catch-cry 'Not in My Name' has no place in a responsible democracy.[11]

---

[11] As Robert Saunders argues, 'Why Tutu is Wrong', *The Gladstone Diaries*, 4 September 2012, http://gladstonediaries.blogspot.co.uk/2012/09/why-tutu-is-wrong.html?q=tutu.

My attempt to interpret Iraq does not spring from personal involvement. Iraq is as personal as it gets for those who were directly affected. For many others, it was a puzzling and seemingly faraway event. The state encouraged citizens to support it but mostly as passive consumers of events. For some of us, Iraq seemed desperately important, as it would be consequential over time and space. As a student of international security, Iraq was *the* defining political event of my lifetime after the fall of the Berlin Wall. Working on the academic staff at the British Defence Academy, the daily implosion of Iraq in the autumn of 2006, bombings, kidnappings, and rampant criminality, was a sobering rebuke to the ambitions of the war party. That people I knew who were rotating in and out of Iraq lent added pathos to the issue. Ultimately, Iraq was the decisive point in my own political thinking, towards an aversion to utopias and a wariness of the implicit danger of militarism in liberal foreign policy.

Given this background, I cannot pretend to a personal detachment. Even with arcane subject matter, pure value-free objectivity is impossible. Dispassion is all the more difficult with such a wrenching history. Yet the obstacles to objectivity do not license historians to tell stories without worrying whether they are true. Subjectivity should be resisted, not indulged. I attempt to counterbalance any subjectivity in my account by reconstructing the strongest possible case for the invasion, both with and without hindsight knowledge. In order to grasp what drove the decision, I try to perform a double act, attempting to empathize with those who rolled the iron dice, while retaining enough distance to exercise a clear-eyed judgement.

This book takes a hammer to the war's rationale and the dogmatism and muddled thinking at its heart. At the same time, it is offered as a reproach to the anti-war movement. Opposition to the war was a broad church. Its ranks included the honourable and the conscientious. Those at its commanding heights, though, did not properly confront the dilemmas before them, and their popular slogan 'not in my name' suggested disengagement rather than engagement with the question. As Brendan O'Neill observed, 'Protesting wars today seems to be a way to cleanse one's private conscience rather than effecting public change—a case of opting out instead of getting stuck in and having the hard arguments.'[12] Ian McEwan's novel *Saturday*, set on the day of the mass protest, captured the point. As his character Henry Perowne observes, 'All this happiness on display is suspect…If they think—and they could be right—that continued torture and summary executions, ethnic cleansing and occasional genocide are preferable to an invasion, they should be sombre in their view.' Perowne puts his finger on the war's central dilemma: 'The price of removing Saddam is war, the price of no war is

---

[12] Brendan O'Neill, 'What Kind of Anti-War Movement Is This?', *Christian Science Monitor*, 13 December 2002.

leaving him in place.'[13] This book argues for why leaving him in place was the 'lesser evil'.

At the hands of some critics, the Iraq War became a canvas onto which they projected their discontent with the New Labour project and modern life generally, overstating the sudden rupture that Blair's war inflicted on a once green and pleasant land. Peter Oborne, for instance, claims that:

> The British people used to trust the British State. This trust is the magnificent legacy of World War Two, when we united in common sacrifice to confront fascism. Ever since then, we have regarded our state as ultimately decent and benign. We have understood that civil servants owed their loyalty to the state (symbolically expressed as the Monarch) rather than political parties or sectional interests. It was also understood that there was a secret state which was unaccountable through normal democratic means. This was tolerated because we felt that British intelligence officers...were decent, patriotic people. This trust in the state was shattered by the Iraq War, and its gruesome aftermath. We have learnt that civil servants, spies, and politicians could not be trusted to act with integrity and decency and in the national interest.[14]

Oborne's picture of a once-trusting country losing its faith because of a single military campaign is strikingly ahistorical. Earlier history contained crises of confidence over the integrity of the state, from abuses of power in Northern Ireland to the Brixton and Poll Tax riots to industrial unrest, to long declines in political participation, to the general crisis-ridden decade of the 1970s. Oborne's explanation, that suddenly a gang of bad people took over the country, and that spies, officials, and elected leaders in 2003 were oblivious to any concept of the national interest in a sudden fall from their predecessors' patriotism, is pantomimic. Oborne himself, who admits earlier branding the Major government of the 1990s as 'rotten', reflects a broader tendency to romanticize the past and villainize the present.[15] This tells us little about why the Iraq War was actually fought, and what we should learn.

Above all, the book is a self-reproach. My response to the war was fraught and flawed. Opposed at first, I became a supporter as the violence intensified in Iraq. I was hopeful about the possibilities given life by the fall of Saddam, mindful of the fascistic nature of al-Qaeda and the Ba'ath insurgents, and repelled by the toxic anti-Americanism and 'anyone but Washington' spirit so endemic in sections of the anti-war movement. I believed those in the family of hawkish idealism, the neoconservatives and liberal hawks, were right on the

---

[13] Ian McKewan, *Saturday* (London: Random House, 2005), pp. 69–70.
[14] Peter Oborne, *Not the Chilcot Report* (London: Head of Zeus, 2016), pp. 178–9.
[15] Peter Oborne, 'It's Time to Give John Major the Credit We So Cruelly Denied Him', *The Daily Telegraph*, 4 April 2012.

main point, that the West should not have to choose between tyranny and chaos in the Middle East—indeed, that Western-sponsored tyranny had fed the Islamist beast and unleashed chaos. The hijackers on 9/11 were not Afghan but Gulf men, products of oppressive orders—theocratic, or kleptocratic—that had spawned Wahhabi fanaticism and winked at the Islamist groups who had unilaterally declared war on us all. Given those roots, 9/11 and its aftermath warranted an ambitious project to transform the Arab-Islamic world. I was moved by the eloquence of the hawkish idealists Paul Berman, Christopher Hitchens, Fouad Ajami, and Norman Geras. This was poor judgement. It was born of an attraction to the elegance of ideas over their practical utility, an overestimation of Western power, a disregard for the wildness of war and its unintended consequences, an ahistorical attachment to Munich-Churchill-Hitler analogies as the universal guide to security problems, and a blindness to the historic deadliness of good intentions. Even if a revision of the West's relationship with the Middle East is in order, an ideological crusade to reorder the region at our convenience is no kind of answer. It should not have taken a disaster to grasp these realities. As we will see, some in the 'war party' maintain that the chance of liberating Iraq and the region was 'worth' the vast human price inflicted. Such claims are too reminiscent of Bolshevik 'eggs and omelettes' rationalizations, which also failed. Others argue that victory was at hand, only to be squandered by feckless defeatists, an argument too reminiscent of Weimar-era alibis for another disastrous preventive war.

Before we begin the diagnosis, two further points of justification are needed. In the course of preparing these arguments, a persistent accusation arose that this is an exercise in 'hindsight', and implicitly, that our position of 'looking back' should limit criticism. This is a widespread but defective view of our relationship with the past. Firstly, given the current lack of time-travel capability, it is difficult to examine and judge the past from any other vantage point. Secondly, criticisms of the doctrines that led to war are not purely hindsight creations. The arguments I make here were anticipated and made at the time by concerned observers and participants. Most importantly, we are trying to learn something from the past, to guide decisions to come, always a difficult exercise. That is an exercise both in empathy and criticism. To abandon that task is to tell stories with no purpose.

Conversely, there is another common response, regarding the inquest into Iraq as a waste of time and resources, because the folly of the decision was 'obvious'. The fact that the Iraq Inquiry, launched in 2009, took seven years to complete and issue its report, and followed three other inquiries,[16] induces a

---

[16] See Richard Aldrich, 'Whitehall and the Iraq War: The UK's four intelligence enquiries' *Irish Studies on International Affairs* 16:1 (2005), pp. 1–16.

widespread 'Chilcot fatigue', the dismissal of the inquest as a waste of time,[17] and the desire to reduce Iraq into a sad story that needs consigning to history. That attitude certainly is born of a hindsight distortion. If the imprudence of the Iraq War seems strategically and morally obvious today, it didn't seem so to many at the time. More than most crises, the Iraq War presented a choice of agonies. To oppose the invasion was effectively to argue for continued management of the status quo, which was a bloody one. More people favoured invasion than they care to remember. People remember opposing it, but a plurality of Britons supported it at the time, albeit mostly in muted form, according to twenty-one polls carried out by YouGov between March and December 2003.[18] The *Economist* that later judged it 'obvious' that occupying Iraq made international terrorism worse, that reported the 'damning' conclusion that an adapted strategy of inspections and containment could have succeeded, is the same journal that in February 2003 called for Saddam to be disarmed by force if necessary, because alternative strategies had failed.[19] Iraqis too are divided on the issue, and they most bore the brunt of war's negative consequences.[20] Many resent what happened to the country in the wake of Saddam's fall, yet are glad he fell, and the question of America's withdrawal divides them on largely sectarian lines.[21] Evidently, for those involved, the question is a complex one. Internationally, there was no global consensus at the time. Opinion was conflicted and fluid. The coalition assembled by the United States, that lent diplomatic and material support, was larger than the one that fought the Korean War. It had the support of half the member states of the European Union. Its ranks numbered South Korea, Poland, Japan, Australia, Italy, Spain, Georgia, and the Czech Republic, and after the first phase, New Zealand troops, German money, and Canadian trainers. Mongolian soldiers also came, descendants of Ghenghis Khan the

---

[17] Deborah Orr, 'The Chilcot Inquiry is a Waste of Time', *The Guardian*, 4 February 2010; Daniel Larison, 'Remembering some obvious truths about the Iraq War,' *American Conservative*, 6 July 2016; Simon Jenkins, 'The Chilcot Report merely proves the British love hindsight,' *The Guardian*, 8 July 2016.

[18] Will Dahlgreen, 'Memories of Iraq: Did we ever support the war?', *YouGov*, 3 June 2015, at https://yougov.co.uk/news/2015/06/03/remembering-iraq/.

[19] 'Why War would be justified', *The Economist*, 20 February 2003; 'Stating the Obvious' *The Economist*, 28 September 2006; 'Iraq's Grim Lessons' *The Economist*, 6 July 2016.

[20] The most comprehensive survey on Iraqi opinion, the Zogby Poll of 2011, reflected a largely negative but still 'mixed' picture: 30 per cent of those questioned believed that Iraq was better off at present than before the overthrow of Saddam Hussein, 42 per cent thought it was worse, 23 per cent thought that Iraq was the same, and 6 per cent were not sure. Iraqi Kurds largely endorsed the removal of the regime, unsurprisingly. Iraqis are divided on whether there is now greater political freedom since regime change (33 per cent positive, 48 per cent negative; 16 per cent none); regarding women's rights, the picture was also conflicted (26 per cent positive, 37 per cent negative, 26 per cent no impact). Zogby Research Services, *Iraq: The War, Its Consequences and the Future* (18–20 November, 2011).

[21] See Mark Kukis, *Voices from Iraq: A People's History 2003–2009* (New York: Columbia University Press, 2011).

sacker of Baghdad, who this time aimed 'to rebuild Iraq'.[22] Even if we accept the dubious proposition that we can evaluate the wisdom of decisions by 'counting heads', there wasn't overwhelming international opposition that critics imply. If many thought differently about Iraq then, and warnings went unheeded, that is a matter of important historical inquiry.

The history of Britain's Iraq War is still being written. Far from an exhaustive account of the whole episode, this book is about the most fundamental decision: whether to take part. I explain the decision, critique it, and offer a broader caution, rooted in realism, against warlike idealism, to guide more prudent decision-making in future. It is not an account of how the campaign was rescued. Rather, it asks how Britain got itself into a campaign that needed rescuing in the first place.

---

[22] James Brooke, 'The Struggle for Iraq: Allies, Mongolians Return to Baghdad, This time as Peacekeepers', *The New York Times*, 25 September 2003.

Contents

Introduction	1
1. Warpath	23
2. Breaking States: The Ideological Roots of Regime Change	72
3. Atlantic Ambitions	132
4. Weighing the Arguments	152
5. Virtue Runs Amok: How Realism Can Help	206
Epilogue: Two Speeches	222
Index	227

HE'S GOT EM. LET'S GET HIM.
The Sun, 25 September 2002
I am more afraid of our own blunders than our enemies' designs.
Thucydides, The History of the Peloponnesian War 1.144

Introduction

Bad ideas caused Britain's war in Iraq, ideas that were dogmatically held. Many remember Iraq as a misadventure of bad faith and botched management, of 'dodgy dossiers' and deceit. These are evergreen subjects. But they are not the paramount issue. Mischiefs and falsehoods can facilitate war. They were not its driving force. From its inception as a proposal as the shadows lengthened in 2001 to the invasion fifteen months later, Britain's Iraq venture was a war of ideas, real concepts about the pursuit of security in a dangerous world. Those ideas were occasioned by conditions, a sense of both power and vulnerability. Visions of world order and democracy, and corollary fears of rogue states with deadly arsenals, were not retrospective face-saving fictions. They drove the push for action from the outset. Prime Minister Tony Blair was the chief protagonist and embodiment of ideas that were widely shared. He and his counsellors, congregating in his Downing Street 'den', regarded Iraq as the central front in an epochal struggle against a new, apocalyptic barbarism. Britain's 'deciders' are remembered as deft propagandists, but were idealists at the core. Their endeavour was underpinned by powerful and doubt-proofed assumptions, as sincerely assumed as they were rarely examined. The decision to settle accounts with Iraq after a long stand-off, to topple its regime in Baghdad, was a genuine effort to forestall a hypothetical but terrifying danger, the coming together of dictatorship, terrorism, and weapons technology, to reorder the world with the antidote of liberal democracy. It was also a British effort to play tutor to the United States. British officials were frightened of the superpower that was wounded and inflamed by the 9/11 terrorist attacks. They aimed to prevent America becoming a runaway train. Blair ran grave political risks to turn his Atlantic ambition into policy. A journalist who tailed the prime minister affirmed the intensity of his beliefs and the strain of the hour. The once-cherubic premier of Cool Britannia was thin faced and dark eyed, enduring 'sleepless nights and anxious days'.[1] As the parliamentary vote loomed, without a legitimizing mandate from the United Nations Security

---

[1] Peter Stothard, *30 Days: A Month at the Heart of Blair's War* (London: HarperCollins, 2003), p. 7.

Council, Blair asked his Cabinet Secretary to ready his resignation papers. Joining Washington's war was not an act of geopolitical cynicism. It was more dangerous, a real ideological crusade. As Blair said privately and publicly, 'It's worse than you think. I actually believe in doing this'.[2]

I argue that three bad ideas drove the war. These ideas I refer to as 'warlike idealism', as they blended a pessimistic account of the international security environment, one that demanded bold and decisive action, with an optimistic account of what well-intentioned force could achieve. All three ideas warrant interrogation. The first is 'regime change', a doctrine as much as a practice, that states have little choice but to pursue security by breaking and remaking states, possibly in preventive wars, by fixing the political interior of those states with the expansion of democratic and capitalist institutions, by reordering whole regions, and by exterminating rather than containing threats. In launching this bid to reorder the world, policymakers had internalized revolutionary ambitions that were more radical than they realized. They lost sight of the possibility that their cure was worse than the disease. Behaving as insurgents, breaking states and creating new power imbalances, they believed themselves to be guardians bringing order into chaos. Second, there is the doctrine of 'rogue states', the assumption that defiant 'outrider' states are undeterrable, suicidally aggressive actors that we cannot live with, whose neutralization and removal is so vital that it warrants risky preventive action, and who make any strategies of restraint an invitation to aggression. Third, there is the 'blood price' fallacy, that Britain can secure exceptional influence in Washington by committing significant up-front costs, and with ground forces in America's '9/11 wars'.

As I argue, the explanation that Britain's Iraq War came from bad ideas that were widely held better fits the evidence than alternative explanations. These alternative explanations argue variously that Britain got into the war by accident as a result of a diplomatic process that locked it in, or that it was a war of opportunism masked by rhetoric of democratic liberation, or that it was a good idea that was poorly executed, that it was the result of American pressure, or that it was simply 'Blair's war' and that the British people were his victims. These alternative histories struggle to survive interrogation. From the many things written about Iraq, we can now assemble a range of competing explanations, explicit and implicit, and weigh them.

This book is a work of 'international history', or the historical study of international politics. It explains an historical event and its significance for the future. It focuses on the decision for war, and that decision's consequences. It does so methodologically with the inspiration of two minds, the philosopher

---

[2] A. Campbell & B. Hagerty, *The Alastair Campbell Diaries. Volume 4. The Burden of Power: Countdown to Iraq* (London: Hutchinson, 2012), p. 279; Jackie Ashley & Ewan MacAskill, 'History will be my judge', *The Guardian*, 1 March 2003.

Karl Popper and the historian Marc Trachtenberg. Trachtenberg argues that the historian must also be a theorist. If 'theory' is a set of assumptions that map the world, the historian should examine evidence consciously with a prior set of questions in mind, and then attempt to adjust both until they align and reconcile.[3] Why did Britain join the war, when it had discretion not to, and was already committed to another one? Why did it believe such a relatively weak adversary posed such a security problem? Why, given the latitude of choice, did decision-makers think the matter was obvious and that there was little real choice in the matter? Why did the decision-makers expect such decisive and benign results, or alternatively, why did they think the risks were worth the trouble? Why were they able to succeed in carrying opinion? These questions arise from assumptions that I will defend. In answering these questions, I borrow from Popper. Like Trachtenberg, Popper assumes that theory guides observation, and that observation presupposes theory.[4] In that tradition, we approach an issue like the causes of Britain's war in Iraq as a contest between competing hypotheses. If ever a conflict attracted divergent explanations about motive, influence, and causation, it was this one. Important here is Popper's social-scientific principle of falsification. We cannot hope for a complete, to-scale explanation that is positively 'provable'. We can, though, get closer to a partial rendering or approximation by identifying and dismissing 'disprovable' hypotheses, weighing competing explanations, and, by eliminating inadequate accounts, identify the explanation that comes closest to the evidence we have, in terms of plausibility and consistency. To test my explanation, I pit against it several competing hypotheses, to demonstrate how my argument better fits, and predicts, the rationales, behaviour, and chronology of the time. As one of the first histories written 'post-Chilcot', this is only a first foothold, to prepare the ground for histories to come.

Deploying the large number of primary documents and retrospective testimonies of participants, I reconstruct the assumptions underlying decisions, the policy 'world' that participants inhabited 2001–3, a world that later disappointments have made harder to imagine. I present an account of how governance over the issue 'worked'. As this was a war conceived primarily in Washington, and Britain's preparations grew from interactions with its senior ally, this is also unavoidably a transatlantic story.

Britain's Iraq War has already attracted a large literature. Ever since the withdrawal of international troops, civilian and military officials as well as the commentariat have re-fought the Iraq War a second time in memory. It has drawn in journalistic, academic, and 'grey' literature. Much of it is partisan

---

[3] Marc Trachtenberg, *The Craft of International History: A Guide to Method* (Princeton: Princeton University Press, 2006), pp. 51–140.
[4] Karl Popper, *The Logic of Scientific Discovery* (London: Hutchinson, 1959); *Conjectures and Refutations: The Growth of Scientific Knowledge* (London: Routledge, 1963).

and polemical. There is also more dispassionate analysis to be found. Most of that literature predates the release of the Iraq Inquiry's report in July 2016. Valuable studies of Iraq were produced before the Inquiry's findings were released, but they examine the campaign as a whole and devote much effort to other questions.[5]

In particular, fixations on dishonesty and illegality overshadow the debate. The literature already explores how, and how far, Iraq was a war of false pretences, feints, omissions and exaggerations, and what it means for international law.[6] The Inquiry itself was an honourable undertaking. This book would be impossible without it. But its critique largely focused on other related questions: the process of decision-making, intelligence, truth, legality, whether war was a 'last resort', and how Britain handled the aftermath and subsequent disorder.

Unlike so much of the public discussion, this history of the war is not centrally about the question of 'lies' or legality. The Iraq Inquiry rebuked Blair's circle, if not exactly for lying or fabrication. Rather, it found the government guilty of decision-based and faith-based evidence-making, casting about for evidence to confirm a prior belief and a settled decision.[7] 'Selling' the threat compromised the process of assessing it, as did the effort to harmonize plans with Washington, leading to misplaced certainty and undue weight being placed on ambiguous evidence. The state prepared policies in private,

---

[5] Jack Fairweather's history is mostly an account of the decisions made in the aftermath of the invasion, 'taken by soldiers, diplomats and contractors on the ground', *War of Choice: The British in Iraq 2003–2009* (London: Vintage, 2011), p. 9; Jonathan Steele examines the causes of failure with a particular emphasis on the occupation and the impossibility of Iraqis accepting what looked like a 'colonial' project from outsiders, *Defeat: Why they Lost Iraq* (London: I.B. Tauris, 2008).

[6] Eric Herring & Piers Robinson, 'Report X marks the spot: The British government's deceptive dossier on Iraq and WMD', *Political Science Quarterly* 129:4 (2014), pp. 551–84; 'Deception and Britain's road to war in Iraq', *International Journal of Contemporary Iraqi Studies* 8:2 (2014), pp. 213–23; D. Miller (ed.), *Tell Me Lies: Propaganda and Media Distortion in the Attack on Iraq* (London: Pluto Press, 2003); S. Kettell, 'Who's afraid of Saddam Hussein? Re-examining the "September dossier" affair', *Contemporary British History* 22:3 (2008), pp. 407–26; Brian Jones, *Failing Intelligence: The True Story of How We Were Fooled Into Going Into War in Iraq* (London: Biteback, 2010).

[7] *The Report of the Iraq Inquiry (Report of a Committee of Privy Counsellors) Executive Summary* (HC 264), p. 115: 'The statements prepared for, and used by the UK Government in public from late 2001 onwards conveyed more certainty than the JIC Assessments about Iraq's proscribed activities and the potential they posed'; p. 117: 'intelligence and assessments made by the JIC about Iraq's capabilities and intent continued to be used to prepare briefing material to support Government statements in a way which conveyed certainty without acknowledging the limitations of the intelligence'. Sir John has reiterated these findings since: 'The judgements about Iraq's capabilities in that statement, and in the dossier published the same day, were presented with a certainty that was not justified' in 'Sir John's Public Statement', 6 July 2016 at http://www.iraqinquiry.org.uk/the-inquiry/sir-john-chilcots-public-statement/; see also 'Iraq Inquiry: Full Transcript of Sir John Chilcot's BBC Interview', *BBC News*, 6 July 2017.

to force regime change, that diverged from those publicly articulated, to secure peaceful disarmament. Its plans was locked and loaded well before weapons inspectors could complete their job. Can lying in wartime be justified? This is an important question, but a separate one. Certainly, most of the wars Britain and the United States remember as honourable were also attended by dishonesty and dissembling. Wartime leaders most revered in the Anglosphere—Churchill, Lincoln, Roosevelt—were dissemblers all, suggesting the issue is less obvious than we may assume. This issue has attracted a sophisticated literature.[8] The question of deceit may help explain how states generate consent. It tells us little about the *recourse* to war. Charges of falsehood tell us little about what drove policymakers to war in the first place. This book is concerned less with deception than self-deception, the tragic process by which rulers are gripped by assumptions they fail to scrutinize.

Above all, I focus on the ideological roots of the decision to intervene. I explore three interlocking doctrines that formed the war's intellectual foundations: 'regime change', 'breaking states', and the 'blood price' of the Anglo-American relationship. Iraq, like other wars of this century, was an intellectual war, both opposed by intellectuals and 'made by intellectuals, and cheered on by intellectuals'.[9] President George W. Bush and Blair erected their beliefs on specific theoretical foundations about the world, and they sought intellectual opinion to buttress their doctrines, if not question them. The doctrines warmakers drew upon had a rich intellectual pedigree, such as the 'democratic peace', ideas that were widely accepted at the time, even if many advocates distanced themselves once the war ran aground. This book puts ideas, habitually sustained, collectively shared, and often uncritically accepted, back at the centre of the story. These are enduring habits of mind that led Britain into disaster, and might again.

EXPLAINING IRAQ: INTERPRETATIONS SO FAR

As we refight the war in memory, the most important historical question is the simplest one. Why did Britain take part in the first place? There is already a medium-sized academic literature addressing the question, offering competing explanations. Many accounts appeared before the Iraq Inquiry generated

---

[8] See John M. Schuessler, *Deceit on the Road to War: Presidents, Politics, and American Democracy* (Ithaca: Cornell University Press, 2015), pp. 7, 57–8, 125–6; Sissela Bok, *Lying: Moral Choice in Public and Private Life* (New York: Vintage Books, 1999); John J. Mearsheimer, *Why Leaders Lie: The Truth about Lying in International Politics* (Oxford: Oxford University Press, 2011), pp. 11, 23–4.

[9] As David Rieff observed, 'The Road to Hell', *New Republic*, 23 March 2011.

its documentation. They are often speculative, and replete with half-truths. Five versions can be identified: the 'poodle' explanation, attributing Britain's participation to its servile client status and alliance pressure; inadvertent escalation, identifying an accidental momentum created by a disarmament process that was supposed to avoid a final conflict; 'Blair's war', attributing Britain's entry predominantly to the will and agency of the Prime Minister; and 'virtue/vice', arguing that Britain went to war either for secret and diabolical reasons, or simply in good faith, for the reasons publicly articulated by the government. Each of these captures elements of the truth, but each also distorts the record.

The 'poodle' charge is a common interpretation. It is often vulgarly formulated as a product of Blair's power-worshipping tendencies, or the eagerness of British security elites to please Washington, as a servile client state, a critique famously played out in the 'romcom' film *Love Actually*. According to this theory, Blair invaded Iraq out of alliance pressure, real or anticipated. Those who draw this interpretation charge Downing Street with being seduced and strong-armed by its senior ally, with Blair capitulating to the superpower. Rosemary Hollis presents the decision in these terms, approvingly quoting the memoir of former Foreign Secretary Robin Cook: 'the real reason he [Blair] went to war was that he found it easier to resist the public opinion of Britain than the request of the US President'.[10] Hollis and Cook charge that Blair was 'programmed to respect power not rebel against it'. Sir Christopher Meyer's memoir speculates that Blair was seduced by the awe of Washington DC.[11] Geoffrey Wheatcroft's polemic takes the allegation to fever pitch, accusing Blair of behaving in the manner of a 'puppet or satellite', denouncing his 'servility' to Washington, going to Bush's retreat in Crawford, West Texas because he was 'summoned'.[12] Like many anti-Blair philippics, the portrait is incoherent, painting Blair as a warmongering egotist with 'great power' fantasies about Britain's stature, yet also a slavish vassal willingly subordinating Britain to a foreign potentates' will.

The 'poodle' interpretation of a craven Blair, doing as he is told, is an odd account of the figure who confronted trade union leaders and traditionalists within his own party over its constitution and voting system, a figure who had argued publicly for a decisive confrontation with Saddam Hussein years before Bush became president, and whose persistent pressure on President

---

[10] Rosemary Hollis, 'The United Kingdom: Fateful Decision, Divided Nation', in Rick Fawn & Raymond Hinnebusch (eds), *The Iraq War: Causes and Consequences* (London: Lynne Reiner, 2006), pp. 37–49, p. 39; quoting Robin Cook, *Point of Departure* (London: Simon & Schuster 2003), p. 104; see also Roderic Braithwaite, 'End of the Affair', *Prospect* 86 (2003), pp. 20–3.
[11] Christopher Meyer, *DC Confidential* (London: Weidenfeld & Nicolson, 2005).
[12] Geoffrey Wheatcroft, *Yo, Blair!* (London: Politico, 2007), pp. 7, 8.

Bill Clinton during the Kosovo crisis led Clinton to rebuke him for 'grandstanding'.[13] It is also an interpretation at odds with the observable dynamics of the Anglo-American relationship after 9/11. Blair was not 'summoned' to Bush's ranch, he was invited with flattering overtures, with signals communicated through Condoleezza Rice that the president wanted Blair's advice, not his compliance, advice on assembling a coalition that Blair delivered and Bush heeded. David Manning, his foreign policy advisor, privately advised Blair that it was a chance to exert 'real influence' on the United States, 'to push Bush on the Middle East'.[14] This is not the language of poodles. As we will see in Chapter 3, British Atlanticists desired from their solidarity with Washington not subordination and approval but influence, out of a flawed expectation of a grand strategic pay-off, and a belief that Britain could vicariously reclaim global leadership via its closeness to the US. The 'poodle' charge also misrepresents the dynamics between Blair and the US. It was not a case of the dog owner instructing its pet to come to heel. Bush's administration was not naturally multilateralist in its orientation, and did not feel the need to invest capital in pressuring allies to join the fray. Bush's administration held a growing confidence that while allied support and international mandates were desirable 'extras', it could confidently act alone. Indeed, the relationship is the reverse. Blair took more of the initiative to reach out to the Bush's administration in the aftermath of 9/11 and impose himself on events. There is also a significant recorded detail. In a phone call on the eve of Britain's parliamentary vote, a vote that could be fatal to his premiership, Bush repeatedly and emphatically assured Blair that Washington would sympathize if he dropped out of the warfighting coalition. Bush offered Britain an alternative supporting role through a second wave of peacekeeping. Blair gratefully declined the offer, advising the President 'I absolutely believe in this too ... I'm there to the very end'.[15] America was not making a forceful request for British participation, and stated a preference for the survival of an allied government over its risky participation in Iraq. Rather, Britain's government insisted on taking part. Alliance-related pressure would constrain the UK in other ways, but only later in the causal pathway, through the accelerating dynamics of mobilization, weather, and timetables. The 'poodle charge' flows from a disbelief that the Prime Minister actually believed in the cause. It relies on

---

[13] Kampfner, *Blair's Wars* (New York: Free Press, 2004), pp. 56–7; Christopher Meyer himself averred the sincerity and longevity of Blair's belief in the 'wickedness' of Saddam Hussein: Iraq Inquiry Testimony, 26 November 2009, pp. 41–2.
[14] Letter, David Manning to Blair, 'Your Trip to the US', 14 March 2002.
[15] Bob Woodward, *Plan of Attack* (London: Simon & Schuster, 2004), p. 338; Bush confirmed the conversation in a later interview, Con Coughlin, *American Ally: Tony Blair and the War on Terror* (New York: Harper Collins, 2006), p. 368: 'I told Tony ... rather than lose your government, withdraw from the coalition—because I felt it was very important for him to be the Prime Minister ... he told me, I'm staying, even if it costs me my government.'

a poorly supported demonology about Blair. It fails to distinguish between allied support and allied servility. And it falls back on a crude account of the Anglo-American relationship.

A second and flawed explanation is *inadvertent escalation*. According to this theory, Britain stumbled into war. The invasion was the product of an accidental momentum created by a disarmament process that was supposed to avoid a final conflict. The UK allegedly 'went to war in a comedy of errors, locked into a sequence of events that its government had worked so hard to avoid',[16] falling prey to a 'policy momentum, largely driven from Washington, which became impossible to slow down, still less reverse. The systemic failure to get off the rails that a prime minister, obsessed with leading from the front, had laid down is the real Chilcot story behind Tony Blair's own'.[17] Some versions of this interpretation then stretch to account for what happened next, charging that with the initial 'weapons of mass destruction (WMD)' and counterproliferation rationale discredited, the occupiers went on conveniently to the justifications of democracy promotion and nation-building. This draws partly on a typical 'bureaucratic politics' explanation, where governments reach decisions for functional reasons and then formulate rationales after the fact. This explanation is tied also to assumptions about how the Anglo-American relationship functioned. And it assumes that Blair's circle overconfidently invested their hopes in a UN mandate and process that would force Saddam to yield without a shooting war. As we will see, Britain's multilevel strategy was staked on a strong early assumption of regime change, probably involving participation in a war to forcibly overthrow Saddam, preferably through an attempt to gain UN approval, while publicly legitimizing this endgame as a disarmament process intended for a peaceful resolution. There was nothing accidental about Britain's war in Iraq. Coates and Krieger argue that Britain had no face-saving way out, denied a mandate but facing a defiant Saddam and under American pressure, with its unique-world-role 'arrogance' and imperialist pretensions. This interpretation need not detain us long. To attribute empire nostalgia to the Europhile, multiculturalist architects of New Labour is an odd gambit. And like the 'poodle' explanation, it is self-contradictory, positing a Britain that is both vassal state and great power fantasist. It is also directly contradicted by the historical record.

A third, flawed explanation is the 'One Man's War' account. This narrative recalls the project as overwhelmingly Blair's creation, where a messianic leader dragged his reluctant country to war. One strand of explanation puts weight on Blair's authoritarian 'personality type', stretching insights about the agency of leaders to the point where Iraq becomes a product of Blair's individual

---

[16] David A. Coates & Joel Krieger, *Blair's War* (Polity: Cambridge, 2004), p. 127.
[17] Michael Clarke, RUSI Briefing Note: 'Chilcot, The Judgement of History', 7 July 2016, https://rusi.org/commentary/chilcot-judgement-history.

foibles or obsessions,[18] his autocratic tendencies and gifts of persuasion. A silver-tongued charismatic leader, or a glib falsifier in some versions, almost single-handedly sold Britain the undertaking. The reduction of Iraq to Blair's persona has obvious political appeal. For those who doubt Iraq's legitimacy, the claim that it was conducted against strong domestic opposition is a major theme. For those who regret their support, Blair is a tempting target of blame-shifting. But if the Blair-focused approach is to be consequential to understanding Britain's decision-making, it implicitly must mount a counterfactual claim, that a different type of leader would not have taken Britain to war. 'His faith in his own star convinced him he was right about Iraq's supposed weapons of mass destruction. He then charmed parliament and voters into war. Nobody forgives being seduced and then deceived, which is why most Britons now despise Blair'.[19] This begs questions. Why were people so easily 'charmed', including Blair's most committed and bitter opponents outside and inside his own party, who were not in the habit of being seduced? If Blair did possess such powers, why did he fail when keenly advocated other causes, such as Britain joining the euro currency? Blair, it is true, was prone to dogmatic thinking and assumed a great capacity to control events. His dogmas, though, were rooted in ideas and historical experiences that lay well beyond his character. Neither is it obvious that without Blair, Britain would have kept its distance. Gordon Brown, Blair's Chancellor and who was the recognized future leader in the wings, admitted even when Iraq was imploding that he would have made the same decision, and later reaffirmed that the invasion was 'the right decision' for 'the right reasons' when appearing before Chilcot.[20] We can't know definitively what Brown would have done in Blair's position, but the refusal of Blair's greatest rival to repudiate the decision in hindsight, and even despite the political pay-offs, is significant. To carry the will of Parliament and assemble a wide domestic coalition, Blair needed more than self-belief and charm. His case for war needed the active help of other agents who might withhold support. And it had to resonate with a wider pool of assumptions.

This was Britain's war too, not just Blair's.[21] In public discussion, the former prime minister has since become the tribe's scapegoat, onto whom collective

---

[18] See Stephen Benedict Dyson, 'Personality and Foreign Policy: Tony Blair's Iraq Decisions', *Foreign Policy Analysis* 2:3 (2006), pp. 289–306; reworked in Oliver Daddow & Jamie Gaskarth (eds), 'New Labour, Leadership and Foreign Policy Making after 1997', in *British Foreign Policy: The New Labour Years* (New York: Palgrave, 2011), pp. 63–84.
[19] Simon Kuper, 'The chill behind Macron's charm', *FT Weekend*, 20–1 May 2017, p. 5.
[20] Interview cited in Patrick Wintour, 'Moment Blair and Brown Tied Knot, *The Guardian*, 30 April 2005; Gordon Brown, Iraq Inquiry Testimony, 5 March 2010, p. 3.
[21] See by contrast John Kampfner's title, *Blair's Wars*; for heavily Blair-centric and biographical accounts of the war's origins, framed as a decision by one leader in defiance of most of the nation, see Caroline Kennedy-Pipe and Rhiannon Vickers, 'Blowback for Britain? Blair, Bush and the War in Iraq', *Review of International Studies* 33 (2007), pp. 205–21; Jane M. O. Sharp,

sins are loaded before being driven out of the village. This is not to exculpate Blair or the weight of his decisions. This book will criticize his judgements in detail. To Blair's credit, he asks for understanding not exculpation. Instead, it is to resist the attempt to isolate the issue to one figure, and the attempt to avoid painful engagement with the war through the blood sport of Blair-obsession. Blair fulfils a similar exonerating function in Britain to 'neoconism' in the US, where a once-broad coalition of minds who supported the war claims in hindsight that a narrow cabal of ideologues made America do it.[22] That Blair's inner circle prepared their case in ways that precluded internal scrutiny is the beginning of the story, not the end. Blair could drive and discipline his cabinet but did not, and could not, foist the venture on his other compatriots in the dead of night. He could not have undertaken it had the ground been infertile. Paradoxically, Britain's Iraq decision was both covert and democratic. The inner circle conceived regime change as their goal and kept that ambition close to their chest. Yet when the conditions were fitting, they took it to the country. Iraq became one of the most democratically contested wars in British history, initiated only after a protracted public debate and vote in the House of Commons. Even Blair, armed with a well-honed propaganda machine, could only lead Britain to war because many were already receptive to the doctrines on which it rested. Powerful institutions rallied to the cause with impressive ease, from press barons to security service chiefs to Parliament, as did the military service chiefs whose forewarnings were low volume and gentle. Public figures, including Iraqis in exile, independently joined the coalition of pro-war opinion. Central to the argument was the press magnate Rupert Murdoch and his 175 newspapers worldwide, all of whom supported the invasion. Often depicted as a mere cut-throat businessmen, Murdoch is also an intellectual figure who came to the Iraq question through long-held ideological commitments.[23] He was, in his own words, 'a man of ideas'. Murdoch held and promoted the neoconservative vision of US heroic greatness, that marries democratic idealism with military assertiveness, using its hegemonic might to transform nations.[24] Long before Blair took office, Murdoch sponsored the *Weekly Standard*, America's foremost neoconservative publication whose signature project was the liberation

---

'The US-UK "Special Relationship" after Iraq', in Paul Cornish (ed.) *The Conflict in Iraq, 2003* (London: Palgrave, 2004), pp. 59–75.

[22] On 'neoconism', see Frank P. Harvey, *Explaining the Iraq War: Counterfactual Theory, Logic and Evidence* (Cambridge: Cambridge University Press, 2011), pp. 1–2.

[23] On this dimension of Murdoch, see Frank McKnight, *Murdoch's Politics: How One Man's Thirst for Wealth and Power Shapes Our World* (London: Pluto Press, 2013), pp. 172–93.

[24] On neoconservatism, see Michael C. Williams, 'Morgenthau Now: Neoconservatism, National Greatness, and Realism', in *Realism Reconsidered: The Legacy of Hans Morgenthau in International Relations* (New York: Oxford University Press, 2007), pp. 216–41, 217–27; Jacob Heilbrunn, *They Knew They Were Right: The Rise of the Neocons* (New York: Doubleday, 2009).

of Iraq, and maintained it at a loss, and his media embraced the 'Bush Doctrine' that realized these ideas. 'With our newspapers we have indeed supported Bush's foreign policy', he said, 'And we remain committed that way.'[25] Britain's 'Sun King', like other pro-war newspapers from the *Observer* to the *Financial Times*, were not subject to the government's whip. Of his own volition, Murdoch agitated for Blair to strike. In the week before the Commons war vote, he phoned Blair to urge against delay.[26] The Iraq War attracted major figures from the British intelligentsia across the spectrum, from Paul Johnson, Melanie Phillips, Anne Leslie, Michael Gove, and Max Hastings to David Aaronovitch, John Lloyd, and Nick Cohen. Among these names were ex-leftist radicals, who embraced American military power as an instrument of revolution. Blair's vision was nourished by collective assumptions that had built up before the 9/11 terrorist attacks that defined the period, assumptions about the nature of security, about what war was for, and what statecraft could achieve.

Those MPs who voted for war in Iraq, at times, have since scrambled for alibis, as have some of their supporters. They claim they lent their support only because they believed false intelligence, because they trusted the government, or that the blame lies with others for bad planning. Matthew Parris pleaded, 'we believed what we were told'.[27] Gordon Brown, the then Chancellor, has since claimed that he and his colleagues were 'misled' into supporting the war, and that had he known of one critical intelligence report of September 2002 that was withheld by the US until 2011, he would have doubted the case.[28] The report admitted that there was only a thin evidential base for the Iraqi WMD programme, and that most analysis was based on analytical assumptions rather than evidence.

But this hand-washing is bogus. Journalists and politicians are supposed to scrutinize authority. If they were persuaded by the official intelligence dossier, they were easily persuaded. In Brown's case, why should we accept that he would have weighed the withheld report more heavily than the other seemingly authoritative estimates he was given by the head of the Secret Intelligence Service, Richard Dearlove and his officials, or the seemingly compelling new evidence produced in September 2002 from the Iraqi defector, that he also mentions, about alleged mobile biological weapons production facilities? Even if the secret report had surfaced in time, why should we assume Brown would have believed it and rejected the others? No one was in a position to 'know'

---

[25] Joanna Chung, 'Unbiased Murdoch Stands By His Views', *Financial Times*, 27 October 2004.
[26] Alastair Campbell, *The Burden of Power: Countdown to Iraq* (London: Random House, 2012), Diary entries Tuesday 11 March 2003, p. 490.
[27] Cited in Joy Lo Dico, 'Big Guns of the Press all quiet on the Iraqi Front', *The Independent*, 16 March 2008.
[28] Gordon Brown, *My Life, Our Times* (London: Bodley Head, 2017), pp. 250, 254, 255.

that the secret, sceptical US report represented indisputable truth, or that it should outweigh the multiple other reports. Even that report still judged that Iraq 'is making significant progress in WMD programs', and that more precise knowledge was being obstructed by Iraqi Camouflage, Concealment and Decoys.[29] There was also in existence, in public, alternative credible sources to suggest doubts over the state of the Iraqi WMD Programme. If Brown had been open to dissuasion, he could have accessed the serious and informed doubts that were raised before the invasion, in public, by the head of UN weapons inspections Hans Blix, (as well as Dr Mohamed El Baradei of the International Atomic Energy Agency), to the Security Council on 14 February 2003, that 'so far, UNMOVIC [the United Nations Monitoring, Verification and Inspection Commission] has not found any such weapons [of mass destruction], only a small number of empty chemical munitions'.[30] If Brown had been truly prepared to revise the issue, at the time, on the basis of a weak intelligence base, he did not need access to a secret US report, especially one that still estimated that a progressing and covert WMD programme existed. Recall that one argument of the Blair and Bush governments was that the likely reason for any lack of final proof was Saddam's concealment, and that in a post-9/11 world, given incomplete knowledge, responsible states couldn't take the risk. Brown's own memoir supplies further evidence that early access to the document would probably not have changed his mind. Brown indicates he was predisposed to accept that Saddam, with his serial breaches of UN resolutions and his WMD programme, was a 'threat to regional and global order'. He recalls that he had strong domestic political incentives not to dissent over the war. At the time, he was already on a 'head-on collision' with Blair over the euro, NHS, and tuition fees, and so was 'anxious to avoid a fourth area of dispute, particularly one that was not my departmental responsibility'. Brown's alibi is implausible, that one critical missing document would have overturned a whole set of well-entrenched assumptions about power, order, and security. What mattered was the predispositions of those who, like Brown, consumed intelligence products.

Outside the government, politicians and journalists cannot plausibly reduce the issue to one of betrayed trust. In other policy areas, the tabloids and opposition MPs who supported the war regularly accused the Prime Minister of mendacity. They accepted the state's verdict because, ideologically, they were predisposed to. And they were not only evaluating the government's threat assessment, but were exercising a wider strategic judgement, that invading was a prudent choice and had a strong chance of succeeding. They

---

[29] Joint Staff, 'Iraq: Status of WMD Programs', 9 September 2002.
[30] 'Briefing of the Security Council, 14 February 2003: An update on inspections' at http://www.un.org/Depts/unmovic/new/pages/security_council_briefings.asp.

chose to support the argument that war would work. This, too, drew on assumptions that warrant scrutiny.

The 'Blair's War' alibi also places undue emphasis on administrative incompetence, a shifting of blame to 'bad planning' and administrative bungling, and the assumption that Iraq's 'lesson' is that military force must be aligned to and optimized around the 'reconstruction' of countries after overthrow.[31] The 'incompetence dodge' is a face-saving exercise that glibly suggests the profound political problems inherent to post-Saddam Iraq could have been administered or engineered away. 'Managerialist' accounts of Iraq sidestep questions of 'whether' to fight such wars, and to reduce Iraq's memory to a guide in 'how' to conduct such wars in future. Managerialists infer that the failure of Iraq is attributable to bad planning, rather than the idea of regime change itself. They draw from the campaign insights into nation-building and how to govern states once their own states have seized their capital. Ultimately, their concern is about failure to intervene, not intervention failure, and are determined to keep the flame of interventionism intact. They caution that we must not 'over-learn' from Iraq, lest it erodes our spirit of warlike idealism. They work to limit Iraq's salience as a precedent. Versions of this storyline, of invasion being spoilt by maladministration, and the need to remain predisposed to frequent intervention, are offered by other participants and observers, including grandees of British security policy like former Secretary of State Lord William Hague and former UK ambassador to the UN Sir Jeremy Greenstock. 'Yet action to support global order cannot be totally abandoned because particular campaigns ended badly', as Greenstock's straw-man reductionism has it.[32] To the contrary, the geopolitical storms created by those campaigns suggest that we should maintain global order differently. In finally admitting that the war in Iraq was a 'mistake', Lord Hague presents the error as a problem of proof ('We relied too much on evidence that turned out to be flimsy')[33] and stresses that there will need to be more intervention in the next quarter-century even than the last, returning to his most emphatic theme, based on a misrepresentation of recent history, that the gravest danger is Western passivity: 'We have seen in recent years that when the West pulls back, other actors come in'.[34] By the time Hague finishes qualifying the cautionary lessons of Iraq, the campaign shrinks into an unfortunate 'one-off' with the underlying agenda of liberal war undisturbed. We can identify other defects of managerialism that Chapter 2 will address in more

---

[31] See, e.g., Andrew Dorman, 'The United States and the War on Iraq', in Paul Cornish (ed.) *The Conflict in Iraq, 2003* (London: Palgrave, 2004), pp. 145–59, p. 155.

[32] Jeremy Greenstock, *Iraq: The Costs of War* (New York: William Heinemann, 2016), p. 424.

[33] William Hague, 'I admit it, Iraq was a mistake: but that shouldn't stop us intervening in Syria', *The Daily Telegraph*, 24 November 2015.

[34] Reported comment at the RUSI Land Warfare Conference, 2017, Tweet 27 June 2017, 1.26 a.m.

depth: managerialists underestimate the profound problems of breaking and remaking states and governing foreign populations. Their arguments tend to treat host populations not primarily as active political agents with visions and agendas of their own, but as passive recipients who must be better administered into stable market democracy. In that sense, managerialists carry colonial attitudes to those they wish to assist. They wrongly interpret post-Iraq cases, from Libya to Syria, as instances of Western 'retreat' or 'non-intervention'. In their fixation with staging military operations in order to impress third parties of the West's 'resolve', they treat international life as a narcissistic drama about Western political will, and overstate the prospects of waging peripheral wars in order to impress other major powers into submission. And in their vision of permanent armed revolution, they betray the same attitude as another idealistic and relentless warmaker, Philip II, of whom it was said that 'No experience of the failure of his policy could shake his belief in its essential excellence.'[35] Those who embraced the cause of 'regime change' would hardly deny themselves a share of the credit for the consequences if it had been a cheap and rapid success. They must accept co-responsibility for their 'judgement call'.

A narrow focus on Blair arises also from what we might call the legalist tradition about the Iraq War. Legalists approach the Iraq War primarily as a crime, rather than a blunder. They emphasize above all the war's criminal unlawfulness. The decision-makers, too, devoted much energy and time to building their case and legitimizing it at home and abroad.[36] Legalist critics range from polemicists such as Tom Bowyer and Owen Jones, to scholars such as Glen Rangwala, to former intelligence and weapons experts such as Brian Jones, to jurist Phillipe Sands.[37] They suggest that successful diplomacy relies upon the legitimacy that only the United Nations can bestow. In this prosecutorial tradition, Blair specifically must answer a charge of high crimes and suffer impeachment. But in 2003, warmakers also considered themselves internationalists. They too believed that they were enforcing international principles, to the extent that they were willing to flout the global community's formal rules in order to strengthen its writ. The US and British governments successfully persuaded others to support the invasion, illegal or otherwise.

---

[35] Barbara Tuchman, *The March of Folly: From Troy to Vietnam* (New York: Knopf, 1984), p. 7.

[36] See in particular James Strong, *Public Opinion, Legitimacy and Tony Blair's War in Iraq* (London: Routledge, 2017).

[37] Tom Bower, *Broken Vows: Tony Blair, the Tragedy of Power* (London: Faber & Faber, 2016); Owen Jones, 'The War in Iraq was not a blunder or a mistake. It was a Crime', *The Guardian*, 7 July 2016; Glen Rangwala, *A Case to Answer: A First Report on the Potential Impeachment of the Prime Minister for High Crimes and Misdemeanours in Relation to the Invasion of Iraq* (London, Spokesman, 2004); Philippe Sands, *Lawless World: Making and Breaking Global Rules* (London: Penguin, 2005).

A number of liberal democracies supported Washington's claim that the best way to uphold world order was to overthrow Saddam Hussein after his serial affronts to it, and argued that an insistence on unanimity had paralysed the international community in the past. It was not a case of virtuous internationalists versus malign rule-breakers. It was a conflict between competing visions of global order, as one side stressed the unity of the United Nations, the other its credibility.[38] This division had been anticipated in 1999, when NATO countries and their supporters argued that their unauthorized bombing of Serbia to oppose genocide and war crimes was illegal but legitimate. So too did advocates of the Iraq War in 2003. As the hawkish intellectual Robert Kagan noted, 'In 2003 France and Germany and other European nations were demanding that the United States adhere to an international legal standard that they themselves had ignored, for sound moral and humanitarian reasons, a mere four years earlier'.[39] Iraq stands for a wider question, about competing visions for what it means to uphold international order. A war's legality—or otherwise—can only be determined by a properly constituted court.[40] Ultimately, the difficulty with legalism is pragmatic. In the absence of an international system whereby powerful states will actually be tried, or rulers prosecuted, and in a world where states from time to time believe they must infringe rules to uphold order, these are questions of judgement that cannot be resolved in courts.

Finally, there is the 'virtue/vice' school of interpretation. This approach treats the matter as a morality play, from opposing angles, whereby the British government acted out of simple good faith or bad. One version, centred on 'vice', speculates that Britain's participation was driven by unspeakable ulterior motives covered by deception. Peter Oborne, for instance, insinuates an anti-Islamic motivation on Blair's part, referring to his 'habit of attacking Muslim countries'.[41] The suggestion that Britain attacked those countries because they were Islamic would intrigue the Muslim majority populations of Sierra Leone and Kosovo, on whose behalf the UK intervened before Iraq. It also sits oddly with Blair's well-documented admiration for all Abrahamic faiths, his government's oversight of a mass immigration programme

---

[38] This distinction was outlined by Sir George Young, MP, in the debate on 18 March 2003: 'the debate concerns the credibility of the United Nations on the one hand, and its unity on the other. The Prime Minister's view is that unless firm action is taken now, the UN's credibility will be fatally undermined. The alternative view is that moving too fast will shatter the unity of the UN, thus fatally undermining it'.

[39] Robert Kagan, *Paradise and Power: American and Europe in the New World Order* (London: Atlantic Books, 2003), p. 129.

[40] Neither is there a clear link between legal authorization and strategic success. Most of the violence that occurred in post-Saddam Iraq took place after the United Nations Security Council passed resolution 1546 in June 2004, unanimously authorizing the continuing presence of a multinational force.

[41] Oborne, *Not the Chilcot Report*, p. 166.

including a surge of migration from Muslim majority countries, and his daily reading of the Qur'an.[42]

Hostile accounts of Britain's war in Iraq often share one overriding quality, an assumption there can be no idealism in a war that was allegedly dishonest or illegal. Iraq was such a low gambit, they assume, that it must have been bereft of idealism and dominated by narrow and material *Realpolitik*. As Piers Robinson charges, 'to what extent might have western populations been manipulated into support for a war on terrorism that was as much about geo-strategic opportunism and aggressive wars, as it was about tackling Islamic fundamentalist terrorism?'[43] Notice the structure of Robinson's question, dividing the 'geo-strategic' from the armed struggle against Islamism. The document he builds this case on, 'The War Against Terrorism: The Second Phase',[44] shows Blair clearly linking the broader Islamist threat to seven countries. The idealists who took Britain to Iraq believed that if a geostrategic opportunity presented itself, it was a chance to attack Islamism's foundations, for militant Islamism they believed was one by-product and symptom of a dysfunctional regional order. Because opponents of the war so often cannot bring themselves to imagine that the warmakers also held ideals, they struggle to explain it.

A more widespread version of the 'bad faith' tradition alleges that it was mainly a project to secure Western oil interests, whether by unlocking a rich source of petroleum for the international market, or by seizing a geostrategic foothold to secure access, with other stated rationales working as high-minded 'cover'.[45] This draws too on the demonology about Blair. More subtle observers, like Paul Rogers, frame the issue more gingerly, inferring intention from likely effect:

> A cynical analyst might conclude that one function of the war, at least in the short term and from a US perspective, was to break OPEC, damage the economies of countries such as Iran and Venezuela and ensure price cuts at gas stations in the run-up to the 2004 presidential election.[46]

We may doubt whether the US Democrats who voted to authorize the President's use of force were eager to maximize Bush's chances of re-election, and the oil market plays a strikingly marginal role in the records of US deliberations that we do have. But it is hard ultimately to falsify such theories.

---

[42] Tim Adams, 'This Much I know: Tony Blair', *The Guardian*, 12 June 2011.
[43] Piers Robinson, 'Learning from the Chilcot Report: Propaganda, Deception and the War on Terror', *International Journal of Contemporary Iraqi Studies* 11 (2017), pp. 47–73, 69.
[44] Memo, Blair to Bush, 4 December 2001.
[45] Nafeez Ahmed, 'Iraq invasion was about oil: Maximising Persian Gulf oil flows to avert a potential global energy crisis motivated Iraq War planners—not WMD or democracy', *The Guardian*, 20 March 2014.
[46] Paul Rogers, *A War Too Far*, p. 50.

The totality of motivations are irrecoverable, and hidden motives by definition are hard to reconstruct. In Britain's case, if there were secret alternative rationalizations, they must have been very secret. As we will see, along with a process of alleged deception, we can also identify expressions of intense and consistent beliefs in private communications and in the testimonies of Blair's opponents within cabinet, where oil was mostly marginal, second order or unmentioned, all of which suggests authenticity and genuinely held core convictions.

The 'oil' hypothesis is often formulated simplistically, presenting the Iraq adventure as a war of plunder. Oil, to be sure, had to form part of the calculus. Had Iraq not been a potentially wealthy oil-rich state located in a region regarded by London and Washington as strategically sensitive and adjacent to other sources of threat, policymakers may not have ranked it so highly on their hierarchy of interests, and there was a general aspiration that a liberated Iraq would return to a fully functioning part of the international energy market. Oil mattered less as a 'spoil' of war but more indirectly and generally. Petro-dollars were a strategically potent resource that policymakers feared a hostile state like Saddam's could use to generate threatening capability, such as nuclear weapons.[47] If, on the other hand, profitable access to Iraq's energy resources was the overriding motive, as opposed to a second-order one, Western powers had cheaper means short of invading the country. To get Iraqi oil flowing in greater volumes, and to increase their access, they could have lifted economic sanctions. For twelve years by enforcing sanctions, they had conducted a policy despite, not because of, an interest in maximizing Iraq's oil output. If a prime concern for the US had been to 'lock in' privileges for their own oil companies, overthrowing the regime was not the easiest way to do it. They could have privately bargained with the regime in Baghdad, as did the anti-war statesman, French President Jacques Chirac. Oil is a fungible commodity on the global market, its price is affected by overall supply and demand, and does not require seizure of a country to secure access to it.

The picture that emerges from the documentary sources is different. Oil interests in British decision-making circles, while not overlooked, were an afterthought. Blair's circle and the Parliament predominantly willed the removal of Saddam Hussein for other ambitious, security-related reasons. Only later did they calculate that in the event of his removal, they should ensure their companies a share of the spoils. There was, from 31 October 2002, lobbying by British companies BP, Shell, and BG to the Department of Trade and Industry for a slice of the contracts in post-Saddam Iraq.[48] This date that came after, not before, Blair's circle had privately settled on its decision to

---

[47] See Charles L. Glaser & Rosemary A. Kelanic, 'Getting out of the Gulf: Oil and US military strategy', *Foreign Affairs* 96:1 (2017), pp. 122–31, 128.
[48] Minute Christopher Segar to PS/Baroness Symons, 31 October 2002, 'Iraq Oil'.

participate in military action, so the causal sequence was the reverse of the 'plunder' thesis. Liz Symons, Minister of State for Trade, noted, 'we have been making the case publicly that this conflict is about WMD not oil (as many have unfairly claimed)'.[49] If anything, British firms expressed concern to her that the state was not being ruthless *enough* in pursuing commercial interests in a post-bellum Iraq, and that with momentum for war building, Britain was losing out to American and French firms in an emerging market. In the words of Colin Adams, of the trade association British Consultants and Construction Bureau, as relayed by Symons to Straw, 'insufficient action appears to be happening at the political level to safeguard UK interests when the situation in Iraq is finally normalised'. British envoys were in the awkward position of emphasizing that security interests were paramount, but that the state would still lend support in Washington to British oil companies. Britain pushed the US to ensure more rigorous international oversight over the management of Iraqi oil revenues. The British embassy advised UK oil companies that 'US motivation as regards Iraq parallels our own: this is a matter of national security, not oil',[50] while also urging Downing Street to take up the matter with the White House. Britain's main decision-makers did not think, even in private, that a grab for Iraq's oil was the main purpose. A paper from the Foreign and Commonwealth Office set down as a principal aim of a stable Iraq selling oil on world markets, but described securing reconstruction contracts for British companies as a 'second order objective'.[51] With the campaign underway, Blair urged Bush to outline a vision of Iraq's political and economic future 'to dispel the myth that we were out to grab Iraq's oil'.[52] British policy settings were not optimized around exploiting opportunities for its oil companies. US rules enabled Washington to favour American companies in disbursing reconstruction contracts, whereas Britain's rules from April 2001 denied preferential treatment to British firms. There evidently was concern within government to ensure a pay-off once war was underway. But an anxiety to receive incidental material benefits once a decision is taken is not the same as core prior motive. Nor does it falsify the other aims that Blair's circle repeatedly and fulsomely asserted.

The other side of the 'virtue/vice' approach is the 'good faith' version.[53] This account of Britain's participation is a sympathetic one, and arises partly out of discontent with the sometimes hysterical allegations of anti-war critics.

---

[49] Memo Liz Symons to Jack Straw, 1 November 2002, 'Iraq: Commercial Aspects'.
[50] Christopher Meyer to David Manning, 15 November 2002, 'Iraqi Oil'.
[51] Mark Sedwill to David Manning, 'Scenarios for the Future of Iraq after Saddam', 20 September 2002.
[52] Nicholas Cannon to Simon McDonald, 31 March 2003, 'Iraq: Prime Minister's Conversation with Bush, 31 March'.
[53] Vernon Bogdanor, 'The Iraq War, 2003', Lecture, Gresham College, 17 May 2016; Christoph Bluth, 'The British road to war: Blair, Bush and the Decision to Invade Iraq',

Britain's war, it argues, was waged in good faith and, without the luxury of hindsight, in circumstances that were compelling. As well as accepting the basic honesty of the government's case, it also accepts Blair's calculation about the problem. It supports, or at least sympathizes with, the premise that failing to strike Iraq would amount to an imprudent failure to act. Britain in March 2003 had no 'good' choices, and given the risks implied in restraint, was on balance wise to take the difficult path of conflict. A later chapter tackles these apologetic arguments, and the dubious counterfactual claims on which they rest.

Elements of the above interpretations contain some truths. As we will see, there was an Anglo-American relationship consideration, though not a 'poodle' version; oil was indirectly relevant, not an overriding driver; Blair was a driving force who needed other conditions in place to succeed; and perceptions and presentation of threat mattered in implementing a genuine calculation about security. The best question is how these elements ranked and interlocked, and what inferior interpretations leave out.

CHAPTER SUMMARY

In Chapter 1, 'Warpath', I argue that Britain's war in Iraq was enabled and driven by an interaction of power and ideas, a particular blend of fear and confidence. A set of ideas about how best to pursue security, ideas enabled by the capabilities of the US, created the warpath, and those ideas were insulated and taken for granted. Like Bush, Blair's circle decided on war because it hardly occurred not to, or to entertain alternatives. Dogmatic ideas were not merely the property of the decision-making elite: they could thrive, even in the glare of parliamentary debate. Decision-makers were ideologically predisposed to war, and thus neglected the most important question of whether to strike. A set of basic assumptions, flowing from a pre-existing and widely held ideology, and the logic of preventive and coalition war, went unexamined, and proved decisive. Blair and his inner circle assumed war was inevitable—the only prudent choice was to force the issue now, on their terms, rather than later, on Saddam's. They worried predominantly about how to create conditions that would legitimize a British military campaign, that would generate enough support, and that would predispose the country against further postponement of the final reckoning. By taking this wandering course, however, they were moving towards a fixed end. They imposed on their compatriots the tightening pressures of mobilization, the impatience of their senior ally, and

International Affairs 80:5 (2004), pp. 871–92; John Rentoul, 'Let's Have a Serious Debate about Chilcot, and stop claiming Blair is a war criminal', *Middle East Eye*, 5 July 2016.

the mounting fear of the reputational costs of standing down. Even when the degraded quality of Iraq's arsenal and its relative weakness was declared by inspectors on the eve of war, they calculated that only a complete capitulation by the regime would do. They reckoned they could no longer live with the ambiguities and frustrations of the status quo. The ghosts of Suez taught them that they could only influence the superpower by aligning with it. Ultimately, Britain followed America to war because recent experience and embedded ideas taught them a simple truth, that war worked.

Chapter 2 forms the core of my argument. In this chapter, I trace the ideological roots of 'regime change', identifying regime change as an underlying form of security-seeking. Though it took the structural fact of American power and the contingent event of the 9/11 terrorist attacks to make the assault on Saddam possible, it was also conditioned by the rise in the previous decade of a set of ideas about liberalism and security. Those ideas bred a 'common sense' that presented disputable ideas as obvious: that 9/11 was a harbinger, not an aberration, warranting high-risk and radical measures; that designated 'rogue' actors are undeterrable aggressors who we cannot live with; and that given the obvious 'arc' of history towards democracy and capitalism, Western power can be applied to transform whole regions if only Westerners have the will. I then refute an alternative argument, made by two liberal-internationalist scholars John Ikenberry and Dan Deudney, that the intellectual foundations of the Iraq War were primarily realist, and that the ideological tradition of liberalism had little to do with it. As I demonstrate, liberals and liberalism were deeply implicated. The forceful reassertion of American primacy was not an amoral exercise in power maximization. It was infused with an idealism that has deep historical roots. Moreover, liberalism and the pursuit of hegemony are not antithetical, as the authors imply. Liberalism married with the capabilities of a superpower gives America a proclivity for reckless military adventures. So long as liberalism, untampered by prudential balance-of-power realism, remains a central engine of American grand strategy, the US will be prone to further such tragedies.

Chapter 3 turns to the Anglo-American relationship, and the ambition that by aligning with the United States and paying the 'blood price', Britain can win great influence over its strategic direction. Rather than subordinating itself to receive material benefits, British decision-makers believed that by aligning with the US in the War on Terror, they were generating the ability to steer a superpower that otherwise might run amok and jettison itself from the international community. The belief that Britain could have this leverage was encouraged by apparent success in steering the Bush administration towards the United Nations and its authority as the framework through which to confront Saddam. However, the experience of preparing and waging war as junior partner revealed the contradictions within the 'special relationship' mindset. Influence, so the theory goes, must derive from acquiescence, and continued acquiescence to the outlines of US policy is necessary to retain influence.[54] This renders any influence highly circumscribed. Having pledged support for a policy, that support must continue and Britain can only influence its execution (and the course of the campaign revealed the limits on Britain's ability even to shape that). Otherwise, the ability to influence policy will be withdrawn and estrangement or even punishment will follow. Past solidarity creates a path-dependent pressure to tow the line, in order to obtain an influence that Britain in the most critical hour dare not exercise or test. Ultimately, the 'special relationship' ambition misconceives the complexity of policymaking in Washington, confusing historical sentiment for geopolitical leverage.

In Chapter 4, I weigh the arguments, and construct the strongest possible case in favour of 'regime change' both with hindsight, and without. Hawks pose serious 'what if' questions: what were the alternatives to war? What risks and costs would US-led allies have borne if they had refrained from invading? I demonstrate that the defences of the war rest on counterfactual historical claims that are implausible and, in any case, less grave that what actually happened, even on 'worst case' calculations. The strongest retrospective case for war still involves fragile gains made at costs so heavy, with such serious unintended consequences, that decision-makers would have judged them prohibitive, had they known them in advance. As I will argue, not invading was a lesser evil than invading. Saddam's Iraq was a diminished and wretched force that posed little serious threat, the US-led coalition had successfully shackled the regime by 2003, weakened its ability to threaten the region, and had established effective deterrence. But there is no avoiding the implications of restraint: restraint would have constituted effective toleration for continued Ba'ath party's predatory rule, with all the consequences. The West, I argue, could have coexisted with and contained a weakened Iraq even in a situation where sanctions were breaking down. There was already evidence, before March 2003, that Saddam's regime could be deterred and restrained by clear Western signalling, there are strong reasons to assume that a 'rogue state–terrorism nexus' had not and would not form in Iraq, and that there was time and capacity to disrupt any rearmament or threatening behaviour. Between 'regime change' and 'doing nothing' there was a prudent middle way of vigilant 'overwatch' available to US-led forces.

In Chapter 5, I argue that a return to realism of a prudent and sceptical kind can help temper the pathologies that led to the Iraq War, on several fronts. It can counsel governments against excess certainty. In particular, it cautions against the 'Gordian Knot' temptation, the impatient urge to eliminate sources of insecurity and impose decisive solutions on problems, in particular the

---

[54] For a similar critique, see Alex Danchev, 'Greeks and Romans: Anglo-American Relations After 9/11', *The RUSI Journal* 148:2 (2003), pp. 16–19, 18.

perennial demand for the downfall of adversary regimes. Realism can inform policymakers what war can affordably achieve. As well as placing princes on their guard against predation, it encourages prudent war avoidance. Mindful that states cannot avoid living with insecurity, uncertainty, and risk, we can draw upon realist insight to restore deterrence and consequential diplomacy as the central foundations of security. And with realism, we can guard against the temptation to view international life as a morality play requiring ideological crusades, recognizing it instead as a tragedy where good intentions can be deadly, as a conflicted world where not all good things go together, and where major powers can be their own worst enemies.

In the Epilogue, I offer two speeches to leave the matter for readers to judge. First, there is the televised address Blair gave on the eve of war. And there is an alternative address he could have given, setting out an alternative logic of restraint. It draws on arguments and warnings made and neglected at the time.

1

Warpath

> The wandering course to a fixed end which is the pattern of the rage of Achilles...[1]

In this first chapter, I reconstruct Britain's road to war. I explain how various impulses, pressures, and temptations came together between the terrorist attacks of the autumn of 2001 and the invasion of spring 2003. I do so with an eye to the interaction of three levels of explanation and causation, as taxonomized by the political scientist Kenneth Waltz.[2] The interlocking causes worked through the international system, the domestic level and the 'unit' level of decision-makers. In divining this war's causes, as with any war, there is one central analytical problem. Even if the world is a perpetually insecure place with a dismal recurrence of conflict, most states most of the time do not enter armed conflict with most other states, including their main adversaries and rivals. The 'constant' of insecurity does not in itself explain variation. We must, therefore, not only give an account of threat perception, or why British decision-makers regarded Saddam Hussein's regime as threatening. They had regarded him as threatening for the thirteen years prior to invasion. We must explain how a long period of enmity and active hostility—that had not translated into all-out war—then did so. We must identify a process of change, how low- to medium-level hostility escalated into an actual clash.[3] Even if we accept that Britain had effectively been at war with Iraq by using force and sanctions to punish breaches of an earlier ceasefire, we must still explain how a long, grinding siege then transformed into a different and more direct campaign to decapitate the enemy. What impersonal forces and prior choices delivered the actors to this point? What did they consciously think they were doing? How did the three leaders and their inner circle get into such a fatal

---

[1] From Bernard Knox, introduction to *The Iliad* (trans. Robert Fagles, New York: Penguin, 1990), p. 12.

[2] Kenneth Waltz, *Man, the State, and War* (New York: Columbia University Press, 1959).

[3] On the need for explanation for how general 'structural' constants like insecurity translate into actual war, see Jack Levy, 'The Causes of War and the Conditions of Peace' *American Review of Political Science* 1 (1998), pp. 139–65, p. 142.

dance? In brief, I argue that the 9/11 attacks of 2001 coincided with a period of growing confidence in the US and Britain that the West <u>could</u> remake international conditions, and a mounting fear that it <u>could *only*</u> <u>be secure by doing so</u> in a dangerously globalizing planet. Britain's decision-makers genuinely shared this outlook, and took part out of a confidence that they could guide and restrain the superpower.

This chapter attempts to explain a single conflict. To that end, I attend to the particularities and unique circumstances of the context, to offer the most accurate possible portrayal of the war's origins and its causal hierarchy. To do so also requires us to go beyond a close study of the documentary record, and borrow assumptions from the study of the origins of wars generally, to assist our analysis with more generic concepts. Iraq, like all individual cases, was unique in its particular combination of people and circumstances. But its defining 'parts'—a preventive war, a coalition war, a war of regime change, were not *sui generis*. It bears comparison with other cases where rulers role the dice. We should therefore go beyond single-case analysis, to help us learn something from Iraq. This chapter, therefore, enters into a dialogue between the case of Iraq and general theory, helping them inform one another. A trade-off of rigour and richness is needed in explaining any conflict. Without rigour, assumptions go untested. Without richness, the dominance of generic categories makes us lose sight of complexity, and human agency, and raises inflated hopes of scientific predictability.

The chapter has three parts. In Part I, we begin in Baghdad. Saddam Hussein's choices are a point of entry into a wider problem, the propensity for dogmatic miscalculation to cause war. In Part II, we move to Washington. At the international level, the defining reality and permissive cause was one of unchecked American power and how its wielders made their calculations in the wake of 9/11. This was a war conceived and designed primarily in America. As early signals from Washington indicated, it was very likely going to happen. Britain's choice was whether and how far to join in. London had some influence over decisions about how and when to proceed, and over the declared rationale. Indeed, Blair's role was to articulate the cause of regime change most effectively for Americans and the wider world. The reality, however, was that the American drive to war in Iraq worked as a 'juggernaut', in the words of Blair's Private Secretary and foreign policy advisor Matthew Rycroft, that those outside the interagency process could only hope to influence, push or pull, but rarely stop.[4] In the circumstances of a wounded and determined superpower striking out, not even America's primary ally could have stopped the war happening. President Bush was moving inexorably towards forced regime change in Baghdad.

---

[4] Matthew Rycroft, Iraq Inquiry Testimony [Henceforth abbreviated 'IIT'], 10 September 2010, p. 7.

In Part III, we move to London. London, like Washington, approached the issue as a preventive war. As I argue, that type of initiative typically flows from a particular alchemy of fear and confidence. Blair's inner circle believed in what it was doing, that it was prudent to align Britain with the effort to eliminate a gathering threat. It believed Britain and its allies were vulnerable enough to make Saddam Hussein an unacceptable menace, yet powerful enough to make him an easy target, and that liberating Iraq was a natural step on the right side of history. Beyond assessments of Iraq, there was a wider momentum towards 'visionary world-ordering', a growing idea that the optimal response to 9/11 was an ambitious effort to transform the Greater Middle East, the crucible of a global conflict of ideas.

In Part IV, we examine how the main decision-makers persuaded Britain to go to war by investing urgency and a sense of imminent peril into the question, framing a genuine perceived threat as a 'clear and present' danger, and steering the confrontation with Iraq to a point of escalation where relaxing pressure and refusing invasion was hard to accept, and where urgency was reinforced by fears of reputational cost. Path dependency (or the constraining effect of prior decisions on later decisions) also exerted greater force over time. By the time Parliament debated the question in March 2003, British forces were mobilized in the Gulf at an unsustainable level, the government had made open commitments to coercive disarmament, had warned of the penalties of standing down, and America was unmistakably readying its sword. Climbing down or moderating was difficult to accept. Blair as the principal agent in the process had deliberately led Britain down the path to this point.

PART I. BAGHDAD'S WAR

Before moving onto the invaders' calculations, we should consider Iraq's.[5] Britain's war in Iraq took three to tango. The First Armoured Division that it committed to the fight would not have found itself advancing through southern Iraq to guard America's flanks in the spring of 2003 if Washington had not

---

[5] On Saddam's miscalculations and the regime's estimates, see Gregory D. Koblentz, 'Saddam versus the Inspectors: the impact of regime security on the verification of Iraq's WMD disarmament' *Journal of Strategic Studies* (2016) published online only at http://www.tandfonline.com/doi/abs/10.1080/01402390.2016.1224764; *Comprehensive Report of the Special Advisor to the DCI on Iraq's WMD* (the 'Duelfer Report'): 'Regime Strategic Intent' section, pp. 1, 29–32, 47; David D. Palkki & Mark Stout, *The Saddam Tapes: The Inner Workings of a Tyrant's Regime, 1978–2001* (Cambridge: Cambridge University Press, 2013); Kevin Woods, James Lacey & Williamson Murray, 'Saddam's delusions: The View from the Inside' *Foreign Affairs* 85:3 (2006), pp. 2–28; Michael R. Gordon & Bernard E. Trainor, *Cobra II: the Inside Story of the Invasion and Occupation of Iraq* (New York: Atlantic Books, 2006), esp. pp. 55–75.

chosen war. And they wouldn't have met resistance had not Iraq also made certain choices. For an attack to become armed struggle, the opposing party must also willingly resist. And resist the adversary did, though not well.

In the twenty-fourth year of his rule, the Fifth President of Iraq had come to seem permanent. Sycophantic poets hymned Saddam Hussein as part of nature, 'the peak of the mountains and the roar of the seas'.[6] Saddam had long marinated in power, surviving purges, CIA-backed revolts, wars, defeat in the Gulf War of 1991 and the economic strangulation of his regime from outside. And this in a country historically vulnerable to invasion. At a vulnerable crossroads, Iraq bordered six other states. Its flat, alluvial plains had no natural barriers. Aggressors had fallen upon it again and again. Endurance in such lethal conditions can breed fantasy. Saddam became a victim of his own mythologized longevity, or in the words of one British MP who graced his court, his 'indefatigability'. Increasingly detached, the self-styled modern-day Nebuchadnezzar who had debauched the public sphere with the vulgar architecture of self-celebration now devoted more time to writing novels, delegating the job of governing to his lieutenants. He had become insensitive to the shifts going on around him. Saddam believed he had America's measure. He had told his own subordinates that if Iraq rode out the siege that had lasted since the withdrawal from Kuwait, America would be revealed as incapable of overthrowing the state. Iraq's forces, he bragged, had sustained losses in the battle of the Fao Peninsula in the war against Iran that were equal to America's entire losses in the Vietnam War. Saddam distributed to his army the film *Black Hawk Down* about the battle of Mogadishu that triggered America's retreat from Somalia. As Saddam told it, America's flight after only eighteen soldiers were killed—at the hands of 'pagans' who had ruined and shamed them—was symptomatic of the superpower's reluctance to pay the price of invasion.

Saddam's defiance in 2002–3 has long puzzled outsiders. With strident demands for disarmament at the point of a barrel, and hostile forces gathering on his border, surely there were compelling reasons to yield. It would never have been possible to prove the negative of final disarmament. He could, though, have cooperated more fully with weapons inspectors, admitted them without restriction, permitted his scientists to be interviewed outside the country, and ceased all evasion, concealment, or non-compliance. This would have weakened the Anglo-American rationale for military action. Cooperation and certification by international inspectors of his disarmament would have allowed Iraq to export oil again, after the annual loss of tens of billions of dollars in revenue.

---

[6] Cited in Joseph Sassoon, *Saddam Hussein's Ba'th Party: Inside an Authoritarian Regime* (Cambridge: Cambridge University Press, 2011), p. 181.

Why, then, didn't he realize the game was up? Some argue that Saddam refused to cooperate fully because he wished to practise 'deterrence by doubt', to bluff adversaries into believing he had deadly capabilities in reserve. Thanks now to captured records of the regime's inner deliberations, we can trace a path to war that was less about deterring adversaries and more about securing the regime from outside penetration. Like Stalin whom he aped, Saddam Hussein reigned through studied paranoia. He was determined to coup-proof his rule. Iraq's previous rulers had been violently deposed, their bodies dismembered and dishonoured: in July 1958 the regent Abd al-Ilah was dragged through Baghdad to be hung, only for the architect of the coup, General Abd al-Karim Qassem, to be shot dead four years later. Abdal Rahman Arif was luckier, being deposed into exile, while Saddam's immediate predecessor Ahmed Hassan al-Bakr wisely took his deputy's advice to retire for health reasons. This background makes it easier to understand Baghdad's reluctance to give unrestricted access to international bodies to comb the country at will. The regime regarded international inspection bodies, from UNSCOM (the United Nations Special Commission) to the IAEA (the International Atomic Energy Agency), as vehicles of subversion infested by foreign spies, potentially giving Washington the coordinates of his own location for a cruise missile strike. Even if there was a danger of the US and UK making good on their threats, full cooperation with the international community would expose his security apparatus to foreign infiltration. He must also have been nervous that unlimited capitulation would invite challenge and revolt. It would be a capitulation and a death sentence. In the process of surveillance, verification, and disarmament, the stakes were existential. Saddam therefore walked a precarious line, cooperating enough to divide and weaken the coalition enforcing sanctions, and resisting enough to insulate his regime.

Saddam's apprehension about weapons inspections being tied to a hostile campaign to topple him were not entirely unfounded. The inspections process had an abiding difficulty. The superpower demanding inspections and threatening punishment also demanded Saddam's removal from power. Anglo-American ultimatums, that Saddam must disarm 'or else', were undercut by their refusal to guarantee he could stay in power if he actually disarmed. Deterrence works only when the actor on the receiving end can be confident that choosing to be deterred, and avoiding forbidden behaviour, will make a difference and help them survive. Throughout the interwar period between 1991 and 2003, there were demands for Saddam's overthrow or assassination within the political class and commentariat.[7] US security services had attempted to kill Saddam during and after Gulf War One and later in a failed coup

---

[7] Thomas L. Friedman, 'Head Shot', *The New York Times*, 6 November 1997; George Stephanopoulos, 'Why We Should Kill Saddam', *Newsweek*, 1 December 1997, p. 34.

attempt in June 1996.[8] Even when the UN issued Resolution 1441 in November 2002 demanding Iraq's full and final disarmament, a senior US administration official suggested Saddam would still be tried for war crimes even if he disarmed.[9] Disarmament, therefore, could not be counted on as a path to survival to reduce his adversaries' hostility. To the contrary, that the diplomatic campaign for his disarmament was coupled with a continuous death threat created incentives to ride out the pressure and hold ambitions for rearmament.

Saddam's response to this dilemma was to manipulate and divide his coalition of enemies, mindful that France and Russia were more biddable to eventual reconciliation and a resumption of business. 'Gaming' the international community might have worked before. But in the wake of 9/11, it was now too cute a ploy. Saddam's error was his failure to sniff the new impatience in Washington, or to recognize, in time, that war was almost definitely coming. Even as the American sheriff rounded up its posse over 2002–3, and publicly insisted that the violations of concealment and partial obstruction were proof enough of a clear and present danger, Saddam failed to revise his calculations about America's fecklessness and casualty aversion. In a fatal misperception, he estimated as though it was still 10 September 2001, believing until the final hours that America did not have the stomach for a ground war. His greatest adversaries, he maintained, were local and internal, his own subjects, as well as Iran and Israel. France and Russia could be counted on to sabotage America's bid for a UN mandate and even to upset its advances once invasion was underway. Saddam never took seriously the possibility that US-led forces would reach deep into the country and always prioritized the internal threat of revolution over external adversaries.

In his preoccupation with the threat of internal uprisings, from hostile populations or from his officers, he created paramilitary units designed primarily to suppress revolts, at the expense of the conventional forces needed to defend the country. Saddam could have delayed and frustrated invasion by scorching the earth of infrastructure, and could have prepared a bloodier, more formidable strategy of defending cities as fortresses, forcing invaders into an undesired siege as Western strategists feared he might.[10] Such a strategy would reduce the stronger invaders' advantages in stand-off strikes,

---

[8] Saïd K. Aburish, *Saddam Hussein: The Politics of Revenge* (London: Bloomsbury, 2000), p. 136.
[9] David Singer, 'US Plans to Pressure Iraq by Encouraging Scientists to Leak Data to Inspectors', *The New York Times*, 9 November 2002.
[10] Michael R. Gordon, 'Saddam's Likely Plan: Make a Stand in Baghdad', *The New York Times*, 4 March 2003; Kenneth M. Pollack, 'The Defence of Baghdad', *Brookings Institute*, 4 April 2003; Mike Allen, 'US Increases Estimated Cost of War in Iraq', *The Washington Post*, 26 February 2003.

firepower, manoeuvre and precision, as one of his generals had unsuccessfully proposed.[11] Yet Saddam deployed his regular and Republican guard forces outside Baghdad in order to distance them from the seat of power, entrusting his more lightly armed paramilitary forces with city defence, and left his professional military with no doctrine of urban combat.[12] The bungler of Baghdad could have mounted a more attritional urban strategy to delay and bleed the invaders and force a more protracted battle. Instead, he chose to maintain defiance, while weakening his ability to hold on by stubbornly deploying his main forces 'out in the open'. Baghdad fell three weeks later. The world's twelfth largest army was swept aside and the paramilitary units were gunned down in short order.

As Operation Iraqi Freedom neared, he could have taken up President Bush's offer to leave Iraq within forty-eight hours to settle abroad in voluntary exile and immunity,[13] an offer backed by Saudi Arabia and Egypt, and by Britain's Foreign Secretary Jack Straw. Russian President Vladimir Putin's envoy also offered Saddam an opportunity to abdicate. Bahrain's King Hamad made an offer, hours before the expiry of America's ultimatum for he and his sons to leave Iraq or face military invasion.[14] Past rulers have sometimes fled and survived in exile, such as Kaiser Wilhelm II. Of course, survival could never be guaranteed, and Saddam could have been killed or arrested. That option still conceivably offered higher odds of success than accepting war and the near-certain consequence of violent death or flight, pursuit, and then trial and violent death. In a meaningful sense, Saddam chose war. He at least got to rail incessantly at his subsequent trial. The ultimate dividend was the gallows. As the fabled survivor finally perished, a chorus of balaclava-clad executioners chanted sectarian slogans while filming his death, a fitting emblem of the time, as vendetta and zero-sum competition tore a whole society apart.

Saddam's blinkered choices made possible his toppling. And it was not just he who fell prey to the errors of closed thinking. While the Bush and Blair governments were hardly the equivalent of Saddam's abattoir autocracy, all three centres of decision proved to be insulated, organized around like-minded cabals. For decisive stretches of time, the two Atlantic democracies did not operate democratically in their preparations for war. The American and British leaders did not willingly subject their case to an open 'marketplace of ideas', or even to cabinet-level scrutiny, until late. Instead, they shaped the

---

[11] Paul Martin, 'Iraqi Defence Chief Argued with Saddam', *The Washington Times*, 21 September 2003.
[12] Stephen T. Hosmer, *Why the Iraqi Resistance to the Coalition Invasion Was So Weak*, (Monterey: RAND 2007), p. 51; Stephen Biddle, *Toppling Saddam: Iraq and American Military Transformation* (Calisle: Pennsylvania, April 2004), pp. 26, 27.
[13] 'Straw backs Exile Deal for Saddam', *BBC News*, 20 January 2003.
[14] Gerald Butt, 'Bahrain offers exile as Egypt reviles Saddam', *The Daily Telegraph*, 20 March 2003.

circumstances in the shadows, in order then to persuade wider government and the public. The words of Colin Powell's former chief of staff about Bush's style could be applied to London: 'Its insular and secret workings were efficient and swift—not unlike the decision-making one would associate more with a dictatorship than a democracy'.[15] Democracies can be decidedly undemocratic in their national security decision-making, even in wars that are fought in democracy's name.[16] The fact of secrecy is not in itself reprehensible. Worthy of regret is not any crime but a blunder, the failure to subject the most basic decision to robust internal scrutiny. And worthy of regret is the ease with which their ideas, once presented, succeeded, and for that the blame is wider.

PART II. WASHINGTON'S WAR: CONFIDENCE AND FEAR

As the World Trade Center collapsed and as bodies were being carried out of the Pentagon, a former colleague of mine asked a well-placed American official about the contours of Washington's likely response. The reply: 'It's going to be big. It's going to be American'. There is visible in American history whereby the US in response to surprise attack on its soil—in 1814, 1941, and 2001—raises its ambitions, enlarges its sphere of responsibilities, and embarks on 'visionary world making'.[17] It did not take long for American-sized ambitions to form. As Britain contemplated the warpath, its principle ally was the most powerful state that has ever existed. The action-enforcing events that prompted Britain to make plans and prepare dossiers flowed mostly from Washington. There were declaratory signals: Bush's 'axis of evil' claim in the State of the Union speech of January 2002, his West Point speech of June 2002 announcing a shift from containment and deterrence to anticipatory war, the National Security Strategy. And there were in private communications the persistent signals of a policy shift and military preparations.

A concurrent rise in fear and confidence turned Washington's longstanding enmity with Iraq finally into a direct clash. The overthrow of

---

[15] Lawrence B. Wilkerson, 'The White House Cabal', *Los Angeles Times*, 25 October 2005.

[16] See Michael C. Desch's study of Israeli decision-making about conflict in its invasion of Lebanon in 1982, which 'was exempted from normal democratic procedures' or cabinet scrutiny. *Power and Military Effectiveness: The Fallacy of Democratic Triumphalism* (Baltimore: Johns Hopkins University Press, 2008), pp. 100–1.

[17] I borrow the phrase 'visionary world making' from Nicholas Kitchen, 'Systemic Pressures and Domestic Ideas: A Neoclassical Realist Model of Grand Strategy Formation', *Review of International Studies* 36:1 (2010), pp. 117–43, 141; see the history of American responses to strategic shock in John Lewis Gaddis, *Surprise, Security and the American Experience* (Cambridge: Harvard University Press, 2004), p. 37.

Saddam Hussein was already formal policy in Washington, as the commitment to a post-Saddam Iraq was fully codified in the Iraq Liberation Act of October 1998, a bill passed unanimously in the US Senate spelling out unambiguously that 'It should be the policy of the United States to support efforts to remove the regime headed by Saddam Hussein from power in Iraq'.[18] After 9/11, the will quickly grew to realize that policy directly and in full. Americans, including those in government, were scared. They had suffered the greatest act of urban terror by a non-state group in history. An anthrax scare one week after the 9/11 attacks compounded fears that a serial wave of terrorist attacks was underway. By the close of 2001, they were also emboldened. America had enjoyed unexpected early success in its campaign in Afghanistan, toppling the theocratic Taliban regime with an agile mix of air strikes, indigenous allies, special forces, and bribes. And it had achieved this rapid dominance in what was notoriously a zone of exclusion, the so-called 'graveyard of empires'.[19] With al-Qaeda and its hosts on the run, the superpower now exhibited a mix of fear, vengefulness, and self-confidence. Its declared ambitions were boundless. In the words of President George W. Bush in the State of the Union address in October 2001, 'Our war on terror begins with Al Qaeda, but it does not end there. It will not end until every terrorist group of global reach has been found, stopped and defeated'.[20] With the Afghan Taliban scattering, the 'Bush Doctrine', with its mix of democracy promotion, anticipatory war, and belief that bold unilateral action would attract coalitions, was hammered out in a matrix of insecurity and confidence from combat success.[21] Ever since 9/11, those in close contact with

---

[18] *Iraq Liberation Act of 1998*, Public Law 105–338, 105th Congress, section 3.

[19] As Bob Woodward relates, among Bush's advisers there was great apprehensiveness about Afghanistan, its history of 'rebuffing outside forces', and the prospect of mountain fighting, quagmire, and even overspill into Pakistan: *Bush at War* (London: Simon & Schuster, 2002, 2003 edn.), pp. 82–3; but success created momentum and optimism: *Plan of Attack* (New York: Simon & Schuster, 2004), p. 5; on 21 November 2001, the day Bush instructed Rumsfeld to prepare plans for Iraq, he declared that the Taliban were 'on the run', 'President Shares Thanksgiving Meal with Troops', at https://georgewbush-whitehouse.archives.gov/news/releases/2001/11/20011121-3.html. Memoirs by administration officials also recall the emboldening effect of initial success in Afghanistan: Richard B. Meyers, *Eyes on the Horizon: Serving on the Front Lines of National Security* (New York: Simon & Schuster, 2009), pp. 187–96; Hugh Shelton, *Without Hesitation: The Odyssey of an American Warrior* (New York: St Martin's Press, 2010), p. 482, discussed further by Melvyn Leffler, 'The Foreign Policies of the George W. Bush Administration', *Diplomatic History* 37:2 (2013), pp. 190–216.

[20] President George W. Bush, 'Address to the Joint Session of the 107th Congress', 20 September 2001, in *Selected Speeches of President George W. Bush, 2001–2008*, pp. 65–75, p. 68, at https://georgewbush-whitehouse.archives.gov/infocus/bushrecord/documents/Selected_Speeches_George_W_Bush.pdf (accessed 30 September 2017).

[21] See President of the United States, *National Security Strategy of the United States of America* (Washington, DC: US Government Printing Office, 2002); Robert Jervis, 'Understanding the Bush Doctrine', *Political Science Quarterly* 118:3 (2003), pp. 365–88.

Bush reported his real and sincere ambition to transform the world. 'I will seize the opportunity to achieve big goals'.[22]

The collapse of the Soviet Union had removed the last check on America's power, or so it seemed. Because of their country's relative strength and a long-held set of beliefs about America's exceptional historical mission, American elites were able to swagger, and to congratulate themselves for their country's singularity and prescience in global affairs. Secretary of State Madeleine Albright had declared that 'If we have to use force, it is because we are America. We are the indispensable nation. We stand tall, and we see further than other countries into the future'.[23] In 2002–3, well before China's rise seriously gathered pace, neither were there any plausible great power candidates to counterbalance the US. Such an imbalance was the permissive cause of the war in Iraq.

This was a unipolar war, made possible and therefore tempting by the uniquely lopsided distribution of material and structural power. Unipolarity entails the constant impulse to use force and tame the world back into order. A superpower with global reach, and without major opponents, is unfettered by the kinds of constraints that most major powers must reckon with. Coupled with that, Washington was not contemplating a strike on Iraq from a blank sheet of paper. Elite habits, built up over decades, predisposed policymakers towards a worldview where American predominance was the only natural and legitimate aspiration. Unlike at earlier crossroads, after World War I, or even after World War II when America's sudden acquisition of global power prompted a serious debate about its international course, the grand strategy of 'primacy' was entrenched and unquestioned.[24] This meant that the emergency set off by 9/11 was interpreted as evidence of a need for more American power projection, not less.

New conditions made preventive war thinkable. A similar venture, to topple a lesser regime in a power centre like the Gulf would have been vastly more risky and less attractive during the Cold War, when the Soviet Union was then Iraq's main diplomatic ally. A unipolar world power that styles itself the 'world leader' will be tempted to use the muscle that those very conditions allow it to. America's preponderant levels of power enabled it to identify far-flung and remote threats for elimination. Whatever benefits it has wrought, American

---

[22] President George W. Bush, cited in Bob Woodward, *Bush at War*, p. 339; Bush privately told his close counsellor Karen Hughes a week after 9/11, 'We have an opportunity to restructure the world toward freedom, and we have to get it right'. Frank Bruni, 'A Nation Challenged: White House Memo; For President, a Mission and a Role in History', *The New York Times*, 22 September 2001.

[23] Statement on NBC *Today Show*, 19 February 1998.

[24] As I argue elsewhere, 'Why the United States' Grand Strategy Has Not Changed: Power, Habit and the U.S. Foreign Policy Establishment,' *International Security* (Forthcoming, Spring Edition, 42:4, 2018).

unipolarity is not peaceful. The first two decades of the *Pax Americana* after 1989 that made up less than 10 per cent of America's history generated 25 per cent of the nation's total time at war. Measured in percentage years that great powers spend at war and the incidence of war involving great powers, the period of American unipolarity by an order of magnitude is more bellicose than the preceding eras of bipolarity and multipolarity, in terms of frequency if not intensity.[25] On the road to Saddam's fall, America embarked as an already busy, ambitious and warlike hegemon that was willing to project power while initially wary of open-ended ground commitments. In response to 9/11, America's casualty aversion was lowered, and its muscular idealism was roused. America's level of material strength had existed throughout the 'interwar period' between the Cold War and 9/11. Now, its rulers had rediscovered a new appetite for military action, including large-scale ground action, beyond raiding and 'missile diplomacy'.

Bush's newfound vision of transformation through American power, and promoting peace through the solvent of free elections and free markets, would be developed in world-historical terms by hawkish intellectuals. Charles Krauthammer, regarded as America's most influential commentator especially on the right,[26] defined the Bush Doctrine in world-historical terms. Birthing pro-Western, peaceable states in Afghanistan and Iraq and their neighbours 'like the flipping of Germany and Japan in the 1940's, change the strategic balance in the fight against Arab-Islamic radicalism...the undertaking is enormous, ambitious and arrogant. It may yet fail. But we cannot afford to try'. The 'monster behind 9/11' was not bin Laden, but the 'cauldron of political oppression, religious intolerance, and social ruin' of the Arab-Islamic world, 'deflected into murderous anti-Americanism', a condition to be corrected.[27] As Krauthammer realized, the Bush Doctrine was not an aberration but an extension of US foreign policy traditions and practices. Though articulated more abrasively with only slight regard for international opinion, in fundamental ways it held commonalities with the Clinton-era National Security Strategy of 1999 and Obama's formal strategic documents, sharing a commitment to primacy, a willingness for unilateral action, an imperative to spread democratic institutions and free markets, an emphasis on dealing with rogue states, and a stress on the links between WMD and terrorism. In the months succeeding 9/11, as Bush and his senior ministers took dead aim at a familiar adversary, the high-minded belligerence of the moment was simultaneously visceral. On the evening of 9/11, Bush insisted 'we are going to kick

---

[25] See Nuno Monteiro, 'Unrest assured: Why Unipolarity is not Peaceful', *International Security* 36:3 (2012), pp. 9–40, 11, 19–20; Bruce Porter, 'The Warfare State' *American Heritage* 45:4 (1994), pp. 56–69, 56.
[26] Lionel Barber, *The Financial Times*, 20 May 2006.
[27] Charles Krauthammer, *Democratic Realism: An American Foreign Policy for a Unipolar World* (2004 Irving Kristol Lecture, American Enterprise Institute), pp. 16–17.

some ass'.²⁸ 'Fuck Saddam', Bush insisted in March 2002, interrupting a meeting of senators with his National Security Advisor. 'We're taking him out'.²⁹

As well as a unipolar war, this was a preventive war. Preventive war is one kind of anticipatory war. It is distinct from pre-emptive war, which is a type of conflict-initiation against what a pre-emptor believes is an imminent attack, to secure first-move advantages. Secretary of State Daniel Webster 1842 argued that pre-emption is only justifiable when a state can show a necessity of self-defence, 'instant and overwhelming, leaving no choice of means, and no moment of deliberation'.³⁰ By contrast, to wage preventive war is to attempt to forestall a threat that is distant, usually produced by an 'adverse shift in the balance of power', driven by 'better now than later logic'.³¹ Preventive war is directed against more hypothetical future threats, and a different time horizon. For a concrete comparative case, a pre-emptive war would have been an attack on the Imperial Japanese fleet before it reached Pearl Harbor in 1941, whereas a preventive war would have involved bombing Japanese factories in 1921 on the basis that it could be used to threaten US later. Not all deliberately initiated wars are designed to forestall a direct threat. There are also military activities initiated for purposes of territorial conquest (like Saddam's invasion of Kuwait in 1990), or to interrupt an anticipated atrocity (the Anglo-American-French bombing of Colonel Gaddafi's forces as they neared the rebel city of Benghazi in 2011), without anticipating any direct aggression by the target. Practitioners of preventive war choose conflict in the short term in exchange for what would effectively be a 'worse war' in the long term, or a worse direct threat, such as nuclear proliferation by a hostile state.³² In practice, 'preventers' mindful of opinion and claims about legitimacy will work hard to position the target as the aggressor, and may seek to induce the target to conduct themselves in an allegedly reckless and provocative way. In 2002–3, the initiators worked hard to position their target, Iraq, as the true source of the conflict, framing Saddam's failure to fully comply and his breaches of UN resolutions as evidence of his aggressive intent. Preventive war and reserving the right to

---

[28] Jean Edward Smith, *Bush* (New York: Simon & Schuster, 2016), p. 225.
[29] Michael Elliott & James Carney, 'First Stop, Iraq', *Time*, 31 March, 2003; George Packer, *The Assassins' Gate: America in Iraq* (New York: Farrar, Strauss and Giroud, 2005), p. 45.
[30] Daniel Webster, letters to British Foreign Minister Lord Ashbutton, 6 August 1842, and to Mr Fox, 24 April 1841, cited in Louis Henkin, Richard Crawford Pugh, Oscar Schachter & Hans Smit (eds), *International Law: Cases and Materials* (3rd edn., St Paul, MN: West. Pub. Co. 1980), pp. 890–1.
[31] Jack S. Levy, 'Preventive War and Democratic Politics', *International Studies Quarterly* 52 (2008), pp. 1–24, p. 1; see also Richard Ned Lebow, *Between Peace and War* (Baltimore: Johns Hopkins University Press, 1981).
[32] On the latter, see Francis J. Gavin & Mira Rapp-Hooper, 'The Copenhagen Temptation: Rethinking Prevention and Proliferation in the Age of Deterrence Dominance', Annual Meeting of the American Political Science Association, 2011.

'act alone' if necessary is not an alien practice in US diplomatic history but a mainstream idea that presidents often entertained and occasionally waged.³³ True to the pattern of preventive wars, heightened and disproportionate fear and confidence mingled.

Preventive war historically is a gamble.³⁴ It presumes great prescience, confidently assuming that the initiator can ride all the typical hazards of war that are in fact hard to forecast. By definition, it 'removes the evidence that would convince people of the wisdom of waging war'.³⁵ Preventive wars have been urged before. When they were adopted and failed they were catastrophic, such as the *Kaiserreich*'s preventive strike on the Franco-Russian alliance in 1914. In the US, preventive wars were proposed against Stalin's Soviet Union and Mao's China, and were refused by presidents Truman and Johnson. It is hard to argue that the results of such attacks would have been preferable to the successful deterrent relationships that formed with the US in both cases. Because the initiator (in this case, the US) would oppose a world order where other great powers also choose preventive wars—China over Taiwan, or India over Pakistan—it implicitly claims a privilege that the initiator would deny to other states, it has the cost of damaging one's moral authority. And by striking first even before an unavoidable crisis has emerged, it may incentivize irreconcilable adversaries (or potential adversaries) to prepare deterrent capabilities or even to strike first themselves. The sad history of great powers overreaching and inflicting self-harm suggests it would be difficult for any major power to avoid restraint if it possessed this much capability, especially in circumstances so frightening and exhilarating.³⁶

With the campaign in Afghanistan proceeding, a range of potential targets loomed in the discussion about 'Phase II' of the War on Terror, a phase British policymakers were made aware of. Iraq had already been raised in Bush's inner circle after 9/11, and it emerged as the target of choice for several reasons. The regime's historical behaviour, its prior use of chemical weapons, its sponsorship of terrorism, its genocidal campaigns and attacks on neighbours suggested a present and future threat.³⁷ Iraq's position at the heart of a strategically

---

[33] See Marc Trachtenberg, 'Preventive War and US Foreign Policy', *Security Studies* 16:1 (2007), pp. 1–31; Melvyn Leffler, 'Think Again: Bush's Foreign Policy', *Foreign Policy* 144 (2004), pp. 22–7.

[34] For critiques of preventive war as a means of security, see Richard Betts, 'Suicide for Fear of Death?', *Foreign Affairs* 82:1 (2003), pp. 34–43; Michael Lind, 'Preventive Wars: The Antithesis of Realpolitik', *The National Interest*, 26 July 2016.

[35] Michael Mandelbaum, *The Case for Goliath* (New York: Public Affairs, 2005), p. 60.

[36] On the history of great powers and adjustment failure, see Charles A. Kupchan, *The Vulnerability of Empire* (Ithaca: Cornell University Press, 1994), pp. 3–4, 33–105; Karen Rasler & William R. Thomson, *The Great Powers and Global Struggle, 1490–1990* (University Press of Kentucky, 2009), p. 146.

[37] See Jeffrey Record, *Wanting War: Why the Bush Administration Invaded Iraq* (Washington: Potomac Books, 2010), pp. 85–103. Blair shared this reasoning, that Saddam's historical behaviour

valuable and oil-rich region also made it both a promising basis for reinforcing US hegemony, and a potential springboard for the transformation of the region. And there was a practical dimension. If Saddam presented a grave threat, his regime was also disposable, an easier target than North Korea or Iran. There was too much doubt about earlier proposals that the regime could be brought down through a US-supported Iraqi ground force, emulating the Northern Alliance of Afghanistan model. Washington decided to attack head-on.

While we cannot identify the exact combination of America's exact motivations for war, what matters for this analysis is the 'law of the instrument', the objective power realities that made possible the superpower's ambitions, the temptation to broaden their use to preventive regime change in Iraq, even while participants had disparate, overlapping, and sometimes conflicting rationales.[38] The reasons swirled: to eliminate a threat, kick-start a revolutionary democratic and pro-American wave, to signal a willingness to use force, to create an alternative client state to Saudi Arabia, and to remove an enemy of Israel, American's only democratic ally in the Middle East. Deputy Secretary of Defence and hawkish intellectual Paul Wolfowitz recalled there were multiple rationales within the administration for attacking Iraq, and they made counterproliferation and WMD the central basis because 'it was the one reason everyone could agree on'.[39] Wolfowitz' recollection was accurate. Each of these rationales flowed from the fact of America's power position and the ambition to double down on its advantages.

Hours after 9/11, leading officials sensed an opportune moment to strike out globally and take problems off the board. On the afternoon of 9/11, an aide recorded Rumsfeld's reaction, 'Judge whether good enough to hit S.H. [Saddam Hussein] at same time. Not only UBL [Osama bin Laden]. Go massive. Sweep it all up. Things related and not'.[40] This went beyond terrorist groups and rogues. As Bush's 'West Point' address and *National Security Strategy* made clear, America's response to 9/11 was to reaffirm and reinforce its primacy, to prevent 'any other state from surpassing, or even equalling, the power of the United States'. 'Iraq was—and doubtless was intended to be—a shot across the bow of America's potential great power rivals: Don't even think

and present capability made his regime a threat, in his letter to Bush, 'The War Against Terrorism: The Second Phase', 4 December 2001.

[38] For this interpretation, see also Noah Feldman, *What We Owe Iraq: War and the Ethics of Nation Building* (Princeton: Princeton University Press, 2004), p. 19; Stephen Holmes, *The Matador's Cape: America's Reckless Response to Terror* (New York: Cambridge University Press, 2007), p. 108.

[39] Sam Tannenhaus, *Vanity Fair*, May 2003; Wolfowitz specified that the main four reasons were WMD, terrorism, the criminal mistreatment of the Iraqi people, and the linkage between the first two: Jamie McIntyre, 'Pentagon Challenges Vanity Fair Report', *CNN*, 30 May 2003.

[40] David Martin, 'Plans for Iraq Attack Began on 9/11', *CBS News*, 4 September 2002.

about messing with the United States'.[41] Thus was America both scared, and not scared enough. As it prepared to storm Baghdad, the Bush administration was in a state of exaltation, overinterpreting initial success in Afghanistan as proof of America's general transformative might and its destiny. The campaign proceeded with a hyperbolic and operatic quality, stressing both unprecedented peril and supreme power.

US officials signalled early to London their intention to spread the conflict beyond al-Qaeda and international terrorism to Iraq as a designated 'rogue state'. They signalled their dissatisfaction with the existing strategy of containing Iraq via inspections, sanctions, and coercion. British officials became aware in late November and early December 2001 that Bush's attention was turning towards Saddam, and that a consensus was hardening for a final settling of accounts. Bush made vague but threatening comments about the consequences of Saddam failing to cooperate with weapons inspectors in a press conference on 26 November 2001.[42] The British embassy and the Deputy Prime Minister reported that an 'overwhelming majority' of Senators favoured removing Saddam.[43] British Ambassador Christopher Meyer reported that the long-standing lobby for toppling Saddam was now getting increased reception with the President.[44] The prospects of American 'direct action' against Iraq was the subject of discussion in December 2001 between Richard Dearlove, the head of Secret Intelligence Service (SIS), and David Manning, then Blair's foreign policy advisor.[45] And it was President Bush's 'axis of evil' speech on 30 January 2002, and a planned meeting with Bush in April 2002, that prompted Blair to commission advisory papers on WMD proliferation.[46] The Cabinet Office's main advisory document, the 'Iraq Options Paper' of March 2002, indicated that the US had already lost confidence in containment, distrusted the UN process/inspections, and the momentum flowing from Operation Enduring Freedom in Afghanistan. It shared the US assessment that toughened containment was unlikely to work and that the sanctions regime may break down.[47]

It is difficult to pinpoint when precisely Bush settled on removing Saddam militarily, beyond an approximate time window of April to July 2002. The very

[41] Christopher Layne, *The Peace of Illusions: American Grand Strategy From 1940 to the Present* (Ithaca: Cornell University Press, 2006), p. 135.
[42] The White House, 26 November 2001, *The President Welcomes Aid Workers Rescued from Afghanistan* at https://georgewbush-whitehouse.archives.gov/news/releases/2001/11/20011126-1.html/.
[43] Telegram 1616 Washington to FCO London, 29 November 2001, 'Deputy Prime Minister's Visit to Washington: Afghanistan and Iraq'.
[44] Telegram 1631 Washington to FCO London, 1 December 2001, 'The Wider War against Terrorism: Iraq'.
[45] Letter, Richard Dearlove's Private Secretary to David Manning, 3 December 2001.
[46] See *Report of the Iraq Inquiry*, 4:1, 166, p. 45.
[47] Cabinet Office, Overseas and Defence Secretariat, 'Iraq Options Paper', March 2002.

opacity of the process suggests a problem in both capitals, that there was a lack of rigorous internal review over 'whether' to attack, beyond small coteries around the President and Prime Minister.[48] Principals and participants in Washington who could reasonably have expected to be alerted to the process reported that it happened 'elsewhere' and they were informed after the fact. As one senior administration official told journalist Nicholas Lemann, it was 'somewhere in the first half of 2002... What I can't explain to you is exactly the process... That's a mystery that nobody has yet uncovered'.[49] Senior officials agree on this point. Richard Armitage, deputy Secretary of State, and George Tenet, the head of the CIA, both recall that never, to their knowledge, was the question of whether to strike seriously debated internally.[50] Speechwriter David Frum supports this account:

> You might imagine that an administration preparing for a war of choice would be gripped by self-questioning and hot debate. There was certainly plenty to discuss: unlike the 1991 Gulf War, there was no immediate crisis demanding a rapid response; unlike Vietnam, the U.S. entered the war fully aware that it was commencing a major commitment. Yet that discussion never really happened, not the way that most people would have imagined anyway. For a long time, war with Iraq was discussed inside the Bush administration as something that would be decided at some point in the future; then, somewhere along the way, war with Iraq was discussed as something that had already been decided long ago in the past.[51]

We do know that Bush first tasked Secretary of Defence Rumsfeld with drawing up plans in late November 2001.[52] Tommy Franks, the Commander of Central Command (CENTCOM) recalls that after 28 December 2001, when he presented Bush with an outline concept for a campaign, efforts since then were directed at refining the plan, preparing bases and forces.[53] We also know that by July 2002, the head of policy planning at the State Department was told by Secretary of State Rice 'that decision's been made'.[54]

---

[48] For an earlier summary of the decision-making process, see John Prados & Christopher Ames, 'The Iraq War—Part II: Was There Even a Decision? U.S. and British Documents Give No Indication Alternatives Were Seriously Considered', National Security Archive Electronic Briefing Book No. 328, 1 October 2010, http://www.gwu.edu/~nsarchiv/NSAEBB/NSAEBB328/index.htm.

[49] Cited in Nicholas Lemann, 'How it Came to War', *The New Yorker*, 31 March 2003.

[50] Richard Armitage, 'An Interview with Richard L. Armitage', *Prism* (Journal of the National Defence University), 1:1, p. 104; George J. Tenet with Bill Harlow, *At the Center of the Storm: My Years at the CIA* (New York: HarperCollins, 2007), pp. 305, 308.

[51] David Frum, 'The Speechwriter: Inside the Bush Administration during the Iraq War', *Newsweek*, 19 March 2013.

[52] Bob Woodward, *Plan of Attack* (London: Pocket Books, 2004), p. 1.

[53] Tommy Franks with Malcolm McConnell, *American Soldier* (New York: HarperCollins, 2004), pp. 346–56.

[54] Richard N. Haass, *War of Necessity, War of Choice: A Memoir of Two Iraq Wars* (New York: Simon & Schuster, 2009), pp. 4–6.

Dogmatism was not confined to the Bush circle. The American political class as a whole was predisposed to accept a final confrontation with Saddam Hussein without seriously considering alternatives. When the debate was brought before the US Congress in October 2002, in the form of a 'blank check' bill to authorize the presidential use of force, even the minority of dissidents framed their opposition mostly around operational and procedural reservations concerning timing and relative priorities with Afghanistan, not on 'the broader wisdom of occupying Iraq and overthrowing its government'.[55] Most of those who did vote to authorize military action exhibited incuriosity about the evidence. To inspect the CIA's National Intelligence Estimate on Iraq's weapons programme, Congress members had to travel to a secure location on Capitol Hill, yet only six senators and a handful of House Members were logged as reading the document.[56] Preventive war logic was assumed, without scrutiny.

If a state of this magnitude, governed by an administration that cared little about wooing allies, had shed many of its fears with early success in Afghanistan, and was independently determined to strike Iraq, there was little Britain could realistically do to stop it. Secretary of Defence Donald Rumsfeld gave a glimpse of this reality in the week before military action, suggesting that if Britain was unable to participate there would be 'work-arounds'.[57] Britain's path to war, too, was shaped by America's timetable and momentum. The question facing the UK would be whether, how, and how much, to join in. Emma Sky, former Political Advisor to the Commanding General of US Forces, rightly argued looking back that 'given the limited influence of the UK on both the US and the new Iraqi elites, it is not clear that this would have made much difference to the tragic outcome of events in Iraq'.[58] If this is true, Britain could still have decided not to participate, a consequential and morally serious choice for its own national interest.

The case of Iraq is distinct from America's most significant premeditated 'minor' war, in Vietnam. As Frederik Logevall has shown, American officials in the eighteen-month period of decision, between August 1963 and February 1965, were not gripped by hubris about the deepening of military commitment to South Vietnam. They did not take the prospects of their commitment for

---

[55] Benjamin H. Friedman & Justin Logan, 'Why Washington Doesn't Debate Grand Strategy', *Strategic Studies Quarterly* (2016), pp. 14–45, p. 19; see also Jane Kellet Cramer, 'Militarized Patriotism: Why the US Marketplace of Ideas Failed before the Iraq War', *Security Studies* 16:3 (2007), pp. 489–524.

[56] 'Records: Senators Who OK'd War Didn't Read Key Report', *CNN*, 29 May 2007.

[57] Donald Rumsfeld, cited in "US Defence Secretary Donald Rumsfeld's Comments about UK Involvement in War" *The Guardian*, 12 March 2003, https://www.theguardian.com/uk/2003/mar/12/usa.iraq.

[58] Emma Sky, 'Chilcot Report: Post-Invasion Planning', *Political Quarterly* 87:4 (2016), pp. 486–7.

granted. To the contrary, the Johnson administration deliberated extensively whether to escalate its ground commitment and 'Americanize' the war. Even as the executive worked hard to foreclose options for a diplomatic settlement, senior American officials who favoured heightening the war remained pessimistic about the chances of success.[59] The contrast with the warpath of 2003 is stark. In a period of, at most, four months, decision-makers rarely assessed their own underlying optimism. They worried primarily about carrying opinion. It's time to meet Tony Blair.

PART III. LONDON: BRITISH CALCULATIONS

In explaining Britain's decision for war, we must address two questions: what caused the desire to strike Iraq? And how did decision-makers persuade the country to agree? In their comparative study of the causes of blunders in war, David Gombert Hans Binnendijk, and Bonny Lin argue that botched wars share common features that revolve around the mishandling of information: the ignoring, filtering, or manipulation of information to fit predispositions; excessive reliance on intuition and experience; unwarranted confidence; a rigid strategic concept; the neglect of potential contingencies, the underestimation of potential resistance, and the stifling of dissent.[60]

This explanation broadly fits Britain's war, yet begs a further question. What causes dogmatism? And how do decision-makers persuade? Even dogmatic war initiators must still persuade others to agree. In this case, Blair committed to war early not only because of an authoritarian style of governance, but because some powerful, pre-existing, and flawed ideas about security prevailed in wider society, and proved impervious to challenge. Blair and his circle adroitly steered the crisis over Iraq so that feasible options eventually narrowed into a choice, whether to join a war that was happening anyway against an adversary who had seemingly been given every chance for a peaceful resolution, or back down in ways that would invite first-order threats, damage the United Nations' credibility, and incur the risks and shame of capitulation.

My primary focus lies with Prime Minister Tony Blair and his 'inner circle' of informal advisors. Blair was the chief protagonist. As the Iraq Inquiry and the earlier Butler Inquiry found, he oversaw and decided on the major decisions of foreign policy through a small group, most apart from cabinet

[59] Frederik Logevall, *Choosing War: The Lost Chance for Peace and the Escalation of War in Vietnam* (Berkeley: University of California Press, 2001), p. xix.
[60] David Gombert Hans Binnendijk & Bonny Lin, *Blunders, Blinders and Wars: What America and China can Learn* (Santa Monica: RAND, 2014), pp. xvii–xviii.

and its committee machinery, and often apart from Whitehall mandarins.[61] The earlier Butler inquiry identified the 'the informality and circumscribed character'[62] of Blair's decision-making style, just as Andrew Turnbull, the head of the civil service and Cabinet Secretary, observed that in this period, Blair was 'less and less interested in hearing contrary opinions'.[63] I work on an assumption already well-substantiated, that the main decision-making centre lay in Blair's office, which is where the rationale and strategy were conceived. This is not the whole story. Decision flowed from Blair's den, but we must also explain why it flowed outwards successfully. Within government and beyond, attention to the arguments against war was more popular after the invasion went wrong. The drive for regime change enjoyed support or sympathy from within the Joint Intelligence Committee (JIC), the SIS, the Cabinet Office, the lion's share of print media, most of the government, and almost all of the Conservative opposition. Centres of scepticism within government there were, in the Foreign and Commonwealth Office (FCO) and Ministry of Defence (MOD) in particular, as well as among a minority of the cabinet. But even the FCO's advice was at times borderline naïve, badly underestimating the dilemmas of invasion and occupation. The undercurrents of doubt at the MOD were counterbalanced by an anxiety to be included in campaign preparations and an instinctive Atlanticism that had long been part of British strategic calculation, as Chapter 3 will demonstrate. As for the cabinet, Iraq was discussed on multiple occasions, but almost never did it deliberate whether military action was feasible. Under Blair, the cabinet was largely emasculated, and complicit in its own emasculation. Discussion of Iraq in cabinet rarely rose above protestations of loyalty to the Prime Minister.

In his response to the Iraq Inquiry's report in July 2016, Blair claimed 'I weighed it carefully'.[64] In one important way, this is untrue. Blair weighed carefully, to the point of personal distress, 'with the heaviest of hearts', how, when, under what auspices, and with what diplomatic and military strategy to remove Saddam. He hardly weighed, though, the most vital question of all,

---

[61] This group comprised Blair, Alastair Campbell the Director of Communications, Jonathan Powell the chief of staff, and Sally Morgan, Director of Government Relations. Also intimate were the 'diplomatic knights' in Downing Street, foreign policy advisor Sir David Manning, and Private Secretary Matthew Rycroft. Campbell identified himself, Powell, Morgan, and Manning as the principal advisors 'what you would call his inner circle', as well as John Scarlett, then Chair of the Joint Intelligence Committee, and Richard Dearlove, head of Secret Intelligence Service. Alastair Campbell, IIT, 12 January 2010, pp. 6, 8, 10.

[62] *Review of Intelligence on Weapons of Mass Destruction: Report of a Committee of Privy Counsellors*, Chairman: The Rt Hon The Lord Butler of Brockwell HC 898 (London: Stationery Office, 14 July 2004), p. 148.

[63] Cited in Andrew Rawnsley, *The End of the Party: The Rise and Fall of New Labour* (London: Viking, 2010), p. 114.

[64] 'Chilcot Report: Read Tony Blair's Full Statement in response to the Iraq War Inquiry', *The Independent*, 6 July 2016.

'whether' to commit in the first place. The most striking fact about Blair's decision to strike Iraq is that this dog hardly barked. There lacked intensive internal discussion about this basic issue. The essential belief that success was likely was implicit in the imbalance of effort. The Blair government invested itself heavily in the enabling process leading up to the war more than problems that would flow from it, particularly its intensive diplomatic effort to win over international opinion and secure a clear United Nations mandate. The later, public discussion was conducted only once commitments had been made, and under circumstances that pressured the country not to reverse Britain's course. Blair was conscious, at times, of potential difficulties. Tragically, he did not allow this awareness to disturb his basic optimism, his assumption that the war was necessary and achievable. Difficulties were considerations to be mitigated in execution, not reasons to reconsider the decision to act. Let us now reconstruct Britain's road to war.

The Road to War

Britain's road to war was long and crooked. It was a complex interaction of public justification, military mobilization, alliance politics, and the management of domestic opinion. This tapestry of detail can obscure the simpler and overriding point. While the path was wandering and public rationales shifted, the calculus of Blair's inner circle was consistent. If military action could be successfully framed and sold, it was necessary. Saddam's Iraq, they believed, embodied a growing systemic threat. Removing his regime would begin the positive transformation of the Middle East, and taking part would create influence over their senior ally. A leaked memorandum from Secretary of State Colin Powell to President Bush in the lead-up to the Crawford talks in April 2002 neatly summarized it: 'On Iraq, Blair will be with us should military operations be necessary. He is convinced on two points: the threat is real; and success against Saddam will yield more regional success'.[65] This is consistent with the record of Blair's private deliberations in Downing Street, his personal notes to Bush, his memoirs, and the public case he advocated in March 2003 on the eve of invasion. To those two parts a third element should be added, a determination to act as a guiding influence on American power.

In and around the Iraq Inquiry, there has been much discussion of 'when' the final decision for war was made. But the decision/no-decision binary does violence to the way the choice unfolded. Downing Street decided early that it

---

[65] Internal memo to Bush ahead of Crawford meeting, 'Memorandum for the President, Your Meeting with the United Kingdom Prime Minister Tony Blair, April 5–7 2002 at Crawford', at https://foia.state.gov/searchapp/DOCUMENTS/April2014/F-2012-33239/DOC_0C05446915/C05446915.pdf (accessed 25 July 2017).

wanted to unseat Saddam with force. It was too canny to box itself in entirely, though, as it engaged in public diplomacy and in a rolling negotiation with the Bush administration. Instead, they agreed in principle to attack if they politically could, and if they could align the stars to facilitate it. The consistent theme of David Manning, who conveyed the Prime Minister's views in Washington, was that Downing Street favoured regime change but required a 'clever', carefully managed strategy, one which crafted a coalition and induced enough defiance by Saddam of international inspections to warrant action.[66] A desire to attack Saddam if it could be politically achievable was fixed from early on, as we will see, even if the final resolution to do so had to await the resolution of the political struggle at home and abroad. Barring a major impediment, they would strike.

Tony Blair's conception of the nature of the security problem formed quickly over the months between September 2001 and January 2002. If Bush's immediate response was that 9/11 was a 'Pearl Harbor' equivalent,[67] Blair's immediate private and public response was that 'mass terrorism' was the 'new evil in our world', and the world's democracies must rally to 'eradicate it'.[68] He believed the attacks flowed from a systemic failure, namely an absence of liberal market democracy, and demanded a systemic cure, a clash of ideologies no less, matched with ambitious global combat. Testifying before the Inquiry, Blair clearly articulated a rationale that is also to be found in declassified documents, namely that in a post-9/11 world, the American-led West had to act decisively, and with anticipatory action, to defeat 'religious fanaticism' and transform the global security environment.[69]

9/11 was significant not because in itself it increased risks. Rather, it captured the imagination and exposed risks, or risks as they were perceived, revealing the potential deadliness of the globalizing world and the need to reimpose order on it. Blair's Foreign Secretary wrote to him that although 'the threat from Iraq had not increased as a result of 11 September', America was losing its 'tolerance' for Saddam, 'the world having witnessed...just what evil people can these days perpetrate'.[70] Like Bush and his advisors, Blair's circle believed the 9/11 attacks revealed an environment of clear and present dangers. The assault on the Twin Towers, the Pentagon, and the failed strike on

---

[66] Minute, David Manning to Jonathan Powell, 22 January 2002, 'Talks with Condi Rice, 21 January: Iraq'. Letter Manning to Simon Mcdonald (Blair's Principle Private Secretary), 7 December 2001, 'The War Against Terrorism: The Second Phase'.

[67] On the evening of 9/11, President Bush wrote in his diary 'The Pearl Harbor of the twenty-first century took place today'. Bob Woodward, *Bush at War* (New York: Simon & Schuster 2002), p. 33.

[68] 'Blair's Statement in Full', *BBC News*, 11 September 2001.

[69] Tony Blair, IIT, 29 January 2010, p. 49.

[70] Memo, Jack Straw to Tony Blair, 25 March 2002, at http://downingstreetmemo.com/strawtext.html.

the Capitol demonstrated possibilities of even greater destruction. This 'harbinger theory' held that 9/11 was obviously a portent of things to come in 'a new order of terror'. This was a simple and powerful extrapolation from events.[71] The 9/11 mass-casualty attack, he assumed, was not an aberration in a world where most violent threats on a comparable scale can be kept at bay, but part of a serial wave of catastrophic, first-order threat events that directly threatened the West's heartlands.[72] Though powerful, it was a fallacy. That one disastrous attack has been mounted indicates such an attack is possible, but not that it can be easily repeated. The many points at which such attacks can be disrupted suggests that robust counter-terrorism as an alternative to preventive wars should not have been dismissed so swiftly as an alternative.

The threat matrix included the possibility of a linkage between rogue regimes, the most destructive weapons technology, and terrorist networks. Unless systemic action was taken to dismantle the sources of insecurity, including preventive war, indefinite detention, mass surveillance, and targeted killing, unthinkable larger versions of 9/11 would come, with nuclear terrorism as the apex of possible dangers. Incumbent governments were on notice. Containing, limiting, or disrupting threats and certainly deterring them was no longer adequate. Blair gave an internationalist and social democratic twist to an assumption that was rapidly seizing the commanding heights of debate in Washington, advanced by American neoconservatives and 'liberal hawks', that a proper response to 9/11 entailed not only wiping out threatening actors, but altering the Middle East ideologically, correcting its tumult with the antidote of democracy.[73]

Predisposed to regard 9/11 as the trigger of a global and fundamental conflict, Blair in a private note one month after the attack shared Bush's drive for 'extending war aims', 'confronting terrorism in all its forms' and eventually confronting Iraq as well as intensifying the Middle East Peace Process (MEPP).[74] By 4 December 2001 at least, Blair's focus on Iraq had hardened. He privately wrote to Bush that Iraq was a threat because of its WMD, its historic willingness to use it, its capacity to export it, and its linkages to Palestinian terror groups, but that given reluctance of world and British opinion, 'we need a strategy for regime change that builds over time'.[75] There was a rationale for ranking Saddam's Iraq as the principal adversary: past

---

[71] For an outline and critique, see Robert Diab, *The Harbinger Theory* (Oxford: Oxford University Press, 2015), pp. 2, 99, 102, 189.

[72] A distinction observed by John Mueller, 'Harbinger or Aberration? A 9/11 Provocation', *The National Interest* 69 (2002), pp. 45–50.

[73] See Benjamin Miller, 'Explaining Changes in US Grand Strategy: 9/11, the Rise of Offensive Liberalism, and the War in Iraq', *Security Studies* 19:1 (2010), pp. 26–65, p. 56.

[74] Letter Blair to Bush, 11 October 2001.

[75] Private note, Blair to Bush, 'The War Against Terrorism: The Second Phase', 4 December 2001.

performance (he had used chemical weapons before), his known links with Palestinian terrorists, his role as regional spoiler and keystone rejectionist Arab regime, undermining peace prospects over Israel–Palestine, his continual flouting of international accords and inspections, and his history of serial aggression. Potential targets of this wave of liberation in the 'Second Phase' of the War on Terror, in Washington and London, ranged through Syria, Iran, Libya, Somalia, Sudan, Yemen, and the Philippines.[76] There was also the expectation of a benign domino effect, as the overthrow of Saddam would embolden democratic reformers.

'Regime change' could take a number of forms. Earlier on, as the battle for Afghanistan was playing out, the government entertained scenarios of internal overthrow assisted by a more limited external campaign, either a general revolt or higher level coup, without an 'industrial strength war'.[77] There was the possibility that the armed confrontation with Saddam could successfully buckle his regime without an invasion. 'Saddam may crack', Blair would later speculate to Bush.[78] The hope that international pressure without an invasion could create an internal collapse short of war existed into the summer of 2002, but it was always seen as unlikely.[79] Short of these possible paths, determination grew to ensure Saddam's fall directly. Building the case remained the inner circle's main concern, or more specifically, 'to encapsulate our casus belli in some defining way' as he put it to Bush privately on 28 July 2002,[80] or as David Manning summarized it in September 2002 long before the process of resolutions and inspection reports was complete, 'We must look reluctant to use force, making it clear that we saw the current situation as a challenge to the credibility of the UN, and to the international community'.[81] To wage a preventive war while looking reluctant, and in order to strengthen the liberal world order, is the thread that tied together the words and deeds of the period.

For Blair, 9/11 altered his calculus. Although Saddam's WMD programme had not noticeably increased since Operation Desert Fox in December 1998, the shock of the terrorist attacks in Washington and New York served a didactic purpose. By revealing the capabilities and potential capabilities of

---

[76] Memo, Blair to Bush, 4 December 2001; see also Philip Gordon, 'Bush's Middle East Vision', *Survival* 45 (2003), pp. 155–65.

[77] Richard Norton-Taylor, 'Blair orders invasion force this month', *The Guardian*, 8 October 2002; R. Beeston, & T. Baldwin, 'Washington Hawks under fire for ignoring advice', *The Times*, 28 March 2003.

[78] Private Note, Blair to Bush, 24 January 2003.

[79] This was discussed at the September 2002 Camp David Meeting: Minute David Manning to Prime Minister, 8 September 2002, 'Your Visit to Camp David on 7 September: Conversation with President Bush'. See also Minute, Manning to Prime Minister, 3 November 2002, 'Visit to Washington: Talks with Condi Rice'.

[80] Private Note, Blair to Bush, 'Note on Iraq', 28 July 2002.

[81] David Manning to Blair, 10 September 2002, 'Iraq: Conversation with Condi Rice'.

dangerous actors, it 'taught' him that the world should no longer tolerate the risk of Saddam's survival. Blair has continuously defended his decision on the basis of the precautionary principle, the logic that the high stakes made preventive action necessary even if the risk was distant and for the time being, remote. In particular, the possibility of a WMD transfer to a terrorist group was intolerable. The JIC, Britain's interagency committee responsible for intelligence assessment, coordination, and oversight, in November 2001 advised that the threat of Iraqi WMD terrorism was 'slight' unless the regime faced imminent collapse,[82] yet for precautionary minds, a low-odds severe scenario still warrants major preventive action. At the same time, the fact of 9/11 created a new political opportunity to take measures that were not possible before 9/11. A year before invasion, in March 2002 Blair wrote privately to his chief of staff and his foreign policy advisor that the case should be strategically and morally 'obvious'. It is worth quoting at length. The note distils the rationale and the ambition that Blair's private communications would express over the following year:

> 1) In all my papers, I do not have a proper worked-out strategy on how we would do it... I need to be able to provide them with a far more intelligent and detailed analysis of a game plan...
> 2) The persuasion job on this seems very tough. My own side are worried. Public opinion is fragile.
> International opinion—as I found out at the EU—is pretty sceptical.
>
> Yet from a centre-left perspective, the case should be obvious. Saddam's regime is a brutal, oppressive military dictatorship. He kills his opponents, has wrecked the country's economy, and is a source of instability and danger in the region... a political philosophy that does care about other nations eg Kosovo, Afghanistan, Sierra Leone—and is prepared to change the regime on the merits, should be gung-ho on Saddam.
>
> So why isn't it? Because people believe we are only doing it to support the US, and they are only doing it to settle an old score. And the immediate WMD problems don't seem obviously worse than 3 years ago.
>
> So we have to re-order our story and message. Increasingly, I think it should be about the nature of the regime. We do intervene—as per the Chicago speech. We have no inhibitions, where we reasonably can, about nation-building ie we must come to our conclusion on Saddam from our own position, not the US position.[83]

Visible here is Blair the 'double facing leader'. In one direction, there is the warlike idealist and nation-builder, confident that war is right and can work, and diagnosing the problem's roots in the regime itself, not its arsenal. This Blair viewed the confrontation with Saddam as an extension of his Chicago

---

[82] JIC Assessment, 28 November 2001.
[83] Note, Prime Minister Tony Blair to Jonathan Powell, cc'ing David Manning, 17 March 2002.

doctrine of the international community, but with its limitations relaxed, with a vision of reordering the world in response to global terror.

In the other direction, there is Blair the propagandist, attuned to the difficulties of persuasion. As Blair knew, despite the endless statements about the special Anglo-American relationship, the political context in Britain was significantly different. The US had suffered the 9/11 attacks on its soil. Britain had not. Al-Qaeda had slaughtered sixty-seven British people in that attack, but it had not taken place in Britain, nor was Britain the primary target. In the case of striking a separate target not directly linked to 9/11, British people were less likely to accept the urgency of the cause than a terrorized and vengeful American population. British politics demanded more forcefully that the country strive to adhere to international law, and frame its case within those boundaries, and support the authority of the UN Security Council, whereas the Bush administration with its unilateralist tendencies had to be persuaded to approach the Iraq question through the United Nations. Britain's government was more sensitive to demands that any action against Iraq be accompanied by a parallel effort to revive the Israeli-Palestinian peace process. Moreover, there was a general, diffuse anti-Americanism that bred suspicion about American motives and Blair's Atlanticist solidarity with Washington. Blair calculated that any strategy to legitimize a decisive campaign against Saddam's Iraq must be attuned to these constraints. The use of force would attract support, but only if the country were satisfied that alternative diplomatic measures had been exhausted and only if the regime had breached the will of the UN Security Council, which would eventually be expressed in United Nations Security Council Resolution (UNSCR) 1441. To make war possible, Blair had to manage the build-up to conflict within these constraints.

By the summer of 2002, and probably months before, Britain's calculus focused on how to legitimize and facilitate military action, not whether a war would or should happen. This claim is disputed by Alastair Campbell, who maintains that Britain's desired end-state throughout was disarmament through the United Nations.[84] Blair too had assured the House of Commons in September 2002 while presenting the 'September Dossier' that 'our purpose is disarmament. No-one wants military conflict. The whole purpose of putting this before the UN is to demonstrate the united determination of the international community to resolve this in the way it should have been resolved years ago: through a proper process of disarmament under the UN'.[85]

These claims are misleading. They are at odds with the private notes from Blair that we have already seen. Because of a scheduled meeting at President Bush's ranch in Crawford, Texas in April, Blair's circle was motivated to clarify and firm up its position. In February 2002, a 'Phase 2 War Meeting'

---

[84] Alastair Campbell, IIT, 12 January 2010, p. 23.
[85] *Hansard* 6:390, 'Iraq and Weapons of Mass Destruction', 24 September 2002, column 6.

decided that military action against Saddam's Iraq was a 'public persuasion' issue, implying a preference already reached, and an in-principle commitment to helping overthrow the regime.[86] British Ambassador Meyer recalled being instructed by David Manning in March 2002 to cease advocating an alternative containment strategy, and shift the basis of talks to advising the US to adopt an internationalist, UN-sanctioned path to regime change.[87] Meyer's recollection is consistent with what Manning conveyed to National Security Advisor Condoleezza Rice on 14 March 2002, in his own words reporting back to Blair, 'you would not budge from your support for regime change but you had to manage a press, a parliament and a public opinion that was very different than anything in the States'.[88] Between the March 2002 cabinet Iraq 'options paper' and Crawford, Blair asserted that the central problem was the nature of Saddam's regime, 'in part because of WMD but more broadly because of the threat to the region and the world'.[89] In the same month, Blair met with Vice President Cheney, and the pre-meeting FCO briefing advised that Blair should signal 'In complete agreement on objective. World a better place without Saddam in power. Need to ratchet up the pressure on Iraq',[90] while Blair indicated a 'clever strategy' was needed, as it would be 'highly desirable to get rid of Saddam'.[91] A note from Foreign Secretary Jack Straw ahead of Crawford, on 25 March 2002, indicates that the government was working towards framing and selling a 'regime change' strategy. Warning of the potential post-invasion difficulties, Straw advised also that the core of the strategy for military action against Saddam would have to draw on the international rule of law.[92] Along similar lines, on 8 May 2002 Straw communicated to his counterpart Colin Powell that Blair had always taken the view 'that if in the end President Bush decided on military action, the UK had a duty to support him'.[93] So by the spring, the UK's private position

---

[86] Chilcot cited a report of the meeting, *Report of the Iraq Inquiry* 3.2, para. 67, p. 398; see also 'Blair and Bush to plot war on Iraq', *The Guardian*, 24 February 2002; Campbell also refers to the meeting in his diaries: *The Burden of Power: Countdown to Iraq* (London, Random House, 2012), Tuesday 19 February 2002, p. 170.

[87] Christopher Meyer, IIT, 26 November 2009, pp. 41–2.

[88] Private Note, David Manning to Tony Blair and Jonathan Powell, 14 March 2002, from National Security Archive, at http://nsarchive.gwu.edu/NSAEBB/NSAEBB328/II-Doc05.pdf.

[89] Alastair Campbell, *Diaries: The Burden of Power* (London: Random House, 2012), 2 April 2002, p. 198.

[90] Note FCO, 'Visit of US Vice President Dick Cheney 11 March: Iraq', attached to Letter, Simon McDonald to Matthew Rycroft, 8 March 2002, 'US Vice President's Call on the Prime Minister, 11 March'.

[91] David Manning to Simon McDonald, 11 March 2002, 'Conversation between the Prime Minister and Vice President Cheney, 11 March 2002'. Cited in *Report of the Iraq Inquiry*, 3.2, 358, p. 450.

[92] Declassified Letter, Straw to Blair, 25 March 2002: 'Full Text of Jack Straw's Letter to Tony Blair' *The Daily Telegraph*, 18 January 2010, at http://www.telegraph.co.uk/news/politics/7012529/Full-text-of-Jack-Straws-letter-to-Tony-Blair.html. Accessed 30 September 2017.

[93] Minute Straw to PUS [FCO] 9 May 2002, 'Powell/Straw Tete-a-Tete' 8 May 2002.

had shifted away from discussion about containment versus regime change, and towards setting the conditions for war by advising the US to accommodate British preferences in its strategy.

The timing matters because it suggests the decision for war was moving on two tracks: an earlier, unscrutinized and covert resolution for regime change, and a public process of carefully framing and escalating the issue as one of disarmament undertaken in a way that could avoid war. We cannot know for certain what Blair and Bush privately discussed in their conversation during the meeting at Crawford, Texas in April, though afterwards one official in attendance believed 'The whiff of inevitability mingled with the smell of barbeque at the Bush ranch'.[94] Blair's speech at the George Bush Senior Presidential Library in College Station, after the Crawford meeting, reaffirmed the logic of the 'Chicago doctrine', setting out that, 'if necessary the action should be military and again, if necessary and justified, should involve regime change. To allow WMD to be developed by a state like Iraq without let or hindrance would be grossly to ignore the lessons of 11 September and we will not do it'.[95] The terms of debate were set for the following year, framed not as degrees of activity, but action versus inaction, loading all of the risks onto a mythical path of 'inaction' which few were advocating.

By the summer of 2002, a 'likely' campaign had become almost inevitable. In mid-May 2002, Britain's military leadership first received unambiguous indications that war was going ahead. Air Chief Marshal Sir Brian Burridge recalls an informal meeting between General Tommy Franks, CENTCOM and the UK Chiefs of Staff, indicating 'it was not if but when'.[96] Sir Richard Dearlove, the head of MI6, returned from Washington 'convinced that the Administration have moved up a gear'.[97] As the quiet campaign in Washington to refine the case for war took wing in July 2002, British efforts and capital were spent on diplomatic legitimization. British senior officials put the lion's share of their work into persuading Washington to organize their armed confrontation with Iraq around the enforcement of international law under the UN's banner. They were trying to influence the bureaucratic interagency battle within the US administration over the 'UN route' and inspections, to persuade a doubtful president whose first instinct was to act unilaterally and strike. Britain's leading envoys pressed their opposite American numbers on the point: David Manning with Condoleezza Rice, Jack Straw with Colin Powell, Blair with Bush.[98] Advice from the British Ambassador to Downing

---

[94] Anonymous British official, cited in Philip Stevens, *Tony Blair: The Making of a World Leader* (New York: Viking, 2004), p. 211-12, p. 212.
[95] Speech at the George Bush Senior Presidential Library, College Station, Texas, 7 April 2002.
[96] Air Chief Marshal Sir Brian Burridge, IIT, 8 December 2009, p. 6.
[97] David Manning to Blair, 'Iraq Meeting: 23 July: Anotated Agenda', 23 July 2002.
[98] Jeremy Greenstock, *Iraq: The Cost of War* (New York: William Heinemann, 2016), pp. 104-5.

Street in the same period focused on how to garner international support, with a need to focus on the aftermath.[99] This battle endured until Bush opted against the preferences of the Defence Department and Vice President, and addressed the United Nations on 14 September 2002. Those, like Britain's UN Ambassador Jeremy Greenstock who were kept out of the inner decision-making, pursued a process they believed could prevent war, by maximizing pressure on Iraq to cooperate, but this brought about an escalation that would make relaxation or delay hard to accept.

Any doubt about the Blair circles' agreement on and desire for regime change should be dispelled by the leaked 'Downing Street Memo' of July 2002. It was conducted in preparation for the Prime Minister's phone call with Bush, involving the Defence Secretary, Foreign Secretary, Attorney General, Sir Richard Wilson, John Scarlett (JIC), Francis Richards, the Chief of Defence Staff, chief of SIS Richard Dearlove, Jonathan Powell, Sally Morgan, and Alastair Campbell.[100] The emphasis of the meeting was on how to strike, on what basis, the feasibility of military plans and the building of domestic consent. While no 'firm decision' had yet been taken, there was a basic predisposition to commit: 'we should work on the assumption that the UK would take part in any military action'. There was real anxiety that Saddam might use his WMD on troops stationed in Kuwait, or on Israel, suggesting the authenticity of the circle's fears about his arsenal. 'C' (Dearlove) reported that 'military action now seen as inevitable', while the Foreign Secretary reported that 'Bush has made up his mind to take military action'.

The most notorious phrase from the memo is the line summarizing Dearlove's assessment that in Washington, 'the intelligence and facts were being fixed around the policy'. There has been much exegetical debate about the meaning of the term 'fixed', and whether it referred to deliberate manipulation or outright fabrication, or the more innocent organization of intelligence around policy. Regardless, it is significant that because of a hard assumption that they 'knew' of the WMD programme, policy was shaping intelligence, and marshalling intelligence for already-determined goals, even though that intelligence was inconclusive.[101] Straw, who acknowledged the case was 'thin', argued that the UK should work up an ultimatum, that 'this would help with the legal justification for the use of force'. Blair's concern was making the strategy work—'The Prime Minister said it would make a big difference

---

[99] Christopher Meyer, IIT, 26 November 2009, pp. 26–8.
[100] Matthew Rycroft to David Manning, 23 July 2002, 'Iraq Prime Minister's Meeting, 23 July'.
[101] As Fred Kaplan suggests, 'Either way—"fixed" or "fixed around"—Bush and his aides had decided to let policy shape intelligence, not the other way around; they were explicitly politicizing intelligence...But that doesn't necessarily mean they thought their claims were false...They just *knew* Saddam had WMD, and if the facts didn't quite prove he did, they would underscore and embellish the titbits that came close'. 'Let's Go to the Memo', *Slate*, 15 June 2005.

politically and legally if Saddam refused to allow in the UN inspectors... If the political context were right, people would support regime change'.

The taken-for-granted quality of the basic judgement in both capitals that Britain and its major ally *ought* to remove Saddam Hussein is all the more striking, if seen from a wider historical perspective. Like America's decision for war, Britain's was discretionary and premeditated. It was chosen to forestall a perceived threat, well in advance. Unlike most of Britain's modern wars, this choice was not a response to an obvious imminent threat—as Blair privately admitted—or to an adversary's direct pressure or hostile act. It was not a pre-emptive war against an imminent danger. It was a preventive war, to eliminate a potential threat before it fully materialized.[102] In this case, by contrast, the potential 'axis' Britain sought to disrupt was hypothetical and did not take place within a major war. The architects of the Iraq War saw in this confrontation with a weakened third-world regime stakes as vital as Britain's major historical conflicts with nineteenth-century French imperialism and twentieth-century fascism. They believed that the 9/11 shock had revealed a world transformed, one where the empowerment of traditionally minor adversaries meant that the US-led West had to strike first. It was self-consciously a 'historic' decision, in the terms Blair still uses.

Neither Washington nor London had to interpret 9/11 this way. 9/11 did not speak for itself, and the road from the Twin Towers and the Pentagon did not have to lead to Baghdad.[103] There were several ways of interpreting the significance of the 9/11 attacks, and whether and how they linked to the perceived WMD–rogue state–terror nexus. It could be reasoned that terrorism was still a manageable problem to be suppressed, disrupted, and reduced to a tolerable nuisance, without preventive wars to overthrow states. 9/11 could have led to a focus on Islamist terror networks and their known sponsors, with other authoritarian regimes conciliated or bargained with as part of an anti-terrorist coalition. Alternatively, the 9/11 attacks could be seen as a regrettable cost of projecting power and maintaining a strategic presence in the Gulf and the wider Arab-Islamic world, costs to be mitigated but never eliminated. But these alternatives hardly got a hearing.

Instead, decision-makers instinctively framed the terrorist threat as part of a wider ambitious agenda, of reordering the world ideologically, and widening the scope to other adversaries. The view that the confrontation with Iraq was part of an effort to alter the course of the global system enjoyed some

---

[102] On the distinction between pre-emptive and preventive wars, see Lawrence Freedman, 'Prevention, not pre-emption', *Washington Quarterly* 26:2 (2003), pp. 105–14.
[103] As Ronald R. Krebs & Jennifer K. Lobasz argue, 'Fixing the Meaning of 9/11: Hegemony, Coercion and the Road to Iraq', *Security Studies* 16:3 (2007), pp. 409–51, p. 413.

support in government. The FCO's planning department after 9/11 discussed the prospects of 'draining the swamp' in neglected areas of the world that produced threats.[104] This phrase echoed throughout the wider public debate, on both sides of the Atlantic. Secretary of Defence Rumsfeld and Deputy Secretary of Defence Wolfowitz had already used the phrase to define the strategy of countering the new security threats by transforming geopolitical conditions.[105] Advice from the SIS acknowledged the difficulties of invasion, but also sensed a major geopolitical opportunity to change the region. It would be a stride towards wider disarmament and it would alter mentalities, affecting a

> climatic change in the psychology of regimes in the region, a precondition for progress in the Arab-Israel dispute; and revealing a further horizon of intention to address the regional issue of WMD. The problem of WMD is an element in driving for action against Iraq. In turn, this should open prospects for Arab-Israeli talks, and, beyond, regional work to reduce the WMD inventories which threaten Europe as well.[106]

Like Blair, the advice from SIS spoke of the result of removing Saddam as a 'prize', namely, an altered Gulf. Such optimistic projections assumed that the warmakers could impress as wide an audience as they wished, including potentially dangerous third parties, and that military forces could reliably send signals that would be properly received. 'High intensity warfighting at large scale', suggested the Policy Director of the MOD in April 2002, 'would send a powerful deterrence message to other potential WMD proliferators and adversaries'.[107] One could strip Saddam of weapons, only he would want them back. Instead, killing his regime would help stem proliferation generally. Blair privately averred that regional and world order was at stake. Regime change was the ultimate goal, not disarmament, as he explained in a meeting with the Chief of the Defence Staff on 2 April 2002, refuting General Tony Pigott, who claimed the issue 'was WMD'. As Campbell noted, 'TB felt it was regime change in part because of WMD but more broadly because of the threat to the region and the world'.[108] With invasion underway later in March 2003, Blair wrote privately to Bush that 'Our fundamental goal

---

[104] Stephen Pattison, (former Head of United Nations Department, FCO, 2001–2003), IIT, 31 January 2011, p. 12. They soon dropped the phrase, according to Pattison, but the logic underpinning the concept persisted.
[105] 'Rumsfeld: US must "drain the swamp"', CNN, 19 September 2001; Ambrose Evans-Pritchard, 'US asks NATO for help in "draining the swamp" of global terrorism', *The Daily Telegraph*, 27 September 2001.
[106] Letter, Richard Dearlove's Private Secretary to David Manning, 3 December 2001.
[107] Declassified Memorandum, Simon Webb, Director of Policy to Permanent Secretary/Secretary of State, 'Bush and the War on Terrorism', 12 April 2002, p. 4.
[108] A. Campbell & B. Hagerty, *The Burden of Power: Countdown to Iraq* (London: Hutchinson, 2012), 2 April 2002, p. 198.

is to spread our goals of freedom, democracy, tolerance and the rule of law. Though Iraq's WMD is the immediate justification for action, ridding Iraq of Saddam is the real prize'.[109]

Beyond Blair's circle, the choice between 'tough containment' and threat elimination would be quietly canvassed, but mostly with a leaning heavily towards threat elimination. The Cabinet Office's Overseas and Defence Secretariat produced an 'Iraq Options Paper' in March 2002 in preparation for Blair's first visit with Bush at Crawford, Texas. This paper spelt out the 'endgame', which had long been 'to integrate a law-abiding Iraq, which does not possess WMD or threaten its neighbours into the international community. Implicitly, this cannot occur with Saddam Hussein in power'. The first option was 'toughened containment', a strategy that was only 'partially' successful, which had lost the faith of the US administration, and which would not achieve Britain's long-term aim of reintegrating Iraq into the international community. The second option was two alternative forms of regime change: the replacement of Saddam with a Sunni strongman in a system that might regress back into military coups and the acquisition of WMD, or the creation of a representative democracy that renounced proliferation and aggression, but only through a long nation-building campaign.[110] This was the main Cabinet Office paper on Britain's strategic choices, and Blair invoked it before the Inquiry to support a conclusion he had already reached: 'we couldn't go on like this'.[111] Crucially, the paper was discussed with a small group of officials at Chequers, the prime minister's country estate, but not with cabinet. The position before cabinet, as reflected in the declassified Briefing Paper to the Parliamentary Labour Party on 5 March 2002, was that military action was possible and could not be 'ruled out', but that the government was 'doing everything possible to re-establish under UN auspices an inspection programme within Iraq'.[112] In May 2002, an informal cross-departmental group was formed to define the 'end-state' to inform the MOD's military planning, also involving the intelligence agencies, the JIC, and the Cabinet Office. This group's advice demonstrates just how easily, and widely, was accepted the assumption that the endgame should be the political transformation of Iraq. While it baulked at 'regime change' as a possibly illegal formal objective, like the Cabinet Office it advised a far-reaching ambition for the transformation of Iraq: 'A stable and law-abiding Iraq, within its present borders, co-operating with the international community, no longer posing a threat to its neighbours or to international security, and abiding by its

---

[109] Blair to Bush, private note, 'The Fundamental Goal', 26 March 2003.
[110] Cabinet Office, Defence and Overseas Secretariat, 'Iraq: Options Paper', March 2002.
[111] Tony Blair, IIT, 29 January 2010, p. 19.
[112] Declassified Iraq Briefing for the Parliamentary Labour Party, 5 March 2002, part 10, attached to Letter, Mark Sedwill to Matthew Rycroft, 6 March 2002.

international obligations on control of its WMD'. In other words, war should work as a political surgery, not merely neutralizing or limiting an adversary's behaviour, not even overthrowing a government, but curing the whole body politic of a rogue country.[113] This implied a demanding effort at re-engineering a whole state. The advice was caveated, indicating that a future regime might well pursue WMD for rational purposes, given the fear of Iran, and that 'behaviour change' might be more achievable than 'regime change', but the main goal they defined of turning Iraq into an inoffensive state effectively precluded limitation.

In settling on regime change, a choice that would demand intensive military action, Blair did not seek the counsel of his Chief of Defence Staff Admiral Boyce about military options in Iraq before April 2002. Boyce was not apprised of the dialogue between the Prime Minister and the White House about the possibility of widening the War on Terror to Iraq. Blair advised Boyce that British policy was not regime change.[114] Thus not only did Blair fail to consult the military over the prospects for a regime change policy until after he decided it was his preference—he kept them in the dark over the fact of the choice.

Regarding Iraq, Blair and his circle perceived the regime itself as the source of the problem. The Ba'ath order was pathological and vicious, they believed, incapable of reform, incorrigible in its deadly intentions and its determination to reconstitute its WMD programme. 'Regime change' was the only reliable way to counter it. Disarmament was desirable, and the demand for disarmament and cooperation with the international community in the course of disarmament was the most promising basis to create legitimacy for regime change. But the abandonment of Saddam's weapons programme was not in itself the desired end-state. The objective from the formative period until the invasion was to bring the regime to an end. Jonathan Powell, his chief of staff, had already advised in November 2001 that 'our over-riding objective is the removal of Saddam not the insertion of arms inspectors', as 'only a new regime' could ensure the end to chemical, biological, radiological, and nuclear (CBRN) proliferation, hostility to neighbours, and terrorism, and Blair scribbled 'I agree with this entirely' on the note.[115] Blair had also penned his agreement to David Manning's report of December, stressing that Saddam

---

[113] Letter, Peter Ricketts (then Political Director, FCO) to Simon Webb, MOD, 3 May 2002; Minute Ricketts to Private Secretary [FCO], 25 April 2002, 'Iraq Contingency Planning'.

[114] Admiral Lord Boyce (Chief of Defence Staff February 2001 to November 2003), Iraq Inquiry, Witness Statement; IIT, 27 January 2011, pp. 6, 10; in sending British military planners to assist CENTCOM's preparation, Boyce passed on the Secretary of Defence's instruction that 'no political decisions have been taken in the UK on our participation in an operation against Iraq'. Declassified Letter, Chief of Defence Staff to General Richard B. Myers, Chairman of the Joint Chiefs of Staff, 4 July 2002.

[115] Minute, Jonathan Powell to Blair, 15 November 2001, 'The War: What Comes Next?'

would only be overthrown if there was an effective strategy that sustained a coalition.[116] In an early and prescient advisory note on 30 November 2001, Powell advised that a 'change of heart' by Saddam would be a plausible public demand that the US and UK could build support around, but only a 'change of regime' with a compelling pretext would do.[117] Likewise, in his note of 28 July 2002 to Bush, Blair himself indicated in unmistakably clear terms to President Bush that Britain was committed 'whatever', that it was a war to neutralize a 'potential threat', that it was necessary to assemble a persuasive case, that there were difficulties in assembling allies, in post-war reconstruction and in the Middle East Peace Process, and that the main focus was developing a realistic military and political strategy.[118] By this time, as Blair made plain, this was not a government carefully considering the case for and against striking Iraq. It was gathering intelligence, wooing allies, and building legitimacy for a decision that had essentially been taken.

By July 2002, if not before, Blair and his inner circle knew that war was coming, and their chief anxiety was its legitimation. Blair's note to Bush on 28 July urged him to seek an ultimatum through the UN, once Anglo-American forces had begun to raise their presence and preparation in the Gulf from October. As the Iraq Inquiry found, this was a covert message. It was not discussed or agreed with colleagues, and 'set the UK on a path leading to diplomatic activity in the UN and the possibility of participation in military in a way that would make it very difficult for the UK subsequently to withdraw its support for the US'.[119] With the exception of a final authorizing UNSC resolution, the chain of events envisaged by Blair and his advisors was precisely what happened.

Like Bush, Blair was a 'proliferation pessimist'. He believed, rightly, that Saddam aimed to reconstitute his weapons programme if or when international sanctions collapsed. In government, there was the added fear that Saddam rearming would trigger wider proliferation, and that forestalling this threat would deter others. The government and the opposition also believed, less accurately, what a number of intelligence agencies and security officials believed, that Saddam's Iraq had a highly developed latent capacity to proliferate, and under an imperfect and weakening sanctions regime could

---

[116] David Manning to Simon McDonald, 7 December 2001, 'The War Against Terrorism: The Second Phase'.

[117] As Powell advised Blair, the objective should be 'the removal of Saddam and replacement by a new, more moderate regime' as well as the ending of the WMD programme and stocks, the ending of support for terrorism and peace with neighbours. But the 'public line' should be that if there is 'no return of inspectors will consider what further action. Not ruling anything in or out. Change of regime obviously desirable but not our immediate aim'. Regime change would need a pretext: 'if he does allow in the inspectors need to find a new demand to justify military action'. Powell to Blair, 'Iraq: Change of Heart or Change of Regime', 30 November 2001.

[118] 'Note on Iraq', Tony Blair to Bush, 28 July 2002.

[119] *Report of the Iraq Inquiry*, Volume II, p. 3.

develop his clandestine nuclear programme quickly and covertly.[120] This was partly drawn from a widespread misreading of the lessons of the so-called 'near-miss' after the Gulf War of 1991 and its aftermath, when IAEA inspectors and intelligence analysts were allegedly caught off guard at the advanced state of Saddam's nuclear programme. As an MOD assessment assumed in February 2002, 'Iraq came close to developing nuclear weapons before the Gulf War', that without an intervention in the Gulf War, it 'might have produced a crude nuclear device by late 1993', and the 'high level of technical capacity that Iraq has sustained' means they could move forward quickly'.[121] In fact, though observers had underestimated the 'inputs' or scale and investment of the project, the technical 'outputs' or results of Iraq's ten-year, billion-dollar project were extremely modest. In the words of former IAEA inspector Robert Kelley, Iraq's isotope separation programme was a 'spectacular failure', the centrifuge effort had not accumulated any enriched uranium.[122] Its weaponization effort was barely preliminary, vindicating the JIC's estimate in December 1990 that technical difficulties and a lack of fissile material meant that proliferation within four years was only a 'worst-case' scenario, possible only in 'ideal conditions'.[123]

Despite this evidence that Saddam's Iraq faced imposing obstacles to proliferating, Blair then and subsequently maintained that in an alternative world where Saddam was not overthrown, he could have readily acquired a nuclear weapon under the erosion of sanctions. He cited in January 2010 and again in January 2011 the influential pre-war analysis of former CIA intelligence analyst and National Security Council official Kenneth Pollack.[124]

---

[120] William Hague MP, posed this question and its implications in the House of Commons on 24 September 2002 and Blair concurred:

'Does the Prime Minister recollect that, in the half-century history of various states acquiring nuclear capabilities, in almost every case—from the Soviet Union in 1949 to Pakistan in 1998—their ability to do so has been greatly underestimated and understated by intelligence sources at the time? Estimates today of Iraq taking several years to acquire a nuclear device should be seen in that context, and within that margin of error. Given that, and the information from defectors five years after the Gulf war, that 400 nuclear sites and installations had been concealed in farmhouses and even schools in Iraq, is there not at least a significant risk of the utter catastrophe of Iraq possessing a nuclear device without warning, some time in the next couple of years? In that case, does not the risk of leaving the regime on its course today far outweigh the risk of taking action quite soon?', Hansard, 24 September 2002, column 13.

[121] Declassified Memorandum, 'Axis of Evil', Simon Webb to Permanent Secretary/Secretary of State, 27 February 2002, pp. 2, 8.

[122] Robert Kelley, 'The Iraqi and South African Nuclear Weapons Programs: The Importance of Management', Security Dialogue 27:1 (1996), pp. 27–38.

[123] JIC Report quoted in Review of Intelligence on Weapons of Mass Destruction: Report of a Commission of Privy Counsellors (House of Commons Report HC 898, London: Stationery Office, 2004), p. 43; see also the discussion in Jacques E. Hymans, Achieving Nuclear Ambitions: Scientists, Politicians and Proliferation (Cambridge: Cambridge University Press, 2012), pp. 84–95.

[124] Blair, IIT, 29 January 2010, p. 18; Witness Statement to the Iraq Inquiry, 14 January 2011, p. 3; he also cited Pollack in his memoir, A Journey (London: Arrow Books, 2010, 2011 edn.),

Pollack had warned in 2002 that Saddam could quickly rearm if left under an eroding sanctions regime. But he has long since renounced that assessment. As Pollack admitted in January 2004, he made his initial flawed assessment on the basis of the CIA's National Intelligence Estimate (NIE), and the post-invasion discovery of the pitiful state of Saddam's infrastructure and programme by the Iraq Survey Group suggests that 'in all probability Iraq was considerably further from having a nuclear weapon than the five to seven years estimated in the classified version of the NIE'.[125] In other words, Pollack rejected his own original pessimistic estimate ten years before Blair cited it as a supporting authority.[126] This fits a larger pattern of self-deception, whereby Blair cherry-picks the most useful factual claims, then closes his mind to further scrutiny.

What about the wider Middle East? As well as the intensive focus on weapons proliferation, Britain's second major goal was to begin the transformation of the region through a benign 'domino' effect. Strikingly, although the 'big picture' of geopolitics often figured centrally in debate, it often neglected Iran. When British debate did turn to the wider geopolitics, including most anti-war opinion, it focused almost exclusively on the Arab-Israeli dimension. Across government, only a few voices cautioned that invasion could tip the balance in a more dangerous direction, by empowering, threatening, and radicalizing Iran all at once. If invasion would likely strengthen the Shia majority, that could enable Iran to assert its patronage in the region. At the same time, placing a US-led military coalition in Iraq would effectively install hostile forces on either side of Iran's borders, a concerning development for the country for obvious historical reasons, especially since it had been officially named as one of the 'Axis of Evil' trio, and this could give extra impetus for its nuclear programme. Iran, with its linkages to Iraqi militias and parties, and cross-border access, would potentially be able to bleed international forces and subvert the occupiers' designs. Britain's near-obsession with the Palestinian question was reinforced by the contingent event of the Second Intifada that had raged since September 2000, and in 2002 as the case for striking Iraq was being prepared, a number of violent flashpoints brought to the fore the relationship of terrorism with the condition of the Arab population of the Middle East. A strong belief persisted that Iraq and Israel–Palestine were entwined. Addressing the latter would build legitimacy for the former, while removing the 'spoiler' regime in Baghdad that had rejected the Saudi Peace Initiative in March 2002 would strengthen the chance to bring

---

p. 384; Blair was referring to Pollack's book that had warned of the erosion of sanctions and Saddam's capacity to reconstitute his nuclear programme, *The Threatening Storm: The Case for Invading Iraq* (New York: Random House, 2002), pp. 211–43.

[125] Kenneth M. Pollack, 'Spies, Lies and Weapons: What Went Wrong', *Atlantic Monthly* 293:1 (2004), pp. 78–92.

[126] In Chapter 4, I examine further the flawed claim that a Saddam left in office could readily have rearmed in a clandestine programme under international scrutiny.

about a political settlement over Gaza and the West Bank. Blair and others were conscious of 'unintended consequences', but their geopolitical horizons rarely stretched to Tehran. In his meeting with Cheney, his warnings were notable for what they left out:

> We must ensure that a campaign to bring about regime change in Iraq did not inadvertently destabilise other countries in the Middle East. The Arab street was very angry... We needed to generate a sense that we were determined to promote a peace process that would give justice to the Palestinians... If this problem were not tackled successfully, it would dominate the way that the Arabs thought about the Iraq problem.[127]

Arabs, not Iranians.

The neglect of Iran, and its capacity to intervene in Iraq, went beyond Blair. In the parliamentary debate of 18 March 2003, Iran was mentioned seven times only, five times only incidentally in relation to Saddam's war against the country, as proof of his aggressive tendencies, once in terms of the nature of repressive dictatorships, and once in relation to deterrence. The Cabinet Office's 'Iraq Options Paper' discusses Iran in general terms but not its inclination or capacity to resist the project: it was likely to be 'prickly' but 'neutral' in the course of the invasion, deserving 'special attention' in building the coalition, and having an 'interest' in opposing Kurdish secession and in the rights of its 'co-religionists' in the south.[128] This did not even come close to Iran's extensive intervention in post-invasion Iraq, revealed by Wikileaks-released reports, the shadow war between militias backed by Iran's Quds force and Western occupiers, and Iran's supply of weapons to insurgents, including 'rockets, magnetic bombs that can be attached to the underside of cars', and 'explosively formed penetrators', or EFPs, which are the most lethal type of roadside bomb in Iraq.[129]

This lacuna around Iran was also a shortcoming of the FCO.[130] As one senior FCO civil servant speculated in laying out the options, 'Removal of Saddam, if achieved swiftly, would be applauded by his neighbours, the GCC and the wider Arab/Islamic World'. This was not only an oversimplification, as Saddam's downfall was cautioned against by a number of Arab governments and opposed by the Arab League. It was also untrue of Iran's reaction, which went well beyond applause.[131] The FCO's longest written assessment,

---

[127] Letter David Manning to Simon McDonald, 11 March 2002, 'Conversation between the Prime Minister and Vice President Cheney, 11 March 2002'. Cited in *Report of the Iraq Inquiry*, 3.2, 358, p. 450.
[128] Cabinet Office Iraq Options Paper, March 2002, Overseas and Defence Secretariat.
[129] Michael R. Gordon & Andrew W. Lehren, 'Leaked Reports Detail Iran's Aid for Iraqi Militias', *The New York Times*, 22 October 2010.
[130] Jonathan Steele, 'Trouble at the FCO', *London Review of Books* 38:15 (2016), p. 10.
[131] Simon McDonald to Michael Tatham (then Blair's Private Secretary, Foreign Affairs), 3 December 2001.

'Scenarios for the future of Iraq after Saddam', estimated that in the event of forcible overthrow, the presence of 'large numbers of forces in sensitive areas' after a 'clear military victory' would generate 'far more influence' than if Saddam fell without an invasion, and optimistically reckoned that the presence of foreign forces' ordering influence would mean that 'The Iraqi population would probably remain relatively passive'. Iran did not feature in this section. Where it did elsewhere, Iraq's Shia majority 'would be suspicious of an increase in Iranian influence and have no desire to see the instillation of a clerical regime',[132] with no recognition that Iranian patronage might become more attractive if the Shia population felt threatened, and that Iran was capable of sponsoring friendly regimes apart from 'clerical' ones. An underlying stability and Shia restraint was presumed. Also presumed was a clear dividing line between military victory and post-conflict policing, as was the role of the West as bringer of order into chaos.

These delusions were able to thrive partly because the information base was poor, as the FCO lacked an embassy and derived much of its information about Iraqi politics indirectly, via a 'watching brief' from Amman and from brief visits to Baghdad, increasing the need to project theories onto the country.[133] Jonathan Steele argues that the forewarnings were only from academics, and 'nowhere' in the published Whitehall documents are papers 'which spelt out that Iran would increase its influence in Iraq and that the region's stability would be threatened'.[134] This is not quite true. There was some advice on the point. Secretary of Defence Geoff Hoon suggested in March 2002 that with regards to WMD, 'Iran may be the greater problem for the UK... There is no current plan to deal with these risks. Ironically, we have Saddam bound into an established control mechanism'.[135] The issue of Iran and the sectarian picture and possible internecine fighting within Iraq and across the Iran–Iraq border did come up, but in the margins, and remained an afterthought. Blair later admitted that the government underestimated external actors, 'people did not think that Al-Qaeda and Iran would play the role that they did', which 'caused the mission very nearly to fail'.[136] What actual failure would have looked like, in that case, is intriguing.

---

[132] FCO Directorate for Strategy and Innovation and Research Analysts, 'Scenarios for the Future of Iraq after Saddam' attached to letter, Simon McDonald to David Manning, 26 September 2002.

[133] As Edward Chaplin, the FCO's director for the Middle East, indicated: IIT, Tuesday 1 December 2009, p. 39. Chaplin's testimony is haughtily dismissive of American naïvety about a post-Saddam Iraq and its policymakers' credulity towards exiles' lobbying, but FCO documents suggest a persistent failure on its part, too, to anticipate the severity of sectarianized conflict and the wider difficulties of occupation.

[134] Jonathan Steele, 'Chilcot Report: Foreign Office', *Political Quarterly* 87:4 (2016), pp. 484–5, p. 484.

[135] Minute Hoon to Blair, 'Iraq', 22 March 2002.   [136] Blair, IIT, 29 Jan 2010, p. 182.

The collective inability to weigh carefully that a new conflict in the heart of the Middle East could attract other adversaries was a bad error of judgement, suggesting an implicit 'best case' expectation that Iraq's neighbours would 'bandwagon' with the momentum of regime change, and that Iran would be impressed or intimidated by the campaign. There were fleeting moments when Blair anticipated darker possibilities. In a sombre private note to Bush in July 2002, Blair invited the President to imagine that invasion triggered a range of problems, and that Syria and Iran might be 'actively hostile'.[137] Crucially, though, Blair raised this scenario in an implementational context, not a deliberative one. He was in that note making the case for the value of an international coalition, arguing that an internationalized effort would be more likely to mitigate the risks of war, suggesting that a coalition would somehow make Iranian resistance less likely. It was not until January 2003 that Blair asked the Chief of the Defence Staff to identify 'worst-case scenarios', and he was advised 'any rapid regime collapse followed by a power vacuum could result in internecine fighting between the Shia and Sunni populations, particularly in Baghdad, and adventuring by adjacent countries and ethnic groups that irretrievably fractured the country'.[138]

The tragedy of Iraq can be glimpsed in that very meeting.[139] Despite the dangers of internecine chaos, the Chief of Defence Staff admitted that the thinking on this issue was still 'woolly'. Blair's response to the warning betrayed a mind already made up. Coalition forces, he said, 'must prevent anarchy and inter-necine fighting breaking out', asking the MOD to develop a 'feasible plan' for the aftermath. The potential for chaos, and for coalition forces not to prevent but to cause anarchy, was therefore apparent, but at no stage was this to disturb the commitment to join the invasion. At the same meeting, Blair indicated his 'strong view that we wouldn't be looking much past the end of February before seeing this take place'. The decision to go to war was insulated from consideration of the grave problems that could be caused by doing so. Tragically, this was a failure throughout. When powerful objections arose within government about the need to invade and the prospects of success, doubters treated their own objections as problems to be overcome in terms of persuasion and alliance-building, not as reasons to think twice about invading. Foreign Secretary Jack Straw, for instance, who had privately been more sceptical about the strength of the case for invasion and emerges as more of a war-supporting sceptic, had suggested in a phone call to Colin Powell that the case against Iraq was 'third or fourth strongest'

---

[137] Blair to Bush, 'Note on Iraq', 28 July 2002.
[138] Minute, SECOS to PS/Secretary of State [MOD] 22 January 2003, 'Record of the meeting between the Prime Minister and Chiefs of Staff to discuss Op Telic', 15 January 2003.
[139] The more revealing record of that meeting is the unofficial account, Minute MA/DCJO (Ops) to MA (CJO) 15 January 2003, 'Briefing to the Prime Minister'.

behind other candidates for attention, and that 'Saddam was evil but not insane'.[140] This was three days after the Downing Street meeting confirmed the working assumption that Britain would take part in 'any military action'. Decision not only defeated doubt, it predated it.

The Blair circle, then, believed that the regime was the problem, and that it posed medium- and long-term threats, though not an imminent one, and that time was running out on a failing containment programme. Blair and his circle sincerely believed that it was in the British national interest to help the US wage a preventive war to destroy an emerging threat before it materialized, with all the other dividends this would bring: 'freeing up' a tumultuous region, signalling to other would-be proliferating rogues that an Atlantic-led international community would not tolerate any mischief, and bolstering British influence in Washington. It was not enough for the inner circle to decide it wanted war. Building a domestic coalition around the issue was the other necessary step.

PART IV. CARRYING OPINION

Decision-makers realized that to succeed in this war, more than most wars, they must carry British opinion, to overcome several reservations. Botching the task of persuasion and acting against majority sentiment could fatally damage the government. Around the core of believed truths, Blair assembled a bodyguard, what Manning called a 'clever' presentation strategy, that worked on three levels. First was the time horizon, presenting a preventive war as a matter of looming urgency by eliding and blurring the distinction between pre-emption and prevention, characterizing the adversary as a near-term menace with imminent capabilities.

Secondly, the government framed the diplomatic process of disarmament as a potential way to avoid war, so that the actual objective of regime collapse would be understood as the regrettable result of Iraqi defiance. Blair persuaded the wider UK government and general public that there was a way out of war, a possibility that a military campaign would not happen, and that the crisis over Iraqi WMD could be resolved and Iraq rehabilitated as a result of diplomatic and military pressure. The purpose of putting a disarmament process before the UN was to build a persuasive case by inducing Saddam either to capitulate and therefore for the regime to change itself, or more likely to tempt Saddam to withhold full cooperation from a legitimate process,

---

[140] Minute, Simon McDonald to Peter Ricketts (then the Political Director of the FCO), 26 July 2002.

creating a pretext for war. To secure their domestic mandate for war, they allowed Britons to believe that a decision for war was avoidable, that peaceful disarmament was still their ambition, long after the decision for war had effectively been made. Thirdly, in making the case through an intelligence dossier with commentary, the state placed great weight on ambiguous evidence to make compelling the forensic case for Saddam's weapons programme.

At the centre of this exercise was the concept of 'conditions'. The decision-makers allowed others to conclude that Britain had specified preconditions for any participation in a military campaign. But the conditions Blair identified were in his mind suggestions for how the strategy to mobilize opinion and build legitimacy should succeed (rather than minimal requirements for UK participation), to support the military campaign he had already decided to commit to. As he advised his Private Secretary for Foreign Affairs in advance of a visit by US Secretary of Defence Donald Rumsfeld, 'We should say we'll be with you. Here's how to make it happen successfully; not: here are our conditions for being with you'.[141] Blair indicated on multiple occasions to Washington that Britain would support American military action, as clearly as it was possible to say. Meeting with Rumsfeld in early June 2002, Blair confirmed that 'The UK will be with the US in any military action'.[142] When asked about the UK's stance towards Iraq in cabinet later that month, Blair did not mention this meeting or commitment.[143]

The government's public case for the severity of the threat was organized around the publication of intelligence dossiers, in September 2002 and February 2003. They were designed to answer a simple question: 'Why Iraq, Why Now?', and by doing so, to seize the initiative against significant public opposition.[144] The process mingled the assessment of threats with the 'selling' of the case for war. Because it was organized to synthesize intelligence, against the clock, to support a case the government already believed in, it jeopardized the principle that intelligence should inform policy but not be led by it.[145] The

---

[141] Manuscript comment Blair on Minute Rycroft to Prime Minister, 30 May 2002, 'Don Rumsfeld'. Cited in *Report of the Iraq Inquiry* vol. II, p. 23; this is supported by the testimony of Matthew Rycroft, Blair's Private Secretary, on 10 September 2010: 'If your follow-up question is if one of those had not been pursued, would the UK have not joined the US in military action, had it come to that, my answer would be they weren't conditions in that sense. They were things that needed to be done...if they hadn't been pursued, they would not have fundamentally altered the equation in our strategy'.

[142] Letter Rycroft to Watkins, 5 June 2002, 'Prime Minister's Meeting with Rumsfeld, 5 June: Iraq'.

[143] Cabinet Conclusions 20 June 2002, cited in Iraq Inquiry vol. II, p. 26.

[144] On the history of the dossier's creation and publication, see Rawnsley, *The End of the Party*, pp. 107–21.

[145] Alastair Campbell even chaired meetings with intelligence officials on 5 September and 9 September, critiquing drafts and requesting/obtaining changes to the wording of the dossier.

base of intelligence itself was thin, while language was hardened and caveats were reduced or removed.[146] The JIC itself had estimated on 15 March 2002 that the intelligence around Iraq's WMD programme was 'sporadic and patchy', subject to the regime's 'concealment and exaggeration',[147] though judging that Iraq continued to pursue WMD and delivery systems. Yet Blair in the Foreword cast the matter as 'beyond doubt',[148] and before the House on 24 September characterized the JIC's picture of Saddam's weapons programme as 'extensive, detailed and authoritative', a claim refuted by both Lord Butler and the Iraq Inquiry as an inaccurate account of the meagre intelligence base.[149] This reflected a wider incuriosity about the strength of the case for the existence and development of Saddam's arsenal. Minds were closing on the issue, as the consumer requested proof of truths that the consumer believed it knew. Senior aide Sir Stephen Wall reported that Blair 'didn't ask a lot of crucial questions' about nuclear capacity because he 'didn't want to'.[150]

In the build-up to war, the government propagated an inflated spectre of Saddam Hussein's supposed capacity for rapid assault with chemical weapons, reporting in September 2002 that Saddam Hussein's Iraq had the capacity to launch chemical and biological weapons within forty-five minutes' notice.[151] A revelation of the inquiry was that policymakers genuinely failed to appreciate the distinction between tactical 'battlefield' and strategic range weapons, and that there was a striking incuriosity about the actual geographical extent of the threat.[152] This captured the public imagination. Anticipating the dossier, *The News of the World* reported that 'evil Saddam has enough chemical and biological stocks to attack the entire planet, and the missile technology to deliver them'. Tabloid newspapers interpreted the government's dossier to mean that Saddam could strike Britons with germ warfare missiles in Cyprus on forty-five minutes' notice, mistaking both the limited range of Saddam's weapons and the time it would take for them to reach their targets even if they

---

[146] As argues Mark Pythian, 'Political Interference in the Intelligence Process', in Rob Dover & Michael S. Goodman (eds), *Learning from the Secret Past: Cases in British Intelligence History* (Washington, DC: Georgetown University Press, 2011), p. 105.

[147] JIC Report, 15 March 2002, cited in *Review of Intelligence on Weapons of Mass Destruction*, p. 67.

[148] As Sir Lawrence Freedman observed, see Jack Straw, IIT, 21 January 2010, p. 60.

[149] *Hansard*, 22 February 2007, column 1231; *Report of the Iraq Inquiry*, vol. IV, Section 4.2, p. 275.

[150] Cited in Rawnsley, *The End of the Party*, p. 115.

[151] *Iraq's Weapons of Mass Destruction: The Assessment of the British Government* (London: Stationery Office, September 2002), pp. 4, 17.

[152] Blair told the House of Commons he had been unaware that the controversial '45 minute' claim in the government's September 2002 Iraq dossier referred only to tactical battlefield weapons, and not long-range ballistic missiles. *Hansard*, 4 February 2004, column 772. See also 'Blair admits misunderstanding "45-minute" claim', *Sydney Morning Herald*, 5 February 2004.

were long-range.[153] In the public debate, Saddam's limited capabilities became 'not a chemical weapon for use on the battlefield, but a weapon of mass destruction for use in an interstate war'. The government did not knowingly deceive on this point. But neither did it attempt to disabuse the public of this fear.

The dossier was part of an effort to define the policy choice in starkly binary terms, as one of precautionary direct action, in the form of final confrontation, versus passivity. The Press Office advised on presentation of the dossier that 'September 11 showed that we cannot safely ignore distant threats simply because we cannot get into the minds of terrorists or the leaders of terror states'.[154] Who exactly was recommending that Britain 'ignore' future threats, they did not say. Likewise, Blair in a press conference on 7 September insisted 'the policy of inaction is not a policy we can responsibly subscribe to',[155] and Rycroft briefed Blair on 20 September 2002 ahead of parliamentary discussion, 'Would be unconscionable to be aware of the threat and do nothing'.[156]

By framing the policy picture in these distorted terms, the government invested the issue with urgency. It took a broad audience from 'why', as most generally agreed that Iraq's weapons programme was a long-term problem, to the question of 'why now'? By doing so, they injected into the Iraq question a dynamic identified by strategic theorist Thomas Schelling, the 'premium on haste', the advantage of the first-move (or getting in the retaliation first), 'undoubtedly the greatest piece of mischief that can be introduced into military forces, and the greatest source of military danger that peace will explode into all out war'.[157] As well as narrowing the time horizon of the perceived threat, war proponents framed the issue as a moral test, to act absolutely or not to act and effectively capitulate. Rupert Murdoch's press reflected and reinforced this framing, painting the question explicitly as a three-part contest between Churchillian heroism, Hitlerian aggression, and the Chamberlain-ites who were spineless and deluded, embodied in Jacques Chirac's France and doubters at home.[158] The government and tabloids' criticisms of France were an important rhetorical foil, presenting Paris's intransigent vow to veto any resolution authorizing force as unprincipled geopolitical opportunism.

Both Blair and former opposition leader William Hague acknowledged that the Iraq–Munich parallels could be overdrawn, before going on to draw them,

---

[153] 'Brits 45 Mins from Doom', *The Sun*, 25 September 2002.
[154] Minute, John Williams, Press Office to PS/PUS 'Iraq Media Strategy', 4 September 2002.
[155] The White House, 7 September 2002, President Bush, Prime Minister Blair Discuss Keeping the Peace, at https://georgewbush-whitehouse.archives.gov/news/releases/2002/09/20020907-2.html.
[156] Minute Matthew Rycroft to Blair, 20 September 2002, 'Iraq: Tuesday's Debate'.
[157] Thomas Schelling, *Arms and Influence* (Yale: Yale University Press, 1966), p. 227.
[158] See David McKnight, *Murdoch's Politics* (London: Pluto Press, 2013), p. 186.

insisting that the world had changed geopolitically from interstate balance of power of the past, while drawing on that past's most extreme and notorious example. For good measure, Hague accused those who were merely in favour of economically punishing, patrolling, and occasionally bombing Iraq of 'appeasement',[159] as though opponents of war were proposing making persistent, unreciprocated concessions to Iraq in order to pacify it, which is what appeasement is. Blair's case to the House added a moral dimension. Not only was there an urgent and growing security problem, there was an urgent moral case, for liberating Iraqis and alleviating them from a destructive sanctions regime, and, as is often forgotten, both a strategic and moral case on behalf of international order. And unlike American neoconservatives, who mostly dismissed international institutions, British hawks argued on liberal internationalist lines that the credibility of the United Nations was at stake.

The final, necessary causal step on the road to war was the parliamentary vote on 18 March 2003,[160] passed by convincing majority of 412 to 149. This debate, too, was conditioned by a sense of urgency and the embrace of impatience as a virtue in the post-9/11 world. In Chapter 2, we will examine the ideological assumptions about 'regime change' as they were reflected in the parliamentarians' deliberations in greater depth. Here, we trace the verdict of MPs that in the escalating confrontation with Iraq, they dare not back down.

Britain had no codified constitutional requirement for parliamentary authorization, and in 2003, there wasn't the growing convention of consultation that evolved later. Traditionally, governments committed military forces through the exercise of the Royal Prerogative, effectively the *fiat* of Downing Street. Parliament historically has been recalled and debated military action, but this was the first time since the Korean War of 1950 that the government requested parliamentary approval for a military deployment. This time, the British people and their elected representatives were presented with an open, democratic debate over Iraq, but not under conditions of their choosing. Blair had resisted earlier demands for a parliamentary vote in early 2002, on the basis that no decisions had been taken about the use of force, until January 2003.[161] This position changed as pressure grew. The government decided that in the absence of a final UNSC resolution and with the question of mandates

---

[159] 'The Prime Minister said that analogies with the 30s can be taken too far, and of course they can, yet in some of the opposition to the Government's stance there is a hint of appeasement'. *Hansard*, 18 March 2003, William Hague, column 791.

[160] The transcript of the debate can be found at https://www.theyworkforyou.com/debates/?id=2003-03-18.760.0 and https://www.publications.parliament.uk/pa/cm200203/cmhansrd/vo030318/debtext/30318-06.htm. Accessed 15 November 2016.

[161] See J. Strong, 'Why Parliament Now Decides on War: Tracing the Growth of the Parliamentary Prerogative through Syria, Libya and Iraq', *British Journal of Politics and International Relations* 17 (2015), pp. 604–22, pp. 608–9.

and legitimacy constant, parliamentary approval had become politically necessary.

There was a genuine discretion to the vote of MPs, and a conscious choice of war. To be sure, it was not purely through force of argument that the motion passed. There was back-room cajoling, coercion, and inducement, with the whip's office applying discipline. But that discipline would have applied also if the debate had been held months before, and it was not all-powerful. This was not a fresh government with a premier at the height of his powers. Rather, it had been worn down by six years in office, and was well into its second term, with the continual threat of a party revolt against the government's alignment with the Bush administration in the War on Terror. As the whips and advisors then estimated, they could still have lost an earlier vote. Neither would it be enough to prevail on the strength of opposition votes of support. It would be politically hazardous to pass the motion with reliance on opposition votes. The ghost of Labour Prime Minister Ramsay McDonald left fear that it was imperative to obtain a majority through the votes of Labour MPs. Even as things stood in March 2003, a point Blair deliberately delayed until, bringing the issue before the Commons threatened the survival of his premiership, something Blair turned to his advantage by making Iraq a vote of confidence, to raise the stakes of opposition.

The question of time and the fact that Britain was already engaged in an escalating crisis was crucial. Parliament deliberated effectively under a self-induced pressure of time sensitivity and apprehension about the dangers of backing off. British troops were deployed in the Gulf, with their coalition partners, in high readiness and awaiting the order. An earlier decision had already been taken, to take a posture ready to strike from a 'generated start', or a longer build-up of forces in Kuwait, which accelerated in the two months before invasion, with 40,000 troops, sailors, and air force personnel in the Gulf and Kuwaiti desert. This in itself pro-war MPs asserted as a moral principle to support already-mobilized troops. The parliamentary resolution included the proposal that the House 'offers wholehearted support to the men and women of Her Majesty's Armed Forces now on duty in the Middle East', thus inverting the civilian-military relationship, implying that rejecting war would betray those charged to serve the state.

The vote came at the end of a process whereby military preparations had run ahead of an intensive diplomatic process.[162] By that time, the UNMOVIC/Blix report of 27 January 2002 had judged that Iraq had offered partial

---

[162] The parliamentary debate followed on from the escalation and breakdown of a diplomatic process: after UNSCR 1441 was passed in November 2002, and then after 700 inspections had been conducted in Iraq from November to March by UNMOVIC; after the reported failure of Iraq to fully cooperate with 1441; after Parliament had voted twice to endorse the UN process in November and February; and after the UNSC had rejected a draft resolution in February 2003, as Russia and France promised to veto any resolution for military action.

procedural cooperation, while it called for more substantive cooperation and did not discount the possibility of the existence of WMD. The absence of full cooperation had been seized upon by Washington and London as evidence enough of a threat. Even if Saddam had given complete compliance and verifiable disarmament, it was difficult to prove a 'negative' beyond reasonable doubt, the absence of the arsenal. By loading a heavy burden of proof on Saddam's shoulders, a regime that had dissembled and defied UN resolutions before, the case of regime guilt had become unfalsifiable. The US and its allies deliberately raised international demands high, to the point where any 'material breach, defined as not co-operating fully, immediately and unconditionally'[163] created a *casus belli*. At the moment inspectors announced progress and increased cooperation, the government could argue that the precautionary principle dictated final military action. Even partial UN inspection processes effectively made war more likely. Those against invasion effectively opted to argue for the continuation of an inspection process that was finite, and which was only occurring because there was a credible threat of force in the Gulf and a mobilization backing it that could not be sustained. The 'finality' expressed in UN Resolution 1441 added to the pressure. Some MPs fearful of war's consequences felt the mobilization pressure. John Randall MP realized that 'the military build-up is like water behind a dam. We cannot keep it there forever. That is why I think that what is going to happen is inevitable'.

Blair formulated the problem not primarily as a decision whether to invade, but a decision not to back down from a crisis that the US-led coalition had deliberately ramped up, and urged them to end the waiting game: 'I am not prepared to carry on waiting and delaying, with our troops in place in difficult circumstances', and 'our fault has not been impatience. The truth is that our patience should have been exhausted weeks and months and even years ago'. 'Back away from this confrontation now, and future conflicts will be infinitely worse and more devastating in their effects', he argued. Restraint was tantamount to fecklessness and would invite further aggression:

> This is the choice before us. If this House now demands that at this moment, faced with this threat from this regime, British troops are pulled back, that we turn away at the point of reckoning—this is what it means—what then? What will Saddam feel? He will feel strengthened beyond measure. What will the other states that tyrannise their people, the terrorists who threaten our existence, take from that? They will take it that the will confronting them is decaying and feeble. Who will celebrate and who will weep if we take our troops back from the Gulf now?

Commons MPs were free to notice the contradictions and flaws in Blair's summons to impatience. Not enough did. By March 2003, the US and the UK

---

[163] As Blair reminded the House, *Hansard*, 18 March 2003, Column 767.

had already struck hard against al-Qaeda and taken on the burden of occupying Afghanistan. To step back from occupying Iraq while maintaining these demanding tasks was not the equivalent of being 'decaying and feeble'. Iraq could still have been subject to modified sanctions, including prohibitions on imports of materials for military use and the illicit export of oil. The case for war erased any sense of a policy middle ground between inaction and regime change. Blair dismissed over a decade of serious sanctions, inspections, no-fly zones, and bombing as 'feebleness' and 'indulgence', the 'lassitude of the past 12 years; to talk, to discuss, to debate but never to act; to declare our will but not to enforce it', and the biggest recruiting influence on anti-Western hostility is 'indecision, and the failure to take action to show that such resolve matters'.

Most MPs accepted the government's case about where to think from, in the middle of a crisis that Washington and London had deliberately reignited. Most accepted the suspect assumption that the international community had been hitherto weak with Iraq. David Trimble MP asked rhetorically: 'Are we just going to strike camp and go away?' Donald Anderson MP, chair of the Foreign Affairs Select Committee, asked,

> should we now stand down our troops, and should we fundamentally change our strategy? In theory, we could indeed fold our tents and glide away, forgetting about the fact that there are men and women representing our country on the borders of Kuwait and Iraq. We have chosen to be engaged. In my judgment, we made a correct strategic decision way back last summer. We remain engaged with our US allies. To withdraw at this stage would be unthinkable... The fact is, however, that we cannot easily now turn back without undermining our own credibility and the authority of the United Nations.

The Leader of Opposition similarly argued that 'the Prime Minister's decision comes at the end of 12 years of what was too often indecision by the international community'. 'I genuinely urge them all to consider the consequences of turning back now'. Further delay would make 'any military action nigh on impossible', which would 'split the international community and wreck the UN'. The imperative to act decisively in order to rescue the United Nations was a powerful uniting theme, as was the rewriting of recent history to suggest that the world had done 'nothing' about Saddam's violations until March 2003,[164] and it gave an internationalist justification to what opponents branded an 'illegal' war. Andrew Mackay MP warned that

---

[164] For instance, Clive Solely MP charged that 'The real criticism of all us is that we did nothing when Iraq first started to breach not just the 1991 resolutions, but the ceasefire itself, which Saddam had never put into effect. That ceasefire was signed with the UN, not the United States, and he breached it time and again with genocide, torture, human rights abuses, weapons of mass destruction and terrorism—the lot—and we did nothing, because of which many people have died and the misery continues'.

the whole international community would suffer if we and our American allies withdrew our troops from the Iraqi border without Saddam Hussein having complied with the UN resolutions that he has flouted. Every terrorist and tin-pot dictator around the world would be given a green light. The harm and damage that that would do, to us and to future generations, is incalculable.

American troops were not going to be withdrawn however, regardless of Britain's decision. John Maples MP recognized this probability, but voiced similar fears with a curious analogy:

> If, on the verge of battle, with our troops and their command structure integrated into an alliance with the United States, playing vital small parts in that military effort, they were withdrawn, that would destroy the credibility of British foreign and security policy for a generation. Just reflect what happened at Suez. It took 26 years, till the Falklands war, for the credibility of British foreign policy to be reasserted.

Suez was a botched and ill-conceived expedition, however, not a decision of restraint.

The suggestion that British credibility would be badly damaged implicitly assumed that the US-led invasion would succeed, unlike Suez, and leave impugned the judgement and nerve of countries that stood back. Long-term credibility would scarcely be guaranteed by the commitment if, as Tony Worthington MP presciently warned, 'We are going to invade a country of Balkanesque complexity where occupying forces will be unable easily to withdraw. We are rapidly in danger of becoming piggy in the middle for every discontented ethnic or religious group in the area'.

'Who will celebrate and who will weep?', asked Blair. Among those celebrating a drive into Mesopotamia would be al-Qaeda, for whom an alienated and frightened Sunni Arab population in Northern Iraq could constitute a new base in the heart of the territory it wished to turn into a caliphate, and Iranian Shia supremacists and hardline nationalists, who could strengthen their hand through Iraq while adding to their domestic arguments for going nuclear. Notice also that in this threat assessment, the terrorists and rogue regimes hawks branded as suicidal and beyond deterrence were also apparently open to the encouragement and discouragement of example. Ultimately, the impulse Blair successfully appealed to was one that has plunged states into draining peripheral wars before, the urge to eliminate rather than contain problems, and the fear of embarrassment and looking weak.

We can appreciate the tactical guile of the government in investing the question with urgency, in placing the burden of proof unfalsifiably on Iraq, and in escalating the crisis to create a fear of backing down and losing credibility. Nevertheless, the responsibility for judgement still lies with the Parliament. It chose to accept Blair's dubious precautionary argument, that the risks lay overwhelmingly on one side of the equation, and that bringing down the government of a country subject to great internal distress amounted to 'caution', compared to containing and deterring the regime's behaviour, all while still shouldering the burden of occupying Afghanistan. The Parliament went along with the self-contradictory claims of Blair, that the Iraq that was groaning and immiserated under the weight of sanctions had yet still amassed a WMD arsenal and could quickly produce a nuclear weapon, with enough infrastructure and scientific-industrial base intact; that the unstable and reckless regime that apparently already possessed stockpiles of chemical and biological weapons had possessed such weapons yet not used them for fifteen years; and that a rogue state that was heavily risk-prone was the same regime that would go to the trouble of transferring weapons to third parties in order to threaten the West while avoiding retaliation. At least some of the MPs who voted for war were responsible for yielding to a more reckless impulse, their built-up sense of fatigue with the Iraq-WMD issue, and the wish to terminate an already-existing conflict in the hope that it would go away, the symptom of a view of foreign policy characterized by the need to find definitive solutions for, and an unwillingness to live with and manage, chronic problems.

CONCLUSION

British warmakers hardly stopped to consider 'whether' to strike. Powerful assumptions drove them quickly beyond the most critical choice, tilting them instead into questions of execution and presentation. Their overriding preoccupation was how, when, with what public justification, and the prospects for getting support at home and abroad. Instead of providing cautionary advice and generating the creative friction needed to scrutinize choices, the main task of intelligence services and the professional military was in effect to service the government as 'customer'. Unexamined assumptions could stand undisturbed: that 9/11 was a harbinger, not an aberration; that there were no viable intermediate measures between invasion and passivity; that any anticipated difficulties with regime change should not disturb calculus whether to invade. Those certitudes, as well as a very politicized time pressure, predisposed the majority of the Parliament to give its blessing. The most important decision of all, whether to kill people and break things to serve policy goals and create a better state of peace, deserved a more serious deliberation.

To conclude the chapter with the most consequential question one can ask of a war's origins, 'Was there a point when the looming collision might have been averted?'[165] This chapter suggests bleak answers. For America, the

---

[165] Michael H. Hunt, *Crises in US Foreign Policy: An International History Reader* (New Haven: Yale University Press, 1996), p. 331.

crossroads point effectively was first reached on 9/11. The balance of opinion, the exact mixture of fear and confidence, were moving heavily in one direction from that point. Had the nineteen hijackers faltered, or homeland security functioned with greater efficiency, Bush would probably have remained a reluctant warmaker, resisting the entreaties of the Iraq war party, with the congress and the American populace unaroused. Absent an equivalent, major strategic shock, a more belligerent Vice President Cheney suddenly promoted would have lacked a pretext. The only identifiable alternative development that could have deflected the Bush administration might have been a more adverse turn of events in its war in Afghanistan. Could the Taliban have chosen a different strategy to better resist America's overwhelming force in the autumn of 2001, reducing their appetite for opening a second front in the War on Terror?

For Britain, it might seem less clear-cut. There was greater opposition to regime change in the UK, and support was more conditional, more concerned for legality and the legitimacy conferred by international institutions. The only decisive potential moment of reversal lay in the House of Commons' vote on 18 March 2003. But as Chapter 2 shows, even that parliamentary debate suggests that the success of the 9/11 hijackers was the principal juncture. A set of ideas about security and Western power had germinated well before, and the 9/11 attacks gave them fresh wind. Provided it was framed as the enforcement of the international community's will, this made a parliamentary revolt beyond the left wing of the Labour Party unlikely. According to a doctrine that was gathering pace throughout the 'interwar' period, not only did globalization make modern states uniquely vulnerable. As an instrument for producing peace and security, liberal war could work. Britain was both too frightened, and not frightened enough. The mid to late 1990s, a period in diplomatic history now attracting renewed attention, created a permissive ideological context. To that era that we now turn.

2

Breaking States

The Ideological Roots of Regime Change

In interpreting Iraq's warnings, commentators rightly call for a more rigorous, self-critical process of decision in government. They call for the revival of the cabinet committee system, and advocate more 'red-teaming', or the organized probing of assumptions through creative exercises.[1] To its credit, Britain's Ministry of Defence has extracted warnings from Iraq about the need for critical thinking, careful defining of problems, attention to the gap between ambitions and capabilities, and wariness of the non-linear and wild tendencies of war.[2]

Since we can never be too sure that our assumptions are warranted, embedding scrutiny in decision-making is a valuable step. But the Iraq blunder flowed from something more profound than an error in Whitehall machinery. In his response to the publication of 'Chilcot', political scientist Robert Jervis observed that flawed process on its own does not sufficiently explain the recourse to war:

> If it turned out that Saddam had had active Weapons of Mass Destruction (WMD) programs, few people would have cared or even noticed that intelligence had expressed too much certainty, had failed to examine its assumptions, or exaggerated the reliability of its sources. In parallel, the degree to which Prime Minister Blair overstated the intelligence and short-circuited standard procedures would have seemed like the normal ways of handling a crisis. Had the American and British forces been greeted as liberators and the local population been able to manage a peaceful transition, the lack of preparation for the less happy events

---

[1] Michael Clarke, RUSI Briefing Note: 'Chilcot, The Judgement of History', 7 July 2016, https://rusi.org/commentary/chilcot-judgement-history; Jean Seaton, 'Chilcot Report: Introduction', *Political Quarterly* 87:4 (2016), pp. 476–80.

[2] Ministry of Defence, *The Good Operation: A Handbook for Those Involved in Operational Policy and its Implementation* (London: Ministry of Defence, 2017).

that actually unfolded would not have been seen as a major failure, although it still would have been one.[3]

Accordingly, the problem was not closed decision-making or a dogmatic mindset in isolation. In an alternative universe, if the Blair government undertook exactly the same process but there *was* a WMD arsenal, and Iraq *was* ripe for stable, democratic evolution, there would now be less inquest. There would be less lamentation about poor decision-making process. The failure over Iraq is not just that the war initiators were dogmatic, but that they held bad ideas dogmatically. Former Prime Minister David Cameron claimed, on Chilcot's release, that government had already learned the lessons, but as historian James Ellison observes, 'those seem mostly about process. The question of principle remains.'[4] Dangerous principles thrived because the instruments of government allowed them to, and because the marketplace of ideas were receptive to them.[5] The invaders assumed that it was in the gift of certain great powers to reorder part of the world as it suited them, all the way into the political interior of states. At the same time, they regarded it as a strategic and moral duty, and that the globalized world demanded it.

From the outset, this was an ambitious war. The architects of Britain's effort always intended the toppling of the Iraqi Ba'ath regime to transform world order. It really was an attempt to change the world for the better, with all the deadliness such good intentions can carry. 'Our ambition is big', Blair wrote privately to Bush one week into the hostilities.[6] The last chapter demonstrated the chronology of these beliefs. Blair's later memoirs were not a retrospective platitude, but an accurate reprisal of his thinking all along: the Middle East 'was urgently in need of modernization. It was an alarming melange of toxic ingredients: a wrong-headed view of the future; a narrative about Islam that was at best inadequate and at worst dangerous; [regimes] under immense internal strain', and it needed a 'fundamental reordering'.[7] The causes of democracy promotion, 'freeing up' the Middle East, and modernization were not *post hoc* inventions designed to provide cover for a counterproliferation war that had found no weapons. The inner circles of Washington and London

---

[3] Robert Jervis, 'The Mother of All post-mortems', *The Journal of Strategic Studies* 40:1-2 (2017), pp. 287-94, p. 288.
[4] James Ellison, 'War guilt, Blair and the Chilcot Inquiry', 12 July 2016, http://www.qmul.ac.uk/media/news/items/hss/178983.html (accessed 15 July 2016).
[5] See, in the US context, Chaim Kauffman, 'Threat Inflation and the Failure of the Marketplace of Ideas', *International Security* 29:1 (2004), pp. 5-48; on the ideological roots of the war in the United States, see Michael MacDonald, *Overreach: Delusions of Regime Change in Iraq* (Cambridge: Harvard University Press, 2014), pp. 7-99; Benjamin Miller, "Explaining Changes in US Grand Strategy: 9/11, the Rise of Offensive Liberalism, and the War in Iraq," *Security Studies*, Vol. 19, No. 1 (2010), pp. 26-65.
[6] Prime Minister Tony Blair, Note to President George W. Bush, 26 March 2003.
[7] Tony Blair, *A Journey* (London: Arrow Books, 2010, 2011 edn.), pp. 386-7.

were led by 'daydream believers' from the very beginning.[8] Though they presented their final reckoning with Saddam Hussein as a regrettable step to remove a defiant rogue after all reasonable efforts to induce 'behaviour change', it was from early on intended to bring about the forcible, externally driven removal of a government and the remaking of the state's institutions, thereby inspiring a benign domino effect.

How did warmakers persuade their countries to share their warlike idealism? Deception is not a sufficient explanation. As Chilcot found, Blair's circle successfully persuaded its domestic audience that the confrontation with Saddam was intended primarily for disarmament, they presented weak and ambiguous evidence as cast iron, and delayed debate about military action until the point of maximum pressure to rally around the flag. But deception could only achieve so much. Remorseful war supporters offer a suspect alibi, that they only gave their support because they believed what they were told. No amount of misinformation or duplicity, however sly, would have sufficed on its own to take Britain to war. Other major states—Germany, France, and China—agreed that Saddam's weapons programme and evasion represented a security problem, but refused to infer that it was an intolerable risk, and argued that more time for weapons inspections was preferable to a hasty invasion. In Britain, as in the US, beneath the immediate arguments about Iraq there was a structure of general ideas about power and security. Because of these well-entrenched assumptions, Members of Parliament, much of the media, the professional military and the public were persuaded that war could *work*, and that the risks of the status quo outweighed the risks of full-scale invasion. If, as Chilcot found, the war was powered by assumptions that were 'seldom challenged', it is to those assumptions we now turn.[9]

Before the invasion of Iraq, there was an idea, and an ideology, of regime change. This idea meant more than the literal overthrow of governments. It stood for an ascendant assumption within government, that countries like the UK could only secure themselves properly by eliminating rather than handling threats. Ultimately, this meant breaking and remaking nation states. This revolutionary idea, that the world demands the application of systemic solutions by far-sighted statesmen, took root so deeply that it became a 'common sense'. The 9/11 attacks heightened the doctrine and made it more politically achievable. It amounted not only to a zero-sum conception of 'absolute security'. It also entailed a form of anti-diplomacy. In the desire to cut the Gordian Knot of problems like Iraq, it flowed from an impatience with and frustration towards the notion that major powers must manage, limit, and contain threats, husband their resources, both compete and bargain even with

---

[8] A phrase I borrow from Fred Kaplan, *Daydream Believers: How a Few Grand Ideas Wrecked American Power* (New York: Wiley, 2008).
[9] *The Report of the Iraq Inquiry: Executive Summary*, HC 264, p. 82.

despotic states, and accept trade-offs. British foreign policy argument as a whole—even mainstream anti-war opinion—had become captured by the conceit that the West's duty is to correct problems, 'fix' or 'sort out' the Middle East, and eradicate the 'root cause' of terror. These developments generated a particular mixture of confidence and fear, and emerged out of the interregnum between the fall of the Berlin Wall and the 9/11 attacks.

In this chapter, I trace the ideological roots of regime change. After contrasting it with traditions of limited war, I track its origins to older arguments about Western power, in frustration with the Gulf War settlement, and in the pathologies of a type of warlike liberalism when applied to foreign policy. I then identify the flaws of the 'regime change' mindset. I argue that the Iraq War marked a loosening of restraint, a tragic forgetting of limitations and the agency of Iraqis, the rise of an undisciplined set of concepts, and a confusion around the concepts of rationality and irrationality.

FROM LIMITED WAR TO REGIME CHANGE

The essence of strategy is limitation, the balancing of power and commitments in ways that rank interests, prioritize, and trade off things that are valued, and compromise with lesser evils. Limitation involves refraining from expending all resources at one's disposal. It also involves tempering expectations of what military force can usefully achieve when applied. In the tradition of realpolitik is the realization that in a world of scarce resources, multiple dangers, and imperfect knowledge, decision-makers most of the time can hope only to restrain dangers and reduce threats, and always with an eye to the unintended consequences of action and inaction. In a nuclearized Cold War world, the concept of limited war gained fresh salience. After Korea, it became apparent that the US could contain Soviet Communism while limiting the scale and intensity of its military activity, and that the nuclear revolution gave them little choice. Western debate about limited war in a global conflict drew on these constraining conditions.[10] Even 'minor' wars remain dangerous enough, as they can aggregate into major wars. Seemingly peripheral struggles can unexpectedly wear down and exhaust major powers.[11] The essence therefore lies not in the size of the opponent, but in the scale of the policy and ambition. Military forces, if husbanded carefully, can be effective means of deterrence,

---

[10] Robert Osgood, *Limited War: The Challenge to American Strategy* (Chicago: University of Chicago Press, 1957).

[11] See Hew Strachan, 'Strategy and the limitation of war', *Survival* 50:1 (2008), pp. 31–54, p. 32.

defence, and disruption—but only with great hazard can they be wielded effectively beyond those functions.

A useful point of entry is Edward N. Luttwak's interpretation of the grand strategy of the Byzantine Empire. In Luttwak's history, the Byzantines looked out on a hostile environment, surrounded by adversaries. They developed an austere 'operational code', and survived by holding on to the concept of limits:

> To wear out their own forces... in order to utterly destroy the immediate enemy would only open the way for the next wave of invaders. The genius of Byzantine grand strategy was to turn the very multiplicity of enemies to advantage, by employing diplomacy, deception, payoffs, and religious conversion to induce them to fight one another instead of fighting the empire... In the Byzantine scheme of things, military strength was subordinated to diplomacy instead of the other way around, and used mostly to contain, punish, or intimidate rather than to attack or defend in full force.[12]

Luttwak used this Byzantine ideal-type to offer strategic counselling to America in 2009, as it reeled from the Global Financial Crisis and its two grinding wars in Afghanistan and Iraq:

> Replace the battle of attrition and occupation of countries with manoeuvre warfare—lightning strikes and offensive raids to disrupt enemies, followed by rapid withdrawals... avoid consuming combat forces, and patiently whittle down the enemy's strength. This might require much time. But there is no urgency because as soon as one enemy is no more, another will surely take his place. All is constantly changing as rulers and nations rise and fall. Only the empire is eternal—if, that is, it does not exhaust itself.[13]

The refusal to pursue absolute war aims, and the preference for limited 'raids', offers other dividends beyond the conservation of resources and the avoidance of self-exhaustion. A successful deterrence relationship rests on the deterrer's willingness to be vulnerable, and to hold back if the 'deterree' complies. Whereas an enemy on the receiving end of a war of annihilation, waged by powers inflexibly committed, has little to lose. In turn, successful deterrence relies upon the continued self-restraint of states that do have the capability to go further. If they wish to deter, they must learn to live with frustrating compromise settlements, and the survival of adversaries that they would ideally prefer to perish.

As Chapter 1 demonstrated, Blair's circle resolved early on to abandon the tenets of limited war, and the associated concepts of deterrence and containment, and use war instead as a problem-solving tool that they hoped would have a major, pacifying impact. They refused to be insecure, and believed they

---

[12] Edward N. Luttwak, *The Grand Strategy of the Byzantine Empire* (Harvard University Press, 2009), p. 415.

[13] Edward N. Luttwak, 'Take me Back to Constantinople', *Foreign Policy*, 15 October 2009.

could wipe out one source of insecurity. Blair's rationales for the Iraq War departed from the limited-war tradition. The Iraq War, and the wider War on Terror, at its core was based on an unbounded concept of Western security interests, and the conviction that the liberal order championed by the West could only be properly secured by defeating and uprooting its rivals, in particular 'rogue' actors and the more amorphous force of 'extremism', and replacing them with constitutional governments and free markets. This entailed a rejection of the doctrine that had defined the long contest with the Soviet Union, that the battle of ideas had to be bounded.

Where does the idea of 'regime change' come from? The Bush and Blair doctrines arose in permissive conditions, namely prolonged economic growth which powered a growth in relative strength, and a relatively benign threat-environment. In such conditions, the governments of major powers were more confident than their predecessors, confident enough to attack distant threats and contemplate military adventures to topple the governments of middling and minor states. A determination to destroy an enemy state, or alter it beyond recognition, and replace that regime is implicit in preventive war. States launch pre-emptive wars to forestall a feared imminent threat, as Israel did in June 1967 and Egypt did in October 1973, to revise the balance of power or seize particular territories without usually wishing to topple those regimes directly. By contrast, states do not usually launch preventive wars just to cut an adversary down to size but to take that adversary off the board, if not to annihilate it. The fewer the 'checks' on this option, the more tempting it becomes.

In the chronicle of preventive wars, war initiators usually wish their gamble of first strike against a more distant threat to result in gains well beyond disrupting their opponent's capacity to harm them. From Stalin's 'winter war' to reduce Finland to a protective buffer in 1939, to the *Kaiserreich*'s preventive strike against feared Franco-Russian encirclement in 1914, to Imperial Japan's effort to evict the US from East and South Asia in 1941,[14] the pay-off was supposed to be the absolute elimination of a threat and the creation of a new security order. Such is the scale of the undertaking and the diversion of resources that lesser goals might seem disproportionate. The more wary decision-maker eschews preventive war for that reason. Chancellor Bismarck considered in his memoirs 'the question whether it was desirable, as regards a war which we should probably have to face sooner or later, to bring it on *anticipando* before the adversary could improve his preparations' and concluded that 'one cannot see the cards of Providence far enough ahead'.[15] To shoot on suspicion is to be frightened enough that the threat is so grave as to

---

[14] On these and other cases, noting the confusion of terms in the title, see Matthew J. Flynn, *First Strike: Pre-emptive War in Modern History* (New York: Routledge, 2008).

[15] Cited in *Bismarck: The Man and the Statesman* (New York: Cosimo, 2007) vol. 2, p. 103.

be intolerable, even if it lurks over the horizon, yet to be confident enough in one's power and foresight that acting now can succeed. The Bush Doctrine was based on the premise that the potential intersection of terrorism with WMD required the adoption of a militarized precautionary principle. In Bush's words, America 'must not ignore the threat gathering against us. Facing clear evidence of peril, we cannot wait for the final proof, the smoking gun that could come in the form of a mushroom cloud'.[16]

The idea of 'regime change' echoes older arguments about how America should wield its preponderant levels of power. If the master concept that guided strategic debate during the Cold War was 'containment', that concept always implied a level of threat tolerance. The notion that the US should limit and abide threats until they withered always attracted opposition. 'Rollback' was the main alternative offered up.[17] The point of division was the question of time. Containment implicitly held that time was ultimately on the side of the United States and its allies against Soviet Communism. It counselled a firm and vigilant but slow wearing down of threats until they failed of their own internal contradictions. Because time favoured the ultimate victory of its political model over competitors, America could avoid a catastrophic major war, deter its major opponent from first-order aggression, preserve its constitution and way of life, and wait out and wear down the threat. The advocates of 'rollback' were more impatient and more pessimistic. Time was against them, as it allowed adversaries to grow and become bolder, and those adversaries could not be reliably deterred. These lines of division were first evident in the 1952 presidential election and periodically revived, with their climax under Ronald Reagan's anti-détente stance in the early 1980s, as 'rollbackers' accused containment's architects of mounting a passive and static strategy, which failed to deter revolutionary adventurism, wrongly appeased a totalitarian regime, and legitimized its conquests in Eastern Europe. The mere existence of the threat, rollbackers argued, was intolerable. Containment settled for more relative security; rollback for a more absolute security. Rollback involved regime changes, such as the subversion of puppet officials or covert operations to support overthrow from within, and led governments to entertain the possibility of preventive war. In practice, even administrations like Eisenhower and Reagan that publicly called for rollback ended up holding on to central tenets of containment, for fear that unrestrained rollback would escalate dangerously.

The same debate about time, and the trade-offs between containment and rollback, resurfaced in Washington after 1991, but without the restraining

---

[16] 'Bush: Don't Wait for Mushroom Cloud', *CNN*, 8 October 2002.
[17] On this background, see Robert S. Litwak, *Regime Change: US Strategy through the Prism of 9/11* (Baltimore: Johns Hopkins University Press, 2007), pp. 109–10.

structure of the Cold War.[18] The issue arose in practical form around the long confrontation with Saddam Hussein between 1991 and 2003. The West's relationship with Iraq was centre stage in the long debate of whether to accept a limited victory for limited gains in 1991, and whether to tolerate imperfect outcomes in exchange for limited costs. Calls for going further and 'regime change' flowed partly from discontentment about the outcome and uncertain trajectory of that Gulf War. The war of 1990–1 was a brief and territorially confined struggle. Although it succeeded in its deliberately circumscribed direct goals, it earnt increasing complaints over time, especially as it became apparent that it was only an opening chapter in the West's protracted struggle with Saddam Hussein. Even while that limited war was raging, it attracted more extravagant goals. The posse led by US forces on one level ended operations once Saddam's forces had been expelled from Kuwait, and President Bush halted the punitive bombing campaign against retreating Republican Guard units, and resisted the call to drive on to Baghdad and overthrow the regime. On another level, the course of that war enlarged American ambitions. While the campaign was on foot, Washington and London pursued a twin formula of not moving directly against Saddam Hussein beyond his expulsion from Kuwait, but openly hoping and expecting that his defeat would result in regime collapse.[19] President Bush in February 1991 incited the Iraqi people to force Saddam out, and in March 1991, intelligence briefings forecast Saddam's downfall within a year. In the twelve years following, this ambition was frustrated but never-ending. Any relief from sanctions was made conditional on Saddam's departure: until then Iraq's Western opponents branded it a delinquent and outlaw state, and a ward of the international community. Neoconservatives and some right-wing nationalists regarded the failure to remove Saddam in 1991 and beyond as symptomatic of weakness, and through the Project for a New American Century, they pushed to make Saddam's removal a test of American leadership. Their letter of January 1998 to President Clinton warned that 'If we accept a course of weakness and drift, we put our interests and our future at risk'.[20]

In an increasingly predominant America, it proved difficult even for strategic minds who had once defended Bush's limited war to remain content with the outcome. Consider leading defence intellectual Eliot Cohen, who in July 1992 argued that the campaign had scored serious gains:

> Were Kuwait's borders restored? Was its territorial integrity sustained? ... Was Saddam Hussein's attempt at extortion frustrated? Were nations the world over

---

[18] On the debate in the context of the War on Terror, see Stephen D. Biddle, *American Grand Strategy after 9/11: An Assessment* (Carlisle: Strategic Studies Institute, 2005), p. vi.

[19] See Lawrence Freedman & Efraim Karsh, *The Gulf Conflict* (London: Faber & Faber, 1993), pp. 411–12.

[20] Letter, 26 January 1998, PNAC to President William Jefferson Clinton.

assured of continuing access to oil at reasonable world prices? Was Iraq's capacity to wage nuclear, chemical, and biological warfare crushed, if not as yet... totally eliminated? Was relative stability in the Middle East secured?

The answers were 'affirmative'.[21] Yet by December 2001, Cohen advocated war on Saddam and resolved that overthrowing 'a menace and a monster' and purveyor of terror that was also 'far weaker' would be easier than the 'cakewalk' of 1991, and 'begin a transformation of the Middle East'.[22] Saddam's Iraq, once a containable limited threat, had become both a peril and an easy target. Blair would share this logic, and critics such as Robin Cook in his Commons resignation speech, attacked the contradiction.

> Ironically, it is only because Iraq's military forces are so weak that we can even contemplate its invasion. Some advocates of conflict claim that Saddam's forces are so weak, so demoralised and so badly equipped that the war will be over in a few days. We cannot base our military strategy on the assumption that Saddam is weak and at the same time justify pre-emptive action on the claim that he is a threat.[23]

Hawks may have countered that Saddam could pose dangers with WMD even while his conventional forces were depleted, but that rests too on a dubious assumption that sanctions devastated the latter while not affecting the former. Despite these fallacies, the marriage of superpower capability and post 9/11 insecurity led American and British Atlanticists alike to lose their patience with the 'first' Gulf War settlement.

Externally forced regime change became tempting partly because of a dilemma, that a defeated Saddam would neither capitulate nor go away. Throughout the 1990s, statesmen, inspectors, and diplomats were exasperated at Saddam's refusal to comply with international inspections and demands. But he had little incentive to do so, given his Western adversaries had demanded his demise, and given they had attempted to make it happen through CIA-backed coups, mutinies, and failed assassination attempts. 'Disarmament' as a discrete and limited demand was never attempted. It was always mixed up with—and compromised by—an absolute demand for overthrow. This is the flaw with Tony Blair's persistent claim that only 'diplomacy backed by force' could bring Saddam to heel, a claim based on only a limited set of overlearned historical analogies. In circumstances where the power exercising such diplomacy is effectively insisting that its target commit suicide, giving the target no secure path to survival if it capitulates, we should not be surprised that the targeted state resisted and refused to moderate its conduct.

---

[21] Letter, Eliot A. Cohen, *Commentary*, 1 July 1992.
[22] Eliot A. Cohen, 'Iraq Can't Resist Us', *Wall Street Journal*, 23 December 2001.
[23] Robin Cook, *Hansard*, 17 March 2003, column 727.

Most of the momentum behind the 'regime change' era flowed from Washington. 'Blair's wars', too, had involved military action to defeat sitting heads of state, with an aspiration to bring about their prosecution, from Serbia's Slobodan Milosevic to the British-backed coercion of Liberia's Charles Taylor. The British version of regime change placed greater stress on the internationalism of law enforcement, even while selectivity over UN mandates suggested that the policing might be conducted through vigilantism. In the era of liberal intervention grew a doctrine that misbehaving states could forfeit their sovereignty, and be subject to the remedy of overthrow by other parties,[24] beyond the replacement of a government to include an overhaul of the institutions of state and their mode of civic life. Iraq loomed as a decent candidate, as it had not been a truly sovereign state since Gulf War One.

The notion that certain regimes are intolerable, even ones that did not command the resources of major states, rested also on assumptions about 'regime type'. Namely, it assumed that the internal political and economic attributes of a state determine state behaviour, and that conversion to democracy promotes general peace. This dubious half-truth advocates for war treated as a law of history, drawing explicitly on international relations theory. With a typically neat antithesis, Tony Blair in July 2003 claimed that 'any time ordinary people are given the chance to choose, the choice is the same: freedom, not tyranny; democracy, not dictatorship; the rule of law, not the rule of the secret police'.[25] This kind of argument rested partly on a selective reading of former Soviet dissident and Israel cabinet minister Natan Sharansky, whose book *The Case for Democracy* Bush bought for Blair, losing sight of the historical conditions and contingencies that make stable democracy possible in the first place.[26] At the time of writing this book in April 2017, according to Freedom House, post-Saddam Iraq, even with regular elections, remains 'not free', with political rights and civil liberties scoring at 5 and 6 respectively out of the lowest score of 7 on the 'free' scale.[27] Assumptions that Iraqis yearned to be free and therefore would embrace democratic peace were naïve. People yearn for security, too, and the introduction of ballots into a fractured population demonstrably made parts of the country more violent, not less. Majority rule did not remove secret detention sites and death squads

---

[24] See W. Michael Reisman, 'Why Regime Change is (Almost) Always a Bad Idea', *American Journal of International Law* 98 (2004), pp. 504–13.

[25] 'Tony Blair's Speech to the US Congress', *The Guardian*, 18 July 2003. On the comic Jon Stewart show in 2008, Blair also surmised that democratization translates into benign external behaviour, as liberal democracies never fight one another.

[26] Chris Suellentrop, 'My Sharansky: Bush's Favourite Book Doesn't Always Endorse his Policies', *Slate*, 26 January 2005.

[27] *Freedom in the World 2017*, https://freedomhouse.org/report/freedom-world/freedom-world-2017.

from the state's apparatus.[28] A majority government, representing majority will, in Iraq at that historical posed a threatening prospect to minorities. Even if democratic peace theory is true in the long run, the process of democracy creation is historically often violent. It was ironic that the leaders of two countries whose own constitutional governments were formed through revolution and civil war would overlook that possibility.

REGIME CHANGE: THE LIBERAL CONSCIENCE, THE REVOLUTIONARY MOMENT

'Regime change' can also be traced to two traditions in foreign policy, of liberalism and revolution. It was haunted by the ghosts of William Gladstone, and possibly Leon Trotsky.

Before dealing with the undeniable force of liberalism, or a form of it, that drove the invasion, there is another possible ideological source. This source is harder to prove. Britain's war in Iraq attracted the support of notable ex-communists. Blair himself has recently admitted that Isaac Deutcher's biography of Leon Trotsky, the communist and Red Army founder, 'changed my life',[29] and a number of high-ranking colleagues who supported the war also had Trotskyite revolutionary pasts, such as Alan Johnson, John Reid, Stephen Myers, and Alan Milburn.[30] While they had long repudiated revolutionary socialism, it is possible that a structure of belief remained in their idealistic internationalism, their vision of foreign policy as a crusade and a planet reordered, that lent itself to ambitious projects to overthrow an *ancient regime* via effective cadres deftly waging political combat.[31] Equally important was what they rejected: conceptions of foreign policy built around the 'national interest', narrowly conceived, or the balance of power. Blair himself explicitly rejected these concepts in addressing the US Congress.[32] If American military

---

[28] Amnesty International, *Annual Report, 2016–17*, pp. 196–8, at https://www.amnesty.org/en/countries/middle-east-and-north-africa/iraq/report-iraq/.

[29] Anushka Asthana, 'Blair reveals he toyed with Marxism after reading book on Trotksy', *The Guardian*, 10 August 2017.

[30] George Eaton, 'Tony Blair Isn't the Only Labour Figure with a Far-Left Past', *New Statesman*, 10 August 2017; 'How Labour's Contenders See the War', *The Guardian*, 21 February 2007.

[31] The ideological linkage of Trotskyism, or one strand of it, and neoconservatism is better documented in the American than the British case: see John B. Judis, 'Trotskyism to Anachronism: The Neoconservative Revolution', *Foreign Affairs* 74:4 (1995), pp. 123–9; Stephen Schwartz, 'Trotskycons?', *National Review*, 11 June 2003. For the argument that it also applied in Britain, see Peter Hitchens, 'Usefully Idiotic', 20 April 2015, at http://hitchensblog.mailonsunday.co.uk/2015/04/usefully-idiotic.html.

[32] Text of Blair's Speech, *BBC News*, 17 July 2003, http://news.bbc.co.uk/1/hi/uk_politics/3076253.stm.

power had become the last remaining revolutionary instrument, Iraq was a revolutionary project, both in the basic sense that it was the toppling of a fascistic ruler intended to help the emancipation of the region, and because it was inspired by a Trotskyite impulse and tradition, or one reading of it. In America, certainly, the case for war attracted Trotskyite company. Kanan Makiya, the Iraqi-American anti-Saddamist was a leading Arab member of the Fourth International. Muscular pro-war idealists like Paul Berman and former labor organizer Stephen Schwartz argued for the 'psychological, ideological and intellectual continuity' between Trotsky and neoconservatism, and noted Trotsky's 'militaristic' and pre-emptive disposition.[33] Leading US neoconservatives had been formed in the intellectual tradition of Trotskyism as purveyed by the commanding American figure Max Schachtman.

The revolution that was to be exported, though, was more directly and primarily a liberal one. By 'liberalism', I do not mean the pluralist tradition of John Stewart Mill and the assumption of fallibility and the value of dissenting opposition. I mean firstly the family of associated ideas that combine ideals of individual liberty, free markets, democratic representation, and equality of opportunity, and a belief in the possibility of irreversible progress. I mean also one strain of 'security' liberalism, the assumption that security is tied to the active spread of liberal institutions and values, if necessary at gunpoint. The strain of liberalism that prevailed in Washington and London in the early twenty-first century resists the notion of limitation. Of necessity, the belligerent liberal impulse is not satisfied with armed efforts that fall short of the toppling of regimes. Those efforts imply the tolerance and management of threats rather than their decisive defeat. Such restraint, they judge, is both immoral and strategically unwise. Liberalism contains the seeds of illiberalism, as it is a jealous faith that is intolerant of rival creeds and ideologies and feels threatened by them. The versions of liberalism held by Blair and Bush were belligerent because they idealized and universalized their country's material interests, conflating them with a global struggle that knew few limits.

Consider the striking parallels between Prime Minister William Gladstone (1809–98) and Blair, who was dubbed 'Tony Gladstone' after his Labour conference speech in October 2001 where he urged solidarity with the poor 'in the mountain ranges of Afghanistan'.[34] Gladstone argued in 1876 for an armed intervention after the Ottoman Empire's atrocious suppression of the April Uprising, demanding that the British government should 'apply all its vigour to concur with the other states of Europe in obtaining the extinction of the Turkish executive power in Bulgaria', and in 1882, invoked Britain's 'moral duty' in the invasion of Egypt to convert it 'from anarchy and conflict to peace

---

[33] Jeet Heer, 'Trotsky's Ghost wandering the White House', *National Post*, 7 June 2003.
[34] R. Shannon, 'History Lessons', *The Guardian*, 4 October 2001; T.G. Ash, 'Gambling on America', *The Guardian*, 3 October 2002.

and order'.[35] Gladstone, like Blair, advocated war as a moral duty, on behalf of the international community but not necessarily with its unanimous consent, with the end goal of ending regimes and starting new ones. And the campaign in Egypt, as in Iraq, lasted far longer than a liberal prime minister intended or expected. In the hands of Gladstone or Blair, liberals at war believe themselves to be essentially peaceable, that the enemy (in this case, Saddam Hussein) embodies the belligerent spirit, so that overthrowing it on behalf of the civilized world serves the cause of peace. At a Press Conference in the earlier crisis with Saddam in December 1998, Blair claimed that 'the first stirrings of a new global reality are upon us. Those who abuse force to wage war must be confronted by those willing to use force to maintain peace, otherwise the simple truth is that war becomes more likely'.[36] Left untampered by realism and a sense of the tragic, the tradition of armed liberalism becomes, as Michael Howard noted, 'the efforts of good men to abolish war but only succeeding thereby in making it more terrible'.[37]

Contrary to some interpretations, the Iraq project was not mainly the product of a cabal of neoconservative fanatics with sinister motives, or the sudden rise of a new and alien ideology. Instead, it drew upon a deeper, broader, and more familiar ideological source, namely the ambitious transatlantic neoliberalism of the post–Cold War era. As scholars who trace the war's intellectual origins observe, the prevailing 'common sense' of the time was a restless form of liberalism that sought to remake the world in its own image.[38] The 9/11 attacks 're-bellicized' it, or reawakened its war-like logic. It bred an underlying confidence in the prospects of regime change. With war underway, Blair averred that the vast majority of Iraqis were 'desperate' to be liberated, for its government to be 'representative of the people', and 'for the human rights of the people to be cared for'.[39] In the odd, fleeting moment, Blair acknowledged the risks of post-war chaos.[40] Overall, however, diplomats and academic experts reported that the government's setting was one of unscrutinized optimism, aversion to contrary advice, and incuriosity about whether

---

[35] John Morley, *The Life of William Ewart Gladstone* (London: Macmillan, 1859), II, pp. 121, 241.

[36] *Report of the Iraq Inquiry*, vol. 1, Transcript of Press Conference, 20 December 1998, p. 104.

[37] Michael Howard, *War and the Liberal Conscience* (London: Hurst, 1978, 2007 edn.), p. 115.

[38] Toby Dodge, 'Coming face-to-face with bloody reality: Liberal common sense and the ideological failure of the Bush doctrine in Iraq', *International Politics* 46:2/3 (2009), pp. 253–75, pp. 262–5.

[39] Tony Blair, 'Remarks by President Bush and Prime Minister Blair on Iraq War, Camp David, Maryland, 27 March 2003', in *We Will Prevail: President George W. Bush on War, Terrorism, and Freedom* (New York: Continuum, 2003), p. 244.

[40] In a note of 24 January 2003, Blair warned Bush, 'The biggest risk we face is internecine fighting between all the rival groups, religions, tribes, etc. in Iraq when the military strike destabilises the regime. They are perfectly capable, on previous form, of killing each other in large numbers'.

occupying Iraq would work.[41] Chilcot's verdict was that the government failed to analyse or manage risks adequately, and planning assumed that 'the UK would be able quickly to reduce its military presence in Iraq and deploy only a minimal number of civilians'.[42] A clue to this failure lies in Blair's later confession that he did not realize, amidst the liberal war to release universal human propensity for democratic liberty, that Iraqis would reject their liberation.[43] This mentality was also evident in the leaked memo of a the two-hour meeting between Blair and Bush on 31 January 2003, authored by David Manning and authenticated confidentially by two officials to *The New York Times*, indicating that the two leaders 'envisioned a quick victory and a transition to a new Iraqi government that would be complicated, but manageable. Mr. Bush predicted that it was "unlikely there would be internecine warfare between the different religious and ethnic groups." Mr. Blair agreed with that assessment'.[44] In other words, inadequate planning derived from assumptions about the relative ease of the mission. The liberators expected the liberated to align themselves with the new state in short order, and wanted it to be true, more in hope than in hard-headed calculation. It was a necessary corollary, too, of Blair's conviction that the threat of 'extremism' had to be decisively confronted and corrected, not merely contained.[45] Such a doctrine dictated regime change, no matter the chances of civil strife and disorder.

Optimism also had an Iraqi face: Iraqi anti-Saddam exiles, organized around the Iraqi National Congress, encouraged belief that native Iraqis would welcome their diaspora compatriots as leaders, and there was an underground democratic movement that would naturally prevail after the decapitation of the regime. Hand-in-hand with this assumption was the view of Saddam's regime as a detachable group that would be separated from the body politic, rather than a whole political movement that had over three decades embedded itself through Iraq's institutions.[46]

The sum of these hopes was an optimism that the US-led strike on Iraq would succeed quickly, without a tortured political aftermath. President George W. Bush's declaration of the end of combat operations on board the *USS Abraham Lincoln* on 1 May 2003 may have been overhyped. The banner announcing 'Mission Accomplished' was not his creation, and his speech acknowledged that there was 'difficult work to do in Iraq'. But the occasion

---

[41] This is the dominant view of academic experts and ex-diplomats who warned of country's intercommunal resentments: cited in Jonathan Steele, *Defeat: Why They Lost Iraq* (London: I.B. Tauris, 2008), pp. 18–19, 163–4.
[42] Executive Summary, *Report of the Iraq Inquiry*, p. 122.   [43] Blair, *Journey*, p. 372.
[44] As reported in Don Van Natta Jr, 'Bush Was Set on Path to War, British Memo Says', *The New York Times*, 27 March 2006.
[45] Blair laid out this logic in his testimony on 21 January 2011, p. 6.
[46] As Toby Dodge observed, in Alan George, Raymond Whitaker & Andy McSmith, 'Inside story: the countdown to war', *The Independent on Sunday*, 17 October 2004.

overall signalled the sense of triumphant finality that also tinged Bush's address to troops in Afghanistan in June of that year, that 'America sent you on a mission to remove a grave threat and to liberate an oppressed people, and that mission has been accomplished.'[47]

American and British versions of warlike liberalism commonly believed themselves to be liberating Iraqis to advance their own security. They were not identical, but Iraq marked a powerful point of intersection and agreement. If the 'Bush Doctrine' was articulated in the form of a strident American hyper-nationalism, the 'Blair Doctrine' consciously sought to build a consensual international community around a vision of progress and liberation, championed by Western arms. True to the tensions within Atlantic neoliberalism, the process of liberation was seen as natural yet necessarily coercive. Iraqis, the objects of liberation, would be made to be free, remade as politically and economically rational citizens, entitled to make a rational choice to become friendly states whose interests self-evidently coincided with the West's. With an illegitimate regime separate from Iraqi society, and then surgically removed, rational individuals would exercise their natural choice to be free. Iraqis, they mostly assumed, were not groups formed by the weight of history and potentially vulnerable to a destructive security dilemma, needing security guarantees from one another in order to reinvent their polity. Rather they were individuals to be exposed quickly in the 'year zero' of liberation to the competitive processes of market democracy, their loyalties to the new state reinforced by development aid. There would be little choice in the matter. New Labour, like the Conservatives, sought to persuade people to accept capital and the discipline of the market as facts of life. It drew upon a crude dualism between the modern and premodern, the old and the new.[48] Globalization was a given fact rather than a set of political decisions. Iraq would be subject to the same logic. Blair's domestic agenda they projected onto the regency in Iraq. As Blair once exhorted trade unions, 'modernise or die'.[49]

Emphatically, not all liberals behave or think in this way. Liberal opponents of the war, such as Charles Kennedy and Menzies Campbell, identified liberalism with strict adherence to international institutions and obedience to international law, and the preservation of the United Nations' unity. Against crusading liberalism, they countered with legalist liberalism. Liberalism for them was supposed to be a restraint, not an enabler, of military adventures, and it prized unity and process more highly than the enforcement of credibility. Warlike liberalism in 2003, however, associated liberalism with

---

[47] Judy Keen, 'Bush to Troops: Mission Accomplished', *USA Today*, 6 June 2003.

[48] See Alan Finlayson, 'Tony Blair and the Jargon of Modernisation', *Soundings* 10 (1998), pp. 11–27, pp. 18–19.

[49] Barrie Clement, 'Abrasive Blair tells unions, modernise or die', *The Independent*, 9 September 1997.

the determined application of power to enforce the United Nations' credibility even in defiance of its veto-wielding members.

Blair's strategic outlook evolved through his experience as a warfighting prime minister. He deployed armed forces five times, from Africa and the Balkans to Central Asia and the Middle East, deployments that mostly resulted in an overthrow. Blair acknowledged the power of these historical experiences, and drew confidence from them. In his speech at College Station, the day after the April 2002 Crawford meeting with Bush, he spelled it out: 'If necessary, the action should be military, and, again, if necessary and justified, it should involve regime change. I have been involved, as British Prime Minister, in three conflicts involving regime change: Milosevic, the Taliban and Sierra Leone'.[50] His judgement, he claimed, was vindicated in these campaigns, against the critics.[51] It was the wars in the Balkans, and the possibilities of military action in the age of the *Pax Americana*, that most roused Tony Blair's liberal conscience, and the campaign over Kosovo in particular that defined his moral and strategic worldview.[52] April to May of 1999 were the most formative months for him. As he formulated his doctrine of the 'international community' and lobbied Washington to threaten the use of ground troops to coerce Serbia's regime to end its butchery of Kosovar Muslims, Blair was also visibly shocked by his encounter with refugee camps in Bosnia. His 'first rudimentary thinking on regime change' took shape at this time as the bombardment of Serbia continued. That this unexpectedly protracted campaign eventually succeeded, after making Blair fear it could be his 'Suez' moment, fortified his ambitions about what political will and force could achieve. The ousting of Milosevic became the minimum for the reintegration of Serbia into the civilized world, or in his own words, 'We can then embark on a new moral crusade to rebuild the Balkans without him'.[53] Blair drew from a flawed world-historical vision that was evident in his address to the Romanian parliament:

> In 1945 Germany was still under Hitler. Within ten years, it had re-established its democracy, rebuilt its cities, joined NATO and was in at the birth of what is now the European Union. Germany reconstructed itself within a decade as a peace-loving nation and an impeccable member of the international community, and today is a resolute and leading player in Operation Allied Force. Serbia can re-join the world community too. But that prospect will only be a reality when its corrupt

---

[50] 'Full Text of Tony Blair's Speech in Texas', *The Guardian*, 8 April 2002.

[51] Jackie Ashley, 'No Moving a Prime Minister Whose Mind is Made Up', *The Guardian*, 1 March 2003.

[52] As Oliver Daddow demonstrates, 'Tony's War? Blair, Kosovo and the interventionist impulse in British Foreign Policy?', *International Affairs* 85:3 (2009), pp. 547-60.

[53] From John Kampfner, *Blair's Wars* (New York: Free Press, 2004), pp. 55-6, 59-60; Tony Blair, 'A New Moral Crusade', *Newsweek*, 13 June 1999.

dictatorship is cast out and real democracy returns to the former Republic of Yugoslavia.[54]

Blair's potted history, on which he built his demand for 'regime change', is misleading. Firstly, in the late 1990s the 'world community' he spoke of included powers with authoritarian and illiberal regimes, from China to Saudi Arabia, that his government conducted high-level diplomacy with. Historically, the post-war 'Germany' Blair referred to was in fact West Germany. East Germany was a Soviet satellite. The fragile peace between East and West Germany was kept partly by mutual deterrence—a concept Blair would disown—and maintained and policed by a deliberate division in the form of the Berlin Wall. West Germany did not recover and prosper simply by casting out its old order. It did not have elections for its first four years, and its proud social democracy, like NATO, retained officials who had been security elites in the Third Reich.[55] Former Nazi mandarins stuffed the Interior ministry, the Foreign Ministry, the Justice Ministry and the highest levels of government. The complicity of its officials and bureaucrats ranged from membership of the Nazi Party to involvement in formulating and executing its repressive policies. Several former Nazi generals would later become senior commanders in the Bundeswehr, West Germany's army. The reasons for this continuity were likely both practical—to retain the capabilities of experienced civil servants, armed personnel and lawyers—and political, geared towards the new emphasis on countering the Soviet threat. Understandable or execrable, it was a compromise that stands in marked contrast to the De-Ba'athification purge of the bureaucracy and the security services carried out by the occupying powers in Baghdad from 2003. Blair's case for absolute regime change as the baseline standard, like the case for occupation of Iraq, relied upon the wrongly remembered case of West Germany's post-war reconstruction.

This was not the last time he would offer a dangerously innocent account of history. In a remembrance service for the 9/11 victims, he claimed that for the generation that 'went through the Blitz', America was 'the one country that stood by us'.[56] This was not only untrue of America's diplomatic stance in 1940, but overlooked the solidarity of Commonwealth and European anti-fascist states such as Greece. Blair's oversimplified and sanitized historical narrative underpinned an oversimplified and sanitized account of political change, which he presented as a bold turning of the page, without compromise or negotiation with the past. Blair and like-minded Atlanticist hawks also sanitized the memory of the campaign in Kosovo. Held up as an exemplar of

---

[54] 'Blair: Cast Out Milosevic', *BBC News*, 4 May 1999.
[55] See 'From Dictatorship to Democracy: The Role Ex-Nazis Played in Early West Germany', *Spiegel Online*, 6 March 2012; Stefan Wagstyl, 'Postwar West German Ministry "burdened" by ex-Nazis, study says', *The Financial Times*, 10 October 2016.
[56] 'We Share Grief, Blair tells America', *BBC News*, 20 September 2001.

righteous force, prudently applied, it also accelerated the flight of Kosovar refugees and enabled counter-ethnic cleansing by the Kosovar Liberation Army, who drove 200,000 Serbs out of Kosovo. These unintended consequences exposed the failure of the war's architects to assist victims by preparing in detail. The acclamation of rescued Muslims, cheering Blair's name as he visited camps, overshadowed the brutal reciprocities of a civil war, and cemented the episode as a case of the strong rescuing the weak from the predator. Tragic historical cases, old and recent, became useful accounts of history, as stripped of ambiguities and problems as the September Dossier.

Blair's original doctrine, adumbrated in his Chicago speech of April 1999, contained the seeds of these errors, but it would take cumulative experience to turn them into dogma. The Chicago speech was not an untampered, crusading outburst. With the input of Sir Lawrence Freedman, who is as much sober strategist as principled liberal, the speech was formulated to bound interventionism with serious preconditions, tests, and caveats. The Chicago doctrine was an attempt to capture an equilibrium between the stability of a world of sovereign states, and the revisionist ambition to topple oppressive regimes that forfeited their sovereignty. As Freedman recalls:

> The question in my mind was not how could the interventionist impulse that had developed during the 1990s be taken to the next stage of toppling dictators—which had not been attempted with Saddam nor in any of the interventions in the former Yugoslavia—but how to keep the impulse under control. On one hand, it seemed that in the circumstances of the time and in the context of the West's apparent predominance, demands to intervene would be regular and in many cases justified. Yet on the other, not all these demands could be met even when the case to act might be morally compelling. It was also important to meet the criticisms surrounding Kosovo that the West was acquiring for itself a carte blanche.[57]

The tragedy of Chicago is not that it was originally a pure doctrine of armed liberalism, but that the limitations it included, the clauses of self-restraint, faded over time.

Around Blair were gathered determined minds, who helped to articulate his vision and impose it on the reluctant. It was not the Foreign Office, the Cabinet Office or the Ministry of Defence that were the main sources of Blair's evolving doctrine. If anything, the Kosovo template strengthened his aversion to using Whitehall machinery for advice. Blair neglected orthodox channels of advice, wrote the lion's share of his own speeches in a personalized process, literally on the fly in April–May 1999, and when he turned to others for intellectual input, he tapped trusted outsiders. Advisor Jonathan Powell,

---

[57] Lawrence Freedman, 'Force and the International Community: Blair's Chicago Speech and the criteria for Intervention', *International Relations* 31:2 (2017), pp. 107–24, p. 115.

former diplomat from the British embassy in Washington, was a committed Atlanticist and 'true believer' in the cause.[58] Also central was Secretary of State for Defence and future NATO Secretary General George Robertson. This son of a village policeman, from a long family tradition of policing, would become a hawkish Labour grandee and member of the transatlantic foreign policy establishment, and would retain a constabulary view of the West's global role. He pronounced in his NATO capacity four days before 9/11 that 'in the global village, I am the bobby on the beat'.[59] There is great confidence implicit in such statements, framing the world as a domesticated small place that can be pacified by the authority of the transatlantic alliance 'cop'. Robertson was significant not only ideologically, but because he believed in backing up liberal ambitions with ground troops. To US officials, he had repeatedly pledged '50,000 troops' to a proposed NATO ground force campaign in the Kosovo conflict. Rightly sceptical about the promise of air power as a self-sufficient instrument, 'regime change' visionaries believed in armies as the tools of democratic modernization.

Robertson had overseen the Labour government's *Strategic Defence Review* (SDR) of 1998.[60] The Review did not offer a hardened doctrine of regime change or preventive war, but the early traces of the core assumptions can be found there. Saddam Hussein's regime is a ranked focus—appearing four times, more often than any other named adversary, embodying with his military forces and WMD projects the 'significant sources of instability', threats that 'may grow'. There is a strong emphasis on anticipatory security measures, a preventive orientation, assuming Britain's ability to avert conflicts long in advance, while paying little heed to the potential unintended consequences of well-intentioned activism. Evident overall is a desire to forestall threats with the confident application of power. The fading of great power threats is treated not as an impermanent development incidental to the collapse of the Soviet Union, but almost as a permanent transformation of the world, licensing expeditionary ventures to suppress instability far beyond Britain's region:

> In the Cold War, we needed large forces at home and on the Continent to defend against the constant threat of massive attack from an enemy coming to us. Now, the need is increasingly to help prevent or shape crises further away and, if necessary, to deploy military forces rapidly before they get out of hand.

Robertson's underlying notion of the West using anticipatory measures to bring order into chaos was echoed by Secretary of Defence Geoff Hoon in

---

[58] According to Sally Morgan, cited in Rawnsley, *The End of the Party*, p. 114.
[59] Mark Thomas, 'I'm the Global Bobby on the Beat', *Liverpool Echo*, 7 September 2001.
[60] *Strategic Defence Review: Presented to Parliament by the Secretary of State for Defence by Command of Her Majesty* (London 1998): the following references in order refer to pp. 14, 17, 68, 29, 7.

December 2001, that the only certainty in a complex world was that problems had to be met 'upstream'.[61] Above all, Robertson's Review was founded on the 'Munich' worldview, where one model of muscular diplomacy wielded by righteous nations will always work, and is universally applicable:

> Our forces must also be able to back up our influence as a leading force for good in the world and meet our responsibilities towards the UN, by helping to prevent or manage crises. In the words of the UN Secretary General after this year's climbdown by Saddam Hussein, 'You can do a lot more with diplomacy backed up by firmness and force'.

This was only a half-truth. Diplomacy that emphasizes the threat of force and punishment is not always the most effective approach to hostile regimes. Not every regime is analogous to the unappeasable and undeterrable Nazi Germany, and attempts at constructive engagement that de-emphasize military threats can succeed. As the most in-depth study of this tradition argues,

> Long-standing rivalries tend to thaw as a result of mutual accommodation, not coercive intimidation. Of course, offers of reconciliation are sometimes rebuffed, requiring that they be revoked. But under the appropriate conditions, reciprocal concessions are bold and courageous investments in peace. Obama is also right to ease back on democracy promotion as he engages adversaries; even states that are repressive at home can be cooperative abroad.[62]

It was not with overt threats of force, or ideologically fundamentalist claims to be a 'force for good', that Nixon's Washington engaged and rebuilt relations with Mao's China in 1972, likewise when Australia's Keating government forged a security agreement with Suharto's Indonesia in 1995, another case where a bloodstained regime at home could cooperate abroad.

Whether Saddam's Iraq would fit this model is uncertain. It had certainly never been given the chance. The West had not been conducting coherent 'diplomacy' with Iraq from 1991. Instead, it had demanded that for Iraq to return to the international fold, its ruling regime must abdicate. From the outset, the assumption that Saddam must and will depart under international pressure was stubbornly held, even as the evidence mounted that he was determined to ride out the campaigns to bring him down. Perennial escalations against Iraq were not delivering on the hope of regime change, but rather entrenching the status quo. Ironically, in SDR the success of Western strategy in achieving its more realistic and limited aim, of weakening Saddam's capacity for external aggression, did not get the credit it was due. The worldview

---

[61] Geoff Hoon, '11 September: A New Chapter for the Strategic Defence Review', speech to King's College London, 5 December 2001.
[62] Charles A. Kupchan, 'Enemies into Friends: How the United States can Court its Adversaries', *Foreign Affairs* 89:2 (2010), pp. 120–34, p. 121.

inscribed in the SDR of 1998 takes for granted that the currency of international life is one of resolve versus weakness, of forces for good standing up to hostile states and forcing them to climb down, a world where threats remain deadly or get even worse. Any sense of the Byzantine alternative, of judicious management of potential threats, and proportional threat assessment, let alone the possibility of turning enemies into neutrals or friends, or dividing them against one another, goes missing in action. With these assumptions, Britain was already primed for the road to Basra.

The jurist and former national security official Philip Bobbitt both articulated and probably helped define Blair's worldview, through two macro-historical works, *The Shield of Achilles* and its follow-up, *Terror and Consent*. Blair endorsed the latter, that applied Blairite ideas to war on terrorism, as the 'first really comprehensive analysis of the struggle against terror'.[63] In both works, the victorious West, according to historical pattern, must impose world order on the vanquished. Bobbitt's overall prescription drew on a reading of world history, where major powers could pursue peace by expanding the principles of a vaguely defined 'market state' globally and at home, requiring sustained military domination and an ability to fight constant minor wars. Ominously, this must include 'preclusive' wars, waged by societies based on consent against those who practice and embody 'terror'. The leaning towards long, universal, and existential struggles of ideas, waged by increasingly powerful states with moral vision of enforcing rule of law, followed by grand constitutional settlements that restore order to the world, was an oversimplification of history. But it appealed to the type of 'visionary world-making' that is a tendency of the most powerful states,[64] and an obvious fit with Blair's emerging worldview since before 9/11, one that he intended to guide Washington towards.

The manifestoes of Robert Cooper, former diplomat and senior advisor on foreign policy, did most in writing to define and reinforce Blair's case for world reordering. Cooper's public called for a new 'liberal imperialism' drew on his earlier analysis at the think tank Demos, was coined in an attention-grabbing article published in April 2002, and later turned into a treatise,

---

[63] And Blair's speech on Iraq, March 2004 may have drawn on Bobbitt's work, as he spoke of the old Westphalian order being surpassed in an age of globalization.

[64] As Nicholas Kitchen argues, there is a 'tendency of great powers with a surfeit of material capabilities to attempt visionary world-making. With their territorial and political integrity secured, interests offer few constraints to check the progress of grand ideas in the policymaking process, and the international system poses few constraints on a state whose material power and ideational dominance largely defines international structure. The question "what must we do?" is replaced by "what shall we do?"' Nicholas Kitchen, 'Systemic Pressures and Domestic Ideas: A Neoclassical Realist Model of Grand Strategy Formation', *Review of International Studies* 36:1 (2010), pp. 117–43, p. 141.

The Breaking of Nations.[65] Cooper was close to the Blair circle. He was accorded a high status, exempted from the normal civil service prohibitions on publishing his opinions. He was also asked to provide a position paper on the WMD threat, and had access enough to supply the Prime Minister's Christmas reading. Cooper mirrored Blair's assumption, that the central crisis manifested on 9/11 was the proliferation of WMD and 'pre-modern' actors threatening the breakdown of order in a 'borderless' world. His offerings amounted largely to a hyperbolic and rambling discourse about world order. But he was precise on one point. If the world had a civilized core, there was a barbarous periphery, creating a warrant for open-ended force. Cooper's advice was self-fulfilling:

> Among ourselves, we operate on the basis of laws and open cooperative security. But when dealing with more old-fashioned kinds of states outside the postmodern continent of Europe, we need to revert to the rougher methods of an earlier era—force, *pre-emptive attack*, deception, whatever is necessary to deal with those who still live in the nineteenth century world of every state for itself. Among ourselves, we keep the law but when we are operating in the jungle, we must also use the laws of the jungle.

The timing was significant, calling for anticipatory force just as the British government was getting sure signals of Washington's determination to strike Iraq. Cooper, like Blair, framed the issue in stark terms. The choice was intervention in zones of 'pre-modern chaos', that could be risky and unsustainable, but the only other option was 'letting countries rot'. Less ambitious containing measures, from deterrence to counter-terrorism to shoring up defences, let alone diplomatic bargaining, he did not consider. Alongside imperialist military methods, Cooper like Blair advocated systemic neoliberal solutions to 'solve' the 'underlying problems'. He called for a cosmopolitan empire in which the pre-modern voluntarily submit themselves to the discipline of financial institutions, and European technocrats, soldiers, and police keep the peace in disorderly regions. The book version, produced in 2004 as the difficulties of occupying Iraq were becoming apparent, was more chastened than the earlier appeal for a new imperialism. In *The Breaking of Nations*, wars—presumably including the preventive ones he had called for—can 'weaken and destroy' states, and fuel and empower fanaticism. 'Without the wars in Afghanistan there would have been no Osama Bin Laden', Cooper observes, yet still he still sympathizes with the 'doctrine of preventive action' out of which emerged al-Qaeda in Iraq. Like Blair's conception of world order, Cooper's was self-contradictory and reductionist,

---

[65] Robert Cooper, 'The New Liberal Imperialism', *The Guardian*, 7 April 2002; *The Breaking of Nations: Order and Chaos in the Twenty-First Century* (London: Atlantic Books, 2004), pp. x, 64.

offering a false choice of regime change versus passive threat-tolerance. It inflated threats. And it was presumptuous of the West's power and knowledge. His liberal imperialism was impressed with its own cosmopolitan modernity, not knowing its own complicity in disorder.

THREAT INFLATION, POWER INFLATION: THE FALSE LOGIC OF ROGUE STATES

The case for war rested on a broader appraisal of the dangers of globalization and the promise of Western power. The West's free way of life, so it was said, could be gravely threatened from anywhere and any time, and the intensifying circulation of capital, materials, and ideas made the rise of 'rogue states' dangerous. This worldview penetrated the rhetoric and practices of Anglo-American strategic behaviour abroad throughout the War on Terror. It offered a powerful and dangerously overreaching account of national security and how it should be pursued. It inflated threats, underestimated the risks of military action, and was insensitive to the conditions in which liberal democracy and free markets historically need to thrive.

At the core of the case for military action was the notion of the 'rogue state', often invoked and rarely scrutinised. On closer inspection, the idea is overblown and self-contradictory. The notion of the 'rogue' state dates back at least to the early 1980s, when the US government both formally and informally attributed roguery to the suspect states of Cuba, Iran, Iraq, Libya, and North Korea. All were charged with offences from state sponsorship of terrorism to the pursuit of WMD, along with oppressive internal behaviour that supposedly proved they were externally subversive and sub-rational. By Gulf War One, the archetype was in place, whereby a rogue was 'an aggressive developing country that militarily threatened its neighbours and region while seeking to overturn the international order through the sponsorship of terrorism and the pursuit of weapons of mass destruction'.[66] The 'rogue' classification had its obvious uses. It served as a 'certificate of political insanity'[67] and thus licensed anticipatory measures and rougher treatment. It also bore disadvantages. States that technically fit the category Washington may wish to bargain with in pursuit of larger goals. Syria before its latest civil war, for instance, was an

---

[66] Mary Caprioli & Peter Trumbore, 'Rhetoric versus Reality: Rogue States in Interstate Conflict', *Journal of Conflict Resolution* 49:5 (2005), pp. 770–91, p. 777; on the persistent use of the term with similar meanings, see K.P. O'Reilly, 'Perceiving Rogue States: The Use of the "Rogue State" Concept by U.S. Foreign Policy Elite', *Foreign Policy Analysis* 3 (2007), pp. 295–315.

[67] Barry Rubin, 'US Foreign Policy and Rogue States', *Middle East Review of International Affairs* 3:3 (1999).

important part of the 'Middle East Peace Process', just as Gaddafi's Libya was hostile to Al-Qaeda. Branding a state with pariah status made it harder to conduct crisis diplomacy, as was the case, for instance, with North Korea in the 1994 confrontation with the US over its nuclear programme. And the 'rogue' charge was potentially embarrassing. Saddam Hussein's roguery was at least enabled by other states, at times with their active connivance, in his largest scale aggression against Iran, and the debts he accrued in the course of his campaign came from supporting Gulf states. Saddam, as Blair once said, 'had choices', but he was historically able to act because of the wider complicity of other states. The Clinton administration abandoned the category precisely because it limited its political flexibility. The Bush II administration, however, restored it in February 2001. And even the Clinton administration took the actual idea seriously. There was a distinct class of states, that were 'outlaw', 'backlash', or 'renegade', as articulated in detail by National Security Advisor Anthony Lake, with the imputation of irrationality, that the adversary cannot be deterred.[68]

The 'rogue' category rests on a perception of power capabilities and a perception of the rogue's irrationality. It also rests on an assumption that there is a family of such states sharing common disorders, a family that can be effectively combated by treating it as a whole. Blair in November 2002 warned of the danger of 'extremism driven by fanaticism, personified either in terrorist groups or rogue states', claiming that 'States which are failed, which repress their people brutally, in which notions of democracy and the rule of law are alien, share the same absence of rational boundaries to their actions as the terrorist.'[69] Blair maintained the potential threat of Saddam deploying a WMD-armed terrorist group as a proxy, asking in his autobiography,

> Would Saddam want al-Qaeda to be powerful inside Iraq? Absolutely not. Would he be prepared to use them outside Iraq? Very possibly. Was there a real risk of proliferation, not only from Iraq but elsewhere, leaching into terrorist groups who would not be averse to using WMD? I certainly thought so...I still think so.[70]

Because there was a family of such states sharing common pathologies, the strategy of 'taking out' one rogue state would deter and dissuade other rogues. The driving fear behind Bush's post-9/11 grand strategy was the perceived danger of WMD transfer, in order to use weapons by proxy, while gaining anonymity and deniability, thus avoiding punitive retaliation by the targeted state. The central countermeasure was to inhibit proliferation beyond deterrence and counter-terrorism, through preventive war. Bush claimed that 'States like

---

[68] Robert S. Litwak, *Rogue States and US Foreign Policy* (Washington DC: Johns Hopkins University Press, 2000), p. 41.
[69] 'Prime Minister's Address to the Lord Mayor's Banquet', *The Guardian*, 11 November 2002.
[70] Blair, *Journey*, pp. 386–7.

[Iraq], and their terrorist allies, constitute an axis of evil, arming to threaten the peace of the world. By seeking weapons of mass destruction, these regimes pose a grave and growing danger. They could provide these arms to terrorists, giving them the means to match their hatred'.[71] This was the rationale for elevating terrorism to a threat level of first rank in official national security strategy.[72] The likes of Saddam were fundamentally irrational, or at least wildly incautious and risk-prone actors, who could not be deterred and contained. War proponents dismissed deterrence as too passive and noted that Baghdad's development of WMD would have permitted one of 'the world's most dangerous regimes...to threaten us with the world's most destructive weapons'. 'A WMD-armed Saddam would have, in their view, broken out of his containment box and then threatened vital American interests. Finally, war supporters chastised those advocating deterrence as immoral, blind to the terrible suffering of the Iraqi people under the tyrannical Baathist regime'.[73] Secretary of State Powell likewise argued that Saddam 'does have a proclivity toward terrorist activity and he is developing weapons of mass destruction that he might use or perhaps could make available to other terrorist organizations'.[74] National Security Advisor Condoleezza Rice repeated that claim.[75]

Blair invoked the rogue state–WMD–terrorist nexus in every signature expression of threat and need for regime change. WMD terrorism with a rogue state as intermediary was his main summary of the threat picture, anticipated in his 1999 Chicago speech, and spelt out in his speech to Parliament on 18 March 2003, his letter to Bush on 26 March 2003, where 'terrorists and rogue states come together in hatred of our values', and in his Sedgefield Speech of 2004. His testimony before the Iraq Inquiry was that 9/11 changed the calculus of risk for this reason, so that living with dangers was the risk, whereas taking action to exterminate those dangers was the 'safe' option: 'The point about this act in New York was that, had they been able to kill even more people than those 3,000, they would have, and so, after that time, my view was you could not take risks with this issue at all'.[76]

The rogue-WMD threat perception suffers both empirical and logic defects. It is not clear that such a family exists. Most of the states earmarked as rogues

---

[71] Bush, 'State of the Union Address', 29 January 2002.
[72] White House, *The National Security Strategy of the United States of America* (Washington, D.C.: White House, September 2002), pp. 13–16.
[73] As summarized by Elbridge Colby, 'Restoring Deterrence', *Orbis*, 51:3 (2007), pp. 413–28, p. 417.
[74] 'Interview by Tony Snow and Brit Hume on Fox News Sunday' at https://2001-2009.state.gov/secretary/former/powell/remarks/2002/13324.htm.
[75] Condoleezza Rice, speech given to the Chicago Council on Foreign Relations, Chicago, Illinois, 8 October 2003.
[76] Tony Blair, IIT, 29 January 2010, p. 11.

have different risk calculus, and vary in their willingness to compromise. Most were not more likely than other states to be involved in militarized interstate disputes, not more likely to initiate such disputes, and not more likely to use force when such disputes turned violent. Iraq and North Korea had a greater tendency than the other candidates to get involved in militarized interstate disputes and to use force first, but were not usually the initiators of the row.[77] It also conflates North Korea, which has decided to build a deliverable nuclear bomb, with states like Iran, that have historically desired the 'breakout' capacity but not the complete capability. And confidence that destroying one regime would clearly signal a 'deterrence message' to onlooking states was suspect. Demonstrating the will and capability to kill off one regime can be interpreted by other regimes as an added incentive to develop a deterrent of their own, given that it also demonstrates what can happen to vulnerable adversaries, and given that those regimes may not wish to exist only at the permission of the West. The other difficulty with deterrence-via-regime change is that deterrence requires forbearance if the target agrees to be deterred, and thus it requires later governments to respect the precedent, by also restraining themselves from attacking regimes that have, in fact, disarmed. Post-Iraq events worked otherwise. Looking back, Richard Betts summarized the problem as Washington debated whether to attack Iran. The costs

> might seem justifiable if launching a war against Iran dissuaded other countries from attempting to get their own nuclear deterrents. But it might just as well energise such efforts. George W. Bush's war to prevent Iraq from getting nuclear weapons did not dissuade North Korea, which went on to test its own weapons a few years later, nor did it turn Iran away. It may have induced Libyan leader Muammer al-Qaddafi to surrender his nuclear programme, but a few years later, his reward from Washington turned out to be overthrow and death—hardly an encouraging lesson for US adversaries about the wisdom of renouncing nuclear weapons.[78]

The notion that Saddam was an irrational and undeterrable rogue who would transfer WMD to terrorist groups was not uniformly the advice that government received. A psychological profile commissioned by Downing Street in November 2002, based on earlier Defence Intelligence Service appraisal,[79] and received by Manning and Powell, portrayed Saddam as committed above all to survival, a 'judicious political calculator' who was 'by no means irrational', more likely to be aggressive when feeling his back against the wall, otherwise calibrating risks carefully. Likewise, JIC assessments judged that Saddam with his WMD arsenal was potentially aggressive and unpredictable but ultimately

---

[77] See Caprioli & Trumbore, 'Rhetoric versus Reality'.
[78] Richard Betts, 'The Lost Logic of Deterrence', *Foreign Affairs* 92:2 (2013), pp. 87–99, 94–5.
[79] Letter PS/C to Scarlett, 14 November 2002, 'Iraq: Psychological Profile of Saddam' attaching Paper 'Saddam Hussein, DIS Psychological Profile Updated'.

only below a certain threshold, and ultimately concerned for survival. In November 2001, the JIC judged that Saddam would consider WMD terrorism, but if his regime was under serious and imminent threat of collapse. In other circumstances, the threat of WMD terrorism is slight, because of the risk of US retaliation';[80] in September 2001, the JIC estimated that Saddam in calculating whether to use his chemical and biological weapons pre-emptively would weigh up the military utility against their political costs, and would only be likely to use them in desperation with conflict underway or 'at the death';[81] and another in January 2003 judged that 'there is no sign' that Saddam 'is unstable or losing the capacity to make rational tactical decisions'.[82]

Despite the fact that this alternative interpretation of Saddam's rationality was available, the possibility that a regime that had determinedly stayed in power for decades was not recklessly incautious, or effectively suicidal, hardly touched internal debate. The JIC itself departed from its own profiles of Saddam and fell prey to incoherent views of the problem. While preparing the September dossier, a JIC meeting at which Manning was present spelt out an 'important message',

> which needed to be brought out more clearly in the draft, was that if the chips were down, and Saddam believed his regime to be under real threat of extinction, nothing was going to deter him from using such weapons. Readers of the paper needed to be reminded of Saddam's unpredictability, and of the fact that his thought processes did not work in a recognisably Western, rational and logical way. The draft should also distinguish more clearly between the three different ways in which Iraq might use its offensive chemical or biological capabilities: in weaponised form against military targets; in an unconventional attack on military targets; or as part of a sponsored terrorist attack aimed at spreading fear and influencing public attitudes.[83]

There are several difficulties here. Firstly, note the flattering portrait of rational and logical thought processes as predominantly 'Western' qualities, with the implied assumption that deterrence logic was applicable to Westerners only. It is also unclear why using WMD under 'real threat of extinction' amounts to irrational, illogical behaviour. After all, the threat of punitive retaliation is central to British deterrence doctrine. If backed into a corner, would not a 'rational and logical' actor be moved to use every weapon at its disposal? This account also suggests that Saddam has waited until then to use them, suggesting a more careful calculus on his part.

There was an overarching tension in pro-war argument about rationality and irrationality. The family of rogues, hawks argue, is oblivious to the normal

---

[80] JIC Assessment, 'Iraq After September 11—The Terrorist Threat', 28 November 2001.
[81] JIC Assessment, 'Iraq Use of Chemical and Biological Weapons', 9 September 2002.
[82] JIC Assessment 29 January 2003, 'Iraq: The Emerging View from Baghdad'.
[83] JIC Minutes, 4 September, p. 2.

patterns of deterrence or conventional diplomacy, thus deserving of special treatment. Yet the nuclear transfer scenario begs the question, why transfer in the first place? Those same irrational rogues will take rational steps to survive by transferring WMD rather than using it directly. The very fact that the offending state would place itself at one remove from nuclear use indicates a rational concern to avoid detection, remain anonymous, and duck punishment, in turn suggesting a commitment to survival and a capacity for sane means-ends calculation. If, on the other hand, the state contemplating nuclear transfer is aware that nuclear transfer would probably be detected and punished, and attract significant retaliation, therefore that kind of state would probably be deterrable from such behaviour. A risk-prone 'irrational' regime, heedless of its survival, fanatically committed to aggression, and willing to court the retaliation of a major power, by definition would not worry about detection and retaliation. Indeed, it would not bother transferring nukes in the first place with the 'command and control' downsides that would bring, but would use them openly. The wider argument, that a powerful precedent would teach other rogues (or potential rogues) a lesson, likewise suggests that undeterrable 'mad' regimes can be rationally dissuaded and cowed into submission by a strong signal, after one of their number has been made an example of. That implies a process of rational calculation and risk aversion that the 'rogue state' label denies. In the case of a rational state recklessly betting on the possibility of getting away with a nuclear transfer, there are measures short of war that could drive down the risk of such a misperception through signalling measures short of war, as Chapter 5 will argue.

The Bush administration's intra-war posture towards Iraq in the build-up to war rested on a similar contradiction, claiming Saddam was undeterrable yet making punishment threats to induce him to refrain from using the chemical and biological weapons Washington believed it to possess, thereby relying on the very deterrence that it insisted was impossible in relations with Iraq.[84] While stressing the unstable predatory nature of rogue regimes, Blair simultaneously invited Iran and Libya to abandon their nuclear programmes. The orders that were allegedly oblivious to cost–benefit logic were the same orders that were open to diplomatic persuasion backed by force.

The same have-it-both-ways illogic pervaded the parliamentary debates of February and March 2003. Supporting the case for war, Iain Duncan Smith warned that 'if the international community backs away from dealing with

[84] As Robert Jervis argued before the invasion: 'intra-war deterrence implies that goals as well as means will be kept limited, and since the US now seeks regime change it has few coercive tools at its disposal. If Saddam is the monster Bush sees him as, why should he care what happens to his country if he is going to die? And if the US could deter his WMD use in a war, why would extended deterrence fail in peacetime?' 'The Confrontation between Iraq and the US: Implications for the Theory and Practice of Deterrence', *European Journal of International Relations* 9:2 (2003), pp. 315–37, p. 327.

Saddam Hussein now, that will be seen as a green light by every rogue state and terrorist group around the world'.[85] But 'green light' suggests a rational motorist, awaiting a clear signal, not a fanatical driver determined to accelerate. David Trimble MP argued that 'containment and deterrence will not work in the situation that confronts us', in the world of 'WMD, terrorist movements and rogue states', yet also noted that Saddam would only have disarmed 'if he believed that massive force would be used against him if he did not comply', suggesting the rogue ruler was sensitive to the threat of punishment after all.[86] William Hague MP warned about 'rogue states' in a changed post–Cold War world, yet urged action to ensure 'that those who aspire to be rogue states or sponsors of terrorism know what happens and know how the Western alliance responds to such a threat'.[87] That baseline had already been drawn by the retaliation against Al-Qaeda and its host government in Afghanistan, and the argument that clear deterrent lines could be drawn presupposed a limitation on the aggression of rogues. Containment, an active strategy of monitoring, sanctions, occasional military strikes, and embargo, hawks misrepresented as passivity, while at the same time lamenting the devastation wrought on Iraq by the same containment programme.

In the cumulative vision of regime change and its calculus about threat and solution, there was a flip side, an under-scrutinized assumption that in a 'globalised' world, civilized countries could not abide risks linked to WMD. Globalization imperilled liberal world order, Blair reasoned, warranting the direct removal of threats. Interdependence, as Bush and Blair insisted, erased any distinction between values and interests. In plainer language, evil regimes in middling minor states like Serbia or Iraq, or impoverished pariah states like Afghanistan, were not only morally abhorrent, but strategically intolerable. This was the consistent basis for Blair's Chicago speech in April 1999, his address to the US Congress on the eve of the invasion of Iraq in 2003, and one he unrepentantly maintains.[88] To rapturous applause, Blair before Congress portrayed a systemic virus that changed the rules of the international life. Coming together as a species

> provides us with unprecedented opportunity but also makes us *uniquely vulnerable*...the threat comes because in another part of our globe there is shadow and darkness...in the combination of these afflictions a new and deadly virus has emerged. The virus is terrorism whose intent to inflict destruction

---

[85] *Hansard*, 3 February 2003, column 23. [86] *Hansard*, 18 March 2003, column 845.
[87] *Hansard*, 18 March 2003, column 792.
[88] Tony Blair, 'What I've Learned', *The Economist*, May 31, 2007; Owen Bowcott, 'Tony Blair: Military Intervention in Rogue Regimes "More Necessary Than Ever"', *The Guardian*, 1 September 2010.

is unconstrained by human feeling and whose capacity to inflict it is enlarged by technology.[89]

Blair made the formation and spread of WMD terrorism sound easy, an almost inevitable fact of life that had to be countered with determined and far-reaching preventive measures, and beyond a mere *cordon sanitaire.*

This was a bad case of 'threat inflation', or 'concern for a threat that goes beyond the scope and urgency that a disinterested analysis would justify'.[90] WMD terrorism, whether chemical, biological, or nuclear, is difficult to carry off, especially against well-prepared developed states. Executing a bioterrorist attack entails a multi-step process of obtaining, preserving, moving, and detonating the weapon, while employing specialist skills, maintaining secrecy, and moving through highly policed territory. A successful bioterrorist attack requires that

> one must obtain the appropriate strain of the disease pathogen. One must know how to handle the organism correctly. One must know how to grow it in a way that will produce the appropriate characteristics. One must know how to store the culture, and to scale-up production properly. One must know how to disperse the product properly.[91]

To execute nuclear terrorist attack, as John Mueller calculates, the atomic terrorists' task might involve a twenty-step process, from successfully obtaining HEU (highly enriched uranium), to assembling a team of highly skilled scientists and technicians, the smuggling of the improvised nuclear device weighing a ton or more, to the successful detonation.[92] It requires the secure procurement, preparation, and secret movement of a heavy instrument through increasingly monitored space and across borders. Chemical weapons terrorism has also proven more difficult than feared. They are largely ineffective against well-prepared and well-equipped armed forces. To achieve lethality levels against civilian targets sufficient for 'mass destruction', it requires 'access to sophisticated delivery means capable of disseminating CW agents efficiently over large areas'.[93]

WMD terrorism is not impossible. It is, though, considerably more remote a prospect than advocates of regime change assumed. Just as importantly, it is

---

[89] 'Transcript of Blair's Speech to Congress', *CNN*, 17 July 2003, at http://edition.cnn.com/2003/US/07/17/blair.transcript/.

[90] Jane K. Kramer & Trevor A. Thrall (eds), 'Introduction: Understanding Threat Inflation', *American Foreign Policy and the Politics of Fear: Threat Inflation since 9/11* (New York: Routledge, 2009), p. 2.

[91] Milton Leitenberg, *Assessing the Biological Weapons and Bio-Terrorism Threat* (Carlisle, PA: US Army War College, Strategic Studies Institute, 2005), p. 46.

[92] John Mueller, *Atomic Obsession: Nuclear Alarmism from Hiroshima to Al-Qaeda* (Oxford: Oxford University Press, 2010), p. 186.

[93] As Stephen Biddle observes, 'Assessing the Case for Striking Syria', *Council on Foreign Relations*, 10 September 2013, p. 5.

capable of being disrupted by less expensive and high-risk 'rollback' measures. Contrary to Blair's claim that globalization renders every security problem intimate and urgent, states can disrupt threats and reduce them at many points along the chain between 'over here' and 'over there', with gradual, incremental, patient containment to lower probabilities that are already low, reducing the threat into a third-order, chronic nuisance. This would entail measures already underway, but without the inflated rhetoric of threat eradication, without the rushed dismantling of civil liberties, and without the entrapment of living in a perpetual state of emergency and its continual drive to escalation. Combinations would bring together ordinary police work, international cooperation, the cultivation of intelligence within the wider community, continued efforts to secure stored weapons-grade nuclear material, with a more measured and discriminate programme of raids and drone killings to keep 'havens' unsafe. Blair's government blithely brushed off unspectacular, patient counter-terrorism, as an alternative to regime change.

The case for war, therefore, was muddled. It suffered self-contradictions that deserved greater consideration. And it overlooked a basic question.

WOULD WAR WORK?

In a memo of 25 March 2002, Foreign Secretary Jack Straw asked a question that hardly engaged the war's architects:

> We have also to answer the big question—what will this action achieve? There seems to be a larger hole in this than on anything. Most of the assessments from the US have assumed regime change as a means of eliminating Iraq's WMD threat. But none has satisfactorily answered how that regime change is to be secured, and how there can be any certainty that the replacement regime will be better.[94]

Straw's question went neglected. The utility of war, the elementary issue of what it could deliver, and whether it could deliver with acceptable costs, deserved dispassionate probing in cold blood. Those charged with making the decision ought to have drawn on a wide body of historical analogies, to explicitly test assumptions and weigh up counterfactual scenarios.

Overthrowing states followed by military occupations is a difficult undertaking, historically, that usually intensifies security competition within states,

---

[94] Memo, Jack Straw to Tony Blair, 25 March 2002.

and sometimes between them.[95] It has an impressive record of failure. Since 1815, there have been twenty-six completed military occupations where a victor has chosen to stay, reform, and rebuild, but only in seven such cases were occupying powers able to achieve their interests sustainably. Except in unusually propitious conditions where a threatening external power creates a level of consent for the occupier, occupations tend to fall short of their goals, and at a high cost compared to most other forms of statecraft. A 'selection effect' means that the difficulties of occupation are usually inherent. The very fact that a particular state is targeted suggests a level of interior dysfunction and prior conflict, a fraught situation into which the occupier is stepping. 'Outsiders' occupying can all too easily seem alien, thus energizing and internationalizing resistance, breeding hardened forms of violent politics it is supposed to suppress, placing the cost-tolerance of the occupier under strain. Israel in Lebanon, the Soviet Union in Afghanistan, France in Algeria and the US in Vietnam should have stood out as cautionary tales for would-be liberators, alongside more successful examples of West Germany, Japan, and Malaya, and these projects too were long and expensive. Foreign-imposed regime change is frequently a gamble in which the costs outstrip the gains.[96]

Unfortunately, any intellectual process of careful judgement, with these considerations, was not the dominant one. Instead, the issue was clouded by emotive mythologies about power and weakness, appeasement and resolve, good and evil. The plausibility and reasonable probability of 'worst-case' scenario was largely assumed, namely a suicidal rogue state anonymously transferring WMD to terrorists. The state hardly considered other potentially ironic outcomes, such as the empowerment of other rogue states or the spread of the same terrorist networks into Iraq.

Dominating historical memory was the regnant 'Munich' analogy of Churchill, Chamberlain, and Hitler. That particular retelling of history has propelled states into regrettable conflicts from Suez to Vietnam. It does violence to the strategic and moral complexities of the late 1930s. Chamberlain's Britain in the late 1930s had a weak hand. It was depleted by the Great Depression and far-flung commitments left it overstretched. It was gradually rearming to prepare against multiple totalitarian states in Europe and Asia, without economic dislocation. Any preventive war would have lacked the vital support of the United States and the largest Commonwealth countries, and any counter-balancing of Nazi Germany would have inevitably involved appeasing the territorial demands of Stalin's Soviet Union. As it was,

---

[95] See David M. Edelstein, *Occupational Hazards: Success and Failure in Military Occupation* (Ithaca: Cornell University Press, 2008), pp. 2, 5, 8, 9; Stephen Walt, 'Why They Hate Us (1): On military occupation', *Foreign Policy*, 23 November 2009.

[96] Alexander B. Downes & Jonathan Monten, 'Forced to be Free? Why Foreign-Imposed Regime Change Rarely Leads to Democratisation', *International Security* 37:4 (2013), pp. 90–131.

its diplomacy bought valuable time, and ensured that when Hitler struck in 1939, Britain could at least defend its waters and airspace, and that Nazi Germany was positioned unquestionably as the aggressor.[97]

Munich analogies in 2003 damaged the capacity to debate the Iraq issue properly. Appeasement is the unilateral, persistent giving of concessions to a potential aggressor, in order to secure peace. No one in mainstream debate was proposing giving Saddam Hussein Kuwait. If war was moral duty, and refraining from war a moral collapse, there was little room for scrutinizing whether war would serve British security interests better than alternative forms of coercive diplomacy. Some advocates for war were sheepish about their Hitler and appeasement similes, yet they pressed them all the same.[98] Others such as the Murdoch press were less inhibited. The late 1930s—and the vocabulary of the mythologized interwar period—was the main interpretive prism.

Serious calculation was made all the more difficult by a primordial reaction to 9/11 and what it all meant. To belligerent idealists, the terrorist attacks of September 2001 were the outcome of Western weakness, even appeasement. Military action would signal the West's toughness and deter future aggressions, as though Al-Qaeda trafficked on a popular grievance that the West didn't project power often enough. Consider the rationale of George Osborne MP eight months after the invasion, who saw the Iraq War

> as a necessary demonstration of Western resolve. For, with the hindsight forced upon us all by 9/11, it was clear that the West had been woeful in its response to the escalating menace of international terrorism throughout the 1990s. We had also been feeble in our efforts to get Saddam to comply with the will of the UN. Together they created the impression that the West was weak, and that we were not prepared to defend our values or protect our citizens. The campaigns in Iraq and Afghanistan have been potent demonstrations that we will stand up to,

---

[97] See Gerhard L. Weinberg, 'No Road from Munich to Baghdad', *The Washington Post*, 3 November 2002; Christopher Layne, 'Security Studies and the Use of History: Neville Chamberlain's Grand Strategy Revisited', *Security Studies* 17 (2008), pp. 397–437; Norrin Ripsman & Jack S. Levy, 'Wishful Thinking or Buying Time? The Logic of British Appeasement in the 1930s', *International Security* 33:2 (2008), pp. 148–81.

[98] 'Blair Likens Saddam to Hitler', *CNN*, 1 March 2003 (this was a misleading headline, Blair's actual claim was that the war party of the 1930s would have been called warmongers, and the anti-war protesters would have fallen prey to the appeasement arguments of the time); Anton La Guardia, 'Straw warns of dangers threatened by NATO split', *The Daily Telegraph* 12 February 2003; see also R. Gerald Hughes, *The Postwar Legacy of Appeasement: British Foreign Policy since 1945* (London: Bloomsbury, 2014), pp. 164–7; accusations of appeasement were made in both houses of parliament: William Hague MP claimed 'The Prime Minister said that analogies with the 30s can be taken too far, and of course they can, yet in some of the opposition to the Government's stance there is a hint of appeasement', and Julian Lewis MP in the Commons argued that arguments for appeasement 'were wrong then, and they are wrong now' (*Hansard*, 2003, p. 333), and Baroness Sharples in the Lords indicated that the 'present situation' brings memories of the 1930s 'flooding back' (*Hansard*, pp. 194–5).

and defeat if necessary, those intent on causing us harm, and that we can improve people's lives by doing so. That is why it is so important in both countries to show we can also win the peace—which, contrary to the relentlessly negative impression given by the anti-war lobby and their fellow travellers in the media, we are now actually doing.[99]

So much for the liberation of Kuwait, and the downfall of Milosevic and the Taliban. Osborne celebrated the winning of the peace in late 2003, no doubt a claim he is waiting to revisit in print. He dismissed pre-war crippling sanctions as 'feeble': what would serious sanctions look like? His was also an odd account of the causes of international terrorism, which traded on the propaganda that the United States was the 'far enemy' and leader of a Zionist-Crusader occupation of holy soil. It was a strange interpretation of the intentions behind Al-Qaeda's jihad, which hoped to bait the US into an escalation, occupation, and a polarizing armed conflict. It was a naively ahistorical expectation of what potentially long peripheral wars could achieve. And it set a high standard for the struggle, demanding nothing less than the 'defeat' of threats, not their reduction. In any event, those two campaigns Osborne praised for their potency have foreseeably not worked out that way. The Islamic State made its assaults apparently undeterred by the displays of resolve Osborne commended, with their billions invested and thousands of casualties.

The unfounded optimism that war would work, and the pessimism that there was simply no alternative choice, also drew on a facile doctrine of 'newness' shared by the Bush administration. Blairism emphasized modernization and change. The need to fundamentally alter his party and his country was his signature theme, which he now enlarged to the reformation and modernization of the Middle East. He extended it to global politics generally, announcing that in the wake of 9/11 and globalization, 'traditional theories of security' had to be discarded.[100] This lent itself to a self-deluding 'year zero' worldview, where denying or erasing the past was part of creating a better future. Briefed by Foreign Office expert Dr Michael Williams on the weight of history in Iraq, its legacies of ethnic and sectarian division, Blair dismissively replied 'That's all history, Mike. This is about the future'.[101] To dwell on Iraqi's historical legacies was to resist the thrust of revolutionary liberalism, 'for in comparison with the glorious future they would create, the past counted for nothing'.[102] Similar conceits were heard from the Bush administration. Leading hardline 'vulcans' insisted that time had only just begun. Richard Perle

---

[99] George Osborne, 'A Soldier Breaks Ranks', *The Spectator*, 1 November 2003.
[100] Text of Blair's speech, *BBC News*, 17 July 2003.
[101] Cited in Rawnsley, *The End of the Party*, p. 185.
[102] As John Gray argued, 'The End was Nigh', *Times Higher Education*, 31 August 2017.

asserted that 'The world began on 9/11. There's no intellectual history';[103] Richard Armitage, that 'History begins Today';[104] Cofer Black, 'all you need to know is there was a "before 9/11" and an "after 911"'.[105] These statements were at odds with the frequent invoking of the historical lessons of the interwar period. And by dismissing history except the badly remembered atypical case of Munich and Hitler, by repudiating the only guide we have, it foreclosed the doubts that a reflective account of the past might have raised, and left a want of proportionality.

A consciousness of historical legacies does not imply, as some critics do, that Arabs or Iraqis are historically incapable of developing constitutional democracy. But awareness of the past could help to resist the equal and opposite illusion that outside powers can induce others to change in their way, at their timetable, at will. Peoples can change—the democratic wave that spread through post-Soviet Eastern Europe proved that—but not under conditions of outsiders' choosing. Iraqis emerging from the Saddamist period, both from the oppressed majority and from the once-hegemonic ruling minority, had powerful reasons to be fearful of a new, competitive politics, where democratic contest could become a winner-takes-all struggle. Neither is this only a hindsight judgement. As the Iraq Inquiry found,

> Mr Blair told the Inquiry that the difficulties encountered in Iraq after the invasion could not have been known in advance. We do not agree that hindsight is required. The risks of internal strife in Iraq, active Iranian pursuit of its interests, regional instability, and Al Qaida activity in Iraq, were each explicitly identified before the invasion.[106]

They were identified—and rejected—because of the delusion that foreseeable and familiar historical dangers were a thing of the past to be overcome, and that the *Pax Americana* had permanently transformed the world.

There was also a broader flaw in the consensus of the time, an unrealistic view of foreign policy as the search for decisive solutions. Blair and Bush in this respect resembled Margaret Thatcher, who

> tended to see foreign policy, not as a continuum, the stream, largely beyond governments' control, on which, to use Bismarck's image, the powers are borne, but on which they can navigate with more or less skill, the stream on which Lord Salisbury would occasionally put out a punt pole to forestall a collision, but rather as a series of disparate problems with attainable solutions, or even as zero-sum

---

[103] George Packer, *The Assassin's Gate* (New York: Farrar, Straus and Giroux, 2005), p. 41.

[104] Armitage cited in Seth G. Jones, *In the Graveyard of Empires: America's War in Afghanistan* (New York: W.W. Norton, 2010), p. 88.

[105] Mikel Thorrup, *An Intellectual History of Terror: War, Violence and the State* (Oxford: Routledge, 2010), p. 186.

[106] Statement, Sir John Chilcot, 6 July 2016, at http://www.iraqinquiry.org.uk/the-inquiry/sir-john-chilcots-public-statement/.

games, which Britain had to win. She regularly complained that her advisers brought her problems but no answers. The thought that for a middling power in a disorderly world there would be few answers in the crossword-puzzle sense and many compromises seemed not to occur.[107]

In this respect, Blair was indeed an heir to Thatcher.

Liberal Managerialism and The 'Phase IV' Fallacy

Fifteen years on from the invasion of Iraq, there are fewer unambiguous defenders of the Iraq War. Yet defenders of the general idea of 'regime change' are many. It is vital to counter a widespread, convenient and dangerous misinterpretation of the 'lessons' of Iraq. This is what we can term the managerialist 'Phase IV' Fallacy, also known as the 'incompetence dodge', the seductive idea that the war wasn't a bad idea, just its execution.[108] Phase IV is shorthand for the 'aftermath' and 'reconstruction' phase of the operation. It often comes twinned with the assertion that the idea of regime change and intervention more broadly is respectable, indeed inevitable, and that the three-week war to remove Saddam is blameless in the post-mortem. The error in Iraq, allegedly, lay mainly in the maladministration of Iraq by the occupiers, and the invaders went wrong when they lost the peace, especially in the first crucial months.

According to that account, peddled most often by voices keen to hold on to maximalist interventionism as a doctrine, the avoidable errors of the Coalition Provisional Authority in 2003–4 and the American proconsul Paul L. Bremer III were the difference between success and failure. If Iraq holds out lessons, they are administrative and implementational, not deliberative. The inferences drawn by Foreign Secretary David Miliband in February 2008 typified the logic: the lesson to draw was not that Iraq was a mistake but that there were 'mistakes in Iraq', and that 'interventions in other countries must be more subtle, better planned, and if possible undertaken with the agreement of multilateral institutions'.[109] How a United Nations mandate would have forestalled Iraq's sectarian civil war, he did not explain. In particular, the 'planning failure' storyline blames the wrong-headed De-Ba'athification Order, the disbanding of the Iraqi Army and intelligence services, and the failure to provide enough occupying troops and prepare capabilities for civil

---

[107] Percy Cradock, *In Pursuit of British Interests: Reflections on Foreign Policy under Margaret Thatcher and John Major* (London: John Murray, 1997), p. 22. I am grateful to Dr Robert Saunders for bringing this to my attention.

[108] Sam Rosenfeld, 'The Incompetence Dodge', *The American Prospect*, 23 October 2005; see also Benjamin H. Friedman, Harvey M. Sapolsky & Christopher Preble, 'Learning the Right Lessons from Iraq', *Policy Analysis* 610, 13 February 2008.

[109] Foreign Secretary Speech on the Democratic Imperative, 12 February 2008.

reconstruction, steps that created a large pool of alienated Sunni Arab Iraqis who then revolted. This is a widespread interpretation of the Iraq experience in the US. It is also endemic in British political and security circles. It has been offered by other participants, officials, and observers: retired ambassador to the UN Sir Jeremy Greenstock;[110] Major General Tim Cross;[111] Britain's logistical component commander; Secretary of Defence Sir Michael Fallon;[112] former Secretary of International Development Andrew Mitchell, who cites Libya as an example of government actively 'learning' from Iraq, as though that strengthens his case;[113] and Lord Paddy Ashdown. Ashdown drew this conclusion as the violence climaxed in mid-2007:

> Plan even harder for peace than for war; you will probably need more troops to provide security after the war than you needed to win it; make the most of the 'golden hour' after the war ends; creating security should be the first priority; get the economy going fast; you may have to remove those at the top of the old regime, but you will need the rest to run the state; work with the local population and its traditions.[114]

This is a sunny account of post-war reconstruction. It assumes that other societies want, or can be made to want, what the intervening powers want for them. It assumes that the population is a unity with 'traditions' that can be worked with, rather than a disparate and conflicting plurality of groups with conflicting memories and anxieties. It assumes that a limited purge of the old

---

[110] Jeremy Greenstock, *Iraq: The Cost of War* (New York: William Heinemann, 2016), see passages below.

[111] Maj. General Tim Cross, Witness Statement, 'Post Invasion Iraq: The Planning and Reality after the Invasion from Mid 2002 to the End of August 2003', Iraq Inquiry, pp. 25, 27; Cross recalls briefing the Prime Minister on 18th March that 'he did not believe post-war planning was anywhere near ready'. In public, however, Cross struck a cautiously optimistic note and reinforced the impression that the invasion would succeed without major disruption: he dismissed critics for 'overplaying the problems there' and being 'almost disappointed that things weren't worse when we first went in', asserting that 'The coalition fought a magnificent campaign, the humanitarian crisis was not there, the reconstruction crisis was not there'. 'Interview with Major General Tim Cross', *BBC News*, 25 May 2003. Cross reserved his public criticisms for later.

[112] See passages below.

[113] Andrew Mitchell, 'Chilcot Report: Department for International Aid', *The Political Quarterly* 87:4 (2016), pp. 497-7. In limiting and marginalizing Iraq as an educational case in what he euphemistically calls 'stabilisation challenges', Mitchell frames the issue in the typical binary way of warlike liberals: (at p. 497) 'Will we continue to support the cause of liberal interventionism, as we successfully did in Sierra Leone and Kosovo, or will we turn our back on discretionary intervention—even under UN auspices—and be prepared to stand idly by if, God forbid, another Rwanda takes place?' Kosovo came at considerable human cost, as it enabled the counter-terror of the Kosovo Liberation Army. And the case against warlike liberalism need not be that we should abandon intervention outright, but that Britain should restrain itself from state-breaking interventions that overthrow political orders and regimes, and adopt the principle 'first do minimal harm'.

[114] Paddy Ashdown, 'When I look to the future in Iraq, I start by studying the past', *The Guardian*, 27 May 2007.

order will satisfy the majority. And like advocates of war, Ashdown bases this account of Iraq as an educational case study on the atypical case of allied occupation of Germany, where successful occupation was possible over a population shattered by global war, held together by fear of the Soviet Union and relatively unified. The contrast with Iraq is pronounced.

Defence Secretary Sir Michael Fallon interpreted the report of the Iraq Inquiry in similar terms. Fallon stressed the need to enhance the working of institutions and prevent failures of planning, and the imperative to act preventively to rescue fragile states, 'to promote good governance, tackle corruption, and build capacity in defence and security forces'. Paying tribute to the service personnel who had overthrown Saddam, Fallon framed the issue suggestively:

> the initial war-fighting phase was a military success. They did fight to help topple a tyrant who had murdered hundreds of thousands of his own people and the subsequent failures in the campaign at whoever's door they are laid, cannot and should not be laid at the door of those who did the fighting on our behalf.

Notice that 'failures' began only later, and are divorced from the act of invasion. He then placed a limit on the Iraq case, asserting that 'Despite the report and the Iraq campaign, we must still be ready to act'.[115] Neither the Iraq Inquiry nor many of the war's critics suggest otherwise, but the emphasis drives towards quarantining Iraq into merely a cautionary tale about execution and implementation, treating the management of foreign societies as an engineering and logistical problem more than a political one. Ashdown and Fallon's managerial accounts of how to make occupation succeed, bounded by an undisturbed belief in the essential wisdom of ambitious military action, helps explain why their appetite for armed intervention remains undimmed.

Consider also the memoir of Sir Jeremy Greenstock, who was Britain's Permanent Representative to the United Nations from 1998 to 2003. Greenstock's interpretation is a notable case of the drive to quarantine Iraq and its lessons, and reduce its failures to planning failures. Greenstock argues that

> The fundamental error of the Coalition was to have lost control of security almost immediately after the invasion was over ... [we] needed to deliver not just an Iraq without Saddam, but a secure and functioning Iraq without Saddam. This would have required pre-invasion planning for at least a full year after the Iraq forces had been defeated, with detailed estimations of the resources necessary to lay the foundations for the next stage.[116]

---

[115] Michael Fallon, *Hansard* v.613 House of Commons, 14 July 2016.
[116] Jeremy Greenstock, *Iraq: The Cost of War* (New York: William Heinemann, 2016), pp. 418, 419, 423–4.

Greenstock contrasts Iraq with two atypical cases, the careful planning for administration and recovery of Germany and Japan after 1945, selecting on the dependent variable of occupation success, and not considering the many cases of occupation failure. As Greenstock makes clear, invaders must 'deliver' security and design a better future for the liberated through careful preparation ('Libya and Afghanistan are still teaching us that'.) Amongst other vital tasks, invaders must identify and elevate a 'visibly capable leader to assume power after the dirty work has been done'. For Greenstock, the overarching insight is that we should respond to the problems of invasion not by questioning the prudence of invasion in the first place, but by making invasions more efficient. Reluctance to commit ground forces and 'refusal to engage in messy regional conflicts has led to criticism of US passivity in Syria, Libya and indeed Iraq itself'. Greenstock goes further, alleging that 'perceptions of withdrawal from proactive engagement in the Middle East' fed into calculations by China and Russia that America could be challenged more assertively, claiming American retreat contributed to Russia's actions in Ukraine and China in the South China Sea.

Greenstock's critique is partly technocratic and managerial, in its assumptions about how bureaucratic preparation can overcome the security dilemmas of invading a country like Iraq. This argument hardly considers the possibility that the idea of invading itself might be reckless. And the vision is partly colonial. It suggests that Iraqis, like Libyans and Afghans, need to be more efficiently and intensively *administered* into stable market democracy. It reduces host populations into passive recipients of the foreigners' gift. Missing here is any sense of the wiliness and politics of the host peoples and exiles who presume to speak for them. In 2011, with the fall of Colonel Gaddafi imminent, Libyan revolutionaries made clear to coalition allies of the UK, France, and the US that they would not accept international ground forces. It was their country and they were in charge. Likewise, as we will see, Iraqi political elites representing the majority demanded, and did not oppose, the policies Greenstock blames for fuelling chaos, an American purge of Sunni Arabs from the civil service, police, and army. No amount of planning could have eliminated the sectarian fractures that would later be wrenched apart. Greenstock's assertion that Iraq is a lesson in the need to find a prominent national leader after the 'dirty work' is done suggests a strangely apolitical concept of statebuilding. In the case of Iraq, Washington and London believed that in Ahmad Chalabi, the tireless Iraqi exiles and the Iraqi National Congress, they had found such a talisman. These Iraqis in exile effectively exploited their links to the anti-Saddamist 'vulcans' inside the government, and promoted the cause of driving Saddam from office. They helped persuade policymakers that swift, successful liberation was achievable. Chalabi's network supplied willing Iraqi defectors to offer up dubious evidence of Iraq's WMD programme and its alleged ties to Al-Qaeda hijackers, intelligence that was eagerly devoured by the Bush administration to confirm its hypothesis, also attracting a wide media coverage that extended to the British press.[117] 'Dirty work', then, does not finish with regime overthrow, but with the ensuing power struggle.

Contrary to Greenstock, America did not then withdraw from Iraq because its own leaders were feckless. Iraq's government and parliament demanded it, and insisted otherwise that any remaining US troops would be subject to Iraqi law.[118] This reality undermines Greenstock's loose accusation of 'passivity' in Iraq. As for Afghanistan, developmental and governance failures were not primarily a problem of insufficient pre-war planning but flowed from the willing corruption of ruling kleptocratic elites, who have a different vision for their country. Foreign peoples often act as agents, not objects.

The calamitous Syrian civil war, which interventionists falsely present as a case of 'Western non-intervention' has become the counterpoint for those who wish to limit the power of Iraq as a cautionary case. But in Syria, the Obama administration and the British government in fact intervened intensively, along with their Gulf clients. By branding the Assad regime illegitimate and sponsoring a revolt that by 2012 had already become infiltrated by Islamists, they internationalized the conflict and raised the stakes. Washington supported elements of the Syrian rebels with over $1 billion a year through the CIA, training, and equipping approximately 10,000 vetted 'moderate' fighters, supplying intelligence, and coordinating logistical supply, in league with a broader, multi-billion-dollar effort involving Saudi Arabia, Qatar, and Turkey to bolster a coalition of militias known as the Southern Front of the Free Syrian Army.[119] This active programme had perverse results, inadvertently empowering al-Qaeda's Syrian franchise, the al-Nusra Front, and allowing weapons and money to fall into the hands of the Islamic State, a movement energized by conflict in Iraq. In other words, Syria suggests not the defects of restraint as a 'counter-case' to Iraq, but rather the hazards of intervention in support of insurgent forces. Contrary to the claim of a general withdrawal,

---

[117] Jane Meyer, 'The Manipulator: Ahmad Chalabi Pushed a Tainted Case for War', *The New Yorker*, 7 June 2004; Richard Bonin, *Arrows of the Night: Ahmad Chalabi and the Selling of the Iraq War* (New York: Anchor, 2013), pp. 194–200.

[118] Chapter 4 will demonstrate this point further.

[119] Greg Miller & Karen de Young, 'Secret CIA Effort in Syria faces large funding cut', *The Washington Post*, 12 June 2015; Gareth Porter, 'How America Armed Terrorists in Syria', *American Conservative*, 22 June 2017; Julia Harte & R. Jeffrey Smith, 'Where Does the Islamic State Get Its Weapons?', *Foreign Policy*, 6 October 2014; academic and 'grey' literature suggests that external support for rebels, especially in wars as complex as that in Syria, tends to make wars longer, more violent, and more intractable: Doug Mataconis, 'Arming the "Good" Syrian Rebels Would Not Have Prevented the Rise of ISIS', *Outside the Beltway*, 12 August 2014; David E. Cunningham, 'Blocking Resolution: How External States can Prolong Civil Wars', *Journal of Peace Research* 47:2 (2010), pp. 115–27; *The Political Science of Syria's Civil War*, 18 December 2013, pp. 5, 34–6, 61–3; a CIA study prepared for President Obama reached the same conclusion: Mark Mazzetti, 'CIA Study of Covert Aid Fueled Skepticism About Helping Syrian Rebels', *The New York Times*, 14 October 2014.

Obama reduced troop levels in the Middle East to over 30,000 troops, a level of garrisoning that reverted to Reagan/Bush I levels; it was hardly a retreat. Greenstock offers no evidence that Western policies in Middle Eastern conflicts emboldened China's expansion in the South China Sea or Russia's lunge in the Crimea. China's land grabs in contested waters predated America's policies in Syria during the Arab Spring era, and the more likely proximate catalyst was America's military and alliance build-up in Asia. For its part, Putin's Russia did not need to be emboldened by perceptions of American disengagement. After all, Moscow had forcefully pursued its regional interests by invading Georgia in 2008, a strategic partner of Washington and at the height of America's deployment in Iraq. It was more likely moved by the strategic value it saw in the Crimea, Sebastopol, and the Black Sea that it saw threatened, and the fear of EU expansion into its orbit that it denounced, than by Obama's reluctance to commit ground troops in Syria. It is alarming that a diplomat of Greenstock's stature could overlook all of these details, and the profound problems of 'regime change' suggested by the very cases he cites. Despite his title (*The Costs of War*), he treats these costs only as lessons in implementation, and leaves undisturbed a Western-centric view where the US and UK must intervene regularly and intensively, placing themselves in the centre of civil wars and revolutions.

The 'Phase IV' explanation for failure is flawed in several respects. Firstly, it assumes, as a counterfactual, that the ascending power holders in post-Saddam Iraq who represented the majority, in particular the main Shia religious parties and the Iraqi National Congress, would have acquiesced to a new order where the apparatus of Saddam's rule was left intact or only dismantled at the top echelons. It assumes that, given the right physical conditions and equilibrium, the significant Iraqi actors would have aligned their interests and ambitions with those of the occupiers. This was obviously not the case.

Firstly, failure to purge the Baathist order would have alienated the most important wielders of power amongst the Iraqi Shia. At the 'aftermath' meeting on 16 May 2003 between Bremer and seven leaders of Iraqi groups, the Iraqi representatives present demanded that de-Ba'athification proceed quickly and thoroughly, against the threat of Ba'ath resurgence. With the support of all present including Chalabi and the Kurdish leader Talibani, Dr Ibrahim al-Jaafari of the Shiite Dawa Party voiced concern 'about signs that the Baath Party is regrouping. The Coalition must never let this happen. We hope that you act decisively to nip this resurgence in the bud'.[120] Bremer's aide Dan Senor likewise recalled that 'if we hadn't [moved against the Baath Party], there may have been severe retribution against the Sunnis. And the Shia and Kurds might not have cooperated with us. Those symbolic steps were

---

[120] Paul Bremer, *My Year in Iraq: The Struggle to Build a Future of Hope* (New York: Simon & Schuster, 2006), p. 48.

very important early on'.[121] Bremer and Senor had an obvious interest in emphasizing that the momentum for the purge came from Iraqis and the instruction of the Pentagon. But their accounts are supported by former cabinet minister Ali Allawi, who was critical of the order but recognized that De-Ba'athification enjoyed overwhelming initial support, had long predated the invasion, was a staple of exile literature and a demand of Shia and Kurdish parties.[122] Iraqi Shia parties' demands for the sacking of the old order were so great that when the CPA handed over the implementation of the policy to Iraqi politicians, 'they broadened the decree's impact far beyond our original design. That led to such unintended results as the firing of several thousand teachers for being Baath Party members'.[123] De-Ba'athification was not just a fantasy of American officials in the Department of Defence and Vice President's office. It had a strong Iraqi constituency, both of exiles returning and indigenous Iraqis.

Iraq was not in a political condition where the chances of a transcendent shared nationalism were strong. With its dictator overthrown, the country was already a violent and volatile place. Between the completed fall of Baghdad (a few weeks after the recorded fall on 9 April) and before the Bremer purge even took force on 25 May 2003, the Baghdad city morgue was already recording a sharp rise in deaths by bullet or explosive, 458 in May compared to 246 in January 2003, rising again to 612 in June.[124] Much of this is attributable to the onslaught of criminal gangs, but conditions were forming for general heightened insecurity. Political relations were already so disfigured, the sense of the Iraqi nation state as the common property of its citizens so weak, that there was widespread looting across cities and towns as soon as the regime collapsed, with participation by government employees, targeting civilian infrastructure such as power plants and hospitals, Ba'ath elites' property, and national symbols of Iraqi heritage such as the National Museum in Baghdad. It began on the day Saddam's government fell, six weeks *before* the De-Ba'athification Order, and climaxing on the weekend of 11–12 July with what Patrick Cockburn called a 'social revolutionary ferocity'.[125] Crucially for our understanding of cause and effect, Shia Iraqis, at this moment when the occupiers were tilting the balance of power in their favour, still took part energetically in the plunder, especially of Sunni homes and businesses. This all suggests that the majority political groupings would not have peacefully

---

[121] Cited in Richard Lowry, 'What Went Wrong?', *National Review*, 25 October 2004.
[122] Ali Allawi, *The Occupation of Iraq: Winning the War, Losing the Peace* (Yale: Yale University Press, 2007), pp. 150–1.
[123] L. Paul Bremer, 'What We Got Right in Iraq', *The Washington Post*, 13 May 2007.
[124] 'Violence Continues to Plague Bagdhad', *Institute for War and Peace Reporting*, 5 April 2004.
[125] Patrick Cockburn, *Muqtada al-Sadr And the Shia Insurgency in Iraq* (London: Faber & Faber, 2008), p. 161.

reconciled to a less favourable political settlement. One of the most pivotal power figures of the new order, the charismatic cleric Muqtada al-Sadr, in May issued a *fatwa* that entitled his followers to take part in looting, provided they donated a share of the spoils to their local Sadrist office. Sadr himself with his considerable leverage was opposed to the occupation of Iraq from the very outset. Even the most intensively planned and even-handed dispensation that gave greater protection to Sunnis and balanced the claims of all groups would probably not have met with broad support.

The failure to recognize the situation in Iraq in that transitional period also points to a deeper fallacy, the assumption of an alignment between the ambitions of the occupiers and the perceived interests of the host population. Evidently, from the very outset, critical players in the drama and their Iranian patron did *not* want the creation of a new order of social harmony and equitably distributed power and wealth. They wanted to strip away and plunder the old order in its entirety, seize the institutions of the state, pursue vengeance, treat elections as a winner-takes-all contest, and pursue security in a zero-sum competition. Shia parties insisted on the prompt holding of free elections, not out of a desire for a unified democratic state, but because they were rightly confident that they had the numbers. If this was their competitive orientation in conditions where American policies effectively favoured them, it is hard to see how they (or their international sponsors) would have moderated their behaviour if the Ba'ath state and army were left largely intact.

As with many cases of intervention crisis, there was a 'misalignment problem'.[126] It is difficult to bring stable governance to fragile states by increasing their technical capacity to govern, if the new ruling elites don't share the intervening power's vision. Other actors, empowered by Western intervention, often have a separate, and sometimes conflicting view of their interests. Providing predatory or partisan governments with weapons, skills, and money may reinforce rather than reform abusive or kleptocratic behaviour, and implicate the occupier in what victims see as repression, stoking resistance and hardening division. If a host government is predatory on parts of its population, for instance, this can undermine security sector reform, as it did later in Iraq. Given the intense centrifugal forces that were already in play in the spring and summer of 2003, it is naïve to assume that the roots of the problem lay in inadequate administrative preparations. The rapid sectarianization of Iraq in the wake of the regime's fall flowed from an older struggle over competing Iraq visions for the state's identity, ownership, and legitimacy, entrenched in the 1990s era of sanctions, Ba'ath governance, and US-sponsored opposition in exile, which saw the rise of an assertive Iraqi Shia consciousness. Iraqis were not primordial beings forever on a default setting of

---

[126] Stephen Biddle, 'Afghanistan's legacy: Emerging lessons of an ongoing war', *The Washington Quarterly* 37:2 (2014), pp. 73–86, pp. 80–1.

internal conflict, but neither were they merely subjects to be administered badly or well. They were political agents who made choices, in pre-existing circumstances that 'proved conducive to the advent of identity politics'[127] and the exploitation of such politics by skilful entrepreneurs. The main defect of the regime change project was the idea itself, which is inherently flawed in most cases. As soon as the occupiers kicked in the door and decided to stay, there was an appointment with strife.

This is not to pronounce on the wisdom, or folly, of the post-Saddam purge. No doubt, the purge did alienate Sunni Arab Iraqis. The flip side, however, was that without de-Ba'athification, or with a more limited purge, this would court the serious risk of resistance among the Shia groups that were treating the fall of Saddam as an opportunity not to forge a reconciled power-sharing federal democracy, but to compete for power advantage. Either way, the invaders in 2003 could not easily have avoided civil turmoil that would flow, given the strong majority demand for the overturning of the old Ba'ath order, and minority fear of that process of change. The task of imposing order and balance on the post-Saddam settlement, to offset pre-existing centrifugal forces, would have required a very adroit manipulation of competing groups with bribes and threats of abandonment. To meet an adequate troops-to-civilians ratio, it would have taken an estimated 380,000–500,000 troops in total to ensure Iraq's post-Saddam stability.[128] That would have been an unsustainable and indeed imprudent commitment given the demands for deployments elsewhere and the need to relieve and rotate those deployed. The very improbability of getting all of this right makes the whole venture simply too difficult and too complex, beyond acceptable costs. The root problem lay in an intractable and older problem, of competing political visions among Iraqis who in a new and fluid environment had powerful reasons to fear one another, both the Shiite majority with its experience of oppressive minority rule, the Sunni minority who feared retribution (and whose Saddamist elements had long planned a guerrilla resistance should this day come), Kurdish Iraqis who would view restoration of the old order as threatening, other actors from Zarqawi's Al Qaeda franchise, and Iran, which also had a stake in supporting competition over cooperation. These potentialities would very probably have erupted into open conflict whether the occupiers dismantled the old order, purged only part of it, or kept it entirely in place under a milder Sunni strongman. There is no simple resolution of this dilemma. That the choice lay between different poisons was—and is—a powerful reason in itself not to invade in the first place.

---

[127] See Fanar Hadad, *Shia-Centric State-Building and Sunni Rejection in Post 2003 Iraq* (Washington DC: Carnegie Endowment for International Peace, 2016), p. 12.

[128] James Quinlivan, 'Force Requirements in Stability Operations', *Parameters* (1995), pp. 59–69; also James Dobbins, 'Who Lost Iraq?', *Foreign Affairs* 86:5 (2007), pp. 61–74.

A LIBERAL WAR AFTER ALL

We now turn to an argument that challenges my interpretation. According to G. John Ikenberry and Daniel Deudney, two of the world's most sophisticated observers of international relations, this war, for all its democracy-promoting effort and ambitious doctrine, was predominantly a realist war, not a 'liberal' one.[129] Declarations of a higher purpose were merely gestures to carry opinion, especially after WMD claims were proved false. Instead of asking, as others do (Van Rythoven, 2016; Schmidt and Williams, 2008)[130] why anti-war realists failed in their advocacy for restraint and were trumped by neoconservatives and liberal hawks, they suggest that a different faction of realists carried the day. If America's most disastrous war since Vietnam had intellectual foundations, those foundations were allegedly laid more by hegemonic realists like John Mearsheimer, who opposed the war, than 'liberal internationalists' like Anne-Marie Slaughter, who supported it.

In laying the groundwork for Operation Iraqi Freedom, which intellectual tradition is more to blame, realism or liberalism? Policymakers may baulk at the suggestion that theory shapes their behaviour, but theory simply means the map with which we interpret the world, and besides, the Iraq War more than most attracted intellectualized discussion. What theory led them to Baghdad? This historical question has high stakes. By shifting the blame and giving American liberalism an alibi for the disaster, by arguing that the Iraq War mostly reflects the pathologies of a species of realism, the authors try to clean liberalism's scorecard. In other outlets, both give liberal ideas credit for the successes of the post-war international order, like the Bretton Woods financial system and the Marshall Plan.[131] Here, they absolve those same ideas of failure. And if disasters like Iraq are not built into Washington's post-war design, but are instead the result of deviations from liberalism, the argument is stronger that America should persist in leaning forward, maintaining a 'liberal' kind of hegemony, using its power to spread free markets and democracy, a project that is more peace-producing than war-generating.[132] Thus, for their grand strategic vision, the unimportance of liberal ideas to the Iraq War is convenient.

---

[129] Daniel Deudney & G. John Ikenberry, 'Realism, Liberalism and the Iraq War', *Survival* 59:4 (2017), pp. 7–26.

[130] Eric Van Rythoven, 'The Perils of Realist Advocacy and the Promise of Securitization Theory: Revisiting the tragedy of the Iraq War debate', *European Journal of International Relations* 22:3 (2016), pp. 487–511; Brian Schmidt & Michael Williams, 'The Bush Doctrine and the Iraq War: Neoconservatives versus Realists', *Security Studies* 17:2 (2008), pp. 191–220.

[131] Daniel Deudney & G. John Ikenberry, 'The Nature and Sources of Liberal International Order', *Review of International Studies* 25 (1999), pp. 179–96; 'Democratic Internationalism' (Working Paper, Council on Foreign Relations, 2012), pp. 7–12, 13.

[132] Stephen G. Brooks, G. John Ikenberry & William C. Wohlforth, 'Lean Forward: In Defence of American Engagement', *Foreign Affairs* 92:1 (2013), pp. 130–42.

To their credit, Deudney and Ikenberry remind us that realism is heterogeneous and does not necessarily counsel restraint. Realism does indeed contain streams of thought that warrant wars for dominance through 'regime change'. There is such a thing as 'primacy realism'. Officials in the operational policy world espouse it, even if their academic counterparts don't. Their argument also shifts the question. Instead of asking, as others do,[133] why realists failed in their advocacy for restraint and were trumped by neoconservatives and liberal hawks, they suggest that a different faction of realists carried the day. To make their case, however, they offer only an impoverished potted history of the Iraq War's origins and conduct, a re-telling that does little justice to the ideas that shaped it.

The issue is not whether realpolitik can inspire hegemonic wars. It can. The issue is whether the Iraq War was primarily 'the product of liberalism' or 'straightforwardly the result of the pursuit of American hegemonic primacy'. As I demonstrate, liberals and liberalism were deeply implicated. The Bush administration's forceful reassertion of American primacy was not an amoral exercise in power maximization. It was infused with an idealism that has deep historical roots. Moreover, liberalism and the pursuit of hegemony are not antithetical, as the authors imply. Liberalism married with the capabilities of a superpower gives America a proclivity for reckless military adventures. So long as liberalism, untampered by prudential balance-of-power realism, remains a central engine of American grand strategy, the US will be prone to further such tragedies.

This section divides into three parts. In Part I, I define liberalism, realism, and 'liberal' wars, as Ikenberry and Deudney's treatment of all three requires some definitional untangling. The authors don't offer a clear or falsifiable account of what a 'liberal' war is or what it would look like, against which to test the Iraq case and identify its conceptual underpinnings. In Parts II and III, I demonstrate the flaws in Ikenberry and Deudney's effort to get American liberalism off the hook. Firstly, their account is bad and reductionist history. It narrows the causes of the war to three policymakers whose views they wrongly elide, neglecting other significant voices and the wide coalition of liberal minds whose account of security led them to support a preventive and hegemonic war, not as the antithesis but the necessary condition for the spread of liberal values. Secondly, for two internationalists this is a strangely parochial account of the Iraq War. Other international agents also shaped the struggle, from

---

[133] On this issue, see Eric Van Rythoven, 'The Perils of Realist Advocacy and the Promise of Securitization Theory: Revisiting the tragedy of the Iraq War debate', *European Journal of International Relations* 22:3 (2016), pp. 487–511; Brian Schmidt & Michael Williams, 'The Bush Doctrine and the Iraq War: Neoconservatives versus Realists', *Security Studies* 17:2 (2008), pp. 191–220.

Prime Minister Tony Blair to Iraqi exiles, and their visions are not reducible to narrow realpolitik.

Part I. Liberalism, Realism, and War

A restatement of definitions is in order, as well as an account of 'liberal wars' and how to recognize them. Deudney and Ikenberry frame the issue in a way that 'games' the argument.

Realism is a pessimistic intellectual tradition that views international life as insecure and defined by the possibility of war, because the world is anarchic, or lacking a supreme, supranational sovereign.[134] Without a 'Leviathan' to keep the peace, this condition of anarchy places a premium on self-help and a sensitivity to dangerous power imbalances. Realists often disagree on specific policies but are generally concerned for stability over progress, emphasize material capabilities, are wary of overzealous crusading, and are above all averse to the impulse to reinvent the world, and transform other countries, in one's own image and at one's own timetable. This translates into a general unease with waging wars to export American values. Most realists who whisper in princes' ears—from George Kennan to Henry Kissinger to Brent Scowcroft—share this orientation, though not all.

As America became a 'unipolar' superpower without a peer competitor to restrain it, most American academic realists directed their energy both to theory-building and to prophesying about the impermanence of unipolarity and the perils of overstretch. There were limits even to American power, they warned. Despite appearances, the triumph of Atlantic democratic capitalism under Washington's stewardship would not permanently transform the world. Americans were not immune from the historical patterns whereby overexpansion generated resistance and counter-power. And they argued that America's commitment to primacy, often euphemized as 'leadership', and to spreading the 'democratic peace' made the country dangerously war-prone, and endangered the very democratic institutions they were supposed to protect. This critique grew more urgent as the Global War on Terror unfolded.[135]

---

[134] On the realist tradition and its unifying facets, see Joseph M. Parent & Joshua M. Baron, 'Elder abuse: How the moderns mistreat classical realism', *International Studies Review* 13 (2011), pp. 193–213; Michael E. Brown, Sean M. Lynn-Jones & Steven E. Miller, *The Perils of Anarchy: Contemporary Realism and International Security* (Cambridge: MIT Press, 1995); Michael W. Doyle, *Ways of War and Peace: Realism, Liberalism, and Socialism* (New York: W. W. Norton, 1997), p. 45.

[135] See Eugene Gholz, Daryl G. Pressc & Harvey M. Sapolsky, 'Come Home America: The Strategy of Restraint in the Face of Temptation', *International Security* 21:4, (1997), pp. 5–48; Christopher Layne, 'Kant or Cant: The Myth of the Democratic Peace', *International Security* 19 (1994), pp. 5–49; Sebastian Rosato, 'The Flawed Logic of Democratic Peace Theory', *American Political Science Review* 97: 4 (2003), pp. 585–602.

Most senior realists of the academy opposed the Iraq War.[136] They argued that the military adventure was not in the national interest, that overthrowing the Iraqi state would spread instability in the Middle East, that invading this divided society would lead to occupation for years, and that the US should focus its efforts on combating Al-Qaeda and to deterring Saddam's adventurism. More broadly, they warned that the Iraq War was part of Washington's overexpansion, an expansion driven by the lack of a major power competitor and by the motor of liberal ideology. Some observers, including realists critical of the Iraq War, trace a lineage from Woodrow Wilson to the 'Bush Doctrine' in which the Iraq War was grounded.[137]

For Ikenberry and Deudney, realists who argued that their faith dictated opposition to Iraq, failed to understand the breadth and multiplicity of their own tradition. Realism, they rightly note, has several variants. The realism that apparently inspired Iraq was more to be found amongst the 'practical-operational' stable of realists within government. These realists proffered a twofold form of realism that has strong purchase in Washington. It was firstly 'hegemonic realism' or the pursuit of American primacy on the basis that order flows from favourable concentrations of power, and 'interdependence realism' that stresses the dangers of violent interdependence and the need to alleviate anarchy in an increasingly lethal industrial and nuclear age by reversing weapons proliferation. For realists of this stripe, there was obvious appeal to the reassertion of American dominance in a vital oil-rich power centre, and the preventive removal of a WMD threat. Even when liberal internationalists joined them in supporting war, they were actually following a narrower counterproliferation agenda, being driven more by worries about interdependence in a nuclear age than by Wilsonian idealism.

And then there is the family of liberal theories. In the field of foreign policy, American liberalism is committed to the possibility of progress and change. Liberalism combines ideals of individual liberty, free markets, democratic representation, and equality of opportunity. It is optimistic about the ability to replace international anarchy with trustful, harmonious relations, and to forge lasting cooperation. Liberals typically identify three pathways to a better world, through economic interdependence, through the spread of democracy,

---

[136] See the advertisement that a group of academic realists placed in the *The New York Times*: 'War with Iraq is not in America's National Interest', *The New York Times*, 26 September 2002; see also John J. Mearsheimer & Stephen M. Walt, 'An Unnecessary War', *Foreign Policy* 134 (2003), pp. 50–9; Paul Starobin, 'The Realists', *National Journal* 39:37 (2006), pp. 24–31.

[137] Michael C. Desch, 'America's Liberal Illiberalism: The Ideological Origins of Overreaction in U.S. Foreign Policy', *International Security* 32:3 (2007), pp. 7–43; Christopher Layne, 'Wilson's Ghost: Spreading Freedom around the World Will Destroy It at Home', *The American Conservative* 4:4 (28 February 2005), pp. 9–11; Lloyd E. Ambrosius, 'Woodrow Wilson and George W. Bush: Historical Comparisons of Ends and Means in Their Foreign Policies', *Diplomatic History* 30 (2006), pp. 509–43; David M. Kennedy, 'What "W" owes to "WW"', *The Atlantic* 30:5 (2005), pp. 36–40.

and through the creation of international institutions. Liberals generally are oriented to a strategic vision where the world is, or should be, a harmony of interests, altering the political and economic character of other states in order to achieve common security. In the Wilsonian tradition, liberals seeks to institute peace by spreading liberty and creating liberal subjects abroad. 'Wilsonianism' is a conflicted thing. Some liberals emphasize President Woodrow Wilson's historic stress on international law and institutions, others the need to spread democratic freedom at the point of a bayonet if necessary, but Wilsonians agree on the 'basic proposition that America's national security requires a liberal world order'.[138] In turn, that liberal world order flowed from and was underwritten by American primacy, a primacy anchored and legitimized in international institutions.[139]

The American neoconservatives, as they had evolved by the time of the late 1990s, blended democratic idealism and military assertiveness. Like liberals, 'neocons' believe that American security rests on the 'regime type' of other states, and that the world's security relies upon America's benign superintendence. Like liberals, neocons self-consciously reject what they see as an amoral, deluded realism that is alien to the best traditions of the republic. Their frame of reference is the interwar period, the failures of appeasement and the resulting catastrophe. Washington should use its unprecedented power not merely to acquire more material advantage, but to expand the sphere of market democracy. Unlike liberals, who worry more about international institutions, legality, and the cultivation of allies, neocons prefer the unabashed and unfettered assertion of American power, where allies or institutions are means, not ends.[140] But for their common missionary impulse and their presumption in favour of military action, liberals and neocons both belong to the Wilsonian family. As we will see, the 'Bush Doctrine' that embodied neocons' ideas, and the Iraq War that was their signature project, drew on liberal ideas about security.

At first glance, Ikenberry and Deudney's treatment of 'realism' and 'hegemony' seems tautological. As the illogic goes, realism of a certain kind prescribes hegemonic war, Iraq was a hegemonic war, therefore the Iraq War was realist. But a closer look suggests that their error is a historical and conceptual one,

---

[138] John A. Thompson, 'Wilsonianism: The Dynamics of a Conflicted Concept', *International Affairs* 86:1 (2010), pp. 27–48, p. 28.

[139] Though Ikenberry has separately argued that Washington could create the institutional framework to 'lock in' the liberal world order even after the decline of American power: 'The Future of the Liberal World Order: Internationalism after America', *Foreign Affairs* 90:3 (2011), pp. 56–68.

[140] On the history of neoconservatism, see Michael C. Williams, 'Morgenthau Now: Neoconservatism, National Greatness, and Realism', in *Realism Reconsidered: The Legacy of Hans Morgenthau in International Relations* (New York: Oxford University Press, 2007), pp. 216–41, pp. 217–27; Jacob Heilbrunn, *They Knew They Were Right: The Rise of the Neocons* (New York: Doubleday, 2009).

not a logical fallacy. They equate the pursuit of 'hegemony' and wars to perpetuate it exclusively with realism, so that the pursuit of 'hegemonic primacy' is assumed to be antithetical whatever is 'liberal'.[141] If there is such a thing as a non-realist 'liberal' war, at Ikenberry and Deudney's hands it becomes such a small target that it almost disappears, thus setting up the inquest to make practically any assertive military project or enforcement of US dominance necessarily 'realist'. This will not do.

Ikenberry and Deudney skate over it, but a significant wing of liberalism is hawkish. There are anti-war liberals, but there also does exist a group of liberal hawks with privileged access to government and the commentariat, who support the forceful pursuit of material power to promote liberal goals. This group was especially galvanized by debate over intervention in the Balkan Wars of the 1990s. If there is a true divide between liberals and realists over hegemony, it lies not in a disagreement about whether or not to pursue it. The belief that hegemony is a desirable, peace-promoting and security-producing state is a monopoly neither of realists or liberals. It was, after all, Ikenberry's seminal work that cast America approvingly as the post-World War II 'Liberal Leviathan', exercising its hegemony to transform the world, its institutions, and norms in a liberal direction.[142] In that moment of creation, American pre-eminence lay at the core.

A fairer test would be *for what purposes, and according to what theory of security, hegemonic wars are intended.* A 'realist' hegemonic war would eschew larger ideological goals or the creation of a constitutional system of government in Iraq as a result, and focus instead on war generating changes in the distribution of material power as a valued end in itself. It would be conservative, fearing that democratization would increase rather than decrease security threats in the region. Realists of this kind might countenance the preaching of human rights but only as an enabling 'cover' for an exercise in austere geopolitics. A 'liberal' hegemonic war would proceed on a different basis: that accommodation with dictatorships in the region was itself the source of the security problem, and that the purpose of the war would be to alter the destructive convergence of weapons proliferation, rogues, and radical Islamist ideology by replacing dictatorship and corruption with democracy and free markets, beginning in Iraq as part of a benign domino effect. A realist hegemonic war would aim to bring the monarchies and dictatorships of the

---

[141] The authors claim that 'the Iraq War...was straightforwardly the result of the pursuit of American hegemonic primacy. Its origins flowed readily from an ancient and prominent body of realist thought'; they characterize neoconservatism as 'partially liberal and partially primacist'. These statements imply a necessary separation of liberalism from the commitment to 'primacy', which is presented as exclusively a realist concern.

[142] John Ikenberry, *Liberal Leviathan: The Origins, Crisis and Transformation of the American World Order* (Princeton: Princeton University Press, 2011).

Gulf under American tutelage; a liberal war would aim to transform their very character.

Part II. The Liberal Road to Baghdad

It is artificial to ascribe major foreign policy initiatives to a single intellectual source. Both idealist liberals and cut-throat realists, for instance, have their reasons for supporting NATO expansion.[143] The resort to arms, too, normally requires a domestic coalition of factions, interests, and lobbies. Deputy Secretary of Defence and hawkish intellectual Paul Wolfowitz recalled there were multiple rationales within the administration for attacking Iraq. Decision-makers settled on WMD as the central rationale because 'it was the one reason everyone could agree on'.[144] Among multiple agendas was a genuine drive to assert American hegemony, eliminate competitors, and demonstrate strength to great power competitors. Momentum built for 'regime change' in the wake of the grave fears caused by the 9/11 terrorist attacks and the anthrax attacks that followed soon after. Exhilarated by unexpected early success in Afghanistan, US decision-makers felt the wind at their back. A visceral 'rally around the flag' emotion took hold. Henry Kissinger, who had been sceptical of earlier interventions, supported the invasion 'Because Afghanistan was not enough. The radical Islamists, he said, want to humiliate us. And we need to humiliate them.'[145] It will not suffice, however, to settle on the banal observation that wars are caused by a combination of factors. Was liberal idealism central, or marginal?

With startling brevity, Ikenberry and Deudney claim that the principal architects of the Iraq War were three 'hegemonic realists' within the executive, Vice President Richard Cheney, Secretary of Defence Donald Rumsfeld and Deputy Secretary of Defence Paul Wolfowitz. 'There are many ways to describe the political ideologies of these three figures', they note, 'but "liberal-internationalist" is not among them.'

Strangely, in Ikenberry and Deudney's account, the most senior figure who had to sign off on the war is missing in action. Over Iraq, President George W. Bush was a driving force. He was not a puppet of his court, but

---

[143] Liberals could point to the benefit of locking in and extending the democratic peace, realists to the geopolitical gain of acquiring new allies and territorial predominance. See Joshua R. Itzkowitz Shifrinson, 'Deal or No Deal? The End of the Cold War and the US Offer to Limit NATO Expansion', *International Security* 40:4 (2016), pp. 7–44.

[144] Sam Tannenhaus, *Vanity Fair*, May 2003; Wolfowitz specified also that the main four reasons were WMD, terrorism, the criminal mistreatment of the Iraqi people, and the linkage between the first two: Jamie McIntyre, 'Pentagon Challenges Vanity Fair Report', *CNN*, 30 May 2003.

[145] Cited in Mark Danner, 'Words in a Time of War', *Asia Times*, 2 June 2007.

independent and strong-willed in his decision-making style.[146] If the ideas and assumptions carried by Cheney, Rumsfeld, and Wolfowitz are deemed to be evidence of the war's origins, it also matters what the President believed he was doing. Every account from close observers, who independently agree, suggest that Bush's private sentiments about Iraq, and the War on Terror, were predominantly liberal ones that invested American power with ideological ambition. Bush told his counsellor Karen Hughes a week after 9/11, 'We have an opportunity to restructure the world toward freedom, and we have to get it right.' Officials, congressional representatives, and other confidantes agree that the President in private interpreted the historic juncture opened by 9/11 in 'grand, emphatic and even Manichaean terms', his belief in the 'goal of wiping out terrorism',[147] his 'strong moral streak',[148] and his 'propensity to be idealistic and see that democracy is the innate right of mankind'.[149] In an otherwise critical memoir, Bush's estranged former Press Secretary Scott McLellan affirmed the strength of the President's commitment to the 'Freedom Agenda': 'There was nothing I would ever see him talk more passionately about than this view, both publicly and privately'.[150] These rationalizations were not merely *post hoc* ones used to justify the war in public, but prior beliefs articulated in private. The sincerity of Bush's public enthusiasm for idealist visions such as Natan Sharansky's manifesto, *The Case for Democracy*, is suggested by his underreported private meetings with exile groups. If Bush secretly doubted the doctrines he articulated intensely when away from the cameras, those doubts were very secret. And if, as the authors argue, the privately held convictions of Cheney and his 'one per cent doctrine' are

---

[146] For instance, against lobbying by Vice President Dick Cheney, Bush insisted on appointing Colin Powell as his Secretary of State. Bush dismissed Donald Rumsfeld, and refused to pardon 'Scooter' Libby, both against Cheney's opposition. He resisted Cheney's urging for a more hardline stance on North Korea and Iran. And at one stage in 2004 he considered dismissing Cheney from the presidential ticket. See Julian E. Zelizer, '5 Myths About George W. Bush', *The Washington Post*, 7 November 2010.

[147] Cited in Frank Bruni, 'A Nation Challenged: White House Memo', *The New York Times*, 22 September 2001. See also the idealistic fervour reported by Bob Woodward from their conversations: Bob Woodward, *Bush at War* (New York: Simon and Schuster, 2002), p. 340.

[148] Condoleezza Rice, cited in Amy Zegard, 'The Legend of a Democracy Promoter', *The National Interest* 97 (2008), p. 51.

[149] According to Victor Davis Hanson, a classical historian who had private talks with both Bush and Cheney, comparing Bush's idealism to Cheney's more 'tragic' view: cited in Barton Gellman, *The Angler: The Cheney Vice-Presidency* (New York: Penguin, 2008), pp. 250–1; Eliot Cohen reported Bush's real, core belief in the Freedom Agenda and the rejection of the practice of accommodation with 'thuggish regimes'. Cited in Stephen Dyson, *Leaders in Conflict: Bush and Rumsfeld in Iraq* (Manchester: Manchester University Press, 2014), p. 46; and John Lewis Gaddis, also in contact with the White House, saw the Bush Doctrine as powered by a recurrent Wilsonian view of the spread of American values as the path to security: John Lewis Gaddis, 'Bush's Security Strategy', *Foreign Policy* 133 (2002), pp. 50–7.

[150] Scott McLellen, *What Happened: Inside the White House and Washington's Culture of Deception* (New York: Public Affairs, 2008), p. 197.

admissible as evidence for the war's ideological drivers, then so too are those of Bush. Indeed, in assessing the evidential value of rhetoric and what ideas underpinned the Iraq War, the authors are methodologically inconsistent. They treat spoken rationalizations as a reflection of real motives and causes when it supports their case, and as mere surface gloss when it doesn't.

The consistency of Bush's beliefs suggests that there was authenticity to the 'Bush Doctrine', which predated and supplied the rationale for the Iraq War and was laid out in the President's West Point address of 1 June 2002 and the White House's *National Security Strategy* of that year.[151] The Doctrine codified liberal assumptions about security and American interests,[152] and its namesake invoked the Wilsonian tradition in advancing it.[153] These ideas were: that the 'regime type' of foreign states is the primary determinant of their behaviour; that globalized security threats, culminating in the potential marriage of terrorism, destructive technology, and revisionist states, must be met with anticipatory measures such as preventive war; and that the promotion of democracy and capitalism, universally applicable, can transform the world into a more peaceful and secure place. That is not to say that the Doctrine in its entirety conformed with the preferences of liberals. Even pro-war liberals were critical of its unilateralism above collective endeavour and institutions. But in the heavy emphasis on the ascent of American ideology, there was far more for realists to dislike than liberals. Iraq, then, flowed primarily from a liberal view of the sources of foreign policy, namely the character of regimes themselves in which America has a large stake, and a liberal view of the solution, namely enforcing a democratic peace. The proposition of a democratized Iraq that would be better for Iraqis and Americans helped swing American liberals behind the effort.

The summary of the three 'architects' of Iraq is also a simplistic treatment of Wolfowitz. Cheney and Rumsfeld, it is true, were clearly not liberal ideologues. They were conservative nationalists, sceptical of declared liberal war aims such as democracy promotion and nation-building. (Indeed, Rumsfeld for these reasons advocated for a quick withdrawal from Iraq after Baghdad fell, and his failure on this front also suggests hardline realists were not in the ascendancy). Paul Wolfowitz, however, cannot usefully be grouped with these two figures.

---

[151] 'Remarks by the President at 2002 Graduation Exercise of the Unites States Military Academy', White House Press Release, 1 June 2002; President of the United States, *National Security Strategy of the United States of America* (Washington, DC: US Government Printing Office, 2002).

[152] See Robert Jervis, 'Understanding the Bush Doctrine', *Political Science Quarterly* 118:3 (2003), pp. 365–88, p. 367; Andrew Flibbert, 'The Road to Baghdad: Ideas and intellectuals in explanations of the Iraq war', *Security Studies* 15:2 (2006), pp. 310–52.

[153] 'From the fourteen points to the four freedoms to the speech at Westminster (Ronald Reagan), America has put its power at the service of principle'. Speech in Whitehall, November 2003, G.W. Bush, 'Both Our Nations Serve the Cause of Freedom', *The New York Times*, 20 November 2003.

Wolfowitz long held an idealistic concept of the purposes of American hegemony. In battles over dictatorship, democracy, and American patronage, for instance, over ending Washington's support for the Marcos regime in the Philippines in 1986, and in his criticisms of Henry Kissinger's alternative vision of stable equilibriums among major powers, Wolfowitz spearheaded a school of foreign policy 'willing to forsake the *status quo* in pursuit of democratic ideals'.[154] The same Wolfowitz co-drafted the notorious 'Defence Planning Guidance' document of 1992, which envisaged America generating overwhelming military superiority to prevent the re-emergence of rivals.[155] Again, liberal idealism can work in synthesis with ruthless hegemonic assertion. It was Wolfowitz who in late November 2001 oversaw the secret advisory paper 'Delta of Terrorism', that anticipated a two-generation war with radical Islam and called for the overthrow of Saddam's Iraq in order to transform the Middle East out of its 'malignancy'. This went beyond the assertion of material power, and called for a regional political transformation, to reverse what Wolfowitz called the 'stagnation' that produced 'radicalism and breeds terrorism'. The paper had great influence on Bush.[156] As it was not meant for wider consumption or public discussion, and was written fifteen months before the invasion of Iraq, it is hard to dismiss the paper as a rhetorical posture 'to sustain public support for the war and provide a template for post-war Iraqi reconstruction'.

It did not just take a handful of well-placed individuals to translate the idea of war into policy. It took the formation of a broad, bipartisan, and civil-military consensus. What were liberals doing on the eve of war? 'In reality', assert the authors without evidence, 'most liberal internationalists opposed the war'. This is a puzzling claim, since in 2008, Ikenberry wrote that 'After all, many liberals did in fact support the invasion'.[157] He was correct the first time. While there is no exact count available, there was significant support for war among self-identifying liberal commentators and policymakers. Support came from liberal intellectuals, some of whom had been in and out of the revolving door between academia and government: Paul Berman, David Remnick, Peter Beinart, Leon Wieseltier, Anne-Marie Slaughter, Kanan Makiya, Harvard professor and *The New York Times Magazine* contributor Michael Ignatieff,

---

[154] James Mann, *Rise of the Vulcans: The History of Bush's War Cabinet* (New York: Penguin, 2004), pp. 134, 76.

[155] Patrick E. Tyler, 'U.S. Strategy Plan Calls for Insuring No Rivals Develop', *The New York Times*, 8 March 1992.

[156] Bob Woodward, *State of Denial* (London: Pocket Books, 2006), pp. 83–5; Wolfowitz on 'stagnation' in *The Jerusalem Post* (2003) cited in T. Ricks, *Fiasco: The American Military Adventure in Iraq* (New York: Penguin, 2006), p. 30.

[157] G. John Ikenberry, Introduction, to G. John Ikenberry, Thomas J. Knock, Anne-Marie Slaughter & Tony Smith, *The Crisis of American Foreign Policy: Wilsonianism in the twenty-first century* (Princeton, NJ, and Oxford: Princeton University Press, 2009), p. 2.

and former senior officials such as Richard Holbrooke and Madeline Albright. Liberals in Congress lent their full-throated support, including Senator Hillary Clinton and Senator John Kerry. A critical shaper of liberal opinion was Bill Clinton's former national security advisor Kenneth Pollack, whose *The Threatening Storm* was 'the most influential book of the season', helping persuade commentators at the main East Coast liberal organs from op-ed regulars at *The Washington Post* and the editors of *The New Yorker* to *The New Republic* and *Slate*.[158] Liberals' rationales were always mixed but included avowedly liberal causes: 'to liberate the Iraqi people from their dungeon' and to establish 'a beachhead of Arab democracy', for 'Iraq as a secular democracy with equal rights for all of its citizens'.[159] Liberal visions viewed the humanitarian and strategic grounds for war as mutually complementary. As Leon Wieseltier wrote, 'it is quite easy to defend the necessity and the justice of separating Saddam Hussein from his lethal devices, which is the same thing as separating him from his power, which is the same thing as aiding in the formation of a democratic government in Baghdad'.[160]

Ikenberry and Deudney deploy the term 'liberal internationalist' in ways that obfuscate. Does 'internationalist' encompass foreign policy liberals of any kind, since it would be difficult to be a non-internationalist liberal? Elsewhere, Ikenberry has defined the essence of liberalism as follows: 'Autocratic and militarist states make war; democracies make peace. In retrospect, this is the cornerstone of Wilsonianism and, more generally, the liberal international tradition'.[161] In which case, this must include liberals who believe that American primacy is the best vehicle towards that peace, and that the liberal international order needs occasional muscular enforcement. A vocal and influential war party has resided within the ranks of American liberalism and has been at the core of America's most significant wars since Korea. These numbered John F. Kennedy, Lyndon Johnson, and Henry 'Scoop' Jackson in the era of Vietnam, and the likes of Wesley Clark and Bill Clinton in the era of Kosovo. It includes the influential liberal hawks Samantha Power, Susan Rice, and Anne-Marie Slaughter who urged President Barack Obama to conduct airstrikes against Libya in 2011.[162] The latter two also supported the invasion of Iraq, undermining Ikenberry and Deudney's ahistorical claim that liberals

---

[158] Bill Keller, 'The I Can't Believe I'm a Hawk Club', *The New York Times*, 8 February 2003; Kenneth Pollack, *The Threatening Storm: The Case for Invading Iraq* (New York: Random House, 2002); Michael Tomasky, 'Beyond Iraq: Toward a New Liberal Internationalism', in Neil Jumonville & Kevin Mattson (eds), *Liberalism for a New Century* (Berkeley: University of California Press, 2007), pp. 209–19.

[159] Cited in George Packer, 'The Liberal Quandary over Iraq', *The New York Times Magazine*, 8 December 2002, pp. 104–7.

[160] Leon Wieseltier, 'Against Innocence', *The New Republic*, 3 March 2003.

[161] G. John Ikenberry et al., *The Crisis of American Foreign Policy*, p. 10.

[162] Michael Hastings, 'Inside Obama's War Room', *Rolling Stone*, 13 October 2011.

with a preference for 'international arms control and security regime-building' are against 'preventive war and hegemonic rule'.[163] This is also true of the majority of Senate Democrats whose consent to use force in Iraq the President requested and obtained.

Another historical problem confronts the liberal alibi. If America was driven narrowly just to strengthen its hegemonic rule, it went to a great deal of extra trouble voluntarily. Nowhere in their account is there an explanation for the bold experiment in 'year zero' reconstruction and nation-building in Iraq. How do we reconcile cold realpolitik with the determination to purge the old order through De-Ba'athification? This decision was driven partly by Chalabi and Shia and Kurdish demands, partly by America's dogmatically idealistic proconsul Paul Bremer III (who is missing from Ikenberry and Deudney's history), and was approved by Bush at least after the fact and possibly before.[164] The purge of the bureaucracy and army was justified as a wise ideological purification, through appeals to the examples of earlier democracy-promoting efforts in post-war Japan and West Germany. America could have installed a client dictatorship and exerted minimal institutional impact, perhaps with a protective garrison, as it had done in other cases where it wanted a strategic foothold. Instead, it embarked on an ambitious nation-building programme to remake the Iraqi state along liberal lines. Is that realism?

Part III. Beyond Washington

Coalition partners and international policy entrepreneurs go missing in Ikenberry and Deudney's parochial account. Whatever happened to Prime Minister Tony Blair? Iraq was primarily America's war, and it could and probably would have been fought without others' participation. But Blair's inner circle was at the forefront of crafting the international case for war, and the pursuit of an international mandate. The logic and appeal of Blair's arguments cannot adequately be explained by pointing to hegemonic realist theory, to put it mildly. For Blair, this was a great struggle of ideas. Britain's alignment with the US over Iraq was partly fuelled by an attempt to bandwagon for influence in Washington. But it also had a genuine ideological element. Saddam's Iraq, Blair and his circle believed, embodied a growing systemic threat. Removing his regime would begin the positive transformation of the Middle East. A leaked memorandum from Secretary of State Colin Powell to President

---

[163] Benjamin H. Friedman, 'The Real Problem with a Secretary of State Susan Rice', *CATO Institute Commentary*, 27 November 2012; Anne-Marie Slaughter, 'Good Reasons for Going Around the U.N.', *The New York Times*, 18 March 2003.

[164] Allawi, *The Occupation of Iraq*, pp. 150–1; Bremer, *My Year in Iraq*, p. 48.

Bush in the lead-up to the Crawford talks in April 2002 neatly summarized it: 'On Iraq, Blair will be with us should military operations be necessary. He is convinced on two points: the threat is real; and success against Saddam will yield more regional success.'[165] This is consistent with the record of Blair's private deliberations in Downing Street, his personal notes to Bush, his memoirs, and the public case he settled on in March 2003 on the eve of invasion. With invasion underway later in March 2003, Blair wrote privately to Bush that 'Our fundamental goal is to spread our goals of freedom, democracy, tolerance and the rule of law. Though Iraq's WMD is the immediate justification for action, ridding Iraq of Saddam is the real prize'.[166]

It is not clear how far his advocacy helped build a bipartisan consensus in Washington for regime change in Iraq. But it helped internationalize the war. America's coalition in invading Iraq was larger than the coalition it mustered for the Korean War. And it led to Britain occupying southern Iraq, suffering 179 fatalities and almost 6,000 non-fatal casualties. Blair's liberalism reinforced the hopeful ambitions of hawkish liberals on both sides of the Atlantic, that the Iraq War should be waged within a wider effort to advance the Middle East Peace Process, accelerate the economic and social development of the region, refracted through the social democratic and internationalist idiom of Britain's New Labour.[167] These hopes would be disappointed, but they helped build initial domestic and international support.

Whatever happened, also, to Ahmad Chalabi, Iraqi exile and later president? Chalabi's network of Iraqi exiles also invested the war with liberal, indeed revolutionary impulse, and had a tangible intellectual effect on the lobby for creating a new order in Baghdad. Long before 9/11, Chalabi and his network prepared and strengthened the case for regime change in Washington, in the hope that favourable conditions would emerge. Chalabi also cannot be bracketed amongst the hegemonic primacists. Alongside his talent for political operation, he had a life-long dream of a liberated Iraq with himself as the 'Shia's great emancipator'. That is a long way from Machiavelli.

For wars to happen, adversaries must agree to fight each other. There is one other figure whose calculations, and miscalculations, also made war possible, but who is also absent from the liberal alibi: Saddam Hussein. He could have chosen otherwise, to run the risks of complete capitulation to weapons inspections during the escalating crisis. He could have taken up the offer to leave. As invasion was at hand, he could have taken up President Bush's offer

---

[165] Internal memo to Bush ahead of Crawford meeting, 'Memorandum for the President, Your Meeting with the United Kingdom Prime Minister Tony Blair, April 5-7 2002 at Crawford'.
[166] Blair to Bush, private note, 'The Fundamental Goal', 26 March 2003.
[167] See also Tim Dunne, '"When the shooting starts": Atlanticism in British security strategy', *International Affairs* 80:5 (2004), pp. 893–909, p. 898.

to leave Iraq within forty-eight hours to settle abroad in voluntary exile and immunity,[168] an offer backed by Saudi Arabia, Egypt, and Britain. Russian President Vladimir Putin's envoy also offered Saddam an opportunity to abdicate, yet he refused. Bahrain's King Hamad made an offer, hours before the expiry of America's ultimatum for he and his sons to leave Iraq.[169] Past rulers have sometimes fled and survived in exile, such as Kaiser Wilhelm II. Of course, survival couldn't be guaranteed. A certifiably disarmed Saddam could have been overthrown internally. A Saddam in exile could have been killed or arrested. These options were bad, but conceivably offered higher odds of success than accepting war and the near-certain consequence of flight, and violent death. In a meaningful sense, Saddam chose war.

It is strange that Ikenberry and Deudney fail to consider these other figures. Given that the authors believe in an international order of 'cooperative problem-solving' and 'broad international coalitions', writing a more international history of the episode would have been a good place to start.

In trying to get liberalism off the hook, Ikenberry and Deudney stretch definitions, concepts, and history to breaking point. Realism in their hands is a grubby business, tainted by a pursuit of power that is morally empty and self-defeating. Liberalism, by contrast, almost stands outside time as a set of pristine concepts. At the heart of their framework is an ahistorical innocence about liberalism, as though liberalism cannot be complicit in empire, in the assertion of hegemony, in preventive war or other projects of imperial domination. Theirs is the antiseptic liberalism of Davos, with its clean vocabulary of the 'rules-based world order' and 'global norms'. Liberals who fall prey to these conceits seem unaware of the coercive and violent pathologies of their own tradition. It was Woodrow Wilson, whose legacy Ikenberry works so hard to distinguish from Bush, who made war and toppled governments often in the belief that benevolent force would create lasting peace, from Mexico and Latin America to the Russian civil war. Like Bush, Wilson argued in World War I that the US had entered the war for 'the overcoming of evil, by the defeat once [and] for all of the sinister forces that interrupt peace and render it impossible', to leave 'utterly destroyed' the old 'balance of power' order.[170] In 1916, Wilson drafted a speech that claimed 'It shall not lie with the American people to dictate to another what their government shall be'. His Secretary of State added in the margin 'Haiti, S Domingo, Nicaragua, Panama'.[171] This is the imperialism that doesn't know itself.

---

[168] 'Straw backs Exile Deal for Saddam', *BBC News*, 20 January 2003.

[169] Gerald Butt, 'Bahrain offers exile as Egypt reviles Saddam', *The Daily Telegraph*, 20 March 2003.

[170] Woodrow Wilson, *War and Peace: Presidential Messages, Addresses, and Public Papers*, 2 vols (New York: Harper, 1927), 1: pp. 255, 342–3, 547–8, 129.

[171] Cited in Warren Zimmerman, *First Great Triumph* (New York: Farrar, Straus and Giroux, 2002), p. 476.

Ikenberry and Deudney conclude by inviting realists to engage with the central security crisis of our time, the need to transform a world threatened by 'violence interdependence' and weapons proliferation, and implicitly, to downgrade deterrence as a foundation of security. Bush and Blair worked from the same diagnosis. This led them to preventive war and liberal hegemony. That these ideas lead consistently to bad results suggests that the very obsession with fictitious, undeterrable rogue states recklessly transferring WMD to terrorists, the exaggeration of threats linked to globalization, and the temptation to try systemic new 'solutions' to threats, is itself part of the problem. If academic liberals, to adapt their words, 'seek to return to engaging with the pressing security issues of this time', they might consider realists' argument that even in a globalized world, deterring, disrupting, and containing threats is a more prudent path.[172] But first they might reckon with the realization of the young journalist Karl Marx, who noticed in another moment of anxiety over globalization, the mid-nineteenth century, that it was the modernizing liberals who now preached 'red hot steel'.[173]

CONCLUSION

Regime change as a system of ideas rested on a series of misconceptions. There was the warped relationship with history. The makers of war held that the post-9/11 world had transformed from an era marked by the deterrence and containment of threats, changing the rules of the game and demanding a focus on the future as a year zero. Yet still, Britain had to be guided by cherry-picked historical cases showing the failure of appeasement from the late 1930s, and of successful post-war reconstruction in Germany and Japan. Supposing that they were embarking on a new project, decision-makers were in fact conditioned by the cumulative experience of short victorious wars in the recent past. There was also the claim that rogue actors like Saddam were irrational, pathologically aggressive, and undeterrable. Yet they were also apparently calculating survivalists, and would transfer weapons to terrorists for fear of reprisal, and could be disciplined into compliance by example and precedent. Regime change was necessary to deter other undeterrable rogues. Saddam's Iraq, hawks argued, posed a clear and present threat to neighbours and the UK with its growing WMD arsenal. Yet war was necessary because it would relieve

---

[172] On the salience of deterrence and the need to adapt it to today's conditions rather than abandon it, see Keir Lieber and Daryl G. Press, 'Why States Won't Give Nuclear Weapons to Terrorists', *International Security* 38:1 (2013), pp. 80–104; Elbridge Colby, 'Restoring Deterrence', *Orbis* 51:3 (2007), pp. 413–28.

[173] Cited in Douglas Hurd, *The Arrow War: an Anglo-Chinese Confusion 1856–60* (London: Collins, 1967), p. 56.

the country of sanctions that had shattered its economy and degraded its infrastructure, while somehow leaving its WMD programme intact to grow quickly. The Iraq of 2003, beggared by sanctions, somehow retained the capabilities of the Iraq of twenty years earlier. As Chapter 3 explores, the government and the Parliament made one more weighty calculation that the self-styled modernizers drew from the past, that by taking part in the war, Britain could guide the American superpower.

3

Atlantic Ambitions

> To oppose the US administration would be a serious step. But this is a serious matter; and what is influence for?
>
> Sir Michael Quinlan, 2002

> He raised steel tariffs and got very little response.
>
> Alastair Campbell diary, meeting of Prime Minister Blair and Vice President Cheney, 11 March 2002[1]

Britain went to war in Iraq partly driven by an old ambition, to gain and ensure unequalled influence in Washington DC. It was an effort at 'bandwagoning' that is often misunderstood. Rather than subordinating itself to receive material benefits, British decision-makers believed that by aligning with the US in the War on Terror, they were generating the ability to steer a superpower that otherwise might run amok and jettison itself from the international community. As we have already seen, British decision-makers genuinely believed in the merits of striking Iraq, and agreed with their American counterparts on the fundamentals, that in the words of Richard Dearlove, Chief of MI6, that it was 'very much in HMG's interest' and the outcome was of 'enormous significance' for the national interest.[2] The bandwagoning was not hollow. As well as this real convergence, the ambition to influence America was driven by a number of forces: a simple fear of how America might react to the 9/11 attacks; a habitual and reflexive instinct among the British governing and political class that London could play Greece to America's Rome; a desire to shape the consequential military campaigns that were already being conceived in Washington; a concern for Britain's relative place in the Euro-Atlantic pecking order; a confused and sentimental concept of international 'friendship'; and as preparations gathered momentum, a fear of being left out. As before in the history of the Anglo-American relationship, these ambitions proved unfounded on all major fronts, diplomatic,

---

[1] Alastair Campbell, *The Burden of Power*, 11 March 2002, p. 187.
[2] Letter, Dearlove to Manning, 27 December 2001, Iraq Policy.

military, and economic. They are based on a flawed understanding of how American policymaking works. As friendly and as historically intertwined as the two countries are, the United States is a separate great power that pursues its interests remorselessly. It is not open to permanent capture by any one state's lobbying. That does not make America a lesser power. It makes it unexceptional. And as an unexceptional power, the United States quickly met its own limits. Even by the second term of the Bush administration, it was seeking out and cultivating allies and clients for cooperation and burden-sharing. The implication is that Britain within the medium term, if not the short term, could have maintained the capacity to exert influence in Washington even while opposing the war in Iraq. This episode exposed a confusion around the very concept of 'influence': if continual alignment and harmony is required in order to ensure influence, then such influence can never be meaningfully used, and is effectively dormant. On the eve of a reckless military adventure, Britain ought to have tested the limits of its influence, and given its partner some unwelcome but friendly advice.

This chapter divides into three parts.[3] In Part I, I put in historical context the ambition that London has traditionally harboured since the World War II, and its disappointments. In Part II, I examine the first reactions of the Blair circle to the 9/11 attacks, the fears and sense of possibility that it awakened, and the conception of Iraq as a platform for elevating Britain's stature in Washington. In Part III, I identify the flaws in this vision and how those flaws surfaced in the pre-war planning and the course the conflict then took.

PART I. BANDWAGONING AND THE BLOOD PRICE

The history of the 'special' Anglo-American relationship is one of extravagant expectation and disappointment. According to Tony Blair, participating alongside America at risk of serious costs was vital to reforging the relationship with the superpower. As he asked, rhetorically, 'Are you prepared to commit, are you prepared to be there when the shooting starts?'[4] From the outset, the assumption was that participation would yield influence, abstention would reduce it. 'If you just go to someone and say, "You're completely wrong. Forget it, the amount of influence you are likely to have... is less"', reasoned Jonathan Powell.[5] Laying out this doctrine to an assembly of British

---

[3] I am grateful to the journal *International Affairs* for permission to use some of the material from an earlier article: Patrick Porter, '*Last Charge of the Knights*? Iraq, Afghanistan, and the Special Relationship', *International Affairs* 86:2 (2010), pp. 355–75.

[4] *BBC News*, 6 September 2002, at http://news.bbc.co.uk/1/hi/uk_politics/2239887.stm.

[5] Jonathan Powell, Testimony, 8 January 2010, pp. 39–40.

ambassadors in January 2003, Blair explained that the 'first principle' of foreign policy was to remain America's 'closest ally' and to 'influence them to broaden their agenda'.[6] There was always a tension within these claims. That Britain should participate in order to create leverage did not easily sit with the claim that participation against proliferating rogue states was a matter of absolute principle, born of the harmony of morality, strategic interests, and trans-Atlantic ties that was a signature theme of Atlanticist rhetoric. What is the relationship 'in theory', and in practice?[7]

The 'special relationship' conceit expresses a hopeful, vicarious ambition for Britain's role in the world. To 'bandwagon' is to align with a stronger power in the belief that the costs of resisting it outweigh the gains.[8] Britain's bandwagoning, though, carried an unusually optimistic aim. 'Special' means more than a transactional exchange of services, whereby loyalty is rewarded by preference or practical benefits like intelligence sharing, consultation rights, or technology transfer. Britain, allegedly, could guide the direction of American foreign policy by bandwagoning with it. As the Foreign Office advised in 1944, 'we can help to steer this great unwieldy barge, the United States of America, into the right harbour'.[9] In return for its solidarity, as well as a European ally and a strategic base in the UK, there would be a great pay-off. This obviously reflects an assumption about the greater wisdom of the older and declining power, tutoring the new power which was potentially wayward, a concern that endures. This vision was supposedly incarnated in the Roosevelt–Churchill partnership. As former prime minister, Churchill the part-American most famously sketched the lineaments of the relationship in his 'Sinews of Peace' speech of March 1946.[10] Churchill's rationale was both sentimental and hard-headed. Pan-cultural identity, a sense of shared values and history, formed one part of the relationship. America and Britain were kindred, bonded

---

[6] 'Full Text: Tony Blair's Speech', *The Guardian*, 7 January 2003.

[7] On the history and anatomy of the Special Relationship, see John Baylis (ed.) *Anglo-American Relations Since 1939: The Enduring Alliance* (Manchester: Manchester University Press, 1997); Alex Danchev, *A Very Special Relationship: Field Marshal Sir John Dill and the Anglo-American Alliance* (London: Brasseys, 1986); and *On Specialness: Essays in Anglo-American Relations* (London: Macmillan, 1998); for competing arguments on its viability and future, see John Baylis, 'The 'Special Relationship' A Diverting Myth?', in Cyril Buffet and Beatrice Heuser (eds) *Haunted by History: Myths in International Relations* (Providence: Berghahn Books, 1998), pp. 118–34; Jerome B. Elie, 'Many times doomed but still alive: An attempt to understand the continuity of the special relationship', *Journal of Transatlantic Studies* 3 (2005), pp. 63–83; William Wallace and Christopher Phillips, 'Reassessing the Special Relationship' *International Affairs* 85:2 (2009), pp. 263–84.

[8] Quincy Wright, *A Study of War* (Chicago: University of Chicago Press, 1942), p. 136; Kenneth Waltz, *Theory of International Politics* (New York: McGraw Hill, 1979), p. 126.

[9] Cited in David Reynolds, 'Roosevelt, Churchill and the wartime Anglo-American alliance, 1935–1945: towards a new synthesis', in Hedley Bull and William Roger Louis (eds), *The 'Special Relationship': Anglo-American Relations Since 1945* (Oxford: Clarendon, 1986), pp. 85–6.

[10] Winston Churchill, 'The Sinews of Peace', speech, Westminster College, Fulton, Missouri, 5 March 1946, at http://www.nato.int/docu/speech/1946/S460305a_e.htm.

through the common inheritance of Anglo-Saxon blood ties, language, and law. The second was practical and strategic. A marriage of Anglo-American power made sense because of shared security interests and interlinked global economic interests. With the US as the mediator, the UK could work through it to attain a global prestige that exceeded its economic and military muscle. Britain would attain an unparalleled influence in Washington. This would be exercised through close cooperation between bureaucracies, collaboration through both militaries, through intelligence sharing, and after 1958, in relation to nuclear weapons. After 1945, it was quickly reaffirmed, when Britain's Attlee government sent a brigade group to Korea on the basis that meaningful contributions sustained the partnership. In its most self-congratulatory form, Britain as the junior but more seasoned partner would play Greece to America's Rome, 'civilising and guiding the immature giant', in the worlds of Harold Macmillan, the weaker but more seasoned ex-hegemon educating the uncouth overdog.[11] Britain may no longer be a hegemonic world power. But by working through the US as well as preserving its nuclear weapons and its place on the Permanent Five of the UN Security Council, it need never resign itself to being just another European nation state. By steering the American giant, Britain could attain an outsized ability to set the agenda and mediate between the European Union and the US. In the article of faith coined by former Foreign Secretary Douglas Hurd in 1993, it enabled Britain to 'punch above her weight'.[12]

The practice of the relationship is more fraught. Later in the same year that Hurd coined the boxing metaphor, a leaked league table ranked the importance of foreign countries to the US, numbering Britain below Germany and in the wide company of France, China, Japan, Russia, Mexico, Iraq, Canada, and Israel.[13] Already in World War II, as the British Empire and the American republic fought on the same side under the aegis of the Atlantic Charter, there was between them a constant tension and power struggle. This friction was a product of the shifting material power balance between them, as Washington gradually realized its vast latent industrial and mobilization strength to outweigh Britain's bargaining power, and it was driven by conflicting interests. Britain was fighting partly in the hope of retaining its Empire. America opposed the colonialism of old Europe, and fought with the intent to dismantle the financial and trading structures on which it rested, replacing its imperial preference system, the Stirling bloc, and the pound's status as reserve currency with US-designed institutions (the International Monetary Fund and

---

[11] David Reynolds, 'A "Special Relationship"? America, Britain and the international order since the Second World War', *International Affairs* 62:1 (1985/1986), pp. 1–20, p. 2.

[12] Speech at Chatham House, reported in *The Financial Times*, 4 February 1993.

[13] Patrick Cockburn, 'Germany tops the US global pecking order', *The Independent*, 4 July 1993.

World Bank) and the dollar. The 'sheep's eyes' telegrams of March 1944 between President Franklin Roosevelt and Prime Minister Winston Churchill reflected an uneasy mix of collaboration and competition, as America sought to replace Britain as the dominant regional power in the Middle East, and prise open its protected markets.[14] Britain as a victor power emerged as a financial supplicant, almost exhausted by the strain of the conflict, the task of reconstruction and the unforgiven debt burden it imposed.

The fragility and realities of the relationship were highlighted by other points of collision. In the Suez crisis of 1956, the hinge event in the post-war Anglo-American relationship, the US Sixth Fleet stalked and harassed British ships in the Mediterranean, fouling their radar and sonar, menacing them with aircraft and lighting them up at night with searchlights.[15] With Stirling and oil supplies under pressure, President Dwight Eisenhower coerced Britain with the simple formula of no ceasefire: no loans. Patronage could be rapidly withdrawn and regardless of recent history, blood ties, or shared visions of Western-enforced order. Former Commander in Chief Middle East Land Forces, Sir Charles Keightley, spelled out the implications of the crisis as British policymakers saw them: 'This situation with the US must at all costs be prevented from arising again.'[16] Even with its nuclear capability and European garrisons, permanent seat on the UN Security Council, and its far-flung network of bases and territorial possessions, Suez demonstrated brutally that Britain had become part of America's grand strategy. Britain from that moment was anxious to fit its policies to those constraints. At the same time, British governments frequently hoped and tried to steer Washington in favourable directions for the sake of influence as a means as well as an end.

Even so, antagonism periodically flared up when their interests diverged. Prime Minister Harold Wilson walked a carefully ambiguous line in diplomatically supporting President Lyndon Johnson's escalation in Vietnam and covertly contributing intelligence, military hardware, and jungle warfare training, while committing no ground forces.[17] Wilson attracted denunciation at the time for his accommodation of America, whereas in the age of Iraq, he was retrospectively praised for keeping his distance. In the 1973–4 slump in Anglo-American relations, President Richard Nixon and his National Security Advisor Henry Kissinger used coercive diplomacy to punish British

---

[14] *Churchill and Roosevelt: The Complete Correspondence*, ed. Warren Kimball, vol. 3, *Alliance Declining, February 1944–April 1945* (Princeton: Princeton University Press, 1984), pp. 14–17.

[15] Keith Kyle, *Suez: Britain's End of Empire In the Middle East* (London: I.B.Tauris, 1991, 2011 edn.), pp. 411–12.

[16] Cited in Kyle, p. 412. On the legacy of Suez, the power shift, and the American assumption of stewardship leading to Iraq, see Martin Woollacott, *After Suez: Adrift in the American Century* (London: I.B.Taurus, 2006).

[17] Mark Tiley, 'Britain, Iraq and the Special Relationship', *History Today* 63:12 (2013).

non-cooperation over a US-initiated Declaration of Principles and the privacy of bilateral and UK–EEC discussions. Accordingly, they suspended intelligence and nuclear cooperation with the Heath government, and Heath later retaliated by restricting US spy-flight access to bases in the UK and Cyprus.[18] Infamously, the Reagan administration's initial triangulations between Argentina's fascist Galtieri regime and Britain over the contested Falkland Islands created a temporary crisis in relations. And even during the post–Cold War period of general amiability, when Britain consistently supported US interventions from the Gulf to Bosnia, the allies clashed over significant policy divides: the recognition of Sinn Fein, industrial tariffs, and the recognition of the International Criminal Court. Washington's preparedness to set aside historical solidarity to strong-arm its junior partner was displayed most consequentially during Britain's referendum to leave the European Union in June 2016. Despite Britain spending blood and treasure in Afghanistan and Iraq to support the War on Terror and thereby cement its standing in Washington, President Barack Obama made a blunt threat on 22 April of that year, that departing the EU would place the UK at the 'back of the queue' when seeking a bilateral free trade agreement.[19] This ought not to shock. Great powers have a long history of doing what they want. But after constant affirmations over fifteen years of Anglo-American unity and shared sacrifice, it shocked.

Thus, in the transatlantic relationship there is persistently a gap between words and deeds, expectations and reality. Through landmark occasions, such as D-Day commemoration, the Atlantic idea supplies a body of evocative rhetoric and politically charged images that celebrate and legitimize the role of both nations as heroic agents and allies in history. It is often framed as a 'friendship' between two kindred nations. This was instinctively the language President Bush used in thanking Blair for his in-person solidarity when attending the Joint Session of Congress on 20 September 2001.[20] Yet this promise of friendship is bound to disappoint.[21] It falsely personalized the totality of interests that link and separate countries. It misapplies to disparate nation states a social term for relationships between private individuals and groups, holding out the illusion that the alchemy of particular

---

[18] R. Gerald Hughes & Thomas Robb, 'Kissinger and the Diplomacy of Coercive Linkage in the "Special Relationship" between the United States and Great Britain, 1969–1977', *Diplomatic History* 37:4 (2013), pp. 861–905, p. 881.

[19] On this episode, see Tim Shipman, *All Out War: The Full Story of How Brexit Sank Britain's Political Class* (London: William Collins, 2016), pp. 231–2, 234–7.

[20] The White House, 20 September 2001, *Address to a Joint Session of Congress and the American People*.

[21] For a critique of the personalized vision of international friendship within alliances, see Kelly McHugh, 'Bush, Blair and Iraq: Alliance Politics and the Limits of Influence', *Political Science Quarterly* 125:3 (2010), pp. 465–91.

leader-to-leader relationships can supplant deeper interests. The pursuit of friendship can lead to a failure to ask difficult questions, as it indeed did. In the unforgiving history of international relations, there are no permanent friends, indeed there are few friends at all, and even dyads that think of themselves as friends will meet clashing interests, as Britain and the US did over Iraq down the track. The very notion that Britain should align itself with its 'friend' in order to shape its behaviour is an instrumental calculation, and not just born by affection. If harmonious collaboration came naturally between the republic and the parent country it fought to liberate itself from, the 'friendship' between the two would not need such constant and anxious reaffirmation.

PART II. TAMING THE SUPERPOWER

I have already used the term 'bandwagoning'. One feature of this concept, salient to the Iraq case, is that when weaker states align with a stronger state, that stronger state is also the potential source of danger.[22] That Britain would be 'closely identified' with the US was already an operating assumption of government.[23] Part of Blair's first response to the 9/11 attacks was fear, the fear of America's possible reaction, and a desire to open channels with Washington to tame its response. For the first days after 9/11, Blair fretted that Washington's response would be 'immediate, inappropriate, and indiscriminate',[24] one minister recalled weeks later, and that 'TB's immediate concern', diarized Alastair Campbell, 'apart from the obvious logistical steps we had to take, was that Bush would be put under enormous pressure to do something irresponsible.' In the first intelligence briefing after the attack, the Director General of MI5 likewise forecast that 'the pressure on the Americans to respond quickly, even immediately, would be enormous.'[25] With the campaign in Afghanistan progressing in mid-November 2001, Jonathan Powell urged Blair to act as a restraining influence on Bush, to counter the 'right wing of the Republican Party' and the Pentagon, and resist the shift to start bombing Somalia and Iraq.[26] The determination to keep America within the frame of

---

[22] Randall Schweller, 'Bandwagoning for Profit: Bringing the Revisionist State Back In', *International Security* 19:1 (1994), pp. 72–107, p. 80.

[23] As the Joint Intelligence Committee assumed in its assessment of the terrorist threat. Minutes, 14 September 2001, cited in *The Report of the Iraq Inquiry*, pp. 326–7.

[24] David Blunkett in BBC interview, *On the Record*, cited in Con Coughlin, *American Ally: Tony Blair and the War on Terror* (New York: Harper Collins, 2006), p. 147.

[25] Diary note, Tuesday 11 September 2001, Alastair Campbell, *The Blair Years: Extracts from the Alastair Campbell Diaries* (London: Arrow, 2007), pp. 560–1.

[26] Minute Powell to Prime Minister, 15 November 2001: 'The War: What Comes Next?'

existing alliances and institutions—in Blair's own words, to avert the danger of the US 'jumping out of the international system'—was affirmed by a close aide.[27] Contrary to the 'poodle' interpretation,[28] it was not a case of Washington actively leaning on allies for support. In the months after 9/11, London did more to reach out. The Bush administration did not place emphasis on 'outreach, consultation and good relationships'.[29] It was rather Blair who attempted to orchestrate the reactions of nations to Washington, and to steer Washington itself, with a heavy campaign of phone calls, trips, and transatlantic conferences, meeting with fifty-four leaders in the two months after 9/11.[30] The intent, if not the outcome, was to make Britain a tutor, not a vassal.

This fear, of the superpower becoming a runaway train, flowed also from older anxieties. Before 9/11 opened the new era, British officials worried that the new Bush administration was dangerously unilateralist and would dismantle the structures of internationalism and peace, as former ambassador Meyer recalled, 'We were very, very worried that if the Americans went *gung ho* for getting rid of the anti ballistic missile treaty and started dismantling some of the key elements of old *detente* that this could unravel—seriously could prejudice the relationship with Russia and all kinds of other repercussions'.[31]

In retrospect, it is easy to forget the openness of the post-9/11 moment, when the international audience held its breath in anticipation of America's reaction. Consider that the most powerful state in history had just been on the receiving end of a major act of urban terror. It had suffered the butchery of thousands of its citizens and a humiliating attack on its nerve centres. The hijackers had not just slaughtered, but inflicted unimaginable fear on civilians who chose to leap from the skyscrapers rather than burn to death. Anthrax attacks in Washington seemed to have been directed against members of the administration. This had become personal. Amidst expressions of international solidarity, there were eruptions of anti-Americanism, from open Palestinian celebrations in East Jerusalem of disputed size, to a jeering open letter from Saddam Hussein, and before a BBC *Question Time* audience, accusations directed at the US ambassador that Washington had

---

[27] 'He was determined that the US must not feel that it was on its own, and that it had friends that would stand by it... how America responded to these attacks would define its relations with the rest of the world, and Blair believed it was crucial that we were part of that decision-making process'. Cited in Coughlin, *American Ally*, p. 154, 'system' p. 113.

[28] See Samuel Azubuike, 'The "Poodle Theory" and the Anglo-American "Special Relationship"', *International Studies* 42:2 (2005), pp. 123–37.

[29] As Jeremy Greenstock recalled, Iraq Inquiry Statement, November 2009, p. 5.

[30] Peter Riddle, *Hug Them Close: Blair, Clinton, Bush and the 'Special Relationship'* (London: Politico's, 2004), p. 156.

[31] Christopher Meyer testimony, 26 November 2009, p. 12.

brought al-Qaeda's aggressions upon itself.[32] There were rumours, including wild ones, of fifth columnists celebrating and preparing further attacks.[33] Whether or not such displays were truly representative of wider reaction, they were perceived, and a feedback loop formed between hostility, resentment, and retaliation. Going by the historical record, the US was a state that had struck back remorselessly when attacked or when it met resistance. It had interned populations, levelled cities and countrysides, destroyed jungle with napalm, and had been the first and only state to incinerate civilian populations with atomic strikes. The occupant of the White House had a Texan drawl that triggered memories of Lyndon Johnson and his merciless bombing of Indochina. Bush as governor had keenly presided over the death penalty. As president he was deploying the 'dead or alive' language of the Wild West, and at one point, even promised a 'crusade'. Even worse, they were not reacting in the knowledge that, over fifteen years later, 9/11 would remain the only mass casualty terrorist attack of that magnitude. Fair or unfair, crude or sophisticated, there was, especially in Europe, a long-standing nightmare that the familiar, English-speaking power whose capital, protection, and products the world craved could transform quickly into a brutish and culturally different Leviathan, especially when wounded. These fears were magnified for the British government when the NATO Secretary General Lord Robertson rallied the transatlantic alliance to invoke Article V of its Charter, committing members to common defence on the basis that the attack on the US was an attack on them all. This historic step, however, met with perceived indifference in Washington. This perception of indifference may have been unfounded, and may have come about more as a result of procedural delays than disregard,[34] but Robertson and European onlookers feared that American hardliners in the hour of emergency wished to keep their power unfettered.[35] Officials like Sir Jeremy Greenstock who believed that Britain's objective should be to prevent regime change being the default option, feared a policy vacuum over Iraq and argued there 'was an urgent

---

[32] Imtiyaz Delawala, 'What ABC News Footage Shows of 9/11 Celebrations', *ABC News*, 4 December 2015.

[33] Joshua Keating, 'The Long, Strange History of the 9/11 Celebrations Meme', *Slate*, 23 November 2015.

[34] As M.A. Smith argues, 'How NATO Survived George W. Bush: An Institutionalist Perspective', *Journal of Transatlantic Studies* 15:1 (2017), pp. 61–76, pp. 70–1.

[35] Former NATO Secretary General Javier Solana declared that 9/11 and its aftermath had shown Article 5 to be 'Useless! Absolutely Useless!', quoted in Ivo Daalder, 'The End of Atlanticism', *Survival* 45:2 (2003), p. 155; see also John Kampfner, *Blair's Wars* (London: Free Press, 2003), p. 117. Robertson judged that 'The US made a mistake in not taking up our offer of support', interview, Coughlin, *American Ally*, p. 156; James Rubin, 'Stumbling into War', *Foreign Affairs* 82:5 (2003), p. 59.

need' to craft a strategy with the US 'at a level which binds in the whole Administration'.[36]

Therefore, British policymakers could be forgiven for anticipating a faster, bloodier, unilateral, and more indiscriminate response. Only in retrospect do we know that compared with the speed and violence with which it could have responded, the US was at first relatively restrained. Compared hypothetically to other great powers in history, the tentatively and carefully planned military campaign in Afghanistan that did not open until 7th October, almost a month later, and even the programme of torture and rendition, were comparatively limited. How might Ottomans, Mongols, Mughals, Hapsburgs, Romanovs, Caesars, Victorians, Manchus, Shoguns, or Nazis have reacted to an equivalent atrocity, if they had possessed the same destructive capabilities? How patient would they have been to appeals for proportionality, to consult allies, seek the approval of international institutions, or to uphold the nuclear taboo?

A less dramatic fear also presented itself, one rooted in historical memory from Suez. The contemplation of war with Iraq could leave Britain marginalized. In December 2001, the FCO in its communication with Downing Street identified an 'unwelcome dilemma', 'support unlawful and widely unpopular action or distance ourselves from a key US policy'. This suggested in turn that Britain take part in the discussion. Before decisions in Washington took place, 'we need to influence the debate.'[37] Downing Street was already engaged in ways that the FCO and MOD were unaware of, through a traditional channel of Anglo-American dialogue, the discrete communication between Britain's SIS and the CIA.

That the new unipolar Rome would need an experienced Greece to tutor it in the ways of international life was both a private apprehension and a public rallying cry. If Britons were averse to a unilateralist, vengeful, and unruly superpower overreacting to mass terrorism, Blair argued that joining Bush's posse under an international banner was a necessary step in applying restraints. Wariness about America's proclivities itself became a reason to participate. Making the case for war in the Commons in March 2003, Blair warned that standing British forces down at the final hour would damage American internationalism, turning it into a dangerous lone wolf: 'if our plea is for America to work with others, to be good as well as powerful allies, will our retreat make them multi-lateralist? Or will it not rather be the biggest impulse to unilateralism there could ever be',[38] an argument he made also to

---

[36] Letter Greenstock to Manning, 29 October 2001, 'Iraq: Cabinet Office Meeting, 30 October'.
[37] Letter, Simon Mcdonald (Principle Private Secretary) to Michael Tatham (then Blair's Private Secretary, Foreign Affairs), 3 December 2001.
[38] 'Full Text: Tony Blair's Speech', *The Guardian*, 18 March 2003.

the cabinet: 'we must steer close to America. If we don't we will lose our influence to shape what they do'.[39] UK Foreign Secretary Jack Straw also warned that to abandon support for the US at the late stage of March 2003 would accelerate American unilateralism and 'reap a whirlwind'.[40] During a briefing meeting on the campaign plans for Iraq, Secretary of Defence Hoon had asked Blair to use his influence to restrain Bush, who was 'going for it' and whose ideas could inflict lasting damage on Iraq.[41] Hoon's consistent view was that British involvement would enhance US planning, thus putting the Greece-Rome logic into concrete form, but he had added a qualifier, that if the US lacked a credible plan, Britain could hold back support.[42] From the vantage point of military planning, earlier engagement and earlier commitment were pressing, as Britain's lead-time for any deployment to the Gulf was longer than America's, but this pressure circumscribed just how far Britain could exert leverage. As Colin Powell's leaked memo for the Crawford summit indicates, Blair knew this was a commitment of political capital. He 'knows he may have to pay a political price for supporting us on Iraq, and wants to minimise it. Nonetheless, he will stick with us on the big issues. His voters will look for signs that Britain and America are truly equity partners in the special relationship'.[43]

If the 'blood price' was the necessary down payment on continual influence, that blood would be offered through ground forces and a land commitment. The British armed forces are one of the main instruments through which the special relationship is symbolized, asserted, and measured. Britain defines its military-strategic power in relation to its American ally. Its Defence White Paper of 2003, *Delivering Security in a Changing World* (supplemented in 2004), presumes that Britain can only conduct major operations within a NATO or US-led coalition. It asserts that Britain should aim to shape the conduct and outcome of such campaigns, and regards interoperability with US forces as a 'major focus'.[44] At a higher level, Britain designs its forces 'to maintain its influence with America and its place at the international top table'.[45] This asset, of privileged access to Washington, must be recurrently

---

[39] James Naughtie, *The Accidental American: Tony Blair and the Presidency* (Oxford: Macmillan, 2004), pp. 83–4. On Blair's argument, see also Alex Danchev, 'I'm with you: Tony Blair and the Obligations of Alliance: Anglo-American Relations in Historical Perspective', in Lloyd Gardner & Marilyn Young (eds), *Iraq and the Lessons of Vietnam* (New York: New Press, 2007), pp. 45–58, p. 49.

[40] UK Parliament, House of Commons Foreign Affairs Committee, 4 March 2003, column 173, cited in James K. Wither, 'British Bulldog or Bush's Poodle? Anglo-American Relations and the Iraq War', *Parameters* (2003–2004), pp. 67–82, p. 72.

[41] Minute MA/DCJO (Ops) to MA (CJO), 15 January 2003, 'Briefing to the Prime Minister'.

[42] Minute Hoon to Prime Minister, 22 March 2002, 'Iraq'.

[43] 'Memorandum for the President, Your Meeting with the United Kingdom Prime Minister Tony Blair, April 5–7 2002 at Crawford'.

[44] UK Ministry of Defence, *Delivering Security in a Changing World* (London: Stationery Office, 2003), p. 19; *Delivering Security in a Changing World: Future Capabilities* (London: Stationery Office, 2004), pp. 2, 3.

[45] 'Britain's Armed Forces: Losing their way?', *The Economist*, 29 January 2009.

fought for. Thus, General Sir Richard Dannatt, Britain's former Chief of the General Staff, argued in June 2009 that Britain must increase its commitment to Afghanistan because 'maintaining military-strategic "partner of choice" status with the US offers a degree of influence and security that has been pivotal to our foreign and defence policy.'[46] The Army can boast a long history of working alongside American forces. It has been continuously engaged as a coalition partner since 9/11. It has a higher rate of deployment abroad than any other European power since World War II.[47] And it can draw upon a heritage of minor wars cherished within its institutional memory.

> Whitehall behaves strategically rather in the manner of an inveterate gambler with a small pot of chips. Britain wishes to stay in the strategic "game," the rules of which are set in Washington, and it perceives that in order to do so it needs to place a stake on the table. That stake is the Army.[48]

As well as seeking long-term diplomatic influence, Britain sought to influence the Iraq campaign as it was being prepared. Yet paradoxically, this created the pressure to conform. Momentum to participate triggered fears that influence would diminish if Britain pulled back once engaged, and that because of the demands of timetables, failure to engage early enough would result in the door being closed. Except for helping persuade Bush to address Iraq via the United Nations, anxiety to be included in CENTCOM's rapidly evolving plans trumped any concern to set preconditions for British participation. These pressures to make a firm land contribution are reflected in MOD correspondence. On 29 October 2002, the Private Secretary to the Secretary of State for Defence advised David Manning that the US military was beginning to plan its campaign with the assumption that the UK would not be involved, and that,

> If we are to keep the option open, and continue to have the strongest military cards to underpin our political influence, the Defence Secretary believes that we should indicate to the US that they should plan on the assumption that the land contribution should be available, subject to final political approval.[49]

That influence might be better exerted through the threat, implicit or explicit, of withholding support, and a reputation for selective support, even at the risk of exclusion, was hardly entertained. The permanent Under Secretary of State for Defence, Kevin Tebbit, placed emphasis on the need to conform with the

---

[46] 'Army Fury at Refusal to Bolster Afghan Campaign', *The Independent*, 1 June 2009.
[47] See William Wallace, 'The Collapse of British Foreign Policy', *International Affairs* 82:1 (2005), pp. 53–68, p. 53.
[48] David Betz & Anthony Cormack, 'Iraq, Afghanistan and British Strategy', *Orbis* 53:2 (2009), pp. 319–36, p. 326.
[49] Ministry of Defence advice to David Manning, 'Iraq: UK Military Options', 29 October 2002 (from Peter Watkins).

broad outline of US policy in order to exercise influence within in. Reporting back from Washington as the US moved to a 'war footing', he advised 'if we want our advice to be heeded', 'we need to place it in the context of counter-terrorism post 11 September'.[50] Tebbit in January 2003 advised the Secretary of State that were 'HMG' to fail to 'go along' with the US in the event of action against Iraq without a 'further enabling UNSCR',

> there would be significant damage... having valued profoundly the way we have stood shoulder to shoulder with them so far, the US will feel betrayed by their partner of choice... the damage to our interests and influence would be felt most immediately and strongly in the foreign policy and security field.[51]

Later recalling the logic of the decision to commit, Tebbit explained that 'If the United States is making a blunder, we must not allow them to make it alone'.[52]

The flawed logic of the 'special relationship' is here demonstrated. Influence, so the theory goes, must derive from acquiescence, and continued acquiescence to the outlines of US policy is necessary to retain influence.[53] This renders any influence highly circumscribed. Having pledged support for a policy, that support must continue and Britain can only influence its execution. Otherwise, the ability to influence policy will be withdrawn and estrangement or even punishment will follow. Past solidarity creates a path-dependent pressure to tow the line, in order to obtain an influence that Britain in the most critical hour dare not exercise or test. Accordingly, discussion within government of the option of holding back and the potentially pernicious consequences of joining the campaign was only rare and sporadic. When one aide suggested Britain not support the war, Blair dismissed the advice, on the basis that it would be the biggest shift in foreign policy in fifty years.[54] This begs the question of when, precisely, influence that has been painstakingly cultivated can be actually used. This issue was especially troublesome for the MOD. There was always an undercurrent of scepticism about the feasibility of the Iraq project, but it remained largely an undercurrent. It was outweighed by the instinctive traditional Atlanticism reflected in Tebbit's warnings, and by the anxiety that participation was not a simple 'yes/no' choice but required prior involvement with US planning, in ways that made early commitment hard to avoid.

---

[50] Telegram 1684 Washington to FCO London, 8 December 2001, 'Tebbit's Visit to Washington: Wider War Against Terrorism'.
[51] Note 14 January 2003, Kevin Tebbit to Secretary of State, 'Iraq: What If'.
[52] Cited by Michael Clarke, at RUSI Conference, 'The Chilcot Inquiry: Learning Lessons from Iraq', 15 July 2016.
[53] For a similar critique, see Alex Danchev, 'Greeks and Romans: Anglo-American Relations After 9/11', *The RUSI Journal* 148:2 (2003), pp. 16–19, p. 18.
[54] Campbell, *The Blair Years*, 23 July 2002, p. 630.

Reinforcing these pernicious trends was the problem that military plans and political choices were delinked in time. Britain's de facto commitment predated the concrete consideration of war plans, and Blair was only fully briefed on military plans on 17 January 2003. Striking is the overall timidity of military advice regarding the long-term potentiality of the campaign, with the exception of the worst-case scenarios warned of by the Chief of the Defence Staff.[55] Professional military advice only rarely raised problems of inadequate post-war plans and possible worst-case scenarios, even in the run-up to invasion, and the focus was restricted largely to the combat phases. There was scarce discussion between arms of government (MOD, the FCO) about the major implication of Britain's campaign plan to advance through southern Iraq, that it would take responsibility with that region and would be committing not to leave quickly. An earlier warning in September 2002 by the MOD Strategic Planning Group that one potential reason for *not* participating would be that in the US policy vacuum, British commitment would be 'open ended', was a concern that faded quickly.[56]

Between going in and staying out, there was another option that was smothered before it could get the airing it deserved. This was the less dramatic 'Harold Wilson' model of limiting Britain's liability, of offering diplomatic support and limited material involvement, without any appreciable land commitment. One of the most sophisticated pieces of advice came in a memo from Peter Watkins, Private Secretary to the Secretary of Defence on 22 July 2002, pulling together the judgements of key advisors. It judged the case for attacking Saddam 'deeply flawed': because of a lack of need given that containment had kept the WMD programme limited, because the attack could have 'unforeseen geopolitical ramifications' and could be the catalyst for an 'upsurge of violence' from Gaza to Kashmir, and because it could create a focusing crisis that robbed the occupying powers of the capacity to act elsewhere. Watkins also feared a long and destructive 'siege' of Baghdad that would benefit al-Qaeda and other terrorist groups, and given that Saddam could have prepared such a combat, it was a reasonable caution. Yet Watkins also estimated that refusing any support, such as basing access in Cyprus and Diego Garcia would 'severely damage' the relationship. But with the likelihood of a US campaign, the UK should offer 'reasonable' support while avoiding offering more. This option hardly penetrated the decision-making, however. It would not satisfy the requirement of 'being there' when the shooting starts, however, and would forego the prize of being a senior coalition participant.

---

[55] See Lawrence Freedman, 'On Military Advice', *RUSI Journal* (17 July 2017), pp. 1–7, p. 5.
[56] *The Report of the Iraq Inquiry: Volume VI*, HC265-VI, 'Section 6.4: Planning and Preparation for a Post-Saddam Hussein Iraq, mid-2001 to January 2003', p. 185.

PART III. NIGHT AND DAY, THE FLAWS OF EXPECTATION

Evidently, something was wrong with the expectations entailed in the 'special relationship' as it was perceived in London. The UK does not exert exceptional influence, though neither is it 'zero'. Not only does the pursuit of vicarious power exaggerate British influence. More fundamentally, it misconceives the nature of policymaking in the United States. It wrongly treats that country as susceptible to any one country's designs. And conversely, it overstates American power, inflating the long-term costs of opposition or disagreement.

We might reduce the confusion generated by the Anglo-American relationship by framing the duality of American policymaking in terms of 'day' and 'night'. By night, American policymakers (and many ordinary Americans) genuinely revere the memory of the Churchill era, the wartime alliance, and ties of blood, language, and shared history. If anything, the Churchill cult is more intense in the United States than in Britain, as the creators of Winston Churchill High School in Maryland could attest.[57] In the Iraq era, elite Anglophilia was strong. Historian Andrew Roberts, promoting his hyper-Atlanticist *History of the English Speaking Peoples*, was enthusiastically received at the highest levels by elites on an American tour in March 2007.[58] General David Petraeus toured Churchill's map and planning rooms in September 2009, and felt 'transported back to that earlier era of extraordinary US-UK cooperation'.[59] On taking office, President Obama praised British sacrifices in Afghanistan and reaffirmed the common bond of both nations, and the New England Historic Genealogical Society discovered that Obama and Churchill are distant relatives.[60] Blair's rousing speech to the Labour Party conference of October 2001 'resonated' around the United States.[61] The relationship still has mystique. It is a ritual totem to mobilize around.

Affection at night, however, does not necessarily translate into material influence in the cold light of the Oval Office, or the Congress. At the very time that Britain deployed 45 Commando into Afghanistan, the US put tariffs

---

[57] Michael Lind, 'Churchill for Dummies', *The Spectator*, 24 April 2004; see also Christopher Hitchens, 'The Medals of His Defeats', *Atlantic*, April 2002.

[58] Andrew Roberts, 'Diary', *The Spectator*, 21 March, 2007.

[59] Speech, The Fourth Colin Cramphorn Memorial Lecture, 17 September 2009, at http://www.policyexchange.org.uk/news/news.cgi?id=749, accessed 26 September 2009.

[60] 'The special relationship between the US and Great Britain is one that is not just important to me, it's important to the American people. And it is sustained by a common language, a common culture, and legal system that is directly inherited from the English system. Our systems of government are based on those same values...I expressed my extraordinary gratitude for the support in Afghanistan and the young men and women of Great Britain who have made enormous sacrifices'. Macer Hall, 'Obama: We Do Love Britain', *The Daily Express*, 14 February 2009.

[61] As Christopher Meyer observed, IIT, 26 November 2009, pp. 22–3.

on exports from UK of speciality steel.[62] There is a persistent disconnect between the payment of the blood price and the response of the recipient. Sir Christopher Meyer, the British envoy closest to the action in Washington, observed the American capacity to compartmentalize their 'sentimental and sincere affection' from the 'single minded pursuit of national interest', yet claimed that 'It is a gap we have to closel.'[63] How Britain could close that gap was not clear.

Iraq exposed the limits of British influence, in the same campaign that was supposed to confirm its stature as America's leading deputy. Britain, though, only exercised a marginal influence at best. Blair privately and unsuccessfully opposed the siege of Fallujah in 2004.[64] The Coalition Provisional Authority (CPA) overrode British concerns over the De-Ba'athification process of liquidating the ruling party from the entire Iraqi civil service, as well as British advice on economic development.[65] And if one of Britain's explicit aims, declared in its Defence White Papers, is to shape the way America designs and conducts its military campaigns, British officers often did not achieve this ambition. This became clear in the leaked report for the Chief of the General Staff, *Stability Operations in Iraq: An Analysis from the Land Perspective*, which found that the UK was powerfully constrained by the 'timetable and ideological views set in the United States. As one Senior Officer put it: 'the train was in Grand Central Station, and was leaving at a time we did not control.'[66] An interview with Colonel J.K. Tanner, formerly chief of staff, Multinational Division South East, also reflected the disappointments and anxieties of the 'special relationship' mindset.[67] In statements tainted with the suspect myth that colonial experience from generations before gave the British a distinctive capability to 'treat with Arabs', Tanner claimed that dealing with Americans corporately is like dealing with 'Martians', and that Britons were treated the same as other European countries such as Portugal. Americans conducted very little dialogue with them. Worse, they were confronted with the worst fear of British Atlanticists, that America might regard them no differently than other European nations. President Bush, extremely

---

[62] As Christopher Meyer lamented, IIT, 26 November 2009, p. 74.

[63] Letter Christopher Meyer to Jack Straw, 5 November 2001, 'America After 11 September'. Cited in *The Report of the Iraq Inquiry*, p. 344.

[64] Rajiv Chandrasekaran, *Imperial Life in the Emerald City: Inside Iraq's Green Zone* (New York: Random House, 2006), p. 307.

[65] Glen Rangwala, 'Deputizing in war: British policies and predicaments in Iraq, 2003–2007', *International Journal of Contemporary Iraqi Studies* 1:3 (2007), pp. 293–309, p. 300.

[66] *Stability Operations in Iraq (Op Telic 2.5) An Analysis from a Land Perspective*, p. 2, Introduction, paragraph 5.

[67] John F. Burns, 'U.K. Documents Show Friction with U.S. on Iraq', *The New York Times*, 23 November 2009; transcript of interview at http://www.telegraph.co.uk/news/newstopics/politics/defence/6634115/Iraq-war-files-British-colonels-scathing-attack-on-arrogant-bureaucratic-Americans.html, accessed 26 November 2009.

close to Blair, still did not fulfil Blair's vow that British support in Iraq would be repaid by a renewed American commitment to the 'Road Map' resolution of the Israel–Palestine conflict. The one notable anomaly is Blair's successful move to persuade the US against its preferences to pursue a second UN resolution authorizing military action in Iraq.[68] Other than that, if the yardstick was influencing the US to 'broaden its agenda', this demonstrably failed.

More broadly, as a pattern of observed behaviour, America historically and recently has often acted against and despite Britain's expressed wishes, even during periods of apparent closeness. Overriding British warnings, President Ronald Reagan's US invaded Grenada in 1983 and bombed Libya in 1986. In 1994–5, the US went against British advocacy and recognized the Provisional IRA as a negotiating partner. Kinship made Ireland as special to America as Britain. The UK has not altered America's stance on a range of fronts. It has not persuaded America to sign the Kyoto Treaty, nor did it dissuade President Donald Trump from withdrawing from the Paris Climate Agreement. It has not steered it towards signing up to the International Criminal Court. Similar failure is apparent with the Ottawa Convention on Land Mines. The two nations persistently diverge on the missile defence shield, and there is little evidence that President Obama's change of policy was attributable to British influence. British solidarity has not resulted in America making generous concessions on its industrial subsidies and tariffs. Demonstrably, Britain's power and capacity to influence America is more limited than the special relationship mindset allows.

There were tensions in the rationalizations given. At times, Blair publicly stressed that this was a grand transaction, that British participation was a vital brake on potential American unilateralism. Yet at other times, as we have seen, the commitment he articulated was absolute and irreversible. This was born of a simple defect in the 'grand bargain' theory. It overlooked the cold reality that influence can only be exerted with the coercive threat of abandonment or at least non-support, express or implied. Support given regardless of repeated non-reciprocation is more likely to generate complacency, not influence. Junior allies who wish to moderate the hegemon's behaviour are more likely to succeed by playing harder to get. When Blair took the absolute stance on the day of 9/11 to 'stand shoulder to shoulder with our American friends', promising they would 'not rest until this evil is driven from our world',[69] amidst the grand ideological declarations there needed to be hard-headed calculation. That in turn would require a greater dose of realpolitik even in

---

[68] Azubuike, 'The "Poodle Theory"', p. 135.
[69] National Archives, 11 September 2001, *September 11 attacks: Prime Minister's statement*, at http://webarchive.nationalarchives.gov.uk/20080909040211/http://www.number10.gov.uk/Page1596.

the emotive aftermath of the 9/11 atrocity. At the highest levels of government, life is not supposed to be easy.

Subsequent diplomatic history suggests fears that non-participation—or less participation—would damage Anglo-American relations in the long term were overstated. Within only one presidential term, Washington was reaching out to states that had opposed its policy.[70] The Bush administration had initially been truculent in its treatment of countries opposed to Iraq. It looked to punish dissidents, only to discover soon afterwards a need for international cooperation. 'As we were looking to the first proposals for rebuilding Iraq', recalled former National Security Advisor and Secretary of State Condoleezza Rice, 'The Pentagon wanted the contracts to go to the countries which had supported the war... in practice it made the United States look petty. Eventually we would want help from everyone—a *lot* of help—to rebuild Iraq.'[71] The 'Petraeus revolution', with its surge of fresh troops and renaissance in counterinsurgency technique, encouraged greater American engagement with British practitioners. And the Bush administration in its second term worked to reverse its isolation among anti-war European states and ease the strains created by its swaggering unilateralism. The White House altered its personnel, removing figures who had pressed for a swaggering unilateralism—Douglas Feith, Paul Wolfowitz, John Bolton, and later Donald Rumsfeld—and replaced them with pragmatists. It reached out to cultivate allies in the Middle East and in 'Old Europe', and even in March 2006 revealed that it had attempted to open dialogue with Iran over the condition of Iraq.

Against claims that Britain had to join the fight to maintain influence, a suggestive rebuttal is the case of France.[72] French opposition to the invasion of Iraq was strong. Its President Jacques Chirac and Prime Minister Dominic de Villepin expressed it in systemic terms, defining a France–German united Europe as the counterweight to American hyper-power, blocking the attempt to obtain a final UN resolution supporting war in March 2003, and exerting pressure on European states that supported invasion to fall in line with Paris.[73] With Saddam overthrown and America's campaign in its ascendancy, American officials and lawmakers, with the open acknowledgment of Secretary of State Colin Powell, earmarked France for retaliation, entertaining plans to impose

---

[70] See Philip H. Gordon, 'The End of the Bush Revolution', *Foreign Affairs* 85:4 (2006), pp. 75–86.

[71] Condoleezza Rice, *No Higher Honour: A Memoir of My Years in Washington* (New York: Broadway Books, 2011), p. 215.

[72] On Franco-American relations in Bush's second term, see Elaine Sciolino, 'Sarkozy Throws Open His Arms to Bush, and US', *The New York Times*, 7 November 2007.

[73] See 'France, America and Iraq: On the Brink', *Strategic Comments* 9:2 (2003), pp. 1–2; statements cited in James Graff and Bruce Crumley, 'France is Not a Pacific Country', *Time*, 16 February 2003.

trade sanctions, exclude it from international forums, and lessen its influence within NATO.[74] The bitterness of the fallout was impressive. It is therefore significant that within four years of the invasion, France under a new president successfully re-embraced the United States, and within six years of the invasion, it joined NATO's military command. Franco-US relations rebuilt around agreement on other international questions—the Iranian nuclear programme, Afghanistan, and Kosovo's independence. And Paris achieved this without changing its position on Iraq, and while criticizing the Bush administration's position on the environment.

Just as strong British support did not translate into exceptional influence, so too did outright French opposition not lead to permanent exclusion or punishment. Not only did the mythology of the Anglo-American 'special' relationship overstate Britain's capacity to shape American behaviour. It overstated America's level of strength. Even the superpower's abundant resources and appeal could be rapidly spent. Even a swaggering leadership in that superpower did not want to become a pariah amongst a significant share of the nations and with a damaged capacity for collective action. America was a great power of unprecedented relative strength. It was not a 'hyper-power'.

In a counterfactual universe, Britain may not have been able to prevent the invasion of Iraq. But the price for trying would have been neither as steep, nor as lasting, as feared. Opposing war would have alleviated Britain of significant material costs in the meantime, and would have served one intangible but vital interest. In another context, one critic suggested what Australia ought to have done in 1974–5, instead of acquiescing to a more predatory invasion and annexation of East Timor:

> We should have warned the Indonesians that they could not subdue the colony. We should have warned them that they could expect no support, only condemnation, from Australia. And we should have warned them that they were marching into their own Vietnam. Do I believe that this would have made a difference to the outcome? No. The history of East Timor would have been the same. But Australia's history would have been different in one crucial respect. We would not have shamed ourselves.[75]

This forewarning did not happen between 'friends' in 2003, and as a result Britain took part in a disastrous war that brought shame and humiliation in its wake. Such friendly advice did not happen partly because of a misconceived notion of how to pursue and obtain influence. And it did not happen because decision-makers generally agreed with Washington's calculus, and sought to shape its execution.

---

[74] Brian Knowlton, 'Officials Consider Ways to Punish France', *The New York Times*, 23 April 2003; Jim V [sic] & eHei, 'US Lawmakers Weigh Actions to Punish France, Germany', *The Washington Post*, 12 February 2003.

[75] John Birmingham, 'Appeasing Jakarta: Correspondence', *Quarterly Essay* 3 (2001), p. 102.

A fragile assumption lies at the root of any argument for waging war for the sake of credibility and reputation, namely the assumption that the campaign will succeed well enough to generate such dividends. Should a war for credibility falter, should it have the ironic result of raising doubts about one's reliability, commitments create pressure for further commitments. Thus, fighting for the sake of keeping stocks high in another capital can create a 'credibility trap'. One significant consequence of Britain's Iraq campaign, once it found itself overextended, was to raise pressure to succeed in the concurrent campaign in Afghanistan. As Tim Bird and Alex Marshall demonstrate in their account of the fraught 'Af-Pak' war, there was a tragic feedback loop between anxiety over reputation, deterioration of Britain's position in Iraq, and the alternative theatre. By early 2004, Britain's presence in Southern Iraq

> was both increasingly unpopular domestically and onerous in terms of resources. As the Iraqi security situation began to deteriorate markedly through 2004 and 2005, a growing yearning became evident in London to reduce the British commitment. The problem was how to do this while maintaining the positive relationship with Washington that had been at the heart of the British decision to join the invasion of Iraq in the first place. Taking on some of the 'stabilization and reconstruction' burden in Afghanistan appeared to provide a neat solution. UK forces could be presented not as 'going home' but rather as redeploying to the Afghan theatre.[76]

'Stabilization and reconstruction' was an attractive scenario, born of a limited intelligence picture and a concern to deploy and redeem the Iraq failure, ahead of rigorous appraisal. As it happened, British forces were about to deploy into the hardest fighting since the Korean War. Capable of regeneration, the Afghan Taliban had an insolent way of deciding for themselves whether the campaign would now move into a low-intensity stage of development in a fragile state. And the disturbing possibility was revealed within the rationale of fighting for alliance influence. Not only would commitment in Iraq not create meaningful strategic leverage once the shooting started. By 2014, according to a Freedom of Information Request, British forces had fired 46 million rounds of ammunition in Afghanistan.[77] Hunting the Great White Whale of transatlantic stature, the shooting would have to go on, and with no end in sight.

---

[76] Tim Bird & Alex Marshall, *Afghanistan: How the West Lost its Way* (Yale: Yale University Press, 2011), p. 157.

[77] Chris Hughes, 'British Army Fired 46 million rounds at Taliban costing taxpayer £200 million', *Daily Mirror*, 7 April 2015.

4

Weighing the Arguments

> I have mentioned once before in the House the advice that was given by Archidamus to his Spartan allies. He said that slow and cautious may be seen as wise and sensible. Many years later, the Athenian superpower, in its impatience, found out that he was absolutely right: impatience had imperilled it and led to its destruction. I say earnestly and honestly to the Government: their impatience will reap a whirlwind...
>
> Peter Kilfoyle MP, 18 March 2003
>
> I beseech you, in the bowels of Christ, think it possible you may be mistaken.
>
> Oliver Cromwell, 1650

If the spirit of this book is to question assumptions, then the book's critique should also be placed under scrutiny. Was the invasion of Iraq in 2003 a blunder? I will argue that it was. By blunder, I mean more than a military misfortune, or the failure of an institution 'to learn, anticipate, or adapt' to the demands of a mission assigned to them.[1] Rather, I mean a failure of judgement about the most fundamental question, taken by the government with professional advice, on whether or not to invade, the prospects of success, and whether it would be worth it. A blunder is a 'careless error' with results that are much worse than intended or expected, when viable alternative courses are available. If the spirit of this book is to plea for less dogmatism, it is only fair that the arguments against the war, like those in favour, are properly weighed in the balance.

I argue that striking Iraq in 2003 was a major error. To be sure, it does not reach the level of history's major, self-inflicted military misadventures that altered the global balance, like classical Athens' Sicilian expedition in 415 BC or Imperial Germany's gratuitous bid for power in 1914. If it does not match those levels of casualties and financial cost, it was still a consequential overreach. It wasted scarce resources and created significant opportunity costs, for

---

[1] See Eliot A. Cohen & John Gooch, *Military Misfortunes: The Anatomy of Failure in War* (New York: Free Press, 1990), p. 247.

the bad overall return of intensifying the turmoil of a region, making international security problems worse, and damaging the moral authority of the countries involved. The Iraq campaign did not finish off Britain as a major power, just as classical Athens after its calamitous Sicilian adventure found fresh timber and built new ships after the retreat from Syracuse.[2] Both Athens and Britain, and the world, could still have done without these blunders. If it did not match worse historic wars in scale of harm and self-harm, it did match those blunders in type. A major power driven by a mix of fear and optimism gravely injured itself—and others—by gratuitously launching a war that was not triggered by a pressing need, and when there were alternative and workable strategies on offer. That premise still needs defending. Operation Iraqi Freedom, and Operation Telic, still have eloquent advocates. Those of us who judge it a blunder must honestly confront the price, and the implications, of our stance. In this chapter, I lay out a test, informed by classical realist tradition, on which we can make a provisional judgement. I then develop the strongest possible arguments, both the claims made at the time and retrospective ones, and test them against considerations of cost, gain, and as far as possible, counterfactual speculation. I then address each line of defence.

In Part I, I establish a standard or benchmark by which we can evaluate the decision, and develop a 'prudential' test. In Part II, I construct the strongest possible arguments in defence of the invasion, and the counterfactual scenarios they depict. In Part III, I demonstrate that those arguments fail to meet the test. In Part IV, I argue that there was an alternative strategy available, one that steered a course between passivity and overreach, one of containment and deterrence, that would have enabled the international community to monitor and disrupt Iraq's weapons programme and checked any future aggression. In Part V, I refute one of the most forceful arguments in favour of war, made in hindsight by the Labour political advisor John McTernan. McTernan's suggestion that without an invasion, the world would be 'ruled by dictators and jihadists' is the kind of counterfactual argument that anti-war critics often fail to confront, and deserves return fire.

PART I. BY WHAT STANDARD?

Some will regard this chapter's inquiry as banal. *Of course* it was a blunder, as one strand of post-Chilcot opinion assumes. Those who dismiss the Chilcot Inquiry regard the issue as obvious, the inquest merely confirming what was already self-evident. A cabal of decision-makers, they allege, forced a conflict

---

[2] As John R. Hale argues, *Lords of the Sea: How Trireme Battles Changed the World* (New York: Viking, 2014), p. 206.

on an unwilling people and against international sentiment.[3] That Iraq was an error is a position now held by the balance of opinion at home and abroad. With this stance, critics take on the closed-minded attitude they criticize in warmakers. The case should not be considered closed. A proper reckoning is due.

Firstly, we are trying to learn something from the experience. We are doing so to guide future judgements when we find ourselves again in the fog, where we won't have the vantage point of hindsight. By what standard should we arbitrate the issue of whether the war was defensible or disastrous? Cases of military action gone wrong draw lamentation, but so do cases of inaction or restraint, such as Rwanda. If we are not content to retreat into unreflective consensus, or conformity with majority folk memory, or wait until afterwards to commend wars that seem to succeed, and denounce those that fail, we need to ask what exactly makes Iraq a blunder and offer an accounting of how we are to judge in the first place.

The issue deserves closer scrutiny also for another reason. Without a counterfactual case, the indictment against the war is inadequate. Arguments about war are intrinsically counterfactual. To argue that a party ought not to have gone down one path is implicitly and necessarily to suggest that alternative paths were preferable. Yet critiques all too often fail to offer a spelled-out counterfactual assessment of the decision. Alternatives were not self-evidently wiser. As one hawk suggests,

> the basic decision to use military force to remove from power a man who had overseen a regime of unspeakable barbarity and cruelty remains, in my view, the right one. And I mean morally right. The failure to implement that choice competently does not, for me, change that basic moral conclusion. That view has, of course, been badly tested over the last 14 years, but I still hold it for the simple reason that I've yet to hear a convincing counter-factual, not least since most anti-war people can't be bothered to construct that scenario. They should work harder: just shouting 'Blair is a mass murderer, don't you watch the news?' isn't an argument.[4]

Indeed it is not. Hawks pose serious 'what if' questions: what were the alternatives to war? What risks and costs would US-led allies have borne if they had refrained from invading? They deserve answers.

Sceptics should explicitly make the case that is too often left merely implicit: that Britain and its allies could have better coexisted with Saddam's regime or its successors left in power, on acceptable terms. Alternatively, they would have been better off coping from a distance with an imploding post-Saddam

---

[3] Geoffrey Wheatcroft, 'The Tragedy of Tony Blair', *Atlantic* 294 (2004), pp. 56–70.
[4] James Kirkup, 'Tony Blair did not Bewitch us into backing war in Iraq', *The Daily Telegraph*, 6 July 2016.

Iraq. Altruistic concerns also demand a counterfactual evaluation: would Iraqis have fared better if the US-led coalition had avoided war? Those who argue that Iraq was a blunder and a warning against future preventive wars of this kind must confront these questions, or abandon the field to those who would repeat such experiments.

There are divisions too among the war's critics. For some, the error lay in its conduct, not it's conception. Even if it was incompetently waged, Iraq for this group should not cast doubt on the cause of armed interventionism itself. The West, they say, must still be prepared at times to overthrow regimes, occupy territories, and use force to transform regional orders. For those attached to armed idealism as a general orientation, the main response to Chilcot is not to ponder the errors of liberal wars. Counter-intuitively, it has become an occasion for them to reaffirm their belligerence. They do so by quarantining Iraq as a special and atypical case, from which we learn little beyond the limited and technical 'lesson' that it is better to plan thoroughly. For others, the separation of the war's execution from its conception represents an 'incompetence dodge', an alibi for what is, in fact, a suspect idea.

The case is not dead within influential opinion circles and especially in the Anglo-American debate. Defenders of the invasion remain vocal.[5] They defend the original decision and regularly update their defence. Subsequent developments, such as Libyan disarmament in 2003, the Arab Spring revolutions and the civil war in Syria from 2011, and the rise of the Islamic State in 2014 have called forth fresh apologias for the conflict. Blair in particular has made several interventions in the debate. Some critics dismiss these defences out of hand. Abrupt dismissal risks leaving the case for war unanswered, and reproduces the unreflective dogmatism that critics claim to oppose.

When the Iraq Inquiry finally published its report, hawks accused it of misjudgement. They maintain that the war was based on a sound calculus, despite its disappointments. It was ultimately the right thing to do, strategically and morally, even if it proved to be harder and more distressing than expected. Compared to alternative possible worlds in which the invasion did not take place, they maintain the invasion is defensible. If there was a failure, it was in the words of Fouad Ajami a 'noble failure', given the hazardous

---

[5] Philip Bobbitt, 'Chilcot's Iraq War Verdict needs Scrutiny beyond the Headlines', *The Financial Times*, 8 July 2016; Niall Ferguson, 'Tony Blair's Legacy? Don't be Too Quick to Judge', *The Boston Globe*, 11 July 2016; for earlier defences of the war after the fact, see Oliver Kamm, *Anti-Totalitarianism: The Left-Wing Case for a Neoconservative Foreign Policy* (London: Social Affairs Unit, 2005); Robert Kaufman, *In Defence of the Bush Doctrine* (Lexington: Kentucky University Press, 2007); Daniel Henninger, 'If Saddam Had Stayed: Saddam would have joined the nuclear bad-boys club with Iran and North Korea', *The Wall Street Journal*, 2 September 2010.

alternatives and what was at stake.[6] There was nothing inherently 'wrong' or misguided about the decision to eliminate Saddam Hussein.

For unrepentant hawks, the main question for the West is not one of judgement, but one of will. They charge that the error was Western abandonment. Iraq may have been a long and bloody slog, they recognize, but by 2010 and thanks to the leadership of President Bush and General Petraeus, the US wrested a victory out of crisis, a victory that was then spoiled by a feckless President Obama for the sake of domestic politics. A counter-history has now formed.[7] With echoes of 'rightist' American accounts of the loss of China after 1948 and Vietnam after 1975, this is the narrative of the 'lost victory'. For those who blame Obama, the main lesson of Iraq is not to focus on the original sin of its beginning but the failure of its ending, when the US in December 2011 abandoned Iraq prematurely to the Sunni Islamist wolves of the Islamic State and left it vulnerable to violent sectarian breakdown. There was indeed a blunder, only it was Obama's blunder of premature withdrawal. As one defence correspondent wrote in the wake of the Chilcot Inquiry, if we are asking who lost Iraq, we should blame Obama, not Blair.[8]

From the perspective of those who take the 'abandonment' interpretation, the main lesson is precisely not to overlearn the instinct for caution or to agonize over the invasion. If Iraq holds out lessons, they argue, it is two different ones, technocratic and moral. The technocratic lesson is that we need more careful and coordinated planning next time. The moral lesson is that we need the strategic patience to see it through. Advocates of counter-insurgency often begin from the premise that ambitious expeditionary wars like Iraq and armed nation-building efforts are almost inevitable, making it imperative to optimize the West's ability to wage them again.[9] This is a fatalistic stance, that seeks to shift debate from 'whether' to 'how' to conduct similar campaigns in future. It assumes, also, that the choice about when to leave is overwhelmingly the West's to make. As we will see, Iraqis also had a say.

How we remember Iraq, whether we judge the war 'worth it', who or what we blame for failure, will shape contests over diplomacy for a generation at least. It will affect how high a threshold for belligerence is set by states like the

---

[6] Fouad Ajami, *The Foreigner's Gift: The Americans, The Arabs and the Iraqis in Iraq* (New York: Free Press, 2006).

[7] Max Boot, 'What Chilcot Missed about Iraq', *Commentary*, 6 July 2016; James Traub, 'The Mess Obama Left Behind in Iraq', *Foreign Policy*, 7 October 2016; Victor Davis Hanson, 'The Costs of Abandoning Messy Wars', *The National Review*, 25 February 2016; Fouad Ajami, 'The Men Who Sealed Iraq's Disaster with a Handshake', *The Wall Street Journal*, 13 June 2014.

[8] Con Coughlin, 'Don't Blame Tony Blair for the Mess Iraq is in, blame Obama', *The Daily Telegraph*, 6 July 2016.

[9] John A. Nagl, 'A better war in Iraq: Learning counterinsurgency and making up for lost time', *Armed Forces Journal* (2006), pp. 22–8; 'Unprepared', *RUSI Journal* 153:2 (2008), p. 83.

UK. Historical verdicts will shape how British policymakers perceive crises that look similar. Iraq has already cast its shadow over subsequent decisions. The reluctance of intervening powers to insert ground forces into post-Gaddafi Libya in September 2011 reflected a disinclination to repeat the experiment of occupying countries against likely resistance. In the autumn of 2013, led primarily by the Labour opposition, whose leaders have renounced the Iraq War, the UK Parliament voted not to launch punitive airstrikes against Syria's Assad regime in response to its apparent use of chemical weapons against civilians. To some, this represented a calamitous collapse of internationalism that can be attributed to the memory of Iraq. To others, it reflects a prudent presumption against the recourse to war for liberal surgery, a wariness about using force beyond defence or deterrence. The stakes are high.

Any judgements about Iraq must be provisional. Arguments in favour of the war have shifted as circumstances have changed. Avowed supporters of the war, many of whom contributed directly to its public justification, have since shifted their reasoning, repented of some aspects of the policy, while raising fresh justifications. Former Bush speechwriter and neoconservative intellectual David Frum, for instance, judged that Washington overstated the threat that a disarmed Iraqi regime posed, noting the heavy costs of the war and the failure to establish a stable, Western-oriented government for all of Iraq, while pointing to the liberation of the Iraqi Kurds and shifting some blame onto Iraqis for the choice of sectarian misbehaviour.[10] Acknowledging five years after the invasion that the war inflicted worse suffering than he expected, Richard Perle prophesied that 'Iraqis will look back and say, we paid a terrible price, but it's worth it.'[11] The outward public reasoning of Tony Blair, especially, has proved flexible. Blair initially made disarmament the central justification and declared, in Parliament, that the movers of UN Resolution 1441 would delay it 'to give Saddam one further final chance to disarm voluntarily'.[12] He has since claimed that he would have invaded Iraq even in the event that Saddam fully disarmed,[13] and that his main aim was nothing less than to advance the modernization of the Middle East.[14] For a brief period, some hawks credited the war for making possible the Arab Spring revolutions of North Africa and the Middle East.[15] This line of argument has since

---

[10] David Frum, 'Iraq Isn't Ours to Save', *Atlantic*, 17 June 2014.
[11] David Kenner, 'Seven Questions: Richard Perle's Advice for Barack Obama', *Foreign Policy*, 16 November 2008.
[12] *Hansard*, 25 February 2003, col. 124.
[13] 'Blair: I would have removed Saddam Hussein anyway', *CNN*, 12 December 2009.
[14] Tony Blair, *A Journey* (London: Arrow Books, 2010, 2011 edn.), p. 387.
[15] Kanan Makiya, 'The Arab Spring Started in Iraq', *The New York Times*, 6 April 2013; Peter Wehner, 'Vindication for Bush's Freedom Agenda', *Commentary*, 28 January 2011; Christopher Hitchens, 'The Iraq Effect', *Slate*, 28 March 2011; Condoleezza Rice, *No Higher Honour:*

receded, given what became of the revolutions in Egypt, Tunisia, Libya, and the attempted revolution in Syria. It is not clear that Iraq did 'cause' these revolutions. Even if it did, the closeness of war with revolution is not an unambiguously good thing. The debate will doubtless evolve again. Ever since it began, the Iraq War has been a decision in search of a justification.

There is more to this than cynicism or the desire of the war's apologists for self-vindication. The shifting of rationales is inherent to the politics of war. Opinion about wars changes over time because circumstances and contexts change, and these changes condition judgement. At first, many Britons regarded World War I as a hard-won, noble victory over Prussian militarism. It was not until the Great Depression and Europe's interwar crisis that opinion shifted towards regret and disillusionment. As late as 1929, patriotic nationalist poets like Rupert Brooke vastly out-sold poets who stressed waste and futility, like Wilfred Owen.[16] In our own time, only in the light of the crisis in Iraq after 2003 did the Gulf War of 1990-1 (and President Bush I's decision to halt the ground campaign at the Iraqi border) become rehabilitated in collective memory, from missed opportunity to wise restraint. As former commander and Secretary of State Colin Powell observed in 2007, 'in recent months, nobody's been asking me about why we didn't go to Baghdad.'[17]

The purpose of this chapter, then, is not to offer a final verdict. It is to refine the critique of the war in order to strengthen our ability to form judgements. I do so by offering the strongest possible 'case against' to counter the strongest possible 'case for' the invasion. I re-evaluate the decision to go to war, against both the contemporary calculations and *post hoc* rationalizations that have emerged since. As far as possible, we must assess the plausibility of what are counterfactual claims from what we can know and infer, and judge whether they are better or worse.

In conducting this audit, auditors must be especially wary of one particular rhetorical trap. A temptation for either side of the argument over Iraq is to emphasize the violence resulting from policy they opposed, and to 'play down', euphemize or de-emphasize the violence that resulted from policy they support. To guard against that bias, here I deliberately identify the extent and quality of violence at its height, both 'before' and 'after' regime change, as impartially as possible and in plain terms.

A Memoir of My Years in Washington (New York: Broadway, 2011); Colleen Graffy, 'Iraq was a good war: it sparked the Arab Spring', *The Sunday Times*, 11 September 2011.

[16] Hew Strachan, *The First World War* (New York: Viking, 2003), p. xvi: 'the first edition of Owen's poems, prepared for publication by his friend Siegfried Sassoon in December 1920, sold only 730 copies. A further 700 copies, printed in 1921, were still not sold out by 1929. By then the collected poems of another poet, Rupert Brooke, who also died during the conflict, had run to 300,000 copies'.

[17] Colin Powell remark, cited https://www.military.com/undertheradar/2015/09/21-facts-about-the-first-gulf-war.

Through this exercise, I demonstrate that the defences of the war rest on counterfactual historical claims that are implausible and, in any case, less grave that what actually happened, even on 'worst-case' calculations. The strongest retrospective case for war still involves fragile gains made at costs so heavy, with such serious unintended consequences, that decision-makers would have judged them prohibitive, had they known them in advance. The West, I argue, could have coexisted with and contained a weakened Iraq even in a situation where sanctions were breaking down. There was already evidence, before March 2003, that Saddam's regime could be deterred and restrained by clear Western signalling, there are strong reasons to assume that a 'rogue state–terrorism nexus' had not and would not form in Iraq, and that there was time and capacity to disrupt any rearmament or threatening behaviour. Between 'regime change' and 'doing nothing' there was a workable middle way of vigilant 'overwatch' available to US-led forces.

No inquest happens in a vacuum. Though critiques of the war often cast judgement without acknowledging their own assumptions, assumptions are inevitable. They ought to be surfaced. Before we judge the issue, it is best to come clean.

To debate whether a particular war is a blunder is to accept the distinction between wars that are and are not blunders. This premise would be nonsensical to both pacifists and militarists. For pacifists, wars are inherently blunders. For militarists, no war is a blunder, because a state of war (or at least a continual warlike state of being) is intrinsically valuable, regardless of its utility in any one case. These are prior and subjective value judgements that cannot be easily resolved analytically.[18] To take a pacifist stance, that the application of violence is always illegitimate and never worthwhile, is a position that gives absolute precedence to the sanctity of life and anti-violence, a principle that not even the most lopsided balance sheet and cost–benefit analysis could overturn, by definition. At the opposite end of the spectrum, militarism, like pacifism, is an absolute stance that no account of the costs of war will refute. There are other 'absolute' stances that also preclude a debate about whether war is a blunder. For legalists, a non-negotiable precondition is war's legal status. If we estimate that a war is 'illegal', this makes it illegitimate and wrong regardless of all else. For pacifists, militarists, and legalists, there is little to see here.

My argument is pitched at everybody else. I proceed from an alternative and equally subjective value judgement, the premise that there are occasions when the use of force is warranted. Most participants in the Iraq debate contest the issue within this general framework. This position flows from the 'just war' tradition, rooted in classical and medieval Christian thought, that the use of

---

[18] See further Alasdair MacIntyre, *After Virtue: A Study in Moral Theory* (Notre Dame: University of Notre Dame Press, 1981), p. 6.

force can be justifiable if it is waged with just cause, if it secures a better state of peace than if force had not been applied, if waged under legitimate authority, and if it is proportional to the costs involved. Believers in the 'just war' tradition are not necessarily optimistic about the utility of force. Applied violence can, and often does fail because of its brutally tragic nature. Paraphrasing the Prussian soldier Carl von Clausewitz, war's purpose is to serve policy, but its nature is to serve itself. Conflict inevitably harms innocents. It almost always has unintended consequences, some of them damaging. The threshold for justification, therefore, is high. But in principle, in classical and mainstream Christian traditions, it can be met. We can legitimately construct a 'balance sheet', where credits outweigh debits.[19]

To guide the exercise, I will attempt a *prudential* evaluation of Iraq. Prudence is the pursuit of practical wisdom. Defined by the political scientist Hans Morgenthau, prudence is the 'supreme virtue' that weighs the consequences of competing choices in concrete situations, and negotiates the conflicting demands of interest and principle. Ideally, it is animated by a humane scepticism, always aware that choices are bound to produce unexpected results.[20] It weighs the expenditure of resources against outcomes, compared to likely alternative scenarios. Whether war is wise, or a blunder, cannot be determined only or even primarily from the purity of intentions, or through mechanistic devices such as the letter of international law. The wisdom—or unwisdom—of decisions for war rests on hard consequences and weighed alternatives, measured against both immediate circumstances and the wider context of the national interest. In the classical and the later Christian Thomist tradition, prudence is a virtue that forbids action which is likely to be disproportionate.

Prudence, as I attempt to apply it here, flows from a particular worldview of classical realism.[21] Realism is an ancient and pessimistic tradition of political thought, with several different permutations. In common, realists regard the world as an inherently insecure place defined by the possibility of war, where human behaviour is constrained by certain realities that are inexorable, and

---

[19] For one such attempt, applied to America's war in Iraq, see John S. Duffield & Peter J. Dombrowski, *Balance Sheet: The Iraq War and US National Security* (Stanford: Stanford University Press, 2009).

[20] Hans J. Morgenthau, *Politics Among Nations: The Struggle for Power and Peace* (New York: Alfred A. Knopf, 1978), p.12; see also Robert Harriman, *Prudence: Classical virtue, Postmodern practice* (Pennsylvania: Penn. State University Press, 2003).

[21] For a discussion of classical realism as distinct from its realist cousins, see Jonathan Kirshner, 'The tragedy of offensive realism: Classical Realism and the rise of China', *European Journal of International Relations* 18:1 (2010), pp. 53–75; Joseph M. Parent & Joshua M. Baron, 'Elder Abuse: How the Moderns Mistreat Classical Realism', *International Studies Review* 13 (2011), pp. 193–213; Andrew R. Hom & Brent J. Steele, 'Open Horizons: The Temporal Visions of Reflexive Realism', *International Studies Review* 12:2 (2010), pp. 271–300; Richard K. Ashley, 'The Poverty of Neorealism', *International Organisation* 38:2 (1984), pp. 225–86.

where states compete for security in a state of anarchy, where there is no transcendent, supranational authority to enforce the peace. In doing so, states cannot have clean hands. They will deploy human beings as instruments and will practise deception. Classical realism is distinct from *amoral realism*, the attempt to maximize one's material interests regardless of all else. It is also distinct from a more recent *scientific realism* that assumes states operate as rational actors responding to the structural pressures of the world, impersonal forces that operate almost like laws, where agency, the domestic or the non-material only take effect at the margins.

In contrast, classical realism rejects amorality. Realism only makes sense as a dialogue of power with morality. The ultimate political act, war itself, descends into mere slaughter if it is waged without purpose. This kind of realism begins from the recognition of the constraints of material power, but it also looks beyond the material. It acknowledges the force of what people most want: to be secure, to be materially prosperous, and to feel good about themselves. These considerations all count in decisions about war. Classical realists are wary of utopian visions of what war is 'for', or what it can achieve. The world tends towards competition. States should therefore keep their swords sharpened. Even so, prudent accommodation with other states is possible and sometimes vital to prevent catastrophe, while it is almost always difficult, impermanent, and fragile. There is an altruistic element to classical realism, but it is a negative altruism of minimizing excess harm, presuming against actively 'doing good'. From a classical realist lens, the inquest into Iraq must be broad in its regard for national, regional, and international security, for honour as well as material interest.

Classical realism places greater weight in human agency and ideas. Rationality, or the capacity to link means and ends in coherent ways, is more an ambition than a given fact. History demonstrates that states often 'screw up' and miscalculate, fall prey to bad ideas or gamble recklessly, and the international system has a way of punishing imprudent behaviour. Realists of this school accord greater historical importance to consequential diplomacy and the choices made by decision-makers, for good or ill.[22] The future is not a set of regular patterns waiting to be discovered in advance by scientific study. It is unwritten. The pressures that create insecurity are powerful, but states and especially major states have enough latitude to make meaningful choices and to respond to domestic politics and act on non-material interests such as national honour. Iraq was not, in this tradition, primarily the kind of thing states simply 'do' in response to the pressures of the international system. It was a voluntary undertaking, made possible by the West's capabilities, but driven by ideas about how to respond to the structural environment.

---

[22] See Jonathan Kirschner's account of Henry Kissinger as both classical realist and diplomatic actor: 'Machinations of Wicked Men', *Boston Review*, 9 March 2016.

'Just war' theory and classical realism are not identical. Realism, though, resonates with central aspects of the just war tradition. As a recent 'just war' theorist observes, the 'just war' worldview draws on a threefold realism: an anthropological realism, that observes the reality of intractable vice on the international stage; a practical realism that is concerned for the realizability of ideas when put into practice; and a moral realism, a view of the moral order rooted in the nature of things as they objectively 'are', as far as we can perceive it.[23]

Turning to Iraq itself, a prudential approach requires that we assess the decision to invade by weighing the costs, gains, and consequences, according to the strongest possible counterfactual arguments. From a classical realist lens, this must place the national interest at the centre of the equation. The nation state's first duty is to secure its own citizens. Did Iraq effectively serve this purpose? We cannot be satisfied, however, by judging whether 'we' benefited even if others did not. The British national interest does not, and ought not, be narrowly selfish or insular. The consequences for Iraqis and the wider region also matter. It matters in terms of material security. We have limited but real interests in the Middle East, and don't want a hostile imbalance of power to develop in ways that could empower international terrorism or disrupt the flow of oil. And it matters in terms of collective conscience. If the net effect of the Iraq War was to inflict avoidable surplus death, injury, and terror on a population, in circumstances short of a supreme emergency, then our honour is harmed in our eyes and in others'. On the other hand, if the net effect was to prevent worse suffering and destabilization, and if the hypothetical security threat was of the first order, then the war is defensible and the grounds for shame are weaker.

A second reason for judging the national interest broadly is that the war's architects asked us to. Advocates of the war mostly did *not* argue that the invasion was justified by narrow national interest. They argued something more ambitious, claiming that the Iraq War was just and necessary because there was a harmony of interests—what was good for Iraqis was good for us all—and a merging of interests with ideals: our principles and our security interests were synonymous. Disarmament, democratic liberation, and the defeat of terrorism were, they argued, mutually consistent and reinforcing. That values and interests had become 'one' was foundational to the Bush Doctrine, to Blair's 'Chicago Doctrine', and to the reasoning both gave before

---

[23] Nigel Biggar, *In Defence of War* (Oxford: Oxford University Press, 2013), pp. 9–12, 328–9. My critique of the Iraq War shares Biggar's prudential approach, but unlike his more sympathetic evaluation of the decision (at pp. 251–325), judges that the decision falls short.

and after the invasion.[24] This is a harder test, but a self-imposed one, so it is only fair that they are judged by this standard.

Should we judge 'with hindsight' or without? Defenders of the war have at times cautioned against hindsight bias.[25] They claim that their support for overthrowing Saddam Hussein should only be judged circumstantially, by what they could be reasonably expected to know or perceive at the time. In making this historicist argument, they cite the consensus across intelligence agencies at the time that Saddam probably had an active weapons programme, and reasonable and shared suspicions that his record of concealment and non-cooperation suggested grounds for precautionary action. In doing so, they chide others for judging in the rear-view mirror, a luxury that historical actors did not have.

This will not do, however. Even if what we know is only a product of hindsight, it is still reasonable to ask how prudent their risk calculus was in the face of uncertainty. Given a lack of sufficient knowledge, should they have presumed in favour or against military action? Should they have judged more wisely even if they were in the dark? It is also open to us to make *post hoc* evaluations, because hawks use hindsight themselves. Looking back, they point to subsequent developments to make a retrospective defence, claiming that what happened afterwards vindicates their decision. They invoke the Arab Spring and the civil war in Syria, for example, to argue that the creation of a better order in Baghdad released the democratic impulse, or prevented an even more dangerous crisis. If the war had turned out well, it is hard to imagine the same hawks urging us to avoid hindsight bias in the war's favour.

In any event, the notion that the case against the war can only rest on hindsight knowledge is faulty. There were dissenting voices at the time who warned precisely of the war's possible consequences. The civil strife and conflicts that actually happened after invasion were not especially unforeseeable 'non-linear' and shocking events. If anything, to be shocked that violent disorder follows the overthrow of a government is a commentary on the assumptions of the shocked. Here we will probe both kinds of argument, evaluating decisions against the state of knowledge and debate at the time, and against what we learned since.

---

[24] Tony Blair, 'Doctrine of International Community', speech to the Economic Club of Chicago, 22 April 1999; before the US Congress in July 2003, Blair argued, 'The best defence of our security lies in the spread of our values.' 'Tony Blair's speech to the US Congress', *The Guardian* 18 July 2003; in 2004 at Sedgefield, Blair used the same line, 'Blair Terror Speech in full', *BBC News*, 5 March 2004; on board the *USS Abraham Lincoln*, as President George W. Bush declared the end of major combat operations in Iraq on 1 May 2003, he observed that 'American values and American interests lead in the same direction. We stand for human liberty'. 'Bush Makes Historic Speech aboard Warship', *CNN*, 2 May 2003.

[25] See B. Fischoff, 'Hindsight Is Not Equal to Foresight: The Effect of Outcome Knowledge on Judgement Under Uncertainty', *Journal of Experimental Psychology: Human Perception and Performance* 1:3 (1975), pp. 288–99.

PART II. BALANCE POSITIVE? WEIGHING THE ARGUMENTS

Here I lay out the strongest possible case for forcibly removing the regime from power, bearing in mind both what could reasonably have been known at the time, and what we know now. I draw together the strongest rationales that have been advanced, from policy experts such as Ken Pollack, Iraqi exiles and regional authorities such as Kanan Makiya, and from the practitioner who has most persistently defended the decision, Tony Blair.

The strongest possible case would proceed as follows. Looking out from London in March 2003, Britain and the established international order was threatened by a dark form of globalization that had revealed itself on 9/11. If globalization is the circulation of people, capital, ideas, and things, the government's risk calculus in the face of such forces was reasonable. Simply put, the West's security was increasingly threatened over time. Given that decision-makers could not know the future, it was reasonable to suppose that the 9/11 attacks were not an aberration but part of a serial wave of assaults. It was reasonable to judge that the most prudent response to an increasingly dangerous world was decisive anticipatory action. Striking Iraq amounted to anticipatory war, to forestall an emerging future threat before it could fully manifest itself. The world we inhabit cannot afford the luxury of 'last resorts', as required in the Thomist tradition. As some strategic minds advise, we must adapt our conceptions of prudential and just war to a world where time is against us. Regime change in Iraq was an application of the 'precautionary principle'. This principle holds that where an uncertain but potentially catastrophic risk is at hand and where we lack extensive or final knowledge, it is better to err on the side of caution. In the context of Iraq, precaution favoured action over inaction. It placed the burden of proof on opponents of action. In the words of Australian former prime minister John Howard, 'if you wait for perfect proof, you could end up with another Pearl Harbor.'[26] Or as Blair put it,

> The point about this act in New York was that, had they been able to kill even more people than those 3,000, they would have, and so, after that time, my view was you could not take risks with this issue at all, and one dimension of it, because we were advised, obviously, that these people would use chemical or biological weapons or a nuclear device, if they could get hold of them—that completely changed our assessment of where the risks for security lay.[27]

---

[26] Cited in Brendan Nicholson & Paul Cleary, 'New 9/11 fears set off Iraq invasion, says John Howard', *The Weekend Australian*, 8 July 2016.
[27] Tony Blair, IIT, 29 January 2010, p. 11.

Saddam's Iraqi regime represented the sum of all fears, namely the possibility of nuclear terrorism. His regime embodied a potential confluence of several dangerous trends: the pursuit of ultimate weapons technology, the aggressive and genocidal intent entailed within emerging radical and religious forms of terrorism, and the collaboration of rogue states. In assessing the new threat environment, the 9/11 Commission reported that globalization put lethal weapons in the hands of actors in ways that weakened the force of time and space, making deterrence, containment, and geographical barriers almost irrelevant.[28] Neither was this only America's problem. The 9/11 terrorist attacks killed sixty-seven British subjects, revealing a transnational threat. The illicit arms trade, too, was a cross-border and cross-ideological phenomenon. In the early twenty-first century, the traffic in nuclear materials through entrepreneurs like A.Q. Kahn and regressive states like North Korea, Libya, and Iraq itself was dangerously ecumenical. Radical Islamists, like the Al Qaeda network, had been historically willing to collaborate even with ideologically hostile 'godless' states, like the Soviet Union, to wage their jihad. Having endured the 9/11 atrocities, it was not fanciful to recognize that such a threat could metastasize.

By early 2002, Saddam was rightfully becoming the prime candidate for elimination, now that al-Qaeda's host government, the Afghan Taliban, was toppled and reeling. Saddam oversaw an uncommonly sadistic abattoir regime of torture, purges, and state terror. To genocide he added ecological atrocities, such as the draining of the Mesopotamian marshes. He was one of the few states in the world to deploy chemical weapons, both at home (against the Kurds) and abroad (against Iran). These instruments are regarded internationally as abhorrent to the point of taboo. That he turned them against his own subjects indicates that he recognized few limits. His barbarity was exceptional, even judging by the competitive standards of Middle Eastern dictators.[29]

All this would be bad enough, if the Ba'ath Party had confined its predatory behaviour to Iraq. Saddam was also a serial aggressor beyond Iraq's borders. He had invaded Iran in 1979, launching one of the worst conflicts the Gulf had seen in living memory. He waged genocidal war on the Iraqi Kurds. He had invaded and annexed Kuwait in 1990, bombing Saudi Arabia and Israel in the process. This regime was historically willing to collaborate with terrorists. Saddam was a known sponsor of Palestinian suicide bombers in the West Bank. He offered bounties for the murder of UN relief workers in northern

---

[28] *The 9/11 Commission Report: Final Report of the National Commission on Terrorist Attacks Upon the United States* (New York: W. W. Norton & Co, 2004), p. 362.

[29] For the humanitarian indictment of Saddam and the moral case for war, see Thomas Cushman, *A Matter of Principle: Humanitarian Arguments for War in Iraq* (Berkeley: University of California, 2005).

Iraq. His regime had also had sporadic contacts with al-Qaeda. The same regime had pursued weapons of mass destruction. Its persistence was a source of conflict and destabilization. His regime was virulently anti-Semitic and was one of the main 'rejectionist' forces in the region, an obstacle to the effort to end the Arab–Israeli conflict. Indeed, Saddam regarded himself as the leader of a historical pan-Arab movement that would fight and annihilate Israel. Saddam was not an Arab 'Stalin', brutal at home while cold, calculating, and deterrable abroad. And the Hitler analogy is ill-suited and overworked. He was more the Mussolini of the Gulf, head of a risk-taking revisionist regime driven by grandiose visions of empire-building, with a penchant for reckless military adventurism. The regime and system he had built promised to perpetuate oppression at home and aggression abroad, long after his passing. His sons Udday and Qusay, who would be his likely successors, had a record of sadistic brutality that appalled even their atrocious father. This held out little prospect of moderation, reformation, or constructive détente.

What of Saddam's WMD capabilities, or as it turned out, non-capabilities? While the regime turns out not to have possessed a WMD stockpile, reason and evidence persuaded a range of international observers that it did, and these observers included opponents of war. All intelligence experts advised that the regime retained some 'CBW' (chemical and biological weapons).[30] There were also good reasons to suppose that Saddam would probably reconstitute his weapons programme in future. The 'Duelfer Report' of the Iraq Survey Group concluded that though he had disarmed his WMD arsenal and programmes, Saddam still had WMD ambitions.[31] And in an age of non-state actors moved by apocalyptic ideology, without a return address and unconstrained by the traditional logic of deterrence, Saddam might donate WMD to such a group in order to 'cheat' the threat of retaliation and empower a fanatical group which could not be easily targeted for retaliation and didn't care about the threat of punishment in the first place.

Western-led international measures to counter the Iraq threat were proving to be increasingly inadequate and unsustainable. Over a decade of blockade had crippled the Iraqi economy and hurt and killed civilians. According to a United Nations Children's Fund (UNICEF) survey, child mortality was at the

---

[30] See David Fisher, former senior official with the MOD and FCO, senior defence adviser to the Prime Minister in the Cabinet Office, cited in David Fischer, *Morality and War: Can War be Just in the Twenty-First Century* (Oxford: Oxford University Press, 2011), p. 200.

[31] The Duelfer Report found that 'Saddam wanted to recreate Iraq's WMD capability—which was essentially destroyed in 1991—after sanctions were removed and Iraq's economy stabilized, but probably with a different mix of capabilities to that which previously existed. Saddam aspired to develop a nuclear capability—in an incremental fashion, irrespective of international pressure and the resulting economic risks—but he intended to focus on ballistic missile and tactical chemical warfare (CW) capabilities'. *Comprehensive Report of the Special Advisor to the DCI on Iraq's WMD*, 30 September 2004, 'Key Findings', p. 1.

same level as the Congo.³² This was not directly the consequence of sanctions, but the misuse of food and medicine aid by the regime for its own purposes. Perversely, the same sanctions strengthened the regime and fed anti-Western grievance. This, as well as America's garrisoning of Saudi Arabia to check Iraqi aggression, created the kind of resentment that nourished Islamist incitement. The status quo of sanctions and near-permanent military presence left a dangerous enemy intact while enabling propagandists to portray the West as an imperialist interloper. At the same time, those sanctions would become progressively less capable of keeping Saddam in his box. The international programme of sanctions was breaking down, and the regime was noticeably becoming bolder in its defiance. Iraq fired on US and British aircraft patrolling it's no-fly zone. As sanctions eventually disintegrated, we know that the global oil price would rise, linked to the economic surge in India and China after 2004. This would enrich Saddam, who would resurface as a dangerous predator, with the added legitimacy of a defiant ruler who had faced down the West's air war and economic strangulation. The regime's hostility to the US and its allies was open. Saddam was the only state leader to openly celebrate the 9/11 attacks. Under his aegis, Iraq was emerging as a possible centre of what Blair called a 'loose' but 'hardening' nexus between WMD, terrorism, and rogue states. In recent years, Saddam had reinvented the Iraqi state, away from the cause of secular pluralism and towards a realignment with militant Islamism. In an era when violence could be projected by means short of large-scale industrial and military power, and at relatively low cost, Western governments were now on notice.

In removing Saddam from power, the US-led coalition replaced a hostile regime with one that is flawed and corrupt, certainly, but also broadly pro-Western. Unlike the overthrown order, the new government in Baghdad respects international borders. Iraq's small Gulf neighbour, Kuwait, is no longer threatened with predation or annexation, as Saddam attempted in 1990–1 and as he threatened to do by mobilizing on the border in October 1994. In turn, the example of Saddam's demise accelerated Libya's peaceful disarmament of its chemical weapons stockpile in December 2003 and the abandonment of its nuclear programme. The US Air Force and the Royal Air Force were no longer required to patrol the skies above Kurdish areas. The invasion removed one of the foremost obstacles to any eventual Arab–Israeli settlement. More broadly, the process of change, though fraught, inspired the wider region. By releasing the Iraqi movement for political liberty, it helped inspire the democratic impulse in subsequent revolutions across North Africa and Middle East.

---

[32] Mohamed Ali & Iqbal Shah, 'Sanctions and Childhood Mortality in Iraq', *The Lancet* 355: 9218 (2000), pp. 1,851–7.

The price tag for these gains was higher than wished for or expected. Given what subsequently happened in Iraq after 2003, any retrospective case for invasion must contend that the gains were still worth the unexpectedly high costs. Compared to Iraq's prior condition, the cost did not, however, exceed the value of the object. With an oppressive regime gone, Iraqis were free to choose a better future. It brought forth a new constitution, free elections, and open debate. Trade and oil embargoes that had devastated the population were lifted, making possible the economic reconstruction of the country. By 2010, GDP per capita was three times what it had been, and child mortality had improved dramatically. There was a brutal escalation of violence in 2005-7, which gave international terrorism a foothold in the country. Yet the descent of the country into civil war was reversed by an American-led 'surge', as an infusion of troops and resources as well as a renaissance in counter-insurgency technique that depressed levels of violence, defeated al-Qaeda's bid for power in Anbar province, and created space for political conciliation. This was a victory that gave invaluable experience to US and international forces in 'minor wars', nation-building, and stabilization missions. It was also a victory that could have become the basis for an Iraqi national rebirth. By 2010-11, as American troops drew down, Iraq was relatively stable, had consolidated its new democracy, and was rebuilding its economy.

The violent fracturing of the country since then, with the spread of the Islamic State into Iraq, de facto partitioning, and sectarian violence, is not the responsibility of the governments that originally decided on invasion. Iraqis themselves are responsible for their collective decisions. They are agents, not objects, are no longer wards of the international community, and are able to pursue their own course. The West helped created an historic opportunity that Iraqis squandered. As David Frum tweeted after the release of the *Report of the Iraq Inquiry*: 'US-UK intervention offered Iraq a better future. Whatever the West's errors, the sectarian war was a choice Iraqis made for themselves.'[33] Or as Charles Krauthammer reasoned,

> We have made a lot of mistakes in Iraq. But when Arabs kill Arabs and Shiites kill Shiites and Sunnis kill all in a spasm of violence that is blind and furious and has roots in hatreds born long before America was even a republic, to place the blame on the one player, the one country, the one military that has done more than any other to try to separate the combatants and bring conciliation is simply perverse. It infantilizes Arabs. It demonizes Americans. It wilfully overlooks the plainest of facts: Iraq is their country. We midwifed their freedom. They chose civil war.[34]

---

[33] David Frum, @davidfrum, 12:16pm, 6 July 2016.
[34] Charles Krauthammer, 'Who's to blame for the killing', *The Washington Post*, 2 February 2007.

Consistent with this line of argument, weighing agency over structure, is the blame that apologists place on the Obama administration. As the argument goes, if there are other guilty parties, they are the later Western governments. By 2011, US and allies, both foreign and Iraqi, *had won* the war and wrested the country back from the brink, securing a stable, friendly new order in Iraq that was still fragile, that needed Western strategic presence to survive. This was squandered by President Obama in his inflexible determination to withdraw all forces, creating a vacuum for the conflict and destabilization that followed. Indeed, there is a link between the two developments. Without the assurance of Western support as a security provider, Iraqis lost faith in their state and the political process, and turned on each other.

Even allowing for these terrible developments, counterfactually, Iraq escaped a worse alternative world than would likely have come about had war not been waged. Had the Arab Spring come to Iraq, as surely it would have, a rearming and resurgent Saddam Hussein would probably have responded to it with the repressive behaviour that he had used in previous cases of rebellion or dissent. Either he would have crushed the rebellion and emerged as a 'North Korea of the Gulf'. Or Iraq would have suffered a Syria-style implosion. Ba'ath Iraq would have unravelled like Ba'ath Syria. This would have created a vortex into which other regional states intervened with gold, arms, and proxies, against a Sunni supremacist order fighting with an existential stake in the struggle. If Iraq in this alternative world developed as Syria has, in a war that had longevity as well as intensity, this would have killed and wounded civilians on a magnitude comparable or worse than what actually happened. Westerners would be debating the missed opportunity to tip the balance. A major intervention would be possible and increasingly demanded, not to remove a regime and achieve something more stable and acceptable, but to impose order on a more multipolar and more chaotic situation. And, as with Syria today, an imploding Iraq would set the scene for a possible collision between global and regional powers, including the US, UK, Gulf Arab states, Turkey, Iran, and Russia.

British security interests are implicated in each of these considerations. Failure to follow through in March 2003 would have damaged the Anglo-American relationship, and reduced Britain's capacity to shape Washington's behaviour. Leaving it to the US would have spurred American unilateralism. Taking part at least reinforced a norm of collective multilateral effort. Capitulating to Saddam Hussein's defiance would have emboldened other adversaries. An increase in violent chaos in the Arab-Islamic world, especially in the Gulf, or alternatively the emergence of a North Korea–like state there, would have threatened the stability of a region regarded as critical to the UK. The types of threat might vary, though could interlock in dangerous ways: the disruption of energy and commercial flows, the increase in international terrorism, and the collision of major powers all seeking to impose order on the region. If 'major wars can begin as an aggregation of lesser wars',[35] a breakdown in order across Iraq would increase the chance of dangerous escalation. Iraq today is a deeply troubled state, and host to a number of misdevelopments such as sectarian conflict. It has, though, avoided becoming a 'Syria mark two'.

PART III. MORE HARM THAN GOOD: THE CASE(S) AGAINST

Here I outline the strongest possible case against the Iraq War, and offer a critique of the arguments above.

The main indictment of the invasion is that it inflicted more harm than good. In some respects, it perversely brought about and aggravated the very security threats that it was supposed to counter. It brought excess and disproportionate costs, in return for only fragile and modest returns. The decision to strike Iraq fails to satisfy the proportionality requirement, central to prudential judgement, as it harmed the West's security interests in return for insufficient security gains.

Invasion did not confer liberty but anarchy on the Iraqi population, at least for a critical time period. It had perverse results, making Iraq a more lethal environment for many of its inhabitants, worsening rather than reducing terrorism, and demonstrating the value of acquiring a nuclear deterrent. And there were realistic alternatives to war. A 'North Korea scenario', where Iraq's regime survived in the absence of war, would still have been preventable if the invasion had not occurred. With regards to the 'Syria scenario', where Iraq imploded in the absence of war, the actual war helped to create the conditions for wider sectarian breakdown in the region, established a new form of abusive sectarian rule in the country, and thereby ultimately empowered Sunni Islamism and its most radical offshoot, the Islamic State. The 'abandonment thesis' is also historically false: the West did not have the politically realistic choice after 2008 of maintaining a large-scale and lasting presence in Iraq. Regime change unleashed forces that are not the West's to control.

It is sobering to compare what *did* happen in Iraq with what was *supposed* to happen. The architects of the venture expected a lightning strike campaign with light casualties, rapidly leading to a peaceful transfer of power to a

---

[35] Hew Strachan, ' Defence Review: *we are as complacent about* war as the Edwardians', *The Daily Telegraph*, 17 September 2010.

constitutional Iraqi government, and an estimated cost of £2.5–3 billion.[36] Inspectors would locate the WMD stockpile and the interveners would confiscate it. Saddam's overthrow would eliminate a major sponsor of terrorism who probably would have strengthened his relationship with al-Qaeda and its affiliates. Onlooking states would distance themselves from international terrorism and eschew illegal weapons proliferation. Liberated from an atrocious regime, Iraqi civil society would create a new and more humane order. To the extent that the West was historically implicated in the regime's atrocities, by omission and commission, the gift of liberation would repay its debts. With sanctions then lifted, Iraq's oil revenue, trade, recovered assets, and investment would mostly pay for the war and quickly finance reconstruction. Iraq's liberation would promote the cause of human rights and democracy worldwide. The United Nations, through Anglo-American leadership, would have its authority restored. It would avoid the humiliation it was about to suffer, in May 2003, of Saddam Hussein's Iraq taking over the chairmanship of the UN Committee on Disarmament. Anticipating the future verdict on the Blair government's decision, historian Andrew Roberts prophesied that Blair, like Winston Churchill, would be vindicated. The historical act of removing Saddam would reveal the horrifying extent of the threat. Iraqi expatriates who also urged for the war, congregating around Ahmad Chalabi's London-based Iraqi National Congress, were likewise optimistic.

All these expectations have been disappointed. Contrary to the WMD claims that were the centrepiece of the case for war, the US Duelfer Commission found that Saddam Hussein had abandoned his WMD programmes. He ended nuclear weapons research in 1991 and biological and chemical weapons research in 1995. In measuring the human costs of war, the first and paramount step is to count the dead. Planners wildly underestimated the levels and type of violence that would occur from 2003 onwards, from insurgent resistance to civil disorder to proxy and communal conflict. Measuring surplus deaths is a difficult and imprecise exercise, and estimates vary. There is no exact point in time to 'stop the clock' on causation, but a reasonable starting point is to track mortality over a ten-year period from 2003 to 2013, given the magnitude of the change in the removal of the Ba'ath regime, and the causal link suggested by the persistence of many of the same actors who took up the opportunity to exercise power (such as Nouri al-Maliki, prime minister from 2006 to 2014, and the Shia cleric Muqtada al-Sadr, leader of the Mahdi Army). The total casualties caused by the conflict over a decade according to the website *Iraq Body Count* were 174,000; according to *PLOS Medicine* they were

---

[36] £2.5 billion was the initial Treasury estimate in September 2002, while the MOD's estimate for costs of military action was £2 billion in October, which it then raised to £2.5–3 billion in February. The Treasury's first comprehensive estimate in February 2003 was £3.4 billion over three years.

461,000; according to the *Associated Press* they were more than 110,000. At its climax, the violence that followed the overthrow of the government between 2004 and 2007 reached 1,700 civilian casualties per month.[37] To be sure, the occupying powers were far from the only ones implicated in this violence. Their culpability is not directly for each death or casualty, but for the structural situation. In the vacuum that invasion made possible, criminal activity, sectarian conflict, and the Al Qaeda–backed Sunni insurgency all thrived.

How does this compare with life before liberation? Over the duration of his reign, 1979–2003, Saddam Hussein was directly responsible for the killing of approximately 200,000 people, according to Western human rights groups collecting accounts from defectors and émigrés (this figure does not include the fatalities of the Iran–Iraq War that he launched).[38] His body count total represents a rate of 8,333 people a year. If we consider that casualties from 2003 onwards at the most conservative estimate of 110,000, Iraq's annual postwar fatality rate rose to 11,000. In other words, for a decade during the invasion and occupation, Iraq was a *more lethal country* to its inhabitants even than during the Ba'ath tyranny. In turn, this drove a refugee exodus. Initially, the toppling of Saddam led to a return movement of 300,000 Iraqis. The surge of internal conflict from 2006 drove many to flee, especially after the polarizing event of the bombing of the shrine in Samarra and the surge of violence it generated. By July 2014, according to the United Nationals High Commission for Refugees, an estimated 1.9 million Iraqis were external refugees, including approximately half of the country's doctors.[39] This was one of the worst refugee crises the region had seen in living memory.

A prior order of state repression, destructive sanctions, and occasional genocide yielded to a new order of sectarian cleansing, multisided combat in urban areas, rampant criminality, and the continuous damage and destruction of civilian infrastructure. This is not necessarily proof, on its own, of the war's imprudence. It does at least heavily qualify the claim that Iraq was liberated. That the war left the country a more dangerous place to live in even than under Saddam is a mark solidly in the debit column.

As for the child mortality claim, it has been revealed that the claim of an abnormally high pre-war infant death rate and subsequent dramatic reduction is overblown. It was based on a UNICEF report of 1999 (the 'Iraq Child and Maternal Mortality Survey') that was compiled with the support of Iraqi government officials, not a source above suspicion. Four subsequent surveys from UNICEF, the UN Development Programme and the World Health

---

[37] Casualty figures from 'Operation Iraqi Freedom', iCasualties.org.

[38] John F. Burns, 'How Many People has Hussein Killed?', *The New York Times*, 26 January 2003.

[39] See the findings of the Watson Institute at Brown University, http://watson.brown.edu/costsofwar/costs/human/refugees.

Organization, as well as the 1997 Iraqi census, found no evidence for a spike in child mortality in the 1990s.[40] In Kurdish areas that were also subject to sanctions but not under Saddam's control, there was no such rise. Moreover, the Foreign Office (FCO), with the confirmation of the Department for International Development (DFID), had advised that there was no reliable answer about child mortality and that the figure of 131 deaths per 1,000 children under the age of five was suspect.[41] Yet in February 2003, Matthew Rycroft advised Blair that the alleged pre-war high mortality rate was sound, and did not burden the Prime Minister with the doubts raised.[42] Ironically, Saddam Hussein's regime and the Blair government reinforced each other's efforts to persuade opinion that pre-war sanctions had been lethal to children. Incuriosity prevailed, as did the search for evidence to bolster a prior decision.

Torture is another revealing comparison point. Saddam's regime made torture the apex of its system of rule through fear, described by the United Nations' Commission for Human Rights as an 'all pervasive repression and widespread terror'. Amnesty International listed the torture methods, from the gouging out of eyes to tongue amputation, electrocution, and rape, killing some victims and leaving others physically and mentally damaged.[43] Saddam even had a secret torture chamber installed in the basement of the Iraqi Mission to the United Nations in New York. The Ba'ath Party elite enthusiastically ordered torture and at times personally carried it out. We know much about Saddam's tortures, because the regime deliberately exhibited its victims' broken bodies as a public deterrent. Mutilation of targets in order to exhibit the price of transgression was a favoured technique. As Kanan Makiya's authoritative account of 'the republic of fear' graphically demonstrated, after defeat in 1991, the repertoire of barbaric punishments and rewards increased and led to new and bizarre kinds of degradation:

> The number of ways in which the state was publicly disfiguring the bodies of its citizens was mushrooming. Depending on the crime, the foreheads of offenders got branded with a horizontal line three to five centimeters long, or with a circle, along with the X spelled out in Law 109. Some army deserters and draft dodgers, and those who sheltered them, got special treatment: the outer part of one ear was to be cut off for the first offence; a repeat offence resulted in the amputation of the other ear and a circle being branded on the forehead... Only after being caught

---

[40] See Michael Spagat, 'The Iraq Sanctions Myth', *Pacific Standard*, 26 April 2013, at https://psmag.com/the-iraq-sanctions-myth-5b05f6712df5#.i9oh5prjx; 'Truth and Death in Iraq Under Sanctions', *Significance* 7:3 (2010), pp. 116–20; World Health Organization, *Iraq Family Health Survey 2006–7* (2008), p. 63, Table 25, at http://www.who.int/mediacentre/news/releases/2008/pr02/2008_iraq_family_health_survey_report.pdf.
[41] Fax Owen to Rycroft, 14 February 2003, 'PM's Speech Question'.
[42] Minute Rycroft to Prime Minister, 14 February 2003, 'Iraq: Scotland Speech—Additional Points'.
[43] Amnesty International, *2001 Annual Report on Iraq*, 10 July 2001, p. 2.

for desertion a third time would a soldier be executed... The reaction of ordinary Iraqis to the new laws was also unprecedented. Two men whose ears had been cut off immolated themselves in central Baghdad in October 1994. Following the murder of a doctor in the southern city of Nassirriyya by an amputee, and the storming of the headquarters of the Ba'th party in the city of Amara by a crowd that cut off the ears of the Ba'th officials it got its hands on, several hundred doctors went on strike to protest having to carry out the new punishments. Upon being threatened with having their own ears cut off, the doctors called off their strike. Law 117 was then promptly issued, directed at the whole medical profession. It threatened immediate amputation of the ear for anyone who insisted in the cosmetic improvement of an officially disfigured body part. The law's wording ends with this strange acknowledgement of the public's outrage: The effects of the punishment of amputation of the hand or ear and branding 'will be eliminated [by the state] if those so punished go on to perform heroic and patriotic acts.[44]

After Saddam's overthrow, torture did not end. Against expectations, it became increasingly difficult to assume that 'at least' the invasion alleviated Iraqis from repression. Instead, now that torture was no longer a state monopoly, it proliferated and at a higher rate even than under the old order. It was carried out by security forces, insurgents, and militia groups. Consider the report in 2006 of UN officials who examined the bodies of kidnap victims in Baghdad's morgue:

> 64. UNAMI HRO [United Nations Assistance Mission for Iraq, Human Rights Office] has consistently documented the widespread use of torture in Iraq. This matter has regularly emerged as a major concern and has been widely acknowledged as a major problem by Iraqi officials. Periodically, information has been received by HRO regarding the use of torture in detention centres. The bodies that regularly appear throughout the country bear signs indicating that the victims have been brutally tortured before their extra-judicial execution.
>
> 65. UNAMI HRO has received reports and documentation showing the type of torture inflicted on detainees, particularly during interrogation. Detainees' bodies show signs of beating using electrical cables, wounds in different parts of their bodies, including in the head and genitals, broken bones of legs and hands, electric and cigarette burns. Bodies found at the Medico-legal Institute often bear signs of severe torture including acid-induced injuries and burns caused by chemical substances, missing skin, broken bones (back, hands and legs), missing eyes, missing teeth and wounds caused by power drills or nails. Individuals who escaped death in such incidents reported that saw [sic] others being tortured to get

---

[44] Kanan Makiya, *Republic of Fear: The Politics of Modern Iraq* (Berkeley: University of California Press, 1989), pp. x–xi.

information about their sect. For example, an individual reported that he was beaten by members of a Sunni extremist group with electrical cables and iron bars to make him confess the sect to which he belonged. The body of another man kidnapped by Shi'a militias bore signs of facial mutilation, had fingers missing from his hands and had a significant perforation—presumably from a power drill—below his left shoulder.[45]

Iraqis reported to the UN Assistance Mission in Iraq that the new realities of torture were 'worse than it has been in the times of Saddam Hussein'.[46] It may not be easy to evaluate that claim. That post-war conditions were *even credibly comparable* is a judgement against the invasion, given that it was supposed to relieve civilians from oppression. Long occupation of Iraq also became the occasion for Western torture. Allegations of British prisoner abuse were upheld in the case of the Baha Mousa Inquiry, with more still under investigation by the Iraq Historic Allegations Team.[47] Torturers, whether American or British, actively contributed to the terrorization of the civilian population, and by doing so, degraded themselves and the states they represented. This damaged the moral authority of the United States and Britain. It created a recruitment tool for Islamist terrorist groups, making it easier for hostile propagandists to portray Western campaigns not as liberation efforts but as colonial domination.

Given the extent of post-Saddam terror, what of the argument that this was primarily Iraqis' decision and agency, choosing civil war over enlightened nation-building? The flaw in this argument is that it wrongly separates the act of breaking the state from the violent forces that were subsequently unleashed. It is true that other developments before the war are causally implicated in the civil strife that followed, including the deliberately divisive and intentionally terroristic nature of Ba'ath Party rule. The invasion, though, was the proximate cause of the subsequent sectarian conflict and breakdown of order, the mobilization of radical Sunni militias, and the spillover of radical jihadist groups into Syria.[48] To characterize the invasion as an act that 'midwifed their freedom' is a perverse account of what happened when invading forces overthrew a government. If it midwifed anything, it was a state of grave mutual insecurity between Iraqis, spiralling not into liberty, a condition that requires a minimal level of security and social cohesion, but instead into anarchy. Without a Leviathan to restrain competing groups, frightened Iraqis turned to their primary groups for protection and succour. In those conditions, both

---

[45] UN Assistance Mission for Iraq (UNAMI), *Human Rights Report* (1 July–31 August 2006), pp. 15–16.
[46] 'Iraq torture worse after Saddam', *BBC News*, 21 September 2006.
[47] *The Report of the Baha Mousa Inquiry* (London: Stationery Office, 2011), volumes 1–3.
[48] As Malcolm Chalmers assesses it, 'The Strategic Scorecard', in *Wars in Peace: British Military Operations Since 1991* (London: RUSI, 2014), pp. 109–35.

sides found themselves in a security dilemma, where they armed, organized, and competed in order to ensure their security, only to heighten one another's insecurity. In such conditions, the 'choice' of taking up arms was not the irrational awakening of ancient hatreds. With the right triggering event, namely al-Qaeda's bombing of the Golden Dome mosque, an escalation of atrocities followed.

Regarding the net humanitarian and strategic results, the fact that life over a decade became more lethal and torturous even than under Ba'ath Party rule might arguably be less weighty if it could be shown that these horrific developments were at least positively productive, that they purchased a more humane order that was beneficial to British security interests. As things stand, however, we do not know that, and there are disturbing signs pointing in the other direction. Amnesty International reported in October 2016 that Popular Mobilization Units, or *Hashd al-Shaabi* (an Iraqi government-backed organization made up of myriad Shia Muslim militias) now torture and execute Sunni civilians who escaped the Islamic State.[49] The post-Saddam killings and tortures were not the birth pangs of what would become a pluralistic state under a restrained constitutional government. They marked the creation of a sectarian Shiite ascendancy that continues to commit grave human rights violations. British military forces are now deployed in Iraq and Afghanistan to counter the Islamic State, the worst by-product of the regional turmoil that the Iraq War helped to generate.

These distressing outcomes also came at significant costs borne by the US and Britain. According to the Iraq Inquiry, the direct cost to the UK was £9.2 billion for the 2003–9 campaign.[50] Overall costs are greater when we factor in indirect costs, such as the costs of through-life medical care for veterans, and the costs of military replenishment such as the replacement of equipment. It is impossible to quantify objectively or precisely how many casualties or how much expenditure is 'too much' in isolation. Evaluations are inevitably value-laden. We can at least inform judgement through relative rather than absolute measures. The total cost was £7 billion more than anticipated, and as we shall see, for a return of decidedly more mixed results than expected, including perverse and undesired outcomes. Without the distress of the Iraq War, £9.2 billion could have been allocated more productively, in capital stock such as education or infrastructure, in different combinations. The UK government hypothetically could have not spent it, reducing the budget deficit. If spent elsewhere, it could have covered the cost of retaining public services that were reduced in later 'austerity budgets' from 2010, sparing for years local government budgets to be spent on British public

---

[49] Amnesty International, *Punished for Daesh's crimes: Displaced Iraqis abused by militias and government forces* (London: Amnesty International, 2016), pp. 6–7, 13.

[50] *Report of the Iraq Inquiry*, v. 10, Section 13.2, p. 580.

libraries (reduced in total by approximately £150 million in 2010),[51] maintaining the flood defence budget (reduced by £30 million),[52] and the legal aid budget (reduced by £350 million).[53] These alternative uses of money have a concrete and direct impact on the populace. Alternatively, the costs of Iraq could have offset the large-scale defence spending reductions in 2010, such as the reduction in army personnel, or could have contributed to the recapitalization of the Royal Air Force and Royal Navy, or covered annual expenditure on operations in Afghanistan for five of its twelve years.[54]

These financial sums are hardly crippling. They do not equal the major cases of imperial overstretch, such as the ruinously exorbitant campaigns of Hapsburg Spain's King Philip II.[55] As the figures suggest, the Iraq War still represented non-trivial opportunity costs. Those costs should weigh more heavily given the larger consequences of the war for British security interests. To dismiss these costs as relatively inconsequential or easily affordable would be to betray an insouciance about scarce resources. Even marginal reductions or reallocations of such resources strongly affect the vulnerable. Money spent on military operations in Iraq not only contributed to an overall worsening environment for Iraqis, but was money not spend preventing flood damage, maintaining a public library, funding police, or supporting under-resourced troops in Afghanistan.

The expenditure of the United States, on the other hand, does stand comparison with major historical episodes. A war whose total direct and indirect costs amount to approximately $3 trillion helped accelerate America's relative decline, adding a legacy of debt to its already unsustainable liabilities, adding to the ratio of public debt to GDP, worsening the strain on scarce resources in the competition between debt, military commitments, and social welfare, and depleting its relative strength as a unipolar power, although it remains a major power.[56]

---

[51] Local Government Spending on public libraries, drawn from Institute of Fiscal Studies, *Green Budget February 2012*, Table 6.2, p. 140.

[52] House of Commons Library SN/SC/5755, Oliver Bennett & Sarah Hartwell Naguib, *Flood Defence Spending in England* (19 November 2014), p. 3.

[53] Proposals for the Reform of Legal Aid in England and Wales, Consultation Paper CP12/10, November 2010, Cm 7967, p. 5.

[54] The net additional cost of military operations in Afghanistan from 2001 to 2013 was £20.65 billion, according to Malcolm Chalmers, representing an average annual rate of approximately £1.72 billion. 'The Sinews of War', in Adrian L. Johnson (ed.), *Wars in Peace: British Military Operations Since 1991* (London: RUSI, 2014), p. 268.

[55] On this case and the thesis of imperial overstretch, where military commitments exceed and dislocate the state's economic capacity, see Paul Kennedy, *The Rise and Fall of the Great Powers: Economic Change and Military Conflict from 1500 to 2000* (London: Fontana, 1989), pp. 39–89; Geoffrey Parker, *The Grand Strategy of Philip II* (London: Yale University Press, 1998).

[56] On the long-term costs of the Iraq War for the United States, see the cumulative work of Joseph E. Stiglitz and Linda J. Bilmes, *The Three Trillion Dollar War: The True Cost of the Iraq*

British casualties in Iraq were also excessively high, if judged against expectations, and if judged against the modest gains of the war, especially the absence of Saddam's WMD programme and thus the non-imminence of the threat. Casualties are also high against another revealing measure. Britain suffered 179 service personnel fatalities and three UK civilian officials. Of these, 138 were killed as the result of hostile acts, rather than illness, suicide, or blue-on-blue accident.[57] Many thousands were wounded. The full figures have yet to be released. According to the Ministry of Defence's (MOD) official figures, since 2006, there were 5,791 total.[58] These numbers—182 killed, 5791 injured—amount to the equivalent of a major terrorist attack, brought on by inserting forces in Iraq.

Two caveats are in order. Firstly, these were volunteer personnel electing to put themselves in harms' way, rather than civilian bystanders, and they were doing so on expeditionary operations away from the mainland UK, in contrast to a major attack on a city in the British homeland. This arguably lessens the severity to an extent, but the military character of the losses and the fact that they happened 'over there' does not negate the point. Most Britons would certainly regard a terrorist attack on a military facility in the Middle East that killed 182 personnel and inflicted thousands of non-fatal casualties as a major and distressing episode, comparable to America's reaction to the Beirut barracks bombing of 1983. The prolonged duration of the losses matters. Spreading these losses over a decade may be preferable to single attack concentrated on one day, given what a shock of that magnitude could do to the state's functioning and to social cohesion. Given this time period, a better comparison might be to serial, smaller scale attacks over a decade. Going by the casualty figures we have, British losses in Iraq are quantitively the

Conflict (New York: W.W. Norton: 2008); Linda J. Bilmes & Joseph E. Stiglitz, 'The long-term costs of conflict: the case the Iraq War', in Derek L. Braddon & Keith Hartley (eds), *The Handbook on the Economics of Conflict* (Cheltenham: Edward Elgar Publishing, 2011) and 'Estimating the costs of war: Methodological issues, with applications to Iraq and Afghanistan', in Michelle Garfinkel & Stergios Skaperdas (eds) *The Oxford Handbook of the Economics of Peace and Conflict* (Oxford: Oxford University Press: 2012), pp. 1–51; Bilmes, 'The Financial Legacy of Iraq and Afghanistan: How Wartime Spending Decisions Will Constrain Future National Security Budgets', Faculty Research Working Paper Series, March 2013; see also Ryan D. Edwards, 'Post-9/11 War Spending, Debt, and the Macroeconomy', Cost of War Project, Brown University (22 June 2011).

[57] Ministry of Defence, 'Operations in Iraq: British Fatalities', at http://webarchive.nationalarchives.gov.uk/20121026065214/http://www.mod.uk/DefenceInternet/FactSheets/OperationsFactsheets/OperationsInIraqBritishFatalities.htm, accessed 12 November 2016.

[58] I derive this figure from the official MOD figures on British casualties, by subtracting fatalities from the total of Very Seriously Injured (73), Seriously Injured (149), Field Hospital Admissions (3598) and Aero-Medical Evacuations (1971), from Table: Summary of Ministry of Defence Statistics on British Casualties in Iraq, at *Casualty Monitor*, http://www.casualty-monitor.org/p/iraq.html. Note that these figures are incomplete, as the MOD has not yet released the official casualty figures for field hospital admissions and aero-medical evacuations from 2003 to 2005.

equivalent of terrorist attacks killing approximately eighteen people a year and inflicting non-fatal casualties of almost 580 people a year. This is higher than the annual rate of terrorist-inflicted casualties Britain has actually suffered at home over the longer period dating back to 11 September 2001, of 145 fatalities (fifty-three in Great Britain, ninety-two in Northern Ireland), an average of almost ten per year.[59] Given that suppressing and defeating international terrorism was one objective of the Iraq War, and given that it turned out that the Iraqi regime did not collaborate with al-Qaeda, suffering the equivalent of a major terrorist attack or a series of smaller terrorist attacks as a direct result of the war is disappointing.

Tony Blair might respond that removing Saddam at the expense of hundreds of dead and thousands injured is still justifiable proportionately, given that it disrupted a potential link that could have resulted in an unthinkable, catastrophic terrorist attack. Though distressing, the losses Britain suffered were still an expenditure of resources that lowered the chances of a complete disaster, even if the odds of that disaster were low. As Blair implored the Commons in March 2003,

> what was shocking about 11 September was not just the slaughter of innocent people but the knowledge that, had the terrorists been able, there would have been not 3,000 innocent dead, but 30,000 or 300,000—and the more the suffering, the greater their rejoicing. I say to my hon. Friend that America did not attack the al-Qaeda terrorist group; the al-Qaeda terrorist group attacked America. They did not need to be recruited; they were there already. Unless we take action against them, they will grow. That is why we should act.[60]

In the context of urging for anticipatory war, this position rests on the same bedrock assumptions of the Bush Doctrine: that the Iraq regime was a prime candidate for collaboration with the Al Qaeda network or equivalent, and that strategies of deterrence and/or containment and 'raiding' were unrealistic against such threats.

The most immediate objection to Blair's argument is that Saddam Hussein's regime did not have a direct, collaborative relationship with al-Qaeda, and showed no signs of doing so. The most thorough and exhaustive investigation of this issue was issued by the Institute of Defence Analyses (IDA), based on 600,000 captured Iraqi documents. Saddam's regime did have a long-standing programme of supporting various Islamist and other revolutionary groups when their goals coincided, and there were limited communications between his government and al-Qaeda, just as there were overlaps in short-term goals. Abu Musab al-Zarqawi, the future leader of AQI (al-Qaeda in Iraq) did

---

[59] House of Commons Briefing Paper, Number 7613, 9 June 2016, *Terrorism in Great Britain: The Statistics* (London: Stationery Office, 2016), p. 4.

[60] *Hansard*, 18 March 2003, column 769.

operate in northern Iraq as part of *Ansar al Islam* (a linked organization) with the knowledge of Baghdad, but this was Kurdish territory that Saddam could not directly control, Ansar's conflict with Kurds coincided with the regime's interests, and the regime had attempted to locate and capture Zarqawi in vain. The relationship was overall 'one of innate caution and mutual mistrust', and there is no evidence of a direct collaborative connection.[61] According to debriefs from detainees who were ex-officials, Saddam distrusted al-Qaeda and issued a general order that Iraq should not deal with al-Qaeda, and rebuffed requests for operational and material support. This verdict supports the independent findings of the 9/11 Commission, the CIA, the Defence Department in its declassified internal report, and the Senate Select Committee on Intelligence.[62]

The war had not only human and financial costs. It also imposed geopolitical costs, affecting the distribution and use of power in the wider region in ways that bear negatively on British security interests. As Blair himself has partially conceded, without the Iraq War, there would be no Islamic State. One of the war's legacies, and most profound failures, was that it created conditions for sectarian government that persecuted a large Sunni minority, leading to the collapse of large swathes of the country in face of the Islamic State in 2014. Because a Shiite regime governed in sectarian ways to alienate Sunni communities, $26 billion of US investment in the military, police, and justice system (including about $12 billion on supplying the Iraqi army)[63] over a decade created a force that collapsed and fled in the face of the Islamic State's offensive. The net result was to create an army that refused to fight to defend the state. At the same time, the Iraq War directly contributed to the growth of the Islamic State and its precursors. By effectively installing into power Shia supremacists who were backed by Iranian patronage, the US and UK persuaded aggrieved Sunnis that they were undertaking 'a historical pivot towards Iran and the restoration of Persian hegemony'. Mass detention, and the prison system in Iraq that evolved under international occupation, in particular Camp Bucca in southern Iraq, became an incubator and organizing structure for Sunni jihadis.[64] Former detainees liken camp Bucca to an 'al-Qaeda

---

[61] Institute for Defence Analyses, *Iraqi Perspectives Project, Saddam and Terrorism: Emerging Insights from Captured Iraqi Documents* (November, 2007, vol. 1), Abstract.

[62] Department of Defence report, cited by R. Jeffrey Smith, 'Hussein's Prewar Ties to Al-Qaeda discounted', *The Washington Post*, 6 April 2007; *Senate Intelligence Committee, Phase II—Bipartisan Report* on Prewar Iraq *Intelligence* (2006) in Senate Reports Nos 330-1 (2007) pp. 105, 106, 108, 109; see also Press Release of the Committee, 5 June, 2008, available at http://intelligence.senate.gov/press/record.cfm?id=298775.

[63] Special Investigator General for Iraq Reconstruction (SIGIR), *Learning From Iraq: A Final Report From the Special Inspector General for Iraq Reconstruction* (Washington DC, 2013), pp. 90-105.

[64] See Martin Chulov, 'Tony Blair was right: without the Iraq war there would be no Islamic State', *The Guardian*, 25 October 2015.

school', producing jihadists in a factory-like environment. Camp Bucca housed about twenty-four-thousand men...[who] sat at the feet of Salafi-jihadists, who mentored them and converted them en masse to their Islamist ideology'.[65]

The Iraq War disrupted the balance of power in the Gulf, empowering Iran, ironically a state with more extensive ties to terrorist groups. Indeed, decision-makers underestimated the prospect that a post-Saddam Iraq may create a vacuum that would attract Iranian influence. More immediately, invasion opened up a new front in the struggle with al-Qaeda, enabling it to establish a foothold in Sunni territories, to move in and stoke a sectarian war with Iraqi Shiites. Allegations of extensive pre-war Ba'ath–al-Qaeda collaboration proved false. 'Regime change' made this a self-fulfilling prophecy, however. It drove al-Qaeda, former Ba'ath regime officials, and disaffected Sunnis into one another's arms. A similar nexus formed in and around the Islamic State.

Invading Iraq, then, made terrorism worse. Whether or not it energized motivations to attack Britain at home and added to the impetus of the men who carried out the 7 July London bombings, it generated a straightforward and concrete benefit for al-Qaeda. It handed opportunities to al-Qaeda that it otherwise would have lacked, and established the ideological and material conditions for the Islamic State to grow to the point where it could seize control of Iraq's 'second city', Mosul. These were perverse outcomes.

Removing a tyrant from power, a process that led to his prosecution and execution, had another perverse consequence. Blair recalled his 'primary consideration' was to send an 'absolutely powerful, clear and unremitting message that...if you were a regime engaged in WMD, you had to stop'.[66] Yet overthrowing Saddam, and then Gaddafi of Libya, signalled the value for hostile states of maintaining, accelerating, or acquiring a nuclear deterrent. Saddam's inability to prevent his overthrow, trial, and execution, having disarmed, affirmed the reality that disarmament or even ambivalence around the issue makes a state a possible target. This was supposed to be a counter-proliferation war that, by disarming a leading rogue, would dissuade other would-be proliferators.[67] Instead, removing a pre-nuclear Saddam demonstrated that consensual disarmament was simply too dangerous, strengthening incentives for other regimes to pursue their nuclear ambitions.[68] The

---

[65] Fawaz Gerges, *ISIS: A History* (Princeton: Princeton University Press, 2016), p. 133.
[66] IIT, 29 January 2010, p. 24.
[67] See the remarks of Under Secretary of State John Bolton on 13 March 2003, US Department of State, International Information Programs, 'Byliner: Under Secretary Bolton on North Korea, Iraq', *Far Eastern Economic Review*, (13 March 2003), cited in Andrew Newman, 'From Pre-emption to Negotiation: The Failure of the Iraq-as-Deterrent Nuclear Non-Proliferation Model' *Global Change, Peace and Security* 17:2 (2005), pp. 155–69, p. 168, n77.
[68] See Andrew Newman, 'From Pre-emption to Negotiation? The Failure of Iraq-as-Deterrent Nuclear non-proliferation Model', *Global Change, Peace and Security* 17:2 (2005), pp. 155–69.

overthrow of Libya's Colonel Gaddafi, another adversary who had disarmed, has reinforced the pattern. Looking back, President Donald Trump's Director of National Intelligence has acknowledged the probability that Kim Jong-un's regime calculates 'The lessons that we learned out of Libya giving up its nukes... is, unfortunately: If you had nukes, never give them up. If you don't have them, get them'.[69] North Korea has also explicitly referred to these examples while justifying its nuclear and ballistic missile testing. To accompany its fourth nuclear test in January 2016, a commentary published by the official KCNA news agency claimed:

> History proves that powerful nuclear deterrence serves as the strongest treasured sword for frustrating outsiders' aggression... The Saddam Hussein regime in Iraq and the Gaddafi regime in Libya could not escape the fate of destruction after being deprived of their foundations for nuclear development and giving up nuclear programmes of their own accord.[70]

Iran's nuclear ambitions are more ambivalent. When the US-led coalition struck Iraq, Iran temporarily suspended its nuclear programme, only to restart it later, probably to pursue 'nuclear latency', the breakout ability to produce bomb at short notice. The presence of US and coalition forces on its western and eastern borders, in Iraq and Afghanistan, heightened the regime's sense of insecurity. Motivations for proliferation and disarmament in both cases are complex and are not reducible to reactions to the Iraq precedent. We can confidently judge, though, that all these regimes care strongly about survival, and the Iraq and Libyan wars did nothing to dampen the powerful incentives for proliferation, and dealt a strong blow to the message that adversary states can securely renounce their nuclear capability.

What of the 'Syria' counterfactual argument? But for regime change, would Iraq have faced a worse future, where a Ba'ath Party regime brutally repressed an Arab Spring uprising in Iraq, resulting in a Syria-style civil war?

The 'Iraq as Syria' hypothetical is flawed. Firstly, it overlooks what actually did happen. Any notion that 'regime change' spared Iraq an internally devastating and regionally destabilizing civil war that would have required international intervention is eccentric. In 2006–7, as a direct result of invasion, the country *did* descend into civil war, and one with an Islamist presence. It prompted a second intervention, led by the United States, in the form of the 'surge' to restore stability and give the new state some breathing space. The surge was itself a costly effort to wrest back control of a crisis, at the price of five additional brigades totalling 20,000 extra troops. That such a meltdown could have happened independently without an invasion does not change the

---

[69] Daniel Coats, Director of National Intelligence, Aspen Security Forum, 21 July 2017.
[70] Cited in Skand Tayal, 'The North Korea Nuclear Test: Quest for Deterrence', *Eurasia Review*, 25 January 2016.

observation that the actual invasion contributed to the meltdown that did happen, and made it more likely and brought it forward. Secondly, the Iraq and Syrian wars are not separate things. The invasion and aftermath in Iraq contributed directly to the later Syrian conflict, inspiring the creation of new jihadi groups in Iraq and neighbouring countries, such as the Jabhat al-Nusra Front, drawing on veterans from the AQI network. The al-Nusra Front, along with other Islamists, seized control of significant parts of the rebellion against Syria's Alawite regime, and the Islamic State was strengthened by its ability to operate and find sanctuary on both sides of the dissolving Syria–Iraq border.[71] This is not to claim that the Syrian crisis would not have erupted without the invasion of 2003. It is to say that the conflicts unleashed by the Iraq War were the precipitating event for the dramatic increase in militant jihadism, and this played a major part in radicalizing opposition forces within Syria.

Rather than suggesting that invasion spared Iraq a Syria-style civil war, others such as David Frum turn to fatalism to exculpate the invaders of responsibility, arguing that Iraq was destined for an internal struggle regardless. His developing assumption is that Iraq had an historical appointment with internal conflict that it could hardly avoid, and that 'the deluge was coming in Iraq, whatever outside powers did.'[72] This is at odds with his other major claim, that regime change in 2003 offered Iraqis the chance for a better future. Did tectonic forces present for Iraq a historical rendezvous with a bloodbath, alleviating invaders of responsibility, or did Iraqis have the agency to wilfully make bad choices? We can't have it both ways. If Iraq was heading for an implosion that was impossible for outside powers to arrest, then it would have been better not to place American, British, and other lives and treasure in the middle of it, conserving those resources instead for where they could make a positive difference. If not, and if invasion was supposed to give them the chance of a better future, given the sectarian and fractured state of the country, the odds were poor, and the costs were high.

Who Lost Iraq? The Abandonment Thesis

It is necessary also to deal with an argument that has become increasingly prominent since Iraq's implosion in the summer of 2014. This is the claim that the original error was not the invasion, but the premature abandonment of

---

[71] Jessica Stern, 'The Continuing Cost of the Iraq War: The Spread of Jihadi Groups throughout the Region', 18 February 2014, at http://watson.brown.edu/costsofwar/files/cow/imce/papers/2014/The%20Continuing%20Cost%20of%20the%20Iraq%20War.pdf, and 'Terrorism after the 2003 invasion of Iraq', at http://watson.brown.edu/costsofwar/files/cow/imce/papers/2013/Terrorism%20after%20the%202003%20Invasion%20of%20Iraq.pdf.

[72] David Frum, 'The Speechwriter: Inside the Bush Administration during the Iraq War', *Newsweek*, 19 March 2013.

Iraq. We can call this the 'abandonment thesis'.[73] Abandoning Iraq was the source of chaos, allegedly. The US-led West could have stayed, with South Korea and Japan as the model. As Senator John McCain recommended in 2008, 'We've been in Japan for 60 years. We've been in South Korea for 50 years or so. That would be fine with me, as long as Americans are not being injured or harmed or wounded or killed'.[74] Paul Wolfowitz likewise argued that Korea in 1955 offered a model for Iraq in 2010, whereby America would retain a stable and stabilizing presence in a strategically vital region in the long term.[75]

This thesis is triply flawed, however. It assumes that Iraq was 'America's' to lose, in the sense that it overlooks the political reality that this was an Iraqi decision, and the Iraqis that wielded power had a different idea of their interests. It overestimates the restraining effect of America's strategic presence beforehand. Already by 2010, Iraq was on the road to sectarian friction and escalating internal conflict. And it loses sight of the fraught geopolitics of the region, which made the Gulf nothing like the Korean peninsula.

If the 'abandonment' charge were true, this would shift culpability from President Bush and Prime Minister Blair to President Barack Obama. Yet Obama cannot plausibly be blamed for the decision to withdraw the main body of US forces. That was pre-decided by the Status of Forces Agreement between the Bush administration and Maliki's government in December 2008. The more developed accusation is that Obama could have tried harder and possibly kept a smaller residual force in Iraq in a non-combat role to exert a restraint, to signal continuing US security assurance, to keep Iraq's political condition stable, and to stiffen the backbone of its security forces. It was the absence of guarantees to the fledgling 'new Iraq' that loosened restraint, and enabled the Maliki government to indulge its sectarian impulses.

Would it have been politically possible to leave forces on terms acceptable both to Washington and to Baghdad and the Iraqi parliament? The short answer is no.[76] Iraqi politicians insisted on American forces not being protected by legal immunity from local prosecution. Such terms, for such a commitment, were unacceptable to the American Congress and White House, and certainly would have been a deal-breaker for any Republican president. The obstacle to any appreciable military presence, whether a division or a few thousand trainers, was that Iraqis overwhelmingly opposed it. A continuing US presence was opposed by Shiite cleric Moqtada al-Sadr, whose support was vital for Maliki's ruling coalition. The emergence of an Iraqi sovereign

---

[73] This section adapts parts of my article, 'Iraq and Libya were not the West's to Lose', *The National Interest*, 3 November 2016.
[74] 'John McCain's 100 Years in Iraq', *CBS News*, 1 April 2008.
[75] Paul Wolfowitz, 'In Korea, a Model for Iraq', *The New York Times*, 30 August 2010.
[76] See also Colin H. Kahl, 'No, Obama did not Lose Iraq: What the President's critics get wrong', *Politico*, 15 June 2014.

democracy created not an accommodating US client state but a Tehran-leaning government.

There is also a deeper problem with the suggestion that a continued presence was necessary for stability. The state was not respectably peaceful and settled when the US drew down. Sectarian abuse and corruption was already rife in Iraqi governance, and the seeds were already planted for civil strife. Before the last scale-downs from August 2010 to the final withdrawal in December 2011, there was widespread corruption in the officer corps and the withholding of oil revenues from Sunni communities. Prime Minister Maliki was already sectarianizing the army with Iranian-backed Badr Corp fighters. Once the US began drawing down its combat role from 2009, Maliki refused to hire the majority of Sunni Awakening Council fighters, only employing 17,000 and excluding 83,000. There were already crackdowns on demonstrations and torture of detainees. The Erbil power-sharing agreements were already stalling, and the March 2010 parliamentary elections triggered struggle for control over security services, government ministries, and oil wealth. Maliki was already exercising state power both to dole out and withhold patronage, favouring Shiite populations and neglecting to provide sufficient services such as electricity to Sunni Arab cities. Data from the US National Counter Terrorism Center (NCTC) shows that Iraq had a consistently higher level of violence than Afghanistan during 2009–11, with no consistent reduction in violence since mid-2009.[77] As even military advisor Rick Brennan concedes, who blames US withdrawal in 2011 for the state of Iraq, even during the 'surge' with the climax of America's on-the-ground commitment, Maliki 'mostly ignored American pleas to govern in a less divisive manner and find ways to bring the Sunni minority into the political process'.[78] If 160,000 troops at the height of the occupation were not enough to curtail the Iraqi state's abusive behaviour, it is hard to see how a smaller force could have made a meaningful difference. If we accept the analysis that the rise of Islamic State in Iraq is rooted in Sunni alienation, this is causally linked more to Maliki's refusal to work for an 'inclusive, tolerant, multi-confessional democracy' than to whether the US deployed a small counter-terrorism force.[79] A return of US combat and advisory forces was only permitted years later, once the emergency of the Islamic State's rise moved Baghdad to let troops back in.

The 'Iraq as South Korea' analogy is also flawed. South Korea is a cohesive society where the majority wanted long-term US protection, whereas the majority of Iraqis did not in 2010–11. South Korea is a relatively homogenous

---

[77] See CSIS, *Patterns of Violence in Iraq* (Washington DC, 2012), p. 3.
[78] Rick Brennan, 'Withdrawal Symptoms: The Bungling of the Iraq Exit' *Foreign Affairs* 93:6 (2014), pp. 25–36, p. 28.
[79] Paul Pillar, 'The Damaging Myth about "Winning" the Iraq War', *The National Interest*, 17 November 2014.

society, whereas Iraq is fraught with ethnic and confessional divisions. South Koreans are strongly motivated by the proximate and direct threat of a hostile North Korea, whereas Iraq faced no equivalent of a large-scale threat on its borders to unify the population. As one critic notes, 'When one thinks of a long-term occupation of Iraq (even with reduced forces), a closer analogy is the dangerous and frustrating British mission in Northern Ireland from the late 1960's through the 90's'.[80]

The 'abandonment thesis' plays off a common and seductive argument, that Iraq unravelled through poor execution. We can avoid error in future, this implies, if we organize better. Western military activism is a generally good thing, this perspective suggests, only more resources and preparation would have given outside powers a solution to the security problems that beset post-Saddam Iraq. A more efficient and careful invasion would have been made the decisive difference, in particular avoiding a large-scale De-Ba'athification programme and keeping civil service and army intact.

There are good reasons to be sceptical of this mechanical interpretation of the problems of intervention. The alternative course, of avoiding De-Baathification, of limiting institutional impact, not purging the bureaucracy or security services, and preserving greater continuity in the state, may well have made Sunni alienation and resistance less likely. Conversely, how would Iraqi's majority of Shia perceive this development? As we have seen, Shia leaders had broadly supported De-Ba'athfication. The absence of a post-invasion reckoning with the crimes of the Ba'ath Party, and the continuation of Ba'ath officials in power, would probably have been tantamount to confirming Sunni supremacy and re-enthroning the old order, only with Saddam removed and this time, with the support of an international occupying force. It is not hard to imagine how this move, effectively presenting the Shia majority with the dispensation of 'meet the new boss, same as the old boss', probably would have increased their insecurity, and their disaffection with the process of reconstruction, and incentivized them to turn to violent self-help. A concerned Iran would not have looked on such developments passively. Could a fractured population that was mutually suspicious have been bought off with more jobs and functioning services? Not when they held a more basic fear, the need to survive against potentially violent threats. Given the state of the country as Western troops and diplomats found it, we cannot afford to adopt a naïvely developmental account of the crisis that ensued. The invasion was a blunder in the most important sense, not as a sound idea badly executed, but an unsound idea built on unsound assumptions. From these errors of judgement, failures of execution flowed.

---

[80] Ted Galen Carpenter, 'Rapid Reaction: McCain's Folly', *The National Interest*, 1 May 2008.

PART IV. ALTERNATIVE STRATEGIES

It is incumbent for the war's critics to articulate an alternative strategic pathway, if not to prescribe how international powers could have 'solved' or terminated the confrontation with Iraq, at least to suggest how the antagonism could have been handled more prudently.

Pro-war arguments about the counterfactual future in 2003 rest on a number of fallacies: that without the invasion, the sanctions programme would have broken down, leaving Saddam free to reconstitute his weapons programme; that the regime could not be contained or deterred; that time was urgently working against the West as the danger rose significantly; and that the choice for the US and its allies was a polar one, between 'regime change' and 'passivity'. Robert Kaufman makes a representative statement of this argument:

> Without Israel's preemptive attack of May 1981 on the Osirak nuclear reactor in Iraq, Saddam Hussein almost certainly would have possessed nuclear weapons when he invaded Kuwait in August 1990, which would have made the cost of liberating it prohibitive. Without the Gulf War of 1990–1991...Saddam might have achieved a nuclear capability within two years, according to the inspectors of Iraqi facilities...Saddam's propensity for risk taking also fell closer on the spectrum to Nazi Germany's under Hitler than to the Soviet Union's during the Cold War...the Kay Commission and Duelfer Report also affirm that it was only a matter of time before Saddam obtained such capabilities once the sanctions so painful to the Iraqi people inevitably broke down. WMD exponentially increased the potential danger of waiting too long to eliminate Saddam, prudently viewed through the prism of 9/11 and Saddam's refusal to abide by the inspection regime.[81]

As Kaufman then argues, opting for continuing inspections and the status quo rather than fighting would have kept the United States 'paralyzed' and Saddam 'defiant—all while the danger mounted'. Four assumptions are visible in Kaufman's portrait of the situation: a reckless aggressor, a collapsing sanctions programme, the West working dangerously against the clock, and a stark choice between decisive combat and paralysis. All four do not survive interrogation.

In the summer of 2001, the Joint Intelligence Committee and the UK Permanent Representative to the UN did indeed fear that the existing strategy of shackling the Iraqi regime would prove impermanent, that it 'continues to

---

[81] Robert G. Kaufman, *In Defence of the Bush Doctrine* (Lexington: University Press of Kentucky, 2007), pp. 39–40.

erode'.[82] The UK, France, Russia, and US were exploring 'smart sanctions' at that time precisely through the concern that existing 'hard' sanctions would unravel. Not only had they not successfully broken the regime, they had inflicted human cost that fed Islamist propaganda against the West. Oversight in the region and the military presence to support it also came at significant costs, involving a US garrison in Saudi Arabia that focused Bin Ladenists on America as 'the far enemy'.

These fears arose before the 9/11 terrorist attacks, and therein lies the first difficulty with the claim that existing strategies were bound to disintegrate. The 9/11 attacks altered the decision environment not just for those who opted for all-out war, but for states whose political will to contain Saddam increased. For those reluctant to support regime change, the 9/11 attacks raised incentives to maintain a modified and more discriminate containment programme. Accordingly, in May 2002, in the wake of fresh apprehensions about Iraq's weapons programme, the Bush administration successfully rallied the international community around new 'smart sanctions', imposing a tight import control system while allowing more civilian goods, under Security Council Resolution 1409.[83] Selectively tightened sanctions were possible, such as prohibitions on imports of materials for military use and the illicit export of oil, as well as increased monitoring and increased inspection of cargoes.[84] A revised sanctions programme of Resolution 1409, confined to military and dual-use equipment, Jack Straw told cabinet, would also help ensure that sanctions could not be blamed for humanitarian suffering in Iraq.[85] More could have been done to interdict illicit finances, such as Saddam's bank accounts in Jordan, and to curtail smuggling through Jordan, Syria, and Turkey, as Carne Ross attested, the First Secretary for Middle East at UK Permanent Mission to the UN in New York.[86]

There was still a 'menu' of intermediate choices available to the US and its allies, including continued vigilance, aerial and on-the-ground monitoring, shipping patrols, and punitive air strikes. These remained possible, as the 9/11 attacks had focused international attention on the need to disrupt and shut down the traffic in nuclear materials. Alternatively, the US and its allies could have attempted a bolder new settlement with Iraq after 9/11, organized around

---

[82] *Report of the Iraq Inquiry* v. 1, pp. 189–90; Sir Jeremy Greenstock, UK Permanent Representative to the UN, 20 November 2009, p. 2; v. 6, pp. 253–4; Joint Intelligence Committee Assessment, 'Iraq: Continuing Erosion of Sanctions', 25 July 2001.

[83] On the prior success of containment and its prospects for working hypothetically in the future, see G.A. Lopez & D. Cartright, 'Containing Iraq: sanctions worked', *Foreign Affairs* 83:4 (2004), pp. 90–103; Harrer, *Dismantling the Iraqi Nuclear Programme: The Inspections of the International Atomic Energy Agency, 1991–1998* (London: Routledge, 2014), pp. 253–5.

[84] As Richard Betts argued in advance, 'Suicide for Fear of Death?', *Foreign Affairs* 82:1 (2003), pp. 34–43, p. 42.

[85] Cabinet Conclusions, 16 May 2002, cited in *Report of the Iraq Inquiry*, vol. II, part 42, p. 11.

[86] Carne Ross, IIT, 12 July 2010, p. 4.

the common adversary al-Qaeda. Whether disarmament has taken place is difficult to prove, given it involves proving a negative. But there were other diplomatic goods to trade. In return for actionable intelligence on al-Qaeda and its affiliates, as well as Iraq suspending support for Palestinian suicide bombers, Washington could have informally relaxed its prior commitment to regime change in Baghdad and exchanged comprehensive economic sanctions for focused antiproliferation sanctions. Saddam's writ still ran strongly in northern Iraq, and denying that territory from Sunni Islamist terrorist networks would have been a valuable contribution to countering al-Qaeda's spread in the region. In return, Baghdad would benefit from the easing of economic strangulation and enjoy the credit for surviving in a lowered threat environment, but only in exchange for joining other authoritarian regimes in assisting the campaign against al-Qaeda. So there were other choices that deserved to be entertained, modifications of containment of varying ambition. Either way, the alternative to going 'all in' on Iraq was not to walk away from the table and hope for the best, as hawks imply.

Counterproliferation strategies do not always succeed, however. Arguably, the Iraqi regime that had a record of deception and non-cooperation could have resumed an underground weapons programme. If so, the road to constructing a deliverable nuclear bomb would have been expensive, technically demandingn and conducted under the glare of international observation. Running a clandestine programme impedes and complicates proliferation. It would have been years yet before Saddam's regime could complete the job. Saddam's nuclear programme was often self-sabotaged and self-disrupted, falling prey to coercive management and inefficiency. In 1991, inspectors had discovered that Iraq possessed nuclear facilities but not weapons-grade highly enriched uranium (HEU), and even before sanctions and safeguards were imposed, 'after years of coercive, authoritarian mismanagement, Iraq's scientific and technical workers had become exhausted, cynical, and divided.'[87] By 2003, sanctions had gravely damaged the possibility of weapons programmes being restored, as approximately three hundred interviews by the Iraq Survey Group with Iraqi scientists, engineers, and officials revealed.

Scepticism about Saddam's capacity to reconstitute a nuclear programme to completion is not just a retrospective judgement. The hurdles Iraq would have to overcome were known, and knowable, at the time. Firstly, evidence suggested that if there was such a programme, it had made little progress and had to be conducted in extremely clandestine ways, itself an inhibiting factor. On the eve of war, on 7 March 2003, the International Atomic Energy Agency Director General ElBaradei and the UN Special Commission on Iraq led by Hans Blix declared to the UN Security Council that there was no evidence of

---

[87] Jacques Hymans, 'Botching the Bomb: Why Nuclear Weapons Programs Often Fail on Their Own—and Why Iran's Might Too', *Foreign Affairs* 91:3 (2012), pp. 44–53, p. 50.

resumed nuclear activities or nuclear-related prohibited activities, and noted the deplorable state of Iraq's industrial infrastructure. They reported progress from more than one hundred visits to suspect sites and interviews with Iraqi scientists, finding no evidence or plausible indication of the revival of a nuclear weapons programme in Iraq. They predicted that the agency should be able to provide the Security Council with an objective and thorough assessment of Iraq's nuclear-related capabilities 'in the near future'. Destruction of the *al Samoud* ballistic missiles, which had exhibited ranges beyond that allowed by the UN, were also underway. There were no stockpiles of chemical and biological weapons found, though it was not yet possible to document destruction of all weapons produced since before the 1991 Gulf War. The Bush administration's response was swift and negative. In the absence of hard evidence of rearmament, it fell back on the National Intelligence Estimate of 2002, citing Saddam's history of aggression and criminality.

Further progress in WMD rearmament by Saddam would face difficult hurdles. In March 2002, the UK MOD had identified the obstacles Iraq would have to overcome in order to acquire a nuclear capability. According to its Defence Intelligence Staff (DIS), Iraq lacked the fissile material to make a weapon, to rebuild its uranium enrichment programme could take 'years' and require 'extensive foreign procurement' which would 'not be possible with effective sanctions in place'. To make a weapon quickly, Iraq would need to acquire HEU from the 'black market', which would be 'very difficult' though 'credible'. In addition, Iraq would need to acquire a neutron initiator, and had lacked a nuclear reactor since 1991. It would then need the 'theory and practicalities' of how to use such a component, and this could only be quickly done with 'outside expertise'. A missile warhead would take 'at least two years longer'. Alternatively, it could acquire a crude nuclear device that would be large and unreliable and would have to be delivered by large unconventional and unreliable means (such as a lorry).[88] A second opinion broadly agreed, adding that if Iraq against the odds acquired HEU and a neutron initiator from a third party, it would also require engineering integration and explosive trials, with a 'low' signature for detection.[89] This expert's rough estimate for the highly unlikely achievement of all these steps was a period of two to three years. In the meantime, Saddam would need to have achieved the nearly impossible task of indigenously producing enough fissile materials, and this would produce 'relatively large signatures'. While the 'clock' on the worst-case estimates was reasonably brief, note the formidable technical hurdles identified, and the difficulty of keeping it undetected. It would have required tests to

---

[88] Minute, DIS to DI ST, 'What Does Iraq Need to Do to Get the Bomb Quickly?', 20 March 2002.

[89] Minute, Dr Paul Roper, Director Strategic Technology to Policy Director, 27 March 2002, 'Iraq—Nuclear Weapons'.

make any bomb deliverable, and a functioning infrastructure of facilities and capable personnel. Should an alert international community have suspected proliferation activity and attacked his facilities, Saddam did not have the deterrence capability that North Korea does, and could not credibly threaten a neighbouring state's cities.

Even if Saddam did rearm covertly but nevertheless successfully, with chemical and biological if not nuclear weapons, how far can we assume that he was a reckless actor, who may have collaborated with al-Qaeda and transferred technology or expertise into their hands? Even if he failed to acquire a deliverable nuclear bomb, might he have donated chemical or biological instruments to terrorists?

The war's defenders suggest Saddam and the regime were almost impossible to deter because of a general aggressive risk-prone irrationality, bordering on madness, exhibited by the historic persecution of their 'own people' and their attacks on other states. Such a regime was not capable of being restrained by the logic of deterrence-via-punishment. In the words of the UK's Joint Intelligence Committee, Saddam's 'thought processes did not work in a recognisably Western, rational and logical way'.[90] This contention rests on two errors, a historical error and an analytical error. Historically, Saddam was deterrable from the most high-risk aggression with unconventional weapons. And analytically, a regime's repressive quality at home does not necessarily make it pathologically aggressive abroad against major powers with the means to retaliate.

As the recently uncovered tapes of internal regime deliberations suggests, Saddam's government was capable of being deterred once a threshold of first-order interests and significant threat of retaliation was reached. While the exact point of deterrability is not easy to determine, there was a sometimes explicit and sometimes implicit calculation that Iraq's nuclear adversaries could and might well inflict a price that was too high in return for WMD use. His regime was demonstrably not successfully deterred from everything. Saddam was prone to 'shooting the messenger', at times distorting information to fit his predetermined goals. But the evidence recently revealed suggests that despite his regime's suboptimal decision-making and inefficient processing of information, American threats of punishment for the most reckless behaviour remained credible and focused the mind.[91] Saddam had committed notable aggressions on his neighbours, but on both occasions (against Iran from September 1980 and Kuwait in August 1990), the US did not actively try to deter the aggression, and Saddam calculated that he could attack his targets

---

[90] Minutes, 4 September 2002, Joint Intelligence Committee, p. 2.

[91] A point conceded even by a scholar who portrays Saddam as otherwise 'very, very hard to deter': Amatzia Baram, 'Deterrence Lessons from Iraq', *Foreign Affairs* 91:4 (2012), pp. 76–90, p. 85.

without a consequential intervention by major powers. In the Iran case, he was correct. Though Washington gave no explicit 'green light' to his attack, Saddam forecast that the US, while disapproving, would not step in, and that Iraq would inflict a quick and decisive victory on a weakened Iran to seize territory, and thus implicitly did not expect the US to enter the conflict as a belligerent.[92] In the case of Kuwait, Saddam counted wrongly on Washington's aversion to a ground campaign, after meetings with US envoys appeared to signal US reluctance to intervene. When he was given clear signals by the West with the threat of punishment in return for attacks on first-order interests above a threshold of aggression, he was demonstrably deterrable. In the course of the Gulf War 1990-1, Washington threatened him with an unspecified but definite threat of punishment should he use chemical and biological weapons, and he accordingly refrained. Tariq Aziz, along with two defectors (the Head of Iraqi Military Intelligence and the Head of the Iraqi News Agency), recalled that Saddam believed the US would retaliate with nuclear strikes if the Iraqis used chemical or biological weapons on US forces.[93] Saddam's senior ministers feared even threatening to use chemical weapons would lead to a nuclear strike. At a secret meeting of the Revolutionary Command Council (RCC) in the autumn of 1990, Saddam's trusted deputy Izzat al-Douri warned that 'It is dangerous for us to reveal our intentions to use chemical weapons. We should not do that'. Tariq Aziz at the same meeting suggested that Iraqi use of chemical weapons would 'give [the Americans] excuse for a nuclear attack'.[94] Atomic threats were credible in Iraq. Saddam believed there was the real possibility of Anglo-American nuclear attacks in any event, practised civilian evacuations, and his deputies

---

[92] Hal Brands, 'Saddam Hussein, the United States, and the Invasion of Iran: Was there a Green Light?', *Cold War History* 12:2 (2012), pp. 319-43, pp. 330-7.

[93] See James Baker III, *The Politics of Diplomacy: Revolution, War and Peace, 1989-1992* (New York: GP Putnam's Sons, 1995), p. 359; 'Text of Letter from Bush to Hussein', *The New York Times*, 13 January 1991, as reprinted in Mark Grossman, *Encyclopedia of the Persian Gulf War* (Santa Barbara: ABC-CLIO, 1995), p. 396; *Frontline* interview with General Wafic al-Samarrai, cited in Vipin Narang, *Nuclear Strategy in the Modern Era: Regional Powers and International Conflict* (Princeton: Princeton University Press, 2014), p. 294; Victor A. Utgoff, 'Nuclear Weapons and the Deterrence of Biological and Chemical Warfare', Occasional Paper 36 (Washington DC, 1997) p. 2, n. 4; 'Saad al-Bazzaz: An Insider's View of Iraq', *Middle East Quarterly* 2:4 (December 1995); while Tariq Aziz may have had a possible ulterior motive in presenting Saddam as deterrable, in order to weaken the sanctions and inspections programme, the two defectors did not have such incentives, and in fact otherwise presented Saddam as difficult to deter: see David Palkki, 'Deterring Saddam Hussein's Iraq: Domestic Audience Costs and Credibility Assessments in Theory and Practice' (unpublished dissertation, University of California, Los Angeles, 2013), p. 146.

[94] Derived from the Conflict Records Research Centre, SH-SHTP-A-000-848, 'Saddam Hussein and his Advisors Discussing Potential War with the United States', 1990. Cited in Baram, 'Deterrence Lesson from Iraq', p. 85; Palkki, 'Deterring Saddam Hussein's Iraq', p. 124.

warned of behaviour that might increase the chances of it.[95] If the regime was reluctant even to threaten chemical weapons use publicly for fear of raising the probability of atomic retaliation, it is hard to envisage it transferring WMD to actors who had sworn to attack America, actors who were also beyond Iraq's control. Saddam in 1990–1 also wished to reserve his chemical stockpile to deter the invasion of Iraq, and by aiming to be a deterrer as well as deterree, this also suggests he ultimately understood the logic of deterrence.[96] The same logic defined his stance towards Israel. Saddam intended his future nuclear weapons not for 'first use' against Tel Aviv, but to neutralize Israel's nuclear capability with the threat of retaliation, in order to enable him to prevail in a conventional struggle with the state he obsessively hated. Again, this suggests a capacity to understand threat-and-response in a 'rational, logical way'. Once it had been expelled from Kuwait, the Baghdad regime grew capable of being dissuaded, by credible threats, from repeating such aggression. In October 1994, when Saddam's forces mobilized and advanced on the Kuwaiti border, probably to pressure the United Nations to remove sanctions, President Clinton deployed marine and naval forces into the region, along with French and British warships. Saddam backed down in the face of this imposing correlation of forces, whose credible threat was buttressed by America's prior willingness to act on Kuwait, and Saddam soon afterwards recognized the sovereignty of Kuwait.[97] True, threats of retaliatory punishment did not deter Saddam from some provocations, such as burning Kuwaiti oil fields, firing SCUD missiles at Tel Aviv and Riyadh in the Gulf War of 1990-1, or suspending cooperation with UN weapons inspectors. Saddam and his regime were, though, deterred from attacks on US core interests. The main threat scenario suggested by the war parties in Washington and London, whereby Saddam would hand over WMD to terrorists, is therefore wildly unrealistic. He was an imperfect calculator who was ultimately willing to limit his risk-taking, not a one-dimensional, reckless adventurer indifferent to the threat of punishment.

The notion that Saddam's domestic oppression, namely his assaults on Kurds, Marsh Arabs, and Shia dissidents, indicates that he was an irrational and undeterrable actor is also flawed. It is based upon the false inference that the slaughter of a regime's 'own' subjects with conventional and chemical weapons, relatively vulnerable weak targets not in a position to inflict serious

---

[95] See Paul Idon, 'Saddam Hussein Seriously Feared a U.S. Nuclear Strike During the Gulf War', *The National Interest*, 24 January 2017; David Palkki, 'Calculated Ambiguity, Nuclear Weapons and Saddam's Strategic Restraint', in Scott D. Sagan, PASSC Final Report: 'Deterring Rogue Regimes: Rethinking Deterrence Theory and Practice', 8 July 2013, Stanford University.

[96] Hal Brands & David Palkki, 'Saddam, Israel and the Bomb: Nuclear Alarmism Justified?', *International Security* 36:1 (2011), pp. 133–66.

[97] On this operation, *Vigilant Warrior*, see Daniel Byman, Kenneth Pollack & Matthew Waxman, 'Coercing Saddam Hussein: Lessons from the Past', *Survival* 40:3 (1998), pp. 127–51, pp. 137–8.

punishment, necessarily means that (short of immediate self-defence) Saddam might elect to use them against targets that can retaliate at high cost. History is full of authoritarian oppressive regimes who nevertheless limit their aggression against major states outside their borders: Francoist Spain, Stalin's Soviet Union, and Mao's China (once it had acquired nuclear weapons). Indeed, the commitment to survival is the logic that ties together their inward cruelty and their outward caution, putting down resistance that can be neutralized at acceptable cost, while avoiding external threats that cannot. Proponents of war in 2003 argued that Saddam might use his arsenal of chemical and biological weapons, either directly or via a transfer, to attack Western targets. Without the knowledge that he had already disarmed, however, the reasonable objection was that if Saddam actually still possessed a WMD arsenal and was such an incautious and undeterrable rogue, why had he not already used them in this way? His regime was already in a state of continuous conflict and confrontation with the US and its allies, yet had not taken these risks. Saddam was not cautious when he saw opportunities and calculated he would not be overthrown and could ride out the international response. He was cautious when direct and credible threats from major powers focused the mind. He was homicidal, not suicidal.[98]

The *post hoc* estimate that counterfactually Saddam could have raced to a bomb if left in power, is implicitly modelled on the Iraq of the 1980s. Even the Iraq of that earlier period had experienced almost prohibitive difficulties in conducting its nuclear programme. Blair's estimate does not take into account the cumulative degradation wrought by sanctions, or the likelihood of continued international vigilance, and it falsely assumes a well-resourced, externally undisturbed weapons organization. This is part of a wider problem with the justifications for war ever since the British government was making the case in 2002, that the severe threat assessments assumed Iraq in its earlier, pre-sanctions state, rather than an Iraq depleted over time. Iraq by 2003 was generally weakened, and this information was available in open source. According to the assessment of Daniel Byman in 2001, based on the expertise of Anthony Cordesman,

> As Iraq depended on imports for logistical and supply assistance, as well as for complete systems, its military readiness and effectiveness has plummeted. Efforts to meet shortfalls through smuggling and by increasing domestic production have largely failed. Iraqi forces have not been able to conduct routine maintenance, let alone modernization. Iraq's military capacity is less than 20 per cent of what it was in 1990. Information on the progress of Iraq's WMD programs is limited, but an intuitive argument can be made that a regime under tight international scrutiny, with its dual-use exports being controlled, has made at

---

[98] Also making this argument were John J. Mearsheimer & Stephen M. Walt, 'An Unnecessary War', *Foreign Policy* 134 (2003), pp. 50–9.

best limited progress on these programs, particularly when compared to their rapid development in the 1980s.[99]

And as Robin Cook observed of the British dossier in September 2002, around half of it drew upon information about Saddam's weapons capacity before 1998 as though this were a guide to its state by 2003, failing to take into account the decay of biological and chemical agents, and the rest presuming present capacity from historic capabilities.[100] On the same issue looking back, regarding the state of Saddam's Iraq by 2003, consider the argument of Jacques Hymans:

> even if, hypothetically, Saddam had resumed pushing for the bomb as hard as he could, and even if the aluminium tubes had indeed been destined for a reconstituted gas centrifuge uranium enrichment effort, nonetheless the Iraqi state was *no longer organisationally strong enough* to make any progress toward that objective. A decade of crippling sanctions—and more to the point, two decades of Saddam's misrule—had predictably brought both Iraq's society and its state to a shocking level of decomposition. The rising corruption—indeed the criminalisation—of the regime had devoured even its core national security apparatus.[101]

The supposition that if Saddam was left in office, this would lead to a nuclear Iraq wrongly suggests that his weapons programme would be undisturbed, as though there were nothing the US and its allies could have done to disrupt any revived programme short of removing him from power. This injects a false polarity into the argument. As Kaufman's own analysis above concedes, measures such as airstrikes on facilities, the turning back of expansion beyond Iraq's borders, and imposing inspections backed by force, measures short of outright invasion and occupation, could successfully disrupt, delay, and deter. In the Gulf War of 1990–1, US bombing severely degraded Iraq's Tuwaitha nuclear facility.[102] Using such alternative and more limited measures of force would not be risk-free. And it would be hardly satisfying in its inconclusiveness and its concession of time to the Iraqi regime. Down the track, the US and its allies would have had a further debate about how to suppress a revived programme. They may have had an appointment with the 'Osirak dilemma', whereby striking can set back a programme physically, while raising the

---

[99] Daniel Byman, 'After the Storm: US Policy Towards Iraq since 1991', *Political Science Quarterly* 115:4 (2001), pp. 493–516, p. 503.
[100] Robin Cook, *The Point of Departure* (London: Simon & Schuster UK Ltd, 2003), pp. 215–16.
[101] Jacques E. Hymans, *Achieving Nuclear Ambitions: Scientists, Politicians and Proliferation* (Cambridge: Cambridge University Press, 2012), p. 120. (My Italics).
[102] Federation of American Scientists, see https://fas.org/nuke/guide/iraq/facility/osiraq.htm.

target's motivation to nuclearize.[103] Given the alternative, however, this was still the best way of limiting and degrading any threat while avoiding the hazards of occupying a state. There was enough time to manage the risk without embracing the graver risk of occupying the country. Sustained vigilance, over a long time period, and against a higher standard of proof, was warranted.

Taken together, these observations suggest that a containment and deterrence strategy was the least bad option. Treating Saddam's hypothetical rearmament as 'only a matter of time' avoids the reality that this was a weakened state with a demoralized officialdom whose capacity to reconstitute a nuclear programme was depleted. There was still significant time within which other more limited measures could be applied. For the regime to 'go nuclear', it would have had to pull off extremely difficult and multiple challenges within that time. And it would have had to have done so undetected, and even then, to behave so recklessly would have invited devastating retaliation. Given the availability and development of surveillance technologies, and the attentiveness of states to early warnings, it would have been extremely difficult to develop nuclear capabilities undetected.[104]

Alternative strategies and warnings against the unintended consequences of invasion were articulated at the time. In September 2002, thirty-three American scholars laid out the case for vigilant containment, the logic of deterrence, the lack of credible evidence for Saddam's ties with al-Qaeda, and gave a warning that Iraq was a deeply divided society that would require occupation and policing for years, and that invading would damage US interests.[105] In the same spirit, the British government was publicly warned. Sir Michael Quinlan, former Permanent Undersecretary at the MOD, warned in August 2002 that striking Iraq would be an 'unnecessary and precarious gamble', that 'deterrence can be brought to bear', that containment could be refreshed by a clear declaration that WMD use would be treated as a crime against humanity, that governing Iraq afterwards would be difficult, given the difficulty of finding a regime that suited US interests and held popular support, and that while UN Security Council assent should not be an absolute condition, an attack would

---

[103] On the 'state of the art' of this debate, about the slowing and the accelerating effects of a preventive strike on nuclear facilities, see Uri Sadot, 'Osirak and the Counter-Proliferation Puzzle', *Security Studies* 25:4 (2016), pp. 646–76; Sarah E. Kreps & Matthew Fuhrmann, 'Attacking The Atom: Does Bombing Nuclear Facilities Affect Proliferation?', *Journal of Strategic Studies* 34:2 (2011): pp. 161–87; Dan Reiter, 'Preventive Attacks against Nuclear Programs and the "Success" at Osiraq', *Nonproliferation Review* 12:2 (July 2005), pp. 355–71.

[104] On the implausibility of most states acquiring a nuclear weapon undetected for these reasons, see Nuno P. Monteiro & Alexandre Debs, 'The Strategic Logic of Nuclear Proliferation', *International Security* 39:2 (2014), pp. 7–51, p. 25, n. 36.

[105] 'War with Iraq is not in America's National Interest', *The New York Times*, 26 September 2002.

breach the tradition of just cause, proportionality, and right authority.[106] Time has vindicated these judgements.

PART V. JOHN MCTERNAN'S CASE FOR WAR

In June 2016, former Labour political advisor John McTernan made the case in hindsight for invading Iraq.[107] His broadside made a number of counter-factual claims that the war's critics ought to engage with, but often don't. Here I respond to his claims, *ad seriatum*, which are italicized:

> *What would have happened if we hadn't invaded Iraq? Tony Blair's pre-emptive framing of the Chilcot Report proceeds apace. The latest instalment is an interview in which he finally responded to the accusations made against him, and often repeated by Jeremy Corbyn: 'I'm accused of being a war criminal for removing Saddam Hussein—who by the way was a war criminal—and yet Jeremy is seen as a progressive icon as we stand by and watch the people of Syria barrel-bombed, beaten and starved into submission and do nothing.*

The use of Syria as a counterfactual foil against criticism of the disastrous invasion of Iraq is now commonplace among hawkish defenders of the war. It joins 'Rwanda' in the arsenal of analogies deployed by the war parties of London and Washington, being repeated by advocates of war in Iraq from *The Economist* to George Osborne MP in the Commons.[108] McTernan's statement implies that in order to prevent crises like Syria or Rwanda, wars like Iraq are an occasional necessary price, a doctrine that would repeat the experiment with all its costs and unintended consequences. Not only is that price excessive on any reasonable measure. It is self-defeating. For as we have seen, the invasion of 2003 played a central role in the energizing of Islamism in the region, contributing to the chaos across the porous Syria–Iraq border. Consider also that the invasion of Iraq demonstrably did not deter the Assad regime nor Islamist rebel groups from committing atrocities, even though McTernan is about to argue that such wars are necessary to impress and inhibit dictators and terrorists.

In any event, it is not the case that Britain or the US did 'nothing' about the Syrian crisis that erupted in 2011. Both governments openly declared in July 2011 that President Bashar al-Assad was no longer the legitimate ruler of

---

[106] Michael Quinlan, 'War on Iraq: A Blunder and a Crime', *The Financial Times*, 7 August 2002.
[107] John McTernan, 'If Jeremy Corbyn had stopped Tony Blair invading Iraq, dictators and jihadists would rule the world today', *The Daily Telegraph*, 9 June 2016.
[108] 'The cost of inaction', *The Economist*, 24 September 2015; George Osborne, *Hansard*, vol. 618, 13 December 2016.

Syria, and that 'Assad must go'. It is not clear exactly how much this contributed to internationalizing and hardening the conflict. Given the proximity of the West's decrees to the beginning of defections, armed resistance, and increasing repression, and given that the rebels and regime were intransigent in their negotiating afterwards, we can reasonably assume it raised the stakes and prolonged the war.[109] No ruler in 2011 could afford to treat such declarations from these two countries as hollow, given their recent track record of toppling adversaries. Assad was a committed survivor with determined backers in Russia and Iran, and even when cornered would not agree to be shown the door by any international fiat. Yet once again, Western officials underestimated the possibility of resistance to their demands. As well as strengthening Assad's existential stakes in the conflict, the statements emboldened the Syrian opposition and precipitated defections from the regime and the formation of the Free Syrian Army. The UK and US then followed up on their pronouncement by providing further formal encouragement through recognition of the Syrian National Council, and through material support to rebel groups: arms, finance, and sanctuary in Turkey, a NATO ally, and granting a licence to an NGO in Washington to raise money for the rebels. Whether these measures were wise is open to debate. But they amounted to a significant early intervention. A larger intervention may have been more catastrophic, as the downfall of Assad or his heirs may have prompted an implosion in Syria that would likely have created a vacuum for combat-seasoned Islamist groups, endangering Alawites, Kurds, Druze, Christians, secularists, women, and any Muslims averse to the severe demands of militant groups. The experience of other 'regime change' experiments suggests that it was reasonable to presume against it. Wary of the costs of a larger intervention, outside powers did enough to prolong and escalate the conflict. Clashes about who is, or is not, a 'war criminal' or 'progressive' are a poor substitute for judicious analysis of what happened, and why.

> *This provokes the thought—what if the Stop the War march in 2003 had been successful? If the display of public opinion had swayed the Commons and the vote had ended up like that on Syria. What would that alternative universe look like? What would have happened if these marchers had had their way? First, it would have been the end of Tony Blair. His resignation in the face of a rebuff would not only have been followed by a new Labour leader—probably Gordon Brown—but*

---

[109] As Alexander B. Downes observed, 'By declaring that Assad has no future as president of Syria, the United States has effectively torpedoed meaningful negotiations to end the war short of decisive victory for one side or the other. The reasons are twofold. First, in calling for Assad's overthrow, the United States has essentially endorsed the rebels' principal war aim. The knowledge that the world's only superpower supports their primary political objective has unsurprisingly made the rebels more intransigent'. 'Why Regime Change is a Bad Idea in Syria', in Marc Lynch (ed.), *The Political Science of Syria's Civil War* (POMPES Briefings, 2013), pp. 61–3, p. 62.

also by a Tory victory in 2005. Michael Howard would have been swept to power by his campaign on immigration. And, paradoxically, the UK would probably be firmly ensconced within the EU—an early referendum, held well before the current refugee crisis would have seen an easy endorsement of the status quo. Also, Jack McConnell would have been returned in a minority government in 2007 in Scotland, halting the ineluctable rise of the SNP. It wouldn't be a pleasant world, but at least there would be no British forces deployed abroad.

In the event of Britain abstaining from Operation Telic, there would have been forces deployed abroad. Britain's principal deployments in the period April 2003 to April 2004 ranged across twenty-eight countries apart from Iraq, from Afghanistan where the UK contributed to the NATO-led International Security Assistance Force (ISAF), to the NATO Stabilisation Force and Kosovo Force in the Balkans, to security sector advice and reform in Sierra Leone, as well as deployments from Brunei and Nepal to Northern Ireland and the Caribbean. British forces were also deployed continuously at sea in the form of the Trident nuclear-armed submarine force, and the Royal Air Force recorded approximately 19,000 hours on operations outside Iraq.[110] We can forgive McTernan's sarcastic quip, suggesting that non-invasion amounts to global withdrawal, as an error of haste.

Defeat in the Commons may well have ended Blair's premiership. It isn't clear that this would have led to the fall of the Labour government. As Iraq and its chaotic aftermath was an electoral liability for the government in the election of 2005, would non-participation really have induced the British electorate to embrace the Opposition that also supported the war? To the extent that voting motivation can be measured, immigration exerted only a limited salience in the 2005 general election, as those who ranked the issue most highly were either already Conservative voters or were disaffected non-voters, while 'asylum and immigration' were surpassed in pre-election polls measuring issue ranking, by health, education, law and order, taxation and public services, and the economy.[111] Oddly, McTernan claims that the same population that was allegedly so aggrieved about immigration that it would have revolted at the ballot box would have tamely endorsed the status quo in a referendum on the EU and one of its foundational principles, the freedom of movement.

Second, the real change would have been in the Middle East—or rather, the real lack of change. Saddam Hussein, a dictator and a war criminal guilt of genocide,

---

[110] See Ministry of Defence, *Annual Report and Accounts 2003–2004* (House of Commons, London: Stationery Office, 2004), pp. 14–19.
[111] See Robert Ford, 'An Iceberg Issue? Immigration at the 2005 British General Election', unpublished paper, 2005. I am grateful to Professor Ford for his permission to cite; see also ICM/Guardian Opinion Poll discussed in Alan Travis, 'Labour Ahead on Key Issues in Run-Up to Election', *The Guardian*, 22 March 2005.

> would have stayed in place and would be here to this day, strengthened internally by facing down the United Nations and its sanctions and weapons inspectors. Nuclear proliferation would have had a major boost. Under no circumstances would Iran facing a resurgent Saddam abandon its own nuclear programme. Had Jeremy Corbyn prevailed, Saddam Hussein would still be in power.

McTernan confuses two countries. Britain's non-participation would not have prevented the United States invading. Had there been no invasion by the US, Saddam Hussein would have remained in power and won some prestige for surviving. This would hardly make him a 'resurgent' actor. Iraq would have remained a weakened, encircled, monitored country whose capacity for external aggression was depleted, with no WMD arsenal or ties to al-Qaeda. Saddam's recovery to restart his nuclear programme would have faced formidable obstacles within a dysfunctional scientific-industrial base. Internally, the survival of his regime and its control of the army and security services would have made it more difficult for the Islamic State to rise in northern Iraq. It is worth considering that this group was also guilty of genocide, also seeks weapons of mass destruction, and is considered too zealous by al-Qaeda. By not invading, the US and its allies would not have destroyed a regime that had effectively disarmed, and thus would not have set a precedent to encourage nuclear proliferation. There would not be American troops on Iran's western border, and less argument in Tehran that nuclear weapons were a necessary deterrent against encircling powers. The invasion of Iraq did not prevent, and may have encouraged, Putin's Russia going ahead with the modernization of its nuclear arsenal and its aggressive doctrines of warfighting nuclear use.

> Libya too would be well on the way to a bomb—Gaddafi would have had no Blair to persuade him to abandon that programme. Syria would not be the site of a humanitarian crisis with nearly half the population displaced. Not because the country would be more democratic but because of precisely the opposite—Assad would have been an unconstrained hard man. Barrel bombs and gas would have pummelled the Syrian people into submission. The lesson would not be lost around the Middle East and North Africa—the rule of hard men prospers.

One overblown claim follows another. Libya's nuclear programme was not advanced. The invasion of Iraq may have exerted some marginal accelerating effect, but was not a significant cause or catalyst of Libyan disarmament, and was certainly not a precondition for it. Bilateral talks had begun in earnest four years before the war, indeed Colonel Gaddafi had already offered to disarm and it was US preconditions (over the Pan Am 130 question and chemical weapons) and bargaining over the terms that delayed the resolution.[112] While credible force was likely a factor, this was already established, as part of a

---

[112] Martin Indyk, 'The Iraq War Did Not Force Gadaffi's Hand', *The Financial Times*, 9 March 2004.

coming together of concessions, guarantees, and Libya's own desire to end its pariah status.[113] As one of the leading US negotiators explained,

> The Iraq war, which had not yet started, was not the driving force behind Libya's move. Rather, Libya was willing to deal because of credible diplomatic representations by the United States over the years, which convinced the Libyans that doing so was critical to achieving their strategic and domestic goals. Just as with Lockerbie, an explicit quid pro quo was offered: American officials indicated that a verifiable dismantling of Libya's weapons projects would lead the removal our own sanctions [sic].[114]

McTernan claims that the example of Saddam Hussein's survival would have encouraged regional leaders to rule as 'hard men' without restraint, and Bashar al-Assad to act as an 'unconstrained hard man'. The difficulty with this argument is that in history as it actually happened, Saddam's overthrow did not prevent those regimes ruling without restraint. It did not relax their authoritarian grip. Saudi Arabia and Egypt remained internally repressive American client states. The government of Syria, according to Human Rights Watch in 2010,

> continues to rule by emergency powers. Syria's security agencies, the feared *mukhabarat*, continue to detain people without arrest warrants, frequently refuse to disclose their whereabouts for weeks and sometimes months, and regularly engage in torture. Special courts set up under Syria's emergency laws, such as the Supreme State Security Court (SSSC), sentence people following unfair trials.[115]

Syria's regime was not deterred by the overthrow of Saddam. Rather, it acted as a spoiler against US interests in Iraq, hosting and assisting networks of foreign fighters to counterbalance the occupying coalition.[116] The Iraq War did not overawe America's regional rivals like Syria and Iran into self-restraint and caution, but provoked resistance.

---

[113] See Bruce W. Jentleson & Christopher A. Whytock, 'Who "Won" Libya? The Force-Diplomacy Debate and Its Implications for Theory and Policy', *International Security* 30:3 (2005/06), pp. 47–86; Lisa Anderson, 'Rogue Libya's Long Road', *Middle East Report* 24 (2006), p. 46; Gawdat Bahgat, 'Proliferation of Weapons of Mass Destruction: The Case of Libya', *International Relations* 22:1 (2008), p. 107; Joseph Cirincione, 'The world just got safer: give diplomacy the credit', *The Washington Post*, 11 January 2004; Peter Viggo Jackobson, 'Reinterpreting Libya's WMD Turnaround: Bridging the Carrot-Coercion Divide', *Journal of Strategic Studies* 35:4 (2012), pp. 489–512.
[114] Flynt L. Leverett, 'Why Libya Gave Up the Bomb', Brookings Institution Op-Ed, 23 January 2004.
[115] Human Rights Watch, *A Wasted Decade* (New York, 2010), p. 2.
[116] Matthew Levitt, 'Syria's Financial Support for Jihad', *Middle East Quarterly* (2010), pp. 39–48; Anthony H. Cordesman, 'The Department of Defense Quarterly Report on Stability and Security in Iraq: The Warning Indicators', Center for Strategic and International Studies, Washington, D.C., 22 December 2006.

> Third, multilateralism would have collapsed. A triumphant Stop the War coalition would have carried on—targeting all UK troop deployments overseas. The RAF would have been withdrawn from patrolling the no-fly zone over the Kurdish Region of Iraq. British troops would have withdrawn from Afghanistan—destabilising and, ultimately destroying, the fragile achievement of establishing a democracy. Blair's Chicago speech on liberal interventionism would not just have been forgotten, the world order would have returned to amoral pragmatism—if you don't bother us, we won't bother about what you do to your people. The winner would have been Vladimir Putin. The whole of Ukraine, not merely Crimea, would have been reabsorbed back into the Russian Federation, along with Belarus and Kazakhstan.

McTernan's picture of a 'Stop the War' domino wave is at odds with his other claim, that the British people would have flocked to the hawkish and Atlanticist Conservative Party. There is also in McTernan's alternative history a strangely zero-sum view of foreign policy. To oppose the invasion of Iraq was not to oppose all multilateral efforts. Countries opposed to the war, such as Canada and France, remained committed in Afghanistan. Rival major powers China and Russia, who would have vetoed the final UN Resolution authorizing war, nevertheless cooperated in imposing sanctions on Iran's nuclear programme. Outside the Stop the War movement, opposition to the Iraq War did not come hand-in-hand with an outright opposition to containing Saddam Hussein. Indeed, the burden of the mainstream anti-war argument was that containment and inspections under the aegis of a military presence deserved more time. Neither does it logically follow that declining to invade one country necessarily entails a universal retreat into 'amoral pragmatism'. McTernan once again offers a binary morality play, by suggesting that failing to invade Iraq and the subsequent collapse of cooperative security efforts would lead Putin to fall on countries in Russia's 'near abroad'. Isn't it possible, though, that the West could have decided not to invade Iraq, while maintaining NATO and nuclear deterrence and the willingness to use sanctions to impose costs on aggression? But in McTernan's self-fulfilling worldview, the West's adversaries are not so much major powers with legitimate security interests to be both bargained with and resisted, but one-dimensional monsters.

> It wouldn't be a pleasant world, but at least there would be no British forces deployed abroad. It wouldn't be a peaceful world either—the violence would be being done to other people in some far-off country of which we know little. It wouldn't, though, bring peace to Britain. The signal to the forces of jihad would have been unmistakable—Britain is weak, not up for a fight. We would be targeted, not ignored for precisely that reason. Stop the War isn't, in the end, about stopping all war—it's about conceding the right to wage war and inflict violence to some of the nastiest regimes in the world. If Jeremy Corbyn had stopped Tony Blair invading Iraq, dictators and jihadists would rule the world today.

There would be British forces deployed abroad, far and wide, and with more capacity given they would not be sent into Iraq. The world in 2003 may not have been peaceful, but Britain at least would not have taken part in a venture that worsened and spread violence in one region, rather than reducing it. The forces of jihad were not intimidated by the invasion of Iraq. Reeling from Afghanistan, they were inspired and galvanized by it as a rallying point and geopolitical opportunity. The Joint Intelligence Committee warned on 10 February 2003 that the invasion would increase the threat from al-Qaeda at the onset of military action, and lead to attacks elsewhere, especially in the US and the UK.[117] This does not mean that any force used against militant Islamists is futile. Wars tend to provoke retaliation, and such retaliation may be a necessary price of long-term measures to suppress a threat. And there are no guarantees of immunity from Islamist attacks. The range of targets chosen by Islamists is wide and varying. But it does suggest that McTernan's notion of al-Qaeda only attacking the reluctant is false. As it happened, al-Qaeda in Iraq was not impressed by the fortitude shown by the invaders. Among other Islamist groups, it launched continuous attacks on coalition forces. Occupation did not signal strength, but overstretch, with the US appealing for international help by 2004. Unable to defeat insurgent resistance decisively, occupiers were steadily bled to the point of crisis and, in Britain's case, into humiliation.

At the root of McTernan's claims is a crude understanding of the world as a system defined only by machismo, where dictators and terrorists are easily impressed by displays of resolve, and where the only decisive test is to appear tough, and the only way to signal toughness is to be continuously on a war footing. That prescription proved false about al-Qaeda. It proved false about Putin's Russia, which invaded Georgia in the summer of 2008 while the US had over 142,000 troops in Iraq. It proved false in the civil war in the Sudan, which raged concurrently with the Iraq War and led to genocide. Like most international actors, these human organizations are not simply a wolfish killer breed, repelled by strength and preying on weakness. They also wish to look tough, and they also strike to counterbalance or reduce perceived threats. If anything, being attritionally caught in Iraq made the US and its allies appear less capable of intervening elsewhere. Concentration of effort and attention in one area took the question of other major excursions off the table. The worst of two worlds came together: removing Saddam gave a graphic demonstration of why 'rogue states' should ruthlessly protect themselves, while occupying Iraq made the superpower again appear, as President Richard Nixon once said, like a 'pitiful, helpless giant'.[118]

---

[117] JIC Assessment, 'International Terrorism: War with Iraq', 10 February 2003.
[118] Richard Nixon, 'Address to the Nation on the Situation in Southeast Asia', 30 April 1970, at http://www.presidency.ucsb.edu/ws/?pid=2490.

If Britain had not invaded Iraq, dictators and terrorists would not have 'ruled the world', an absurd overstatement of their capability and the distribution of global power. Britain would have remained one of the world's largest economies, armed with nuclear weapons, a veto-wielding permanent seat on the UN Security Council, and a proven capacity to use force abroad to protect its interests. Some steely self-confidence and proportion would have been preferable to the kind of panicked hyperbole offered by McTernan, an attitude that left Britain prone to the disastrous war in the first place.

CONCLUSION

To summarize this chapter's arguments, the invasion of Iraq inflicted so much harm, and damaged British security interests to such an extent, that the material and opportunity costs exceeded any gains. There were alternative strategies available. The effort to remove a perceived threatening regime was simply not worth it. It had already discontinued its weapons programmes, whose modest level of capability could have been monitored and contained, and whose hostile relationship with al-Qaeda could have been subjected to greater standards of proof. The price Britain paid for this undertaking was steep in terms of blood, treasure, and honour. In terms of blood, it was the equivalent of self-inflicting a major terrorist attack while opening Iraq to large-scale Islamist subversion, in a campaign that was supposed to suppress such threats. In terms of treasure, it was billions of pounds that could have been productively spent elsewhere. In terms of honour, the unintended consequences and the abuses that the war unleashed damaged Britain's moral authority and engendered national shame.

Ultimately, the question of whether a war was 'worth it' is a value judgement, not a factual finding. This makes it hard to resolve analytically. It is also a never-ending question. Circumstances are bound once again to change, prompting fresh argument. All we can do is refine this imprecise exercise as far as possible. When Iraq comes up again as an analogical case or parable in future debate, as surely it will, we can at least try to ensure our interpretation is as precise and considered as possible. As the story is not yet finished, it is possible to speculate that 'regime change' gave Iraqis the chance for a better future in the long term. But in the medium term, it made Iraq even more dangerous a place to inhabit. It unleashed violent disorder that made conditions more lethal and more torturous. It had significant geopolitical costs, opening up a new front for an al-Qaeda terrorist network that had been reeling, and empowering Iran, creating a Shia–Iran ascendency in Iraq that, in turn, abused power and precipitated the formation of the Islamic State. The invasion demonstrated the value of retaining a nuclear deterrent, it probably cemented the rationale for proliferation by other 'rogue states', and thus was a blow to the cause of counterproliferation. Even allowing for the possibility that invasion marginally accelerated Libya's disarmament and suspended Iran's, the West eight years later cancelled out this potentially useful diplomatic example by undertaking regime change in Tripoli, and on the same basis that we cannot coexist with what Anthony Lake once called 'backlash states'. Once Iran found itself facing hostile Western forces across both of its borders, it resumed its nuclear programme. North Korea has explicitly invoked these examples in explaining its own programme. If removing Saddam Hussein was supposed to signal a broader warning to other adversaries to submit to the American world order, here too the effects were disappointing.

The central rationale for the invasion flowed from the 'precautionary principle', a flawed principle. It has two general failures. Firstly, it prematurely assumes what it needs to prove, that risk lies overwhelmingly on one side of the equation, not the other. And secondly, it is indeterminate. Precaution can just as reasonably dictate restraint, not action. Yet the principle fails to guide the fearful which to choose.[119] Blair's circle identified risk almost entirely on the side of 'not invading', and treated the calculation as an absolute rather than comparative risk assessment. Quite simply, he, his advisors and the Parliament badly underestimated the risks attached to marching on an adversary's capital and overthrowing the state, and in doing so, were blind to the radical quality of what they were taking on. Historically, external intervention and occupation is one of the most politically fraught acts. Except in atypically excellent conditions, it galvanizes resistance, polarizes host populations, energizes radical forces, and invites other interventions, especially in countries with historically porous borders and accessible geography, located at the intersection of antagonistic powers. To offset one risk, the kind of WMD transfer that is a remote contingency by an order of magnitude less likely than proliferation pessimists claim, Blair courted other risks. Tragically, while insisting that decision-makers could not afford to take risks with terrorism and WMD, British hawks lost sight of the profound risks they were running.

---

[119] For critiques of the precautionary principle, see David Runciman, 'The Precautionary Principle', *London Review of Books* 26:7 (2004), pp. 12–14; Cass R. Sunstein, 'The Paralysing Principle', *Regulation* 5:4 (2003), pp. 32–7.

5

Virtue Runs Amok

How Realism Can Help

> Once the doctrine of universal intervention spreads and competing truths contest, we risk entering a world in which, in G. K. Chesterton's phrase, virtue runs amok.[1]
>
> Henry Kissinger

The debate about Iraq was always about something larger than one conflict in one time. It was about idealism and realism, and how those two impulses could best be fused in the pursuit of security. For Iraqis, too, the downfall of Saddam was only the opening in a bitter contest over how their country should govern itself in a hostile world. As we survey the wreckage, and Iraq's ongoing consequences, and as we contemplate what other pathways lay open in March 2003, the issue will not go away. The best question is not whether idealism or realism should prevail. Rather, as I argue in this chapter, realism of a classical and restrained kind should temper the warlike idealism of our time. If not, virtue runs amok.

I argue that for the future, a dose of realism can help on several fronts. It can counsel governments against excess certainty. In particular, it cautions against the 'Gordian Knot' temptation, the impatient urge to eliminate sources of insecurity and impose decisive solutions on problems, in particular the perennial demand for the downfall of adversary regimes. Realism can inform policymakers what war can affordably achieve. As well as placing princes on their guard against predation, it encourages prudent war avoidance. Mindful that states cannot avoid living with insecurity, uncertainty, and risk, we can draw upon realist insight to restore deterrence and consequential diplomacy as the central foundations of security. And with realism, we can guard against the temptation to view international life as a morality play requiring ideological crusades, recognizing it instead as a tragedy where good intentions can be

---

[1] Henry Kissinger, 'The End of NATO as We Know It?', *The Washington Post*, 15 August 1999.

deadly, as a conflicted world where not all good things go together, and where major powers can be their own worst enemies. Below, I explore each insight.

PART I. IDEALISM, REALISM, AND UNCERTAINTY

In the foreign policy debate of major Western powers, idealism and realism will always be in contest. That is as it should be. Power without morality is purposeless, morality without power is impotent, and morality married to power can be reckless if unchecked. For the realist E.H. Carr, thinking and wishing, utopia and reality, were necessary elements in any sound political thought, and the lurching from one to the other constituted the 'tragedy of political life'.[2] Few idealists are pure idealists. Few disown the suggestion that even if the world can be transformed in the long term, the world 'as it is' imposes constraints and trade-offs. Tony Blair's 'Chicago Speech', his touchstone statement about values and interests in foreign policy, contained caveats and limiting conditions that faded only later in the loosening of restraint that marked the Iraq War. Likewise, few realists are truly amoral in their worldview. The pursuit of the national interest as a collective common good, even narrowly defined, is a morally serious business. Realism itself rests on normative commitments as well as observation. The pessimists of that tradition concern themselves with stability and equilibrium over other, more destabilizing values, but order and peace too are values. If 'First Do No Harm' is an impossible demand in the field of conflict, as a starting ethos the principle of doing minimal harm has merit, so long as it does not become a cast-iron prohibition on intervention of any kind. Neither idealists and realists can afford to unbridle their convictions of all doubt. Idealists must remain wary of the limits of international life 'as it is', and realists wary that power without ideals is hollow. Both are constrained by the limits on knowledge.

A similar balance is needed in the way we interpret the present through the past. Like most wars, Iraq was a war fought through the prism of history, or broad-brush visions of history's lessons. We cannot abandon historical comparison, as it is too hardwired into our brains as a short-cut, and without history we have no source of information. Rather, because of history's power and openness to misuse, an interplay of competing analogies should inform choices. In evaluating the proper use of power, the universe of historical analogies we use should always be conflicted. Collective memory of Hitler, Chamberlain, and Munich haunts our instinct for survival. Vietnam, Suez, and the Sicilian expedition anchors our wariness for misconceived peripheral wars.

[2] E.H. Carr, *The Twenty Years' Crisis, 1919-1939: An Introduction to the Study of International Relations* (New York: Palgrave MacMillan, 1939), p. 87.

208 *Blunder*

The July Crisis of 1914 embodies our fear of stumbling into major war. And the Rwandan genocide stands for the heavy price of non-intervention. Ideally, we would condition our choices by considering a wide range of competing analogies, carefully pondered, to isolate the limited but real circumstances and context where the use of military force can work.

Unfortunately, the question of Iraq re-emerged at a moment when there was no such intellectual balance. In the build-up to war in Iraq, a striking quality of British warmakers' language was the stress on certainty. The language of conviction, a rhetorical drive for clarity and urgency, marked the Blair circle's threat assessment: the phrases 'no doubt', 'no doubt at all', 'without any question', 'no one can deny' punctuated dossiers, testimonies, and speeches.[3] Foreign Secretary Jack Straw assured the Parliamentary Select Committee on Foreign Affairs on 5 December 2001 that Saddam Hussein posed a 'very severe threat' in terms of weapons proliferation, 'of that there can be no doubt.'[4] Tabloids, quality journals, and opposition MPs also presumed that their theory of threat and their optimism about a post-Saddam Iraq amounted to hard knowledge. Just as the anti-war movement rarely paused to consider the dilemmas its position invited, so too did a jaunty self-confidence attend hawkish argument, with a brazen and cocksure recourse to one familiar set of analogies. The historian Andrew Roberts typified the intellectual failure with the following comparison:

> In the face of a danger that the left, the Church of England, much of the establishment, the press and the French denied really existed, a lone voice told the truth unashamedly again and again until events forced the rest of the nation to listen. This brave politician faced public obloquy and collapsing political popularity, until he was proved right, when he became the most popular prime minister in recent memory. For Churchill, this apotheosis came in 1940; for Tony Blair, it will come when Iraq is successfully invaded and hundreds of weapons of

---

[3] Consider Blair's Foreword to the September Dossier of 2002: 'I am *quite clear* that Saddam will go to extreme lengths, indeed has already done so, to hide these weapons and avoid giving them up... What I believe the assessed intelligence has established *beyond doubt* is that Saddam has continued to produce chemical and biological weapons, that he continues in his efforts to develop nuclear weapons, and that he has been able to extend the range of his ballistic missile programme... It is *clear* that, despite sanctions, the policy of containment has not worked sufficiently well to prevent Saddam from developing these weapons. I am in *no doubt* that the threat is serious and current, that he has made progress on WMD, and that he has to be stopped'. *Iraq's Weapons of Mass Destruction: The Assessment of the British Government* (London: Stationery Office, September 2002), pp. 3, 4. In his Sedgefield press conference on 3 September 2002, Blair stated 'And I think when that happens that people will see that there is *no doubt at all*, the United Nations resolutions that Saddam is in breach of, are there for a purpose. He is *without any question* still trying to develop that chemical, biological, potentially nuclear capability'. 'Prime Minister's Press Conference', 3 September 2002, at http://webarchive.nationalarchives.gov.uk/20080909002012/http://www.number10.gov.uk/Page3001.

[4] Select Committee on Foreign Affairs, 5 December 2001, *Minutes of Evidence*, Qs 47–52.

mass destruction are unearthed from where they have been hidden by Saddam's henchmen.[5]

The poor forecast of this mytho-historic argument speaks for itself. One element warrants explicit discussion. Contrary to Roberts, neither Churchill nor Blair were lone voices in the wilderness in confronting their respective crises, the major power of Nazi Germany in Churchill's case and an immiserated Third World state in Blair's. But in the affectation that Blair and his supporters were a small group of brave truth-tellers resisting the tide of mass delusion, there is little room for scrutinizing assumptions. Excess certainty and the mischief it can unleash is a problem that concerns observers of international relations.[6] While fear of the unknown can drive conflict, so too can a misplaced confidence in one's foreknowledge.[7]

A profound failure of imagination attended the matter. Warmakers presented the issue as one of action versus inaction, preventive war versus capitulation, and as they glibly pressed analogies into service, the shadows of Hitler and the Rwandan *Genocidaires* eclipsed those of Tet, Sicily, or the Egyptian Canal. A battery of slogans accompanied the drive for war in Iraq, as debate moved 'away from prudence and moderation toward conceptual boldness'.[8] Background analogies were 'best case' ones, from post-war West Germany and Japan to liberated Kosovo, and they were ahistorically recalled. Grand policy declarations about ambitious goals arose not to give meaning and direction to strategy but to substitute for it, and the word 'strategy' itself as the alignment of means and ends lost its meaning.[9] 'Attaching a Roman numeral to the prospect of war', sighed Todd Gitlin, 'does not make it either just or smart. Metaphorical overstretch bids to be the thought disorder of our time.'[10]

It is not in itself shocking that warmakers and their supporters deployed such assurance. What makes this case egregious is that they did so without responding to an immediate and obvious need, such as the open aggression of the target, and when there was already a grave enough international clash to

---

[5] Andrew Roberts, cited in Matt Seaton, 'Blast from the Past', *The Guardian*, 19 February 2003.

[6] Brian Rathbun, 'Uncertain about uncertainty: Understanding the multiple meanings of a concept in International Relations theory', *International Studies Quarterly* 51:3 (2007), pp. 533–57; David M. Edelstein, 'Managing uncertainty: Beliefs about intentions and the rise of Great Powers', *Security Studies* 12:1 (2002), pp. 1–40.

[7] Jennifer Mitzen & Randall Schweller, 'Knowing the unknowns: Misplaced certainty and the onset of war', *Security Studies* 20 (2011), pp. 2–35.

[8] As Owen Harries noted, 'The Perils of Hegemony', in Gary Rosen (ed.), *The Right War? The Conservative Debate on Iraq* (Cambridge: Cambridge University Press, 2005), pp. 73–87, p. 79.

[9] See Hew Strachan, 'The Lost Meaning of Strategy', *Survival* 47:3 (2005), pp. 33–54.

[10] Todd Gitlin, 'Do Less Harm: The Lesser Evil of Non-Intervention', *World Affairs* 171:1 (2008), pp. 39–47, pp. 39–40.

attend to. Instead, hawks framed a distant and hypothetical threat as a severe danger beyond doubt, and generally assumed that war would work. Time itself was assumed to be a wasting asset, injecting the dangerous element of urgency into the calculus, when a traditional function of diplomacy is to create time as a material commodity. That it was strike or collapse, against the clock, was an a priori position they thought from. Nor can this tilt towards surety be explained away as a ploy to increase domestic support. As we have seen, while decision-makers assured their compatriots that ambiguous evidence was compelling, they were genuinely convinced that the national interest demanded regime change in Iraq. This decision they arrived at early, and it curtailed a properly systematic consideration of the choices. It also bred incuriosity. As Chilcot revealed, decision-makers paid insufficient attention to the nature of the perceived threat, for instance, in their nonchalance about the distinction between battlefield and strategic weapons, and to the geopolitical consequences of breaking a state that was potentially fractured and vulnerable to its neighbours' meddling. That events might 'go wrong' after the invasion was acknowledged, but as an afterthought in early 2003, more than a year after they decided they wanted to invade, and then only as a troublesome planning contingency. In an era before the global financial crisis and indeed the Iraq War, liberal certitudes were strong, precisely as they were about to unleash a force, war, whose logic once begun is to serve itself. As Winston Churchill cautioned in 1930,

> never believe any war will be smooth and easy, or that anyone who embarks on the strange voyage can measure the tides and hurricanes he will encounter. The statesman who yields to war fever must realize that once the signal is given, he is no longer the master of policy but the slave of unforeseeable and uncontrollable events.[11]

The want of care with which analogies were deployed was symptomatic of a deeper failure. The preventive war against Iraq, also intended to be a transformational war, was possible because of the particular alchemy of fear and confidence that normally drives anticipatory war in the first place—inflated fear and misplaced confidence. The world of irrational rogue states converging with WMD and terrorism was dangerous enough to threaten 'mushroom clouds', created by shadowy private networks of barbarians without a return address. At the same time, Western power and the universality of its values meant that it could tame that world into order, and reinvent the Greater Middle East in the Western image.

If we conceive of realism as a sensibility as much as an intellectual tradition, it can help even those who would insist on democracy promotion as the

---

[11] Winston Churchill, *My Early Life: A Roving Commission* (London: Thornton Butterworth, 1930), p. 246.

overriding path to their own security. As Owen Harries lamented, 9/11 shifted the balance in favour of those who saw things in sweeping terms, who interpreted the new emergency as a grand historical mission.[12] As he warned, 'the attempt to force history in the direction of democracy by an exercise of will is likely to produce more unintended than intended consequences.' A realism was needed to temper these ambitions, one that 'calls for restraint and patience, a sense of limits and an appreciation of the wisdom of indirection, a profound understanding of the particularity of circumstances'.[13] During the Iraq War, several lines of disagreement divided realists against hawkish members of the Wilsonian family, neoconservatives, and muscular liberals. These disagreements went beyond competing assessments of the Iraq problem. They were rooted in a fundamental dispute about international politics.[14]

Against the hawks' elevation of democracy as the most powerful force on earth, capable of being released by intervening powers when they chose, realists countered that nationalism and other more particularistic loyalties are generally stronger. Hawks' emphasis on 'regime type' and the repressive nature of Saddam's regime, realists believed, was misplaced. States that are authoritarian at home are not necessarily recklessly aggressive abroad. In any event, except in atypical conditions, not even the United States has the sapience or power to spread the democratic peace. Realists also challenged hawks' assumptions that the world tended towards 'bandwagoning' and that resistance in Iraq would be slight, warning that invading and occupying Iraq would more likely trigger balancing behaviour in Iraq, in the region, and in the world. And in real life, the occupation and the wider 'War on Terror' was met with persistent resistance, from Anbar to Tehran to Pyongyang. With regard to the international system as a whole, realists were averse to the doctrine of 'newness', that the new era of weapons proliferation, religious terrorism, and 'rogue' states altered the rules of the game and rendered classical doctrines of deterrence and containment outmoded. Realism like all paradigms is incomplete and flawed. But on each of these issues that surrounded the Iraq debate, compared to liberal optimism, realists' warnings were sound.

For many realists the imperfections in our knowledge are a reason for restraint. In its classical form in particular, realism recognizes that actors—certainly great powers—have agency even in that constrained world, and that the future is unwritten.[15] An anarchic world may always threaten predation.

---

[12] Owen Harries & Tom Switzer, 'Iraq's Lessons for America', *ABC: The Drum*, 20 March 2013.

[13] Harries, 'The Perils of Hegemony', p. 86.

[14] On these disagreements, see Brian Schmidt & Michael Williams, 'The Bush Doctrine and the Iraq War: Neoconservatives versus Realists', *Security Studies* 17:2 (2008), pp. 191–220, pp. 203–9.

[15] On classical realism and its stress on agency and contingency, see Jonathan Kirshner, 'The Economic Sins of Modern IR Theory and the Classical Realist Alternative', *World Politics* 67:1

That same world makes major powers capable of error. Those unable to place limits on their ambitions and fears are prone in certain circumstances to self-defeating wars. States with ample capacity to defend themselves, deter threats, and survive can be their own worst enemies, from the Habsburgs (under Charles V and Philip II) to France (Bourbon and Napoleonic) to Germany (as *Kaiserreich* and Third Reich) to the Soviet Union or Ottoman Empire. The history of self-harm and adjustment failure is long.[16] Wars against minor powers, such as Saddam Hussein's Iraq, are often imprudent both because their relative weakness makes them containable, and because a war against them creates new circumstances—such as the fall of the regime—that might then involve a protracted and bloody stalemate, despite the low stakes involved.[17] During the Cold War, realists like Walter Lippmann, George Kennan, and Hans Morgenthau exhorted the United States to place prudent limits on itself, particularly with regard to the most important commodity, material power, and thus to bound their security doctrines geographically and politically. In particular, realists exhorted the state to focus its master doctrine of containment on major power centres in Europe and Asia, and resist the urge to universalize it in Vietnam. Making the world safe for American and Western democracy was not the same thing as making the world democratic. In our own time, more 'structural', scientific realists, whose academic writing gives less scope to agency, nevertheless urged the sole superpower to resist the expansionist lunge into Iraq that their theories predict.[18] Precisely because we cannot foresee foreign policy outcomes systematically or reliably, that state of uncertainty means that states should marshal their resources carefully,[19] and retain what Walter Lippmann called a 'surplus of power'[20] with which they could adapt to changing circumstances.

Misplaced certainty and the false insistence on clarity remains a danger. It is particularly tempting for the party of 'regime change' that still issues its demands for decisive Western action. Ever eager to draw the sword in international crises, they also presume the existence of a strong and

---

(2015), pp. 155–83, J. Samuel Barkin, *Realist Constructivism: Rethinking International Relations Theory* (Cambridge: Cambridge University Press, 2010), pp. 100–18.

[16] Karen Rasler & William R. Thomson, *The Great Powers and Global Struggle, 1490–1990* (Lexington: University Press of Kentucky, 2009), p. 146; Charles A. Kupchan, *The Vulnerability of Empire* (Ithaca: Cornell University Press, 1994), pp. 3–4, 33–105; Paul Kennedy, *The Rise and Fall of the Great Powers: Economic Change and Military Conflict from 1500 to 2000* (New York: Random House, 1987); Robert Gilpin, *War and Change in World Politics* (New York: Cambridge University Press, 1981).

[17] As Sebastian Rosato and John Schuessler argue, 'A Realist Foreign Policy for the United States', *Perspectives on Politics* 9:4 (2011), pp. 803–19, p. 807.

[18] See the discussion earlier in Chapter 2, 'A Liberal War After All'.

[19] Barkin, *Realist Constructivism*, p. 158.

[20] Walter Lippmann, *US Foreign Policy: Shield of the Republic* (Boston: Little, Brown, 1943), p. 9.

inoffensive indigenous surrogate that can provide a stable democracy in the new order. As they did during the Iraq debate, they presume democracy with Western support normally trumps nationalism, sectarianism, or other competing loyalties, and are easily encouraged by the lobbying of exiles. In Libya in 2011, as the Foreign Affairs Select Committee found, war advocates gravely underestimated the extent to which rebel groups were pervaded by armed Islamists, and barely inquired into the matter.[21] Without any internal assessment of their extent by the British government, 'a quorum of respectable Libyans were assuring the Foreign Office that militant Islamist militias would not benefit from the rebellion ... with the benefit of hindsight, that was wishful thinking at best.' There was evidence available of a possible strong Islamist element, given that Libyan connections with transnational militant extremist groups were known before 2011, because many Libyans had participated in the Iraq insurgency and in Afghanistan with al-Qaeda. This precedent ought to have cautioned against similar wishfulness over Syria in 2011–13. Yet hawks argue that there was a moderate opposition that could securely have been armed and then installed in power without their rule being compromised by competing Islamist forces. Cast and location changes. The pathology endures.

PART II. PRUDENT WAR AVOIDANCE

Realism can inform policymakers what war can affordably achieve, what war is for, and what kind of wars ought to be avoided.[22] As well as placing princes on their guard, it encourages prudent war avoidance. This orientation draws on the classical and Clausewitzian tradition, whereby force derives its utility, or its non-utility, from political context. War is not a separate field of activity but an outgrowth of politics at its most intense, and can only draw meaning from the political condition of a situation. But more than any other kind of political behaviour, war once initiated is difficult to control as an instrument of policy. It tends towards escalation, passion, and the play of chance. Where its purpose is to serve policy, its nature is to serve itself. The more it is used beyond the more austere purposes of defence and deterrence, towards more positive and ambitious goals, the more it is extended into a more protracted and ambitious process, the harder it is to keep destruction proportionate to outcomes, and the more likely it is to generate perverse consequences.

---

[21] House of Commons Foreign Affairs Select Committee, *Libya: Examination of Intervention and Collapse and the UK's Future Policy Options* (House of Commons, Third Report of Session 2016–17, 14 September 2016), p. 13.

[22] Part of this section draws from my earlier article, 'Goodbye to All That', *Small Wars & Insurgencies* 25:3 (2014), pp. 685–95.

This may appear to be an obvious point. But there is a strong appetite for fresh wars and escalations among security elites on either side of the Atlantic. Realists usually are hawkish about the need to prepare military capabilities. At the same time, a prudent realism would raise a presumption against war of any kind—a presumption and a high bar, not blanket opposition. The regular use of military force can desensitize a society to the political turbulence of violence, even to the presence of violence itself. It is a telling indicator of where sixteen years of military engagements have taken the United States, that critics accuse President Obama of weakness and a belligerence deficit, the president who bombed seven countries, intensified an extrajudicial assassination 'drone' programme and maintained 30,000 troops in the Gulf.

In defence of being on a regular war footing, hawks typically claim that the United States and its allies did not seek its conflicts, and indeed cannot choose its wars. This refrain became especially strong in the era of counter-insurgency (COIN) when in Afghanistan and Iraq, major states found themselves bled and beleaguered by weaker but determined adversaries, and minor wars against shadowy insurgents seemed to be the way of the future. According to General David Petraeus, the architect of America's 'surge' strategy in Iraq who was charged with the rescue of a failing expedition, 'Our enemies will typically attack us asymmetrically, avoiding the conventional strengths that we bring to bear. Clearly, the continuation of so-called "small wars" cannot be discounted. And we should never forget that we don't always get to choose the wars we fight.'[23] British proponents of COIN take a similar line. Insurgencies are here to stay, they argue.[24] We have little choice, apparently, than to learn and relearn the doctrine of COIN, which lays down the need to protect civilian populations, out-govern the enemy, kill off violent rejectionists, and win space and time to build up a friendly host state with strong indigenous security forces.

This is a dangerous fatalism. We should resist it. Major states actually do get to choose the wars they fight. That is especially the case for offshore, nuclear-armed states with strong maritime/air forces and large economies and populations. While adversaries voted for war against the occupiers in Iraq and Afghanistan once the capitals had fallen, the 'coalition of the willing' voluntarily chose to seize the capitals in the first place. Violent resistance in the aftermath of such invasions was not a wildly unpredictable, 'black swan' scenario. It was a foreseeable consequence that the invaders treated with slight regard. And the claim that insurgencies and COIN are inevitably in the West's future loses sight of the nature of war itself. War is a political act and involves

---

[23] David H. Petraeus, 'Reflections on the Counter-insurgency Era', *RUSI Journal* 158:4 (2013), pp. 82–7; 'We Must Be Coldly Realistic over the Use of Force', *The Daily Telegraph*, 10 June 2013.
[24] Alex Alderson, '"Learn from Experience" or "Never Again": What Next for UK Counter Insurgency?', *RUSI Journal* 159:1 (2014), pp. 40–8.

choices. To claim that one side 'does not get to choose' is at odds with the verdict of Clausewitz, for whom wars were reciprocal and only truly started once the 'attacked' decides to defend. After 9/11, the 'attacked' chose to retaliate and defend in particular ways, beyond suppressing their adversaries' capabilities. They chose to wage ambitious liberal wars that had high ambitions from the beginning.

Disorder and armed conflict does not reliably end with an opponent's fall. Politics happens on a continuum, rather than in pre-prepared phases, and conflict persists and can re-erupt. As Stephen Biddle and Jacob Shapiro argue,

> If the 2003 Iraq campaign, the 2001–2 Afghan campaign, or the 2011 Libya campaign tell us anything, it is that taking the enemy's capital does not reliably end the war. Replacing a hostile regime with a weak successor in a splintered society or, worse, catalyzing anarchy, simply launches the war's next phase: insurgency and civil conflict.[25]

PART III. DETERRENCE AND DIPLOMACY

One source of excessive Western belligerence is the widespread logic that our adversaries are mad or irrational, and therefore must be bent to our will or destroyed. As the refrain goes, because they are irrational, they cannot be contained, deterred, or bargained with, and therefore responsible states must pressure them into collapse or eliminate them. This mandates severe measures, from deliberate crisis initiation to preventive war. In Iraq's case, it was borne of a muddled rationale, that Saddam was a reckless aggressor oblivious to deterrence, unhinged enough to use WMD regardless of retaliation but sane enough only to use them by proxy, for fear of retaliation. This mix of anti-deterrence and desire to teach by example lay at the foundation of the War on Terror. It remains the foundation of demands for regime change today. As this book was nearing completion, hostility between the United States and North Korea was intensifying over the 'hermit kingdom's' nuclear and missile programme. Hawks, including Bush and Blair, insisted that the regime was 'mad', dangerous abroad because it violated its own population.

The doctrine of taking irrational states off the board is a radical doctrine, partly because it presumes a world made fundamentally 'new', as it sweeps away core concepts from the history of statecraft. It is radical also because it presumes adversaries are reckless, greedy states, the modern equivalent of the thirteenth-century Mongol hordes, driven only to conquer and devour, or of

---

[25] Stephen Biddle & Jacob Shapiro, 'Here's Why We Can Only Contain the Islamic State', *The Washington Post*, 1 December 2015.

Adolf Hitler, one of the rare cases of an aggressor in command of a major state who could neither be appeased nor deterred. And it is radical because it links adversaries' oppressive behaviour at home to their behaviour abroad, making any kind of offensive rival a candidate for extermination. It is ultimately an expression not only of anti-deterrence, but of anti-diplomacy. It flows from a demand for absolute security, and promotes a narcissistic conceit that resistance to the will of the West is itself a symptom of madness.

It is surely time to revisit the intellectual foundations of coercive regime change and restore deterrence as an imperfect but realistic alternative.[26] Thus far, the dividends of attempts to sack hostile orders have been disappointing, leading either to prolonged and occasionally dangerous confrontation in Cuba or the Korean peninsula; to disaster in North Africa and the Gulf. An idea whose results are often bad, if not uniformly bad, is an unsound idea. In reverse order, statements that America's goal is the demise of the North Korean regime have not dissuaded it from developing a nuclear deterrent, and probably encouraged it. The demand that Bashar al-Assad abdicate power in Syria as a precondition for negotiations did not moderate his behaviour, and neither did the multinational effort to support the rebellion. Overthrowing the Taliban and installing a democratic and constitutional order in Kabul, a large experiment in modernization theory, was not a necessary step in disrupting international terrorism, and sixteen years later Afghanistan remains one of the poorest, most corrupt, and war-torn nations on earth. Libya, the 'model' intervention according to the Responsibility to Protect faction, has disintegrated into rival parliaments, the oil industry is in a state of near-collapse, and torture and abuse thrive under Islamist militias. And we have already surveyed the wreckage of the Iraq adventure, a cure that was worse than the disease. Voiced and practised continually, coercive regime change rests on an extravagant conception of our security interests, and an unrealistic account of how to pursue them.

In each of these campaigns, the invaders misread their adversaries, underestimating their determination to survive and their will to resist. And on each occasion, they misread those they thought were freedom fighters whose interests aligned with the West's. Even seemingly pro-democratic, pro-Western rebel forces have competing interests of their own. The kleptocracy in Kabul conducts an abusive rule on behalf of its clients, thus provoking sympathy with the Taliban's severe commitment to restoring law and order. The abuses of the Shia regime of Baghdad and Iranian-backed militias drove

[26] See Amitai Etzioni, 'American Needs a Foreign Policy that Doesn't Center on Regime Change', *The National Interest*, 17 July 2017; Paul W. Schroeder, 'The Case Against Preemptive War', *The American Conservative*, 21 October 2002; Elbridge Colby, 'Restoring Deterrence', *Orbis* 51:3 (2007), pp. 413-28; Robert Jervis, 'The Confrontation Between Iraq and the US: Implications for the Theory and Practice of Deterrence', *European Journal of International Relations* 9:2 (2003), pp. 315-37.

Sunni Arabs into the arms of the Islamic State. And the armed liberation movements of Libya and Syria turned out to host atrocious, determined Islamist killers, who in turn had learnt their fighting trade in the wake of Iraq. Today, loud death threats made against the Chairman of the Workers' Party of North Korea are being reciprocated.[27] This is creating a reciprocal fear of surprise attack, reminiscent of the Cuban missile crisis, another emergency brought about by an attempt to kill off a regime, the Bay of Pigs fiasco.

A prudent alternative is to restore deterrence, and consequential diplomacy, as the foundations of our security. This is not an absolute principle—we have had quite enough of absolutes applied to foreign policy. It would be artificial to dismiss any possibility of overthrowing a state. For instance, there are good prudential arguments for the measured international support given to the Gulf coalition's campaign to evict the Islamic State from its captured urban centres in Syria and Iraq, and returning those cities to their sovereign's rule, provided major powers confine the effort to suppressing and containing a chronic threat, rather than exterminating it. But as an organizing principle, we should abandon the notion that the US-led West should pursue security by demanding or attempting to force the collapse of other orders, whether through sponsorship of revolt to full-scale preventive war.

Many things distinguish the 'rogue' actors mentioned above. But they share in common a will to survive and are demonstrably deterrable. Many of even the most atrocious actors are driven partly by impulses that are also recognizably our own. Even North Korea, treated often as the extreme case of a rogue state, has not launched an all-out war against South Korea and its allies in six decades, and its restraint at this level must be partly explained by the likely consequences of aggression. In common, there are material things that they value, and which can be held at risk. Deterrence has been successfully created and maintained against much larger, revolutionary rogue states, Stalin's Soviet Union and Mao's China, states whose rhetoric prior to developing the bomb was overtly hostile. But policymakers had to sustain and refresh strategies of deterrence always against the criticisms of anti-deterrent factions within the left and right of American politics, and that argument resurfaced after the Cold War.[28]

It is not, in principle, impossible for there to arise an undeterrable and recklessly high-rolling actor oblivious to the dangers of retaliation and punishment in international politics in the nuclear age. Only it is extremely rare. Even the Islamic State, a revisionist 'insurgent' state committed to creating a medieval caliphate and exterminating heretics, turns out in its interactions

---

[27] See Scott Sagan, 'The North Korean Missile Crisis: Why Deterrence is Still the Best Option', *Foreign Affairs*, 10 September 2017.

[28] See Lawrence Freedman, *The Evolution of Nuclear Strategy* (New York: St Martin's Press, 1983).

with Israel to be susceptible to the logic of punishment and restraint. Israel does what it can to interdict chemical weapons to the group, and punish suppliers, while threatening retaliation for any assaults, and the Islamic State has complied.[29] This does not mean it is prudent, ultimately, to abide the Islamic State holding onto its conquests. But even if the extreme case of a contemporary 'rogue' actor turns out to be deterrable, the prospect of a rogue committed to homicide even at the cost of suicide is remote. The insane and effectively suicidal rogue state has been revealed to be fictitious thus far.

To say that we should restore deterrence and diplomacy is not to assume that we can or will deter everything. Classical instruments are imperfect. Actors can miscalculate. Accidents can intensify insecurity and alarm. In a crisis, a mutual fear of surprise attack can destabilize. Information can be filtered and distorted, cognitive biases hard to shift, and a regime like Saddam's was inhospitable to 'bad news'. These are generic problems that must be managed in adversarial relationships. But the history of nuclear rivalry suggests that the prospect, even the limited possibility, of a nuclear strike tends to resonate with even the most aggressive actors. The best we can do is reduce the probability of miscalculation by strengthening the mechanisms and communication of deterrence. If clearly signalled and believed, deterrence generally succeeds in preventing strikes of significant scale on a deterrer's core interests. As Chapter 4 demonstrated, Saddam, like the head of almost all regimes, was demonstrably deterrable when given unambiguous, credible signals.

Nuclear transfer remains a remote contingency that is an order of magnitude less likely and more preventable than pessimists claim. While the odds of nuclear transfer are low, the potential severity of the threat is undeniably high. There are straightforward, feasible measures by which UK policy can drive the risk lower. The task is thus to reinforce deterrence: helping the small number of potential offenders avoid miscalculation, the incorrect belief that they could get away with it, and thus shape their incentive structure in a more cautious direction. This makes it important for the UK and its allies to advertise their attribution capabilities and make clear its determination to attribute and punish such behaviour.

If the calculus above sounds as though it carries risks, it does. Deterrence is not a naturally existing quality inherent in the means of retaliation, even in nuclear weapons. To succeed, it requires vigilance and signalling, patience and a willingness to reciprocate restraint for restraint, so that the choice of 'being deterred' makes a meaningful difference to the deterree. The most difficult political aspect of deterrence, for major powers, is the implicit choice to accept as a price of stability the toleration of potential threats that they otherwise

---

[29] See Graham Allison, 'Why ISIS Fears Israel', *The National Interest* (2016).

might not. Deterrence is the stance of a 'satisfied power'. The alternative of elimination, however, threatens to create the world it predicts, of adversaries driving harder for deterrence capabilities or even WMD use. A strategy more likely to prompt nuclear or WMD use is to attack countries that possess those capabilities. While it may be wise to resist some proliferation where it is possible, there is no feasible or reliable way of eliminating the security risks of proliferation, especially once it is accomplished. Where nuclear weapons already exist in the inventories of hostile states, where they are a political reality that escalating hostility only makes seem more vital, the choices apart from deterrence are not only bad, but would likely bring about the phenomenon most feared, of nuclear use. The war in Iraq and its stimulation of wider proliferation demonstrated the dangers of searching for definitive solutions. Especially in the shadow of the nuclear revolution, there are dark realities that the West must learn to live with.

PART IV. THE TRAGEDY OF INTERNATIONAL LIFE

With realism, we can guard against the temptation to view international life as a morality play, and recognize it instead as tragic. 'Morality play' visions carry excessive certainty, dividing the world into good states and bad states. According to such a view, the problem of insecurity flows mostly from both the aggression of others, especially dangerous regimes, and the West's weakness, and therefore one cannot be safe until the world converts to one's beliefs. By contrast, though the concept of 'tragedy' has many resonances, it has at its core a great miscalculation and error of judgement—a blunder, in fact—when confronted with a difficult and conflicted choice. Tragedy flows from, and is made possible by, the success of the tragic figure, who is usually a wealthy, powerful, and authoritative figure. In the realm of international relations, as well as inexplicable suffering, tragedy refers to self-defeating behaviour.[30] A tragic world is defined by uncertainty, the possibility of miscalculation, and the need for agents to make choices within the constraints of forces over which they can only exert approximate control. In a tragic world, security threats flow more from tragic clashes of interest than from the malign intent of single groups. The lens of tragedy framed Thucydides account of the Peloponnesian war, with Athens as tragic hero unleashed by the premature death of its restraining guardian, Pericles, then suffering and falling from its own loosening of restraint, its lapse into brutal imperialism and its disregard

---

[30] See Tom Erskine & Richard Ned Lebow, 'Understanding Tragedy and Understanding International Relations', in Richard Ned Lebow (ed.) *Essential Texts on Classics, History, Ethics, and International Relations* (London: Springer International Publishing, 2016), pp. 5–20, p. 8.

for limits.[31] It is not overstraining the comparison to recognize that in 2003, with the contingent event of 9/11 setting the scene, the very success of the Anglo-American powers loosened their restraint, and tempted them to presume almost godlike levels of knowledge and prescience.

Yet if Iraq flowed from tragic failure, the tragedy is incomplete, for in tragedies the flawed protagonist is supposed to learn from their miscalculation and, through *nemesis*, come to new recognition. Tony Blair is not the centre of the problem today. Unrepentant though he is, he at least fully confronts the decision and accepts responsibility. The greatest danger is more diffuse, in the collective memory of Iraq. The tragic recognition has not yet come, that the ideas that propelled Iraq still live, even as we consign the conflict to history.

In mid-2004, just after the city of Falluja bled under terrible battle, and as the Iraq project threatened to implode, the Lebanese-American scholar and hawk Fouad Ajami lamented that the dream was dead. Ajami was one of the intellectuals who drafted the blueprint that had so moved Bush, 'the Delta of Terrorism'. He had hoped invasion would disarm and liberate Iraq, and 'purge Arab radicalism', creating a base for American primacy in the region, 'a beacon from which to spread democracy and reason throughout the Arab world'.[32] But the dream, to him, was dead. If only the dream were dead. In fact, the dream of idealistic campaigns to purge regions and impress rivals into submission, the dream of war (and the threat of war) working beyond defence and deterrence, lives on. In every year since withdrawal, op-ed pages on both sides of the Atlantic carry demands from security elites that one or another offensive regime 'must go', in the name of democracy and reason, and in the name of preserving the American primacy that Britain supports. Those same elites demand the use of force not only to constrain threats, but to make troublesome states from Iran and North Korea to Russia and China more compliant. A presumption endures that our power is potentially overwhelming, if we would only have the will to use it. It lives on in the effort to treat Iraq as a mere lesson in how to nation-build 'better' and administer the locals more wisely. It lives on in the claim that since major states like Britain don't get to choose their wars—an odd assertion, given Britain's maritime geography and capabilities—they have no discretion but to prepare for overthrowing governments and occupying countries again. And it lurks in a dangerous general fatigue about the memory of Iraq, and a desire to isolate the fault to a single leader in another time. If it is treated as merely 'Blair's war' and a singular episode, Iraq will linger merely as a sad story that confers only tactical lessons.

---

[31] As Richard Ned Lebow argues, *The Tragic Vision of Politics: Ethics, Interests, Orders* (Cambridge: Cambridge University Press, 2003), pp. 65–168.

[32] Fouad Ajami, 'Iraq May Survive, but the Dream is Dead', *The New York Times*, 26 May 2004.

But there is no collective escape from Iraq as a historical process. The tides of war that it unleashed are with us yet.

The dilemma over Iraq in 2003 was a choice of agonies. The price of 'no Saddam' was war. The price of 'no war' was Saddam. Consider the verdict of one Iraqi who had to endure both sides of the balance sheet, and intimately knew both the costs of Saddam's reign and of his fall. Kadom al-Jabouri ran a motorcycle spares shop in Baghdad. Built like a mountain, he had been a champion powerlifter and suffered eleven years imprisonment in Saddam's Abu Ghraib prison. As the old order fell in April 2003, he became the face of Saddam's repudiation by Iraqis. An iconic photograph captured him taking a sledgehammer to the fallen dictator's statue in the capital's Firdos Square. In the years to come, violent anarchy proved by a measure worse, and more threatening, even than Ba'ath misrule. On the tenth anniversary of the fall, he lamented:

> I hated Saddam ... I dreamed for five years of bringing down that statue, but what has followed has been a bitter disappointment. Then we had only one dictator. Now we have hundreds. Nothing has changed for the better.... Under Saddam, there was security. There was corruption, but nothing like this. Our lives were protected. And many of the basics like electricity and gas were more affordable. After two years I saw no progress. Then came the killings, robberies and sectarian violence.... And things seem to get worse all the time.[33]

[33] Peter Beaumont, 'Saddam's Statue: The Bitter Regrets of Iraq's Sledgehammer Man', *The Observer*, 9 March 2013.

Epilogue

Two Speeches

Here, in order, are two speeches. The first is the actual televised address Prime Minister Blair delivered when Britain went to war in Iraq. The second is an address I have written, that a decision-maker could have given. It is based on an alternative rationale and warnings that were made at the time.

TELEVISED ADDRESS, PRIME MINISTER TONY BLAIR, THURSDAY 20 MARCH 2003

On Tuesday night I gave the order for British forces to take part in military action in Iraq.

Tonight, British servicemen and women are engaged from air, land and sea. Their mission: to remove Saddam Hussein from power, and disarm Iraq of its weapons of mass destruction.

I know this course of action has produced deep divisions of opinion in our country. But I know also the British people will now be united in sending our armed forces our thoughts and prayers. They are the finest in the world and their families and all of Britain can have great pride in them.

The threat to Britain today is not that of my father's generation. War between the big powers is unlikely. Europe is at peace. The cold war already a memory.

But this new world faces a new threat: of disorder and chaos born either of brutal states like Iraq, armed with weapons of mass destruction; or of extreme terrorist groups. Both hate our way of life, our freedom, our democracy.

My fear, deeply held, based in part on the intelligence that I see, is that these threats come together and deliver catastrophe to our country and world. These tyrannical states do not care for the sanctity of human life. The terrorists delight in destroying it.

Some say if we act, we become a target. The truth is, all nations are targets. Bali was never in the frontline of action against terrorism. America didn't attack al-Qaeda—they attacked America.

Britain has never been a nation to hide at the back. But even if we were, it wouldn't avail us.

Should terrorists obtain these weapons now being manufactured and traded round the world, the carnage they could inflict to our economies, our security, to world peace, would be beyond our most vivid imagination.

My judgement, as prime minister, is that this threat is real, growing and of an entirely different nature to any conventional threat to our security that Britain has faced before.

For 12 years, the world tried to disarm Saddam; after his wars in which hundreds of thousands died. UN weapons inspectors say vast amounts of chemical and biological poisons, such as anthrax, VX nerve agent, and mustard gas remain unaccounted for in Iraq.

So our choice is clear: back down and leave Saddam hugely strengthened; or proceed to disarm him by force. Retreat might give us a moment of respite but years of repentance at our weakness would, I believe, follow.

It is true Saddam is not the only threat. But it is true also—as we British know—that the best way to deal with future threats peacefully, is to deal with present threats with results.

Removing Saddam will be a blessing to the Iraqi people. Four million Iraqis are in exile. Sixty per cent of the population are dependent on food aid. Thousands of children die every year through malnutrition and disease. Hundreds of thousands have been driven from their homes or murdered.

I hope the Iraqi people hear this message. We are with you. Our enemy is not you, but your barbarous rulers.

Our commitment to the post-Saddam humanitarian effort will be total. We shall help Iraq move towards democracy. And put the money from Iraqi oil in a UN trust fund so that it benefits Iraq and no one else.

Neither should Iraq be our only concern. President Bush and I have committed ourselves to peace in the Middle East based on a secure state of Israel and a viable Palestinian state. We will strive to see it done.

But these challenges and others that confront us—poverty, the environment, the ravages of disease—require a world of order and stability. Dictators like Saddam, terrorist groups like al-Qaida, threaten the very existence of such a world.

That is why I have asked our troops to go into action tonight. As so often before, on the courage and determination of British men and women, serving our country, the fate of many nations rests.

Thank you.[1]

---

[1] For the transcript, see http://news.bbc.co.uk/1/hi/uk_politics/2870581.stm.

AN ALTERNATIVE ADDRESS

Britain will not take part in military action in Iraq.

The gravest decision a government can make is whether to apply force. I know this decision divides us. Reasonable patriots can disagree.

Sometimes, there are worse things than war. This country has used force to protect itself from domination, to end slavery and piracy, to protect people from persecution. When there is need, where goals are achievable, we should take up arms to secure a civilised state of peace.

Often, war does not work. Wars launched naively for ambitious purposes in the expectation of quick victory can fail, their price exceeding the value of the aim. Without foreknowledge, we must weigh it carefully.

When the threat is years or decades distant, when there is no clear and present danger, the burden of argument lies with those who advocate force. Those who would join us to this expedition have not satisfied that burden.

As we speak, British forces help hunt down Al Qaeda's terrorist network. The murderers of 9/11 and their fellow travellers are being met with force, and without apology. This is where we must focus our strength: where it is most needed. Rather than opening up another dangerous front with high-risk experiments in nation-building, we must concentrate effort on suppressing and weaken Al Qaeda, while conserving enough strength for the threats of tomorrow.

Iraq would be a dangerous diversion form this task. Given what war could unleash, and put us in the middle of, the case for invading is weak.

Whatever good comes of removing Saddam from power, it will likely cause more harm than good.

Baghdad may fall quickly. But invasion to solve one problem will unleash other, graver problems. Iraq is fractured by decades of sectarian rivalry and misrule. It borders ruthless countries that will also intervene. War in such circumstances would stir up radical forces, not pacify them, harden divisions, not cure them, and intensify conflict. The conditions for a successful, externally forced democratic revolution are not there.

The makers of war say a swift war will release democracy, and help free the region from the diseases of sectarianism, dictatorship and social ruin.

But breaking a state, and creating another, will be a cure worse than the disease.

Occupations against determined locals with international backing are a losing bet, and bad news for the visitors and the locals. History leaves warnings: Israel in Lebanon, the Soviet Union in Afghanistan, France in Algeria. Experts, diplomats and regional governments warn of chaos. Since we don't know, it would be unwise to bet on an unlikely 'best case' scenario.

President Bush says that Saddam is a reckless predator who threatens us. He fears Saddam or his sons will grow their WMD arsenal, and transfer weapons to Al Qaeda, to attack us and dodge retaliation. Therefore, we must overthrow him, and send a message to other rogue states. Some compare Saddam to Hitler.

This is mistaken.

There is no evidence of collaboration between him and Osama Bin Laden. Al Qaeda has no base in Iraq. If we overthrow the state, we might unintentionally create a base in a dangerous new vacuum. We might strengthen Iran, which has known ties to terrorists and a nuclear programme.

Saddam is no Hitler. He leads a weakened, impoverished country, not a military-industrial juggernaut. Unlike Hitler, he can be deterred.

Deterrence is a powerful weapon. It has worked with rogues before—Mao's China, and Stalin's Soviet Union. In the past, when we signalled clearly, Iraq's regime held back from using WMD in 1991, and from attacking the Kuwaiti border in 1994.

If Saddam so fears our retaliation that he would 'cheat' and transfer weapons, that means he cares about his survival. If he cares about surviving, then he can be deterred. We can hold what he values at risk—his palaces, his cities, his territory. If Saddam is an aggressor who cares little for survival, he will not bother transferring WMD to a third party. He will use them directly. In that case, this has nothing to do with Al Qaeda.

Saddam allegedly held an arsenal of chemical and biological weapons for fifteen years. Either he scrapped it, making him less threatening. Or he has not, and didn't use them against US-led forces, even while encircled and sanctioned, which suggests a will to survive. In which case, he's evil, not mad.

Every state should know that Britain will retaliate with overwhelming force against any attack, or any state sponsor of attacks. We and our allies will relentlessly track down the origins of any assault on our people, and our attribution rate is high. We will hold responsible the perpetrators and their supporters, states and non-states alike. We will punish such actions without asking permission. Britain has carrier-born firepower, and nuclear-armed submarines, continuously at sea. We are prepared to use them if needed. We have the forces to raid, disrupt and deter. Anyone complicit in an attack on us will have hell to pay.

We will not allow Saddam to acquire a nuclear weapon. We should apply modified sanctions, stay within striking distance, and watch him like a hawk. This is not the Iraq of the 1980's. This is Iraq now: depleted, lacking resources, without a proper scientific-industrial base.

Some say we must hit Saddam to send a message to other rogue states.

If other rogue states are capable of being dissuaded from pursuing WMD, then they too are not so reckless, and can be deterred.

If those states are ruled by irrational madmen determined to acquire WMD, our war on Iraq won't change their minds. It might send the wrong message. Toppling a non-nuclear Saddam would demonstrate the value of a nuclear deterrent.

Bin Laden will not get the bomb, and without us invading Iraq. We will continue to work with America and the world's leading states, and the IAEA, in shutting down the flow of illicit nuclear materials. It will be hard for Al Qaeda to develop clandestine nukes underground, hunted, in hiding, just trying to stay alive. That is what that miserable gang has brought upon itself.

The Leader of the Opposition accuses the government of weakness. He says this hour is a test of resolve, that we must 'sort out' terrorism and the Middle East, that we must stand with our ally, all the way, to keep our influence.

This is what makes terrorism dangerous. As well as killing and injuring, terrorists scare us, sometimes too much, baiting us into self-harm and misguided military adventures. If you want to see our greatest threat, look in the mirror.

As America's ally, our duty is to give good advice. We advise America to hold back, not to let terrorism provoke it into a reckless war. That is what influence is for.

This is a test of judgement. By holding back, we will not settle the Iraq problem, or eliminate terrorism, or fix the Middle East. But regime change in Iraq will not achieve these things. It will put our blood and treasure in the middle of the chaos to come. That would be neither strong, nor wise.

Thank you.

Index

abandonment thesis 170, 183–6
Adams, Colin 18
adjustment failure, among states 212
aftermath phase 107–15
Ajami, Fouad xiv, 155–6, 220
Albright, Madeleine 32, 126
alternative (to Blair's) address 224–6
Amman, Kofi 59
amoral realism 161
Anderson, Donald 68
Anglo-American relationship 1, 2, 4, 6–8, 20–1, 47, 132–51, 169
anti-Islamic motivation 15–16
anti-terrorism viii
appeasement 104
Arab Spring 155, 157–8, 163, 169
Armitage, Richard 38, 106
Ashdown, Lord Paddy 108–9
Assad, Bashar al- 197–8, 201
Attlee, Clement 135
axis of evil speech 30, 37

bad faith tradition 16
bandwagoning 132–8, 211
Beinart, Peter 125
Berman, Paul xiv, 83, 125
Betts, Richard 97
Biddle, Stephen 215
Binnendijk, Hans 40
bioterrorism 101
Bird, Tim 151
Black, Cofer 106
Black Hawk Down 26
Blair doctrine 77, 86, 89
Blair's War *see* One Man's War
Blair, Tony ix, xi, 1–2, 6–14, 15, 19, 22, 24, 40–64, 69, 73, 77, 80–1, 83–9, 95–6, 99–101, 127–8, 133–4, 138, 141, 144, 146, 164, 167, 179, 184, 197, 198, 202, 207, 208–9, 215, 220
  televised address 222–3
Blix, Hans 12, 66–7, 189–90
blood price 20, 142
  and bandwagoning 132–8
  fallacy of 2
Bobbitt, Philip 92
Bolton, John 149
Bowyer, Tom 14
Boyce, Admiral Sir Michael 52, 54, 60

The Breaking of Nations 92–4
Bremer, Paul L. III 107, 112–13, 127
Briefing Paper to the Parliamentary Labour Party 53
Britain
  in Afghanistan 68, 70
  financial costs to 176–7
  intelligence dossiers 62
  public opinion xv–xvi, 3, 61–70
  road to war 25, 29–30, 40–61
  role in war viii
  taming US response 138–45
  troop deployment Korean War 135
  in UN Security Council 135
  and US interventions 137
  war casualties 178–9
  see also Blair
Brooke, Rupert 158
Brown, Gordon 9, 11–12
Burridge, Air Chief Marshall Sir Brian 49
Bush Doctrine 11, 31–2, 33, 77, 78, 86, 120, 124, 162
Bush, George H.W. 79
Bush, George W. 6–8, 11, 16, 19, 24, 29, 30, 33–4, 37, 43, 48–50, 71, 85–6, 122–5, 128, 137, 140, 147–8, 156, 184, 215
Butler Inquiry 40–1, 63
Byman, Daniel 193–4
Byzantine ideal-type 76, 92

cabinet committee system 72
Cabinet Office 41, 53, 58, 89
Cameron, David 73
Campbell, Alastair 47, 50, 52, 138
Campbell, Menzies 86
Camp Bucca 181
Carr, E.H. 207
The Case for Democracy 81, 123
CBRN (nuclear proliferation) 54
CBW (chemical and biological weapons) 166
CENTCOM 143
Chalabi, Ahmad 110–12, 127, 128, 171
chapter content summary 19–22
Cheney, Dick 48, 58, 71, 122–5
Chicago doctrine/speech 46–7, 49, 89, 96, 100, 162, 202, 207
Chilcot (Iraq) Inquiry x, xiv–xv, 4, 5–6, 8, 9, 40, 55, 63, 72–4, 85, 96, 109, 153–4, 156, 176, 197, 210

Chirac, Jacques 17, 64, 149
choosing war 214–15
Churchill, Winston 134, 136, 146, 208, 210
Clark, Wesley 126
classical realism 161, 162
Clinton, Bill 6–7, 33, 79, 126
Clinton, Hillary 126
Coalition Provisional Authority 107
Coates, David A. 8
Cockburn, Patrick 113
Cohen, Eliot 79–80
COIN (counter-insurgency) 214
conditions concept 62
containment concept 78–80
Cook, Robin 6, 80, 195
cooperative problem-solving 129
Cooper, Robert 92–4
Corbyn, Jeremy 197, 202
Cordesman, Anthony 194–5
The Costs of War 112
counterproliferation 36, 189
CPA (Coalition Provisional Authority) 147
Crawford meeting 42, 47, 48–9, 53, 87, 142
Cross, Major General Tim 108

Dannatt, General Sir Richard 143
Dawa Party 112
Dearlove, Sir Richard 11, 37, 49, 50, 132
De-Ba'athification 107–8, 113, 127, 147, 186
deception 74
Declaration of Principles 137
Defence Intelligence Service 97
Defence Planning Guidance 125
Defence White Papers 142, 147
Delivering Security in a Changing World 142
Delta of Terrorism 125, 220
democracy, in Iraq 81
democratic accountability, lack of 29–30
deterrence
  by doubt 27
  and diplomacy 215–19
Deudney, Dan 20, 116, 117, 119, 120–1, 122, 126–7, 129–30
Deutcher, Isaac 82
diplomacy, and deterrence 215–19
disarmament policy 61
dishonesty/deceit 4–5
dogmatism 39, 40
Douri, Izzat al- 192
Downing Street Memo leak 50
Duelfer Commission/Report 166, 171
Duncan Smith, Iain 99–100

EFPs (explosively formed penetrators) 58
Eisenhower, Dwight 136
El Baradei, Dr. Mohamed 12, 189–90

Ellison, James 73
Euston Manifesto x–xi

Fallon, Sir Michael 108, 109
false intelligence 11–12
falsification principle 3
FCO (Foreign and Commonwealth Office) 41, 50, 52, 58, 59, 89, 134, 141, 145
Feith, Douglas 149
First Armoured Division 25
first strikes vii
flaws of expectation 146–51
Foreign Affairs Select Committee 68, 213
45 Commando deployment 146
Fourth International 83
Franks, General Tommy 38, 49
Freedman, Sir Lawrence 89
French opposition 149–50
Frum, David 38, 157, 168, 183

geopolitical costs, of war 180
Geras, Norman xiv
Gitlin, Todd 209
Gladstone, William 82, 83–4
globalization, and liberal world order 100
Global War on Terror viii
Gombert, David 40
good faith account 18–19
Gordian Knot approach 21–2, 74, 206
Greenstock, Sir Jeremy 13, 50, 108, 109–12, 140
Gulf War (1991) 26, 56, 79, 80, 192, 195

Hague, Lord William 13, 64–5, 100
Hamad, King 29
Harries, Owen 211
Heath, Edward 137
hegemonic realists 122
HEU (highly enriched uranium) 189, 190
hindsight bias 163
History of the English Speaking Peoples 146
Hitchens, Christopher xiv
Holbrooke, Richard 126
Hollis, Rosemary 6
Hoon, Geoff 59, 90–1, 142
Howard, John 164
Hughes, Karen 123
Hurd, Douglas 135
Hymans, Jacques 195

IDA (Institute of Defence Analyses) 179
idealism, and realism 207–13
ideas behind war 2
ideological roots, and intervention 5
Ignatieff, Michael 125

Index

Ikenberry, G. John 20, 116, 117, 119, 120–1, 122, 125, 126–7, 129–30
illegality fixations 4
inadvertent escalation explanation 8
incompetence dodge 13, 107
insecurity, sources of 44
institutional support 10
international life, tragedy of 219–21
interpretations of the war 5–19
intolerable regimes 81
invasion
  alternative strategies 153, 154, 187–97
  case against 152, 153, 170–87
  case for 164–70, 197–204
  evaluation standards of decision to 153–63
Iran
  potential hostility 60
  regional patronage potential 57–8
  supply of weapons to insurgents 58
Iraq
  abandonment thesis 170, 183–6
  bureaucratic purges, post-war 88, 115
  casualty figures 171–2
  child mortality 166–7, 168, 172–3
  coups in 27
  De-Ba'athification 107–8, 113, 127, 147, 186
  GDP per capita 168
  and inspection bodies 27
  internal dissent 28–9
  mas regime 215
  military/intelligence disbanding 107–8
  political aftermath 60, 107–15
  post-war reconstruction 60, 107–15, 167, 171, 183–6
  proliferation potential 56
  refugees 172
  road to war 24, 25–30
  torture 173–6
Iraqi National Congress 171
Iraq Inquiry *see* Chilcot Inquiry
Iraq Liberation Act (1998) 31
Iraq Options Papers 37, 53, 58
Iraq Survey Group 57, 189
Islamic State 111, 155, 168, 217
Israel-Palestine Road Map 148

Jaafari, Ibrahim al- 112
Jabouri, Kadom al- 221
Jackson, Henry 'Scoop' 126
JAM (Jaysh al-Mahdi) ix
Jervis, Robert 72–3
JIC (Joint Intelligence Committee) 41, 46, 50, 53, 56, 63, 97–8, 187, 191, 203
jihadi groups 183
Johnson, Alan 82

Johnson, Lyndon 35, 40, 126, 136
Jones, Brian 14
Jones, Owen 14
just war theory 159–60, 162

Kagan, Robert 15
Kahn, A.Q. 165
Kaufman, Robert 187, 195
Keightley, General Sir Charles 136
Kelley, Robert 56
Kennan, George 212
Kennedy, Charles 86
Kennedy, John F. 126
Kerry, John 126
Kilfoyle, Peter 152
Kissinger, Henry 122, 125, 136–7, 206
Krauthammer, Charles 33, 168
Krieger, Joel 8
Kurdish genocide 165
Kurdish secession 58

Lake, Anthony 95, 205
law of the instrument 36
legalist tradition 14–16
Lemann, Nicholas 38
liberal conscience, and regime change 82–94
liberal internationalist 126
liberalism 20, 83, 118–27, 129
liberal managerialism, and Phase IV fallacy 107–15
Libya
  intervention in xi, 155, 157, 182, 213
  nuclear programme 200–1
limitation strategy 75
limited war, and regime change 75–82
Lin, Bonny 40
Lippmann, Walter 212
Logevall, Frederik 39
Love Actually 6
Luttwak, Edward N. 76

McCain, John 184
McEwan, Ian xii
Mackay, Andrew 68–9
McLellan, Scott 123
Macmillan, Harold 135
McTernan, John 153, 197–204
majority government, realities of 81–2
Makiya, Kanan 83, 125, 164, 173
Maliki, Nouri al- 184–5
managerialist accounts 13–14
Manning, David 7, 37, 43, 45, 48, 49, 54–5, 61, 85, 97, 98, 143
Maples, John 69
market democracy, entry to 110
market state principle 92

Marshall, Alex 151
Mearsheimer, John 116
MEPP (Middle East Peace Process) 44
Meyer, Sir Christopher 6, 37, 48, 139, 147
Middle East Peace Process 55, 95, 128
Milburn, Alan 82
Miliband, David 107
military deterrence 75–6
military occupation, success rate of 102–3
Mitchell, Andrew 108
modernization theory 216
MOD (Ministry of Defence) 41, 50, 52, 60, 72, 89, 141, 145, 190
Morgan, Sally 50
Morgenthau, Hans 160, 212
multilateralism 202
Murdoch, Rupert 10–11, 64, 104
muscular diplomacy 91
Myers, Stephen 82

national interest foreign policy 82, 162
National Security Strategy 33, 36, 124
NATO 15, 90, 140, 142, 150
    Article V 140
neoconservatism 120
newness doctrine 105
The News of the World 63
NIE (CIA National Intelligence Estimate) 57
9/11 attacks, consequences of 24, 30, 31, 33, 36, 43–4, 51, 71, 84, 138–40, 165, 188, 220
Nixon, Richard 136–7
North Korea scenario 170
Not in My Name slogan xi
nuclear terrorism 101
nuclear transfer 218

Obama, Barack 112, 126, 137, 146, 148, 156, 169, 184
Oborne, Peter xiii, 15
oil hypothesis 17–18
O'Neill, Brendan xii
One Man's War account 6, 8–14
one per cent doctrine 123
Operation Desert Fox 45
Operation Iraqi Freedom 29, 116, 153
Operation Telic vii–xi, 153, 199
Osborne, George 104–5, 197
Osirak dilemma 195–6
Owen, Wilfed 158

parliamentary authorization 65–6, 70, 71
Parliamentary Select Committee on Foreign Affairs 208
Parris, Matthew 11
passivity allegation 111

path dependency 25
Pax Americana 33, 87, 106
Perle, Richard 105–6, 157
Petraeus, General David 146, 156, 214
The Petraeus revolution 149
Phase II, in War on terror 35, 45, 47–8
Phase IV fallacy, and liberal managerialism 107–15
Pigott, General Tony 52
policy duality, United States 146–51
policy momentum 8
political insanity 94
Pollack, Kenneth 56–7, 126, 164
poodle explanation 6–8, 19, 139
Popper, Karl 2–3
post-war reconstruction 60, 107–15, 167, 171
Powell, Colin x, 42, 48, 49, 60, 96, 127–8, 142, 158
Powell, Jonathan 50, 54–5, 89–90, 97, 133, 138
power, and morality 207
Power, Samantha 126
precautionary principle 164, 205
pre-emption 34, 77
premium on haste 64
pre-modern chaos 93
presentation strategy 61
preventive wars 34–5, 77
primacy realism 117
Project for a New American Century 79
prudential approach 153, 160, 161, 162, 214
prudent war avoidance 213–15
public opinion xv–xvi, 3, 61–70
punitive retaliation doctrine 98
Putin, Vladimir 29, 129, 202

Quinlan, Sir Michael 196

Randall, John 67
Rangwala, Glen 14
rationality 161
RCC (Revolutionary Command Council) 192
Reagan, Ronald 78, 137, 148
realism 20, 21–2, 118–22, 129, 160–1, 206–22
red-teaming 72
regime change 2, 20–1, 36, 41, 45, 52, 54, 58–61, 65, 164, 181, 212
    effectiveness of war 102–15
    ideological roots of 72–131
    and liberal conscience 82–94
    and liberal war 116–30
    and limited war 75–82
    power inflation 94–102
    revolutionary movement 82–94
    threat inflation 94–102
regime collapse 60

Index

regime type 81, 120, 124, 211
Reid, John 82
Remnick, David 125
Report of the Iraq Enquiry 168
revolutionary movement, and regime change 82–94
Rice, Condoleezza 7, 38, 48, 49, 96, 149
Rice, Susan 126
Roberts, Andrew 146, 171, 208–9
Robertson, Lord George 90–1, 140
Robinson, Piers 16
Rogers, Paul 16
rogue states/regimes 2, 37, 44, 74, 77, 94–100, 103, 130, 217
rollback concept 78–9, 102
Roosevelt, Franklin D. 134, 136
Ross, Carne 188
Royal Prerogative 65
Rumsfeld, Donald 36, 38, 39, 52, 62, 122–5, 149
Rycroft, Matthew 24, 62, 64, 173

Saddam Hussein 26–9, 44–5, 61, 128–9, 139, 165–7, 169, 180, 188, 192–3, 199–200, 215, 218
Sadr, Muqtada al- 114
Sands, Phillippe 14
Saturday xii
Saudi Peace Initiative 57
Scarlett, John 50
Schachtman, Max 83
Schelling, Thomas 64
Schwartz, Stephen 83
scientific realism 161
SDR (*Strategic Defence Review*) 90–2
Second Infitada 57
security, public desire for 81–2
Sedgefield Speech 96
self-harm, among states 212
Senor, Dan 112–13
Shapiro, Jacob 215
Sharansky, Natan 81, 123
Shia restraint 59
The Shield of Achilles 92
SIS (Secret Intelligence Service) 41, 50, 52, 141
Sky, Emma 39
Slaughter, Anne-Marie 116, 125, 126
smart sanctions 188
social revolutionary ferocity 113
Solely, Clive 68–9
Soviet Union, collapse of 32
special relationship *see* Anglo-American relationship
Stability Operations in Iraq: An Analysis from the Land Perspective 147

Steele, Jonathan 59
Straw, Jack x, 29, 43, 48, 49, 50, 60–1, 102, 142, 188, 208
Suez crisis 136, 141
surge strategy 214
surplus of power 212
Symons, Liz 18
Syria
  civil war 111, 155, 163
  Islamic rebellion in xi
  potential hostility 60
Syria scenario 170

Tanner, Colonel J.K. 147
Tebbit, Kevin 143–4
Tenet, George 38
Terror and Consent 92
Thatcher, Margaret 106–7
The Threatening Storm 126
threat inflation 101
threat perception 23
threat tolerance 78
toughened containment 53
Trachtenberg, Marc 2–3
Trimble, David 68, 100
Trotskyite influence 82–3
Truman, Harry 35
Trump, Donald 148
trust in the state xiii
Turnbull, Andrew 41

unintended consequences 58
United Nations
  Security Council 1–2, 8, 14, 40, 61, 65, 135, 144
    Resolution 1409 188
    Resolution 1441 47, 55, 67, 157
United States
  in Afghanistan 31, 35, 68, 70
  assassination attempts on Saddam 27–8, 80
  Britain's relationship with *see* Anglo-American relationship
  financial costs to 176–7
  neoconservatism 120
  policy duality 146–51
  policy shift 30–1
  rise to Global Power 32
  road to war 24, 29–40
  State of the Union addresses 30, 31
  tariffs on UK steel 147
  troop commitment numbers 112
  unipolarity in war 32–4, 118
  see also Bush
UNMOVIC (UN Monitoring, Verification and Inspection Commission) report 12, 66–7

Vietnam, deliberation over 39–40
Villepin, Dominic de 149
violence interdependence 130
virtue, running amok 206–22
virtue/vice interpretation 15–19
visionary world-making 30

Wall, Sir Stephen 63
Waltz, Kenneth 23
The War Against Terrorism: The Second Phase 16
warlike idealism 2
warlike liberalism 86–7
Watkins, Peter 145
Webb, Simon 52
Webster, Daniel 34
Weekly Standard 10–11

Wieseltier, Leon 125, 126
Wilkerson, Lawrence B. 30
Williams, Dr. Michael 105
Wilson, Harold 136, 145
Wilsonianism 120, 126
Wilson, Sir Richard 50
Wilson, Woodrow 120, 129
WMD (Weapons of Mass Destruction) viii, 8, 11–12, 33, 36, 44, 45–6, 49, 50–4, 59, 61, 63–4, 67, 70, 72–3, 80, 90, 93, 95–102, 103, 110, 116, 119, 122, 128, 130–1, 145, 166–7, 171, 178, 181, 187, 189–96, 200, 205, 208–9, 210, 215, 219
Wolfowitz, Paul 36, 52, 122–5, 149, 184
worst-case scenarios 60
Worthington, Tony 69